Miss Weeton
Governess and Traveller

Miss Weeton
Governess and Traveller

Alan Roby

Wigan Archives

First published in Great Britain in 2016 by
Wigan Archives
Leigh Town Hall, Leigh
WN7 1DY

A catalogue record of this book is available from the British Library

ISBN 978-1-5262-0553-7

Typeset in Calisto by Douglas Printers, Wigan, Lancashire
Jacket design by Rice Creative, Southport, Merseyside
Printed and bound in Great Britain by Clays Ltd. St Ives plc

For

Padraig O'Brien O.B.E., M.D.

(1922-2002)

for encouraging me to
reach higher

Acknowledgements

I am indebted to the following individuals, who have helped to make this book a reality: Alastair Gillies (Manager, Wigan Heritage Service, retd.), for publishing some of Ellen (Nelly) Weeton's experiences throughout ten issues of Wigan Council's *Past Forward* magazine, from 1999 to 2001; Alex Miller (Archivist, Wigan Council), who perceptively recognised those *Past Forward* articles about Miss Weeton, represented 'unfinished business'; Rita Musa (Local and Family History Officer, The Museum of Wigan Life), Julie Baker, Lorraine Quilliam and Rachel Sixsmith (Heritage Assistants, The Museum of Wigan Life), for their willing assistance; Andy Heyes, for his investigative expertise concerning Thomas Weeton and Edward Pedder; Roger Hull (Archivist, Liverpool Central Library), also Joyce Culling (Research Volunteer at Liverpool Central Library Archives), for her helpful advice and assistance.

David Tilsley (Archive Collections Manager, Lancashire County Council); Revd Rachel Deigh, for her encouragement; Revd Dr Andrew Pratt for his theological assessment in relation to this period in history; George Gleaves and Eric Unsworth for their helpful suggestions; David Lythgoe, for his diligent proof reading and his critique on Miss Weeton as a poet; Michelle Cooper, for her assistance with Lancaster's historical shipping records; Andrew White, for his historical nautical knowledge and advice concerning Lancaster ship-building; Gerald Marsden for assisting with the Weeton family tree; Anthony Grimshaw (Conservation Architect); Revd Roger Driver, for his interest and support.

David Brady for his support and avid interest in 18th and 19th century Wigan; Yvonne Eckersley (Wigan Archives), for her preliminary research; Lynda Jackson (Community History Manager, The Museum of Wigan Life); Hannah Turner (Wigan Archives); Liz Conroy, for additional proof reading; Catherine Laycock, for her interest in Miss Weeton and Lancashire's history; Dr Ruth Symes for her passionate interest and enthusiasm for the life of Miss Weeton; my son Jonathan, whose skilful computer ability greatly assisted and supported me; Josie, my wife, for patiently tolerating my preoccupation with Miss Weeton and her Georgian world for some three years. Finally the late Edward Hall, editor of 'Miss Weeton's Journal of a Governess' (Oxford University Press, 1936 vol. 1, 1939 vol. 2), without whose determination and painstaking research, this book would not have been possible.

Contents

LIST OF ILLUSTRATIONS   x

INTRODUCTION   xi

WEETON FAMILY TREE   xxii

  1. Prologue – 'He that liveth by the sword . . .'   1

  2. New pastures   6

  3. A sea-port beckons   21

  4. Pleasure and tragedy in Lakeland   81

  5. Sojourn on the 'Isle of Refuge'   166

  6. Spare the rod and spoil the child   190

  7. Betrayal and persecution   237

  8. Rejected   264

  9. Adventure by stagecoach   308

10. Hope awakened   333

11. The call of the hills and valleys   357

Epilogue   376

BIBLIOGRAPHY   383

Appendix   I   Rev John Braithwaite (1754-1812)   385

Appendix   II   Thomas Richard Weeton (1781-1845)   387

Appendix   III   Aaron Stock (1776-1830)   391

Appendix   IV   Edward Pedder (1776-1835)   395

Appendix   V   Rev Alexander Steill (1768-1832)   401

Appendix   VI   Rev John Holgate (1787-1850)   403

Appendix   VII   Rev William Marshall (1792-1861)   405

Appendix   VIII Miss Weeton as a poet   407

'An Essay'   409

INDEX   411

List of Illustrations

FIRST SECTION:

1. Up Holland Village, 1815.
2. Up Holland Church of St Thomas The Martyr, c.1900.
3. 'The Priory,' Up Holland, c.1910.
4. Church Street, Up Holland, c.1920.
5. Dean Wood, Up Holland, c.1895.
6. Map of Lancashire, 1786.
7. Map of the environs of Liverpool, 1768.
8. The Mersey at Liverpool, c.1835.
9. Liverpool Theatre, 1825.
10. Advertisement from the Liverpool Courier, 1809.
11. Castle Street, Liverpool, 1786.

SECOND SECTION:

12. Sample of Miss Weeton's handwriting, 1824.
13. Dove's Nest, Ambleside, c.1835.
14. Regatta and boat race, Windermere c.1810.
15. 'Bridge House,' Ambleside, c.1820.
16. Standishgate, Wigan, 1836.
17. St Paul's Congregational Chapel, Wigan c.1900.
18. Market Place, Wigan, 1831.
19. Handloom Weavers' Cottages, Wigan, 1904.
20. Ladies in fashionable walking dresses, 1808.
21. Jane Weeton, nee Scott (1780-1831).
22. Thomas Richard Weeton (1781-1845).
23. A stagecoach leaving London, c.1820.
24. Greenwich Park, London, 1835.

Introduction

I WAS CAUTIOUSLY pleased to be asked to provide an Introduction to Alan Roby's new edition of the writings of Miss Weeton, the third in their history. Edward Hall (1898-1985), a dealer and collector of manuscripts and books, first came across one of her handwritten letterbooks in a bookstore in Wallgate, Wigan in 1925. A subsequent article of the same year written by Hall and published in the *Wigan Examiner* elicited three more – of what appear to have originally been a set of seven – volumes of letters and other personal writings. In 1969, J.J. Bagley (1908-1989), an academic at Liverpool University, published a new edition of Miss Weeton's work keeping Edward Hall's Introduction and commentary and adding an Introduction of his own.

It is in pursuit of a less editorially-controlled view of Miss Weeton – one that allows for greater freedom of judgment on the part of the reader – that Alan Roby has undertaken this edition. Stripping away Hall's (often irritating) editorial scaffolding, he delivers an uncluttered text in one volume rather than two. Personally captivated by the quality of Miss Weeton's prose and her intelligence, Roby's interventions in the text are respectful and pertinent but not obtrusive, and these features alone will ensure that this edition appeals to a far wider readership than earlier ones. Miss Weeton's story, as Roby recounts it (fluently, with a keen eye for chronology and the bravery to cut duplication where necessary), will make gripping reading for anyone with an interest in a life in the past that was ordinary yet remarkable.

In addition Roby has distinct advantages over both his editorial predecessors in that he is a local man, from Orrell, Wigan, with an intimate knowledge of the landscape in which Weeton spent most of her life. As he has said in our recent correspondence, 'It's all here in my own backyard. I can see the reality of it and feel it.' Roby has discovered the site of the cottage and school where Miss Weeton lived and taught in Up Holland, also the grave slabs in Up Holland churchyard, of Miss Weeton's mother, Mary, and of her uncle and aunt, Thomas and Margaret Barton. He has visited the canal bank where she caught the packet to Liverpool and even walked in Dean Wood, subject of a long poem by Miss Weeton (included in part for the first time in this edition), where he finds that the atmosphere remains unchanged since Miss Weeton's day.

A further aspect of this edition, is that Roby has had sight of Miss Weeton's entire oeuvre, having looked at the original manuscripts in Wigan Archives, the microfiches and the new digitised version (of which more later in this Introduction). We have, therefore, a different and newly considered selection of extracts from which to feed our imaginations and make our judgements of Miss Weeton.

Roby has also, to his credit, added more factual information to our knowledge of Miss Weeton's life and that of her immediate relations. With the benefit of new technical tools – many of them available online – he has discovered where she spent her last years, how she died, where she is buried and how she bequeathed her assets. With the help of other experts, he has also discovered more about the fortunes of Miss Weeton's brother Thomas and her husband, Aaron Stock.

Whilst both of Miss Weeton's former editors acknowledged the importance of social history of the late eighteenth and early nineteenth centuries as represented in her work, (what Bagley calls 'the unusual and useful sidelights upon many parts of England during the exciting times through which [Weeton] lived'), their commentary on this was occasionally hampered by their fascination with Weeton's character. This includes judgements that betray unflattering attitudes towards women in the 1930s and the 1960s; Hall might be criticised for dramatising and eulogising his heroine, whilst Bagley more warily surmises that 'Miss Weeton must have been a trial to her friends and relations.' In consequence, up to this point, the intricate literary, political, social, economic and religious history of Miss Weeton's times in relation to her work has barely yet been touched upon by scholars.

It is in this area that we come to Alan Roby's greatest contribution to our understanding of Miss Weeton. Whilst Hall's version of Miss Weeton's Journals (and Bagley's by extension) downplayed the religious dimension of her life, Roby has sought to recognise her Christian faith and remind the reader of its importance throughout society at the time in which she lived. To this end, he has reinstated some original religious verse (entirely ignored by the earlier editors) and has included elucidatory footnotes on local chapels, churches and ministers (together with an appendix of local ministers). Additionally, in the Epilogue, he helpfully analyses the complexity of Miss Weeton's spiritual belief and practice.

For my part, I first came across Miss Weeton as an undergraduate student in the 1980s. I worked on her again as part of my doctorate in the 1990s, and she has cropped up time and time again in my writing career since then: I remain fascinated, awed, provoked and disturbed by her. For the time being, my tuppenceworth (below) takes up the issues around Miss Weeton as a *woman* at a time when her gender put her at a disadvantage.

Any reader inspired to delve deeper into the writings of Miss Weeton, will be delighted to learn that more of the original will soon be available online. A recent project, jointly funded by the Archives and Local Studies Trust and the National Manuscript Conservation Trust, entitled, 'Dear Diary: Conserving the Edward Hall Diary Collection,' has digitised the whole Weeton oeuvre amongst other diaries of historical interest. Work to make this digitised version available to view on the internet is ongoing. Please visit: Wigan Archives and Local Studies at: http://archives.wigan.gov.uk for up-to-date information. Ultimately the entire digitised version will be viewable at: http://wiganarchives.past-view.com/archive/the-edward-hall-diary-collection/ellen-weeton

So vast and detailed is Miss Weeton's body of writing that it will, no doubt, yield to all sorts of other kinds of scholarly analysis in the future. Alan Roby's new perspicuous and entertaining edition will certainly whet the appetite for that analysis to begin.

'A humble, degraded being indeed'
Miss Weeton as a Woman of Her Times

In January 1810, Nelly Weeton wrote to her Aunt Barton (in Up Holland) from her isolated position as a governess in a secluded spot by Windermere, the Lake District. At this point, Weeton was even further than usual from the worldly conversations of towns and cities and, more than ever, keenly aware of her position on the margins of society:

'Battles have been fought and kings deposed and I have been in perfect ignorance. Tranquility in my bosom, and peace in my habitation, I had almost forgot the political world and all its commotions.'
29ᵗʰ January 1810

One might imagine from this humble assertion that Nelly Weeton was a hermit, content to confine her writings to the minutiae of domestic existence. Nothing, in fact, could be further from the truth. To Miss Weeton 'the political world and all its commotions' probably would have meant royal matters, foreign affairs and parliamentary squabbles. And, in those respects, it is true, the commentary in her journals and letters is virtually non-existent. She ignores the ongoing Peninsular Wars of 1807-1814, for example, apart from one brief mention of 'Buonaparte'. But the political world of her times – as of all times - can, of course, more broadly be understood to include the field of sexual politics – the position of women in society, their opportunities in education and employment, their economic position within marriage and outside it, their rights and responsibilities as mothers, and even their potential as cultural commentators (writers). On these matters, in fact, Weeton is voluble.

First editor of the *Journals*, Edward Hall described the moment in history at which Weeton was writing as 'a man's time, either as mighty employer of money and labour, or raw material of the country's future commercial greatness and prosperity. And woe betide the woman who dared question her place in the scheme of things [n.p. Hall, Weeton, [1939].' In this world Miss Weeton's participation in the discourse of sexual politics was unusual and potentially explosive. The degree to which she does in fact *openly* question woman's place in society is up for discussion. Certainly, at times, she railed against matters affecting the lives of women, but she also, to a degree, frequently accepted things as they were.

Fortuitously for us (though not, sadly, for her), Miss Weeton's own life-as-it-was-lived (as a single woman with a small income, as a working woman, as the wife of a violent man, as the separated mother of a young child, as an aspiring but unpublished writer) exemplifies many of the injustices of an old – and indeed outdated – system in which women's needs, rights and desires were not acknowledged. Crucially, time-wise she stands just before many of the social and legislative improvements in women's position that came about later in the nineteenth century. Had they existed during her lifetime, these improvements would, to some degree, have ameliorated her situation. But, she was not to benefit from them. And so, in the letters, her howls of desperation simply fly into the wind unheard, except by their recipients, who probably did no more than roll their eyes and turn over the page.

In the late eighteenth century when Miss Weeton was a child, there was little schooling provision at all for girls at any social level. As the daughter of a sea-captain, she might potentially have been taught either by a governess or within a small private academy.

Limited, in this way, by an education that was neither as lengthy nor as thorough as that of boys,' most girls from the upper and middle classes rarely had the chance to exploit their true academic potential.

The commonplace inequalities in education, on the grounds of gender, however, were, in a way, irrelevant to Miss Weeton since she was not, in fact, tutored either by a governess or within an academy. Her father died when she was very young leaving the family in a parlous economic situation, and, Up Holland, the village just outside Wigan, where she spent her early days had no suitable girls' school. Weeton had to make do with lessons given to her at home by her mother and with the occasional visits of a tutor – an usher from the establishment to which her younger brother Tom was sent (The Reverend Braithwaite's School for Boys in Up Holland). This was trial enough, but how keenly did she feel the injustice when her brother Tom, younger by four years, was sent on to law school in Preston!

Whilst notions of class were very much in flux in the late eighteenth and early nineteenth centuries, Miss Weeton (owing to the position of her father as described above) certainly came from what might be described as the 'middling sort' of society. She might even have been described as 'genteel' in that, as a single woman, she had a small private income derived from some funds left to her by her mother (and later invested in property in Liverpool). Nevertheless, it would have been expected that her brother, Thomas Weeton, a lawyer, might contribute to the upkeep of his spinster sister (as she grew older), particularly as Weeton had contributed to the funds for his schooling in earlier life. But either because of his personal inclination or the machinations of his wife, Thomas Weeton did not support his sister, and her income as a teacher in the village school remained meagre. To augment it, she would have to look elsewhere.

Many women in the late eighteenth and early nineteenth century worked (local females of the lower classes were occupied in domestic service, factories, mills and sewing sweatshops, for example), but such manual endeavour was not open to Miss Weeton. Such jobs, often dangerous, dirty and badly paid, would have involved a serious loss of caste that would soon have had her expelled from the polite circles in which she had mixed, had she been inclined to try them out.

But in this era of male pre-eminence, the professional jobs for which Miss Weeton was more than intellectually capable (medicine, science, the law, the civil service), were also out of bounds for women. In fact, such professions opened up to the female sex only very slowly from the end of the nineteenth-century onwards. All this was far in the future. In the first decades of the nineteenth century, the career expectations of most women of Miss Weeton's ilk were marriage, children and the management of a home. Those who were not married and did not have enough to live on by way of inheritance were caught between a rock and a hard place. Their choices were stark, teaching in a school, teaching as a governess in the homes of others, or acting as a lady's companion. To her credit, Miss Weeton was to have a go at all three.

For a while after her mother's death and with no teacher training – such a concept didn't really exist - she continued to preside over the small 'dame' school in Up Holland that her mother had run for local children of the lower classes. Here she probably focused on teaching reading and, to a lesser extent, writing skills and basic numeracy. In search of a better income, and perhaps of adventure, she then became a governess (and companion) to the Pedder Family in the Lake District (from December 1809 to February 1811) and the Armitage Family in Yorkshire at High Royd House, Honley, Huddersfield (from July 1812 - June 1814). In later life, Mrs Stock, as she became, taught in a number of Sunday schools in the Wigan area. The Sunday School movement (variously described as beginning in 1751 or 1769) was, in some areas, the only experience that poor children had of the classroom until the Education Act of 1870.

The quality of Miss Weeton's writing alone attests to her suitability to teach, and it might be argued that some aspects of pedagogy, the desire to instruct and to better others, were a key part of her personality, for good and ill. Many of her letters – and especially those to her daughter Mary – were written in a didactic tone as a means of passing on information and instilling her own principles and ideas about the world. A long tradition of epistolary correspondence (letter writing) as a means of educating young people (especially girls), preceded Miss Weeton, and was typified by the author Samuel Richardson in his novel *Pamela* published as early as 1740. It is more than likely that Miss Weeton was aware of her literary and pedagogical predecessors and wrote with them somewhere in mind. She had, for instance, read and appraised the popular *Lord Chesterfield's Letters to his Son* (1774).

Nelly Weeton married Aaron Stock, the widowed owner of a Wigan spinning mill in September 1814. From any perspective, it was a strange match and, in this new edition, Alan Roby makes some useful speculation as to why the union went ahead (Chapter 8). Whilst romance was often a factor in marriage in this period, it was usually combined with social and economic considerations amongst families of Miss Weeton's social standing. Women of the middling sorts and above were valued for their moral qualities and, as an ideal, matrimony was expected to involve love, companionship and mutual respect. But wives were also valued for the capital they might bring with them to the marriage, a sum of money, property or other assets. And, to put matters bluntly, when she married, whether or not she was 'in love,' Nelly Weeton had money, and Aaron Stock (an associate of her brother Tom) was virtually bankrupt.

Whatever the personal reasons for the Weeton-Stock union, however, the legal outcome was uncompromising. From the point of marriage onwards, as the historian Paula Bartley has put it, 'the law stipulated that husband and wife were one, and that the 'one' was the husband,' *The Changing Role of Women*, 1815-1914, p. 11. Under common law, like all other women in her position, on marriage, Weeton lost her independent legal status and was considered to be the possession of her husband Aaron Stock. He became the rightful owner of all that Weeton brought to the marriage including her small private income.

Had she wished to avoid this state of affairs, Nelly Weeton would have had to have set up a marriage settlement under equity law, which protected money and property held by wives. But only 10% of the population could afford the costs of setting up such settlements or trusts and Weeton was not among them, nor, it would seem, did her errant brother Tom advise her to do so. It was not until much later in the century that the need for these expensive marriage settlements was substantially reduced. Via the Married Women's Property Acts of 1870, 1882 and 1893, women gradually gained control of their earnings, property and inheritance within marriage.

All might not have been lost for Miss Weeton, however, even at the earlier date. In the early 1800s, a woman who married could, in theory, be forming a union with somebody who would protect her and provide for her for life. Unfortunately with a man like Aaron Stock, the potential for abuse within marriage was enormous. In addition to their other legal disadvantages, women at the time could not sue, sign contracts, run a business or make a will without the permission of their husbands, nor could they take legal action against domestic abuse. When Stock deprived Weeton of money, threatened her with prison or a lunatic asylum, beat her up or locked her away, she had absolutely no redress. For any woman, but particularly for one of Weeton's intelligence, sensitivity and independence, marriage to Aaron Stock was nothing short of a disaster.

Divorce was not an option for Mrs Stock. Again, she appears in history not long before the law – bending to rapidly-developing Victorian notions of democracy, citizenship and justice – finally acted to improve some matters affecting women. The numerous Matrimonial Causes Acts passed between 1857 and 1937 were slowly to give women better access to divorce, but, in the early nineteenth century, such a course of action was available only to the very wealthy, and even then only by Act of Parliament. Husbands and wives who could not bear the sight of each other could, however, be legally separated – usually at far greater cost to the woman than the man – and this was the fate that befell the Stocks. Having sacrificed all her worldly goods to her husband on her marriage, Weeton now had to rely on Stock for a yearly income – agreed at £70 (not a huge sum at the time) – which he delighted in paying in arrears.

But Weeton's trials as a married woman were not confined to finances. She also faced downright injustice as a mother. A daughter Mary, was born to Weeton and Stock on June 9th 1815. By 1819, Stock had removed Mary from Weeton's direct care and placed her in a boarding school, Parr Hall in St Helen's. The Stocks finally separated legally in January or February of 1822 with Nelly being barred from living within two and half miles of Wigan. After years of ill-treatment, Weeton eventually moved out of her marital home and settled again in Up Holland. Mr Stock, at this point, made it yet more difficult for Weeton to see her daughter, barring her from visiting Parr Hall. In this period, part of a husband's rights over his wife extended to his children. Prior to 1839, that right was absolute; even the Court of Chancery found it impossible to grant a mother access. In the case of the Stocks, Nelly's prohibition from seeing Mary lasted until the little girl was at least ten years old, though we know from the letters that Miss Weeton frequently breached the order of the Deed of Separation, visited her daughter at the school and, on many occasions, intercepted her walks to the local church.

It was not until 1839, when Weeton's daughter was already fourteen, that the Hon. Caroline Norton (afterwards Lady Stirling-Maxwell) (1808-1877) successfully fought the unfair custody laws of the nineteenth century and helped mothers gain rights to their children under the age of seven (in certain circumstances). There was a long way to go. Mother's rights to custody over their children up to the age of 16 (again with caveats) was not granted until The Custody of Infants' Act of 1873. The Guardianship of Infants' Act of 1886 further stipulated that the welfare of a child had to be taken into account when the custody of that child was being determined – a factor which again strengthened the position of mothers over fathers. And, it was only in 1925, that married women gained the right to apply for the custody of their children of all ages, and only after 1973 that they finally gained equal, unconditional, guardianship.

Given the difficulties she faced, it seems all the more remarkable that Miss Weeton developed the eloquence, and indeed found the spirit, the space and the time, so frequently to put her thoughts on paper. As we read, we should remember that the letters we have are, in fact, second versions each copied into letterbooks (sometimes painstakingly over a period of five hours or so), ostensibly solely to give the writer herself pleasure in the re-reading of them at a later date. Let us not forget that Miss Weeton had been dissuaded at an early age, by both her mother and her brother, from trying her hand at published writing – and this, in a period, when many writers, especially novelists, and educationalists (Mary Wollstonecraft (1757-1797), Fanny Burney (1752-1840) and Jane Austen (1775-1817) to name but the three most famous) – were female. Miss Weeton's bitterness at not having the chance to join them is real, and perhaps more keenly felt than all her other female disadvantages. Are her extant letters and journal perhaps more calculated in both content and form than they at first seem? What did Miss Weeton really believe or hope would happen to her letters at her death?

We will never know. But certainly, this third edition of Miss Weeton's writings is testimony to her lasting appeal as a skilful writer of prose (and occasional poetry). With it she finally takes her rightful place as a published woman writer of her times.

Dr. Ruth A. Symes
Hale
Cheshire

Preface

Miss Weeton's Journal of a Governess, edited by Edward Hall and published by Oxford University Press, first appeared as two volumes: Volume 1 in 1936 and volume 2 in 1939. My interest in Miss Weeton began in the early 1970s when I read an article concerning a 1969 reprint by David and Charles Reprints, which included a new introduction by the late historian, J. J. Bagley.

The chance discovery of Miss Weeton's will in Liverpool in 1994, revealed that she had died in 1849, so that her sesquicentenary would occur in 1999. I suggested to Wigan Council's then Heritage Services Manager, Alastair Gillies, that a commemorative article about Miss Weeton in a future issue of the Council's heritage magazine, *Past Forward,* might be appropriate. The idea resulted in 10 articles published over a period of three years.

In 2012, Wigan Council Archivist, Alex Miller asked me if I would consider writing a single volume to bring Miss Weeton's life up to date. He explained that existing sources did not record closure to her life. Coincidentally, I also thought that other errors and omissions needed to be addressed. I also possessed more facts than her earlier biographers and was better equipped to address the speculations, conflicts and schisms that affected Protestantism between 1750 and 1850. These were of interest to Miss Weeton who would often paraphrase Biblical extracts to support a particular viewpoint. Nor was she afraid to express an opinion, when considering diverse forms of worship or the virtues and vices of various clergymen.

This book seeks to offer a context for Miss Weeton's life and writings. To that end I have arranged excerpts from her voluminous letters and journal entries into chapters, with sufficient linking text and introductory chapter narratives to allow the reader to follow the writings without offering over-much editing or interpretation. I have sought, as far as possible, to retain her original writings even when the punctuation or spelling has been somewhat arbitrary. The Epilogue provides an overview and a reflection on the whole.

The need for this book overcame my reluctance to engage with it and I began work in the spring of 2013.

A. Roby
Orrell, Wigan
August 2016

WEETON FAMILY TREE

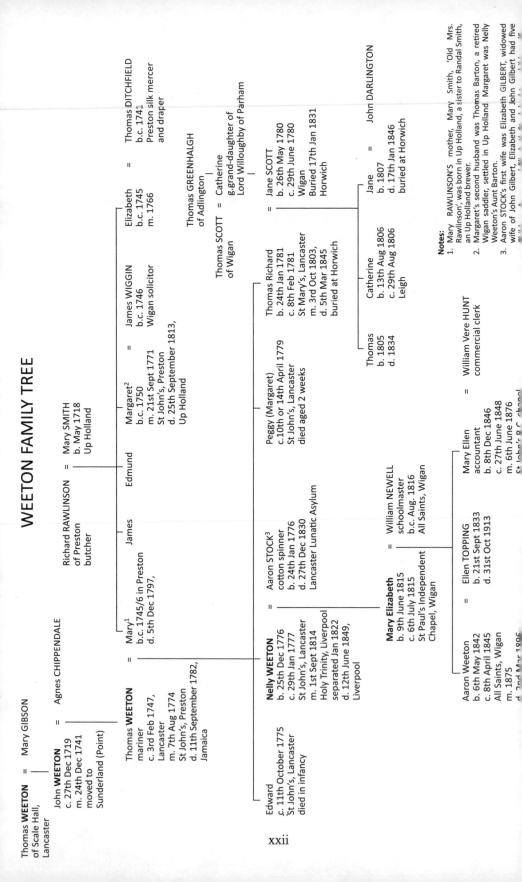

Thomas **WEETON** = Mary GIBSON
of Scale Hall,
Lancaster

John **WEETON**
c. 27th Dec 1719
m. 24th Dec 1741
moved to
Sunderland (Point)

= Agnes CHIPPENDALE

Richard RAWLINSON = Mary SMITH
of Preston   b. May 1718
butcher   Up Holland

Thomas **WEETON**
mariner
c. 3rd Feb 1747,
Lancaster
m. 7th Aug 1774
St John's, Preston
d. 11th September 1782,
Jamaica

= Mary[1]
b.c. 1745/6 in Preston
d. 5th Dec 1797,

James

Edmund

Margaret[2]
b.c. 1750
m. 21st Sept 1771
St John's, Preston
d. 25th September 1813,
Up Holland

= James WIGGIN
b.c. 1746
Wigan solicitor

Elizabeth
b.c. 1745
m. 1766

= Thomas DITCHFIELD
b.c. 1741
Preston silk mercer
and draper

Thomas GREENHALGH
of Adlington

Thomas SCOTT = Catherine
of Wigan   g.grand-daughter of
               Lord Willoughby of Parham

Nelly WEETON
b. 25th Dec 1776
c. 29th Jan 1777
St John's, Lancaster
m. 1st Sept 1814
Holy Trinity, Liverpool
separated Jan 1822
d. 12th June 1849,
Liverpool

= Aaron STOCK[3]
cotton spinner
b. 24th Jan 1776
d. 27th Dec 1830
Lancaster Lunatic Asylum

Peggy (Margaret)
c.10th or 14th April 1779
St John's, Lancaster
died aged 2 weeks

Thomas Richard
b. 24th Jan 1781
c. 8th Feb 1781
St Mary's, Lancaster
m. 3rd Oct 1803,
d. 5th Mar 1845
buried at Horwich

= Jane SCOTT
b. 26th May 1780
c. 29th June 1780
Wigan
Buried 17th Jan 1831
Horwich

Jane   = John DARLINGTON
b. 1807
d. 17th Jan 1846
buried at Horwich

Edward
c. 11th October 1775
St John's, Lancaster
died in infancy

Mary Elizabeth
b. 9th June 1815
c. 6th July 1815
St Paul's Independent
Chapel, Wigan

= William NEWELL
schoolmaster
b.c. Aug. 1816
All Saints, Wigan

Catherine
b. 13th Aug 1806
c. 29th Aug 1806
Leigh

Thomas
b. 1805
d. 1834

Aaron Weeton
b. 6th May 1842
c. 8th April 1845
All Saints, Wigan
m. 1875
d. 2nd Mar 1896

= Ellen TOPPING
b. 21st Sept 1833
d. 31st Oct 1913

Mary Ellen
accountant
b. 8th Dec 1846
c. 27th June 1848
m. 6th June 1876
St John's R.C. chapel

= William Vere HUNT
commercial clerk

Notes:
1. Mary RAWLINSON's mother, Mary Smith, 'Old Mrs.
   Rawlinson', was born in Up Holland, a sister to Randal Smith,
   an Up Holland brewer.
2. Margaret's second husband was Thomas Barton, a retired
   Wigan saddler, settled in Up Holland Margaret was Nelly
   Weeton's Aunt Barton.
3. Aaron STOCK's first wife was Elizabeth GILBERT, widowed
   wife of John Gilbert, Elizabeth and John Gilbert had five

EDITOR'S NOTE

Past writers have referred to Miss Weeton as either 'Ellen' or 'Nelly.' That may have arisen because her correspondence reveals that whilst she mainly signed her letters as 'Nelly', very occasionally she signed as 'Ellen.' In her will, discovered in 1994, she signed herself 'Nelly Stock of Liverpool' (her married name). Her burial record, discovered in the registers for the Necropolis Cemetery, Liverpool, at about the same time, also name her as 'Nelly Stock.' This confirms a brief entry in the registers for St John's Parish Church, Lancaster, that she was christened 'Nelly.' The baptismal register states: 'Nelly', daughter of Captain Weeton. Baptised 29 January 1777.

Nelly Weeton was born on Christmas Day 1776. Until she comes of age in 1797, she is referred to in this edition as 'Nelly.' From then until her marriage in 1814, she is referred to as Miss Weeton. For the duration of the marriage, until she signed the Deed of Separation in 1822, she is referred to as Mrs Stock. Thereafter she is referred to as Miss Weeton.

Prologue

'He that liveth by the sword . . .'

Lancaster

1747 - 84

THE LANCASTER REGISTERED *Nelly*, constructed in 1772, was a swift two-masted square rigged 'snow'[1] merchantman of some 254 tons. Its captaincy fell to one by the name of Thomas Weeton. With a crew of some 35 men aged 18 years and upwards, Captain Weeton's responsibility was to sail the 'triangular' slave trade from Lancaster to the West Coast of Africa. From there he would make slave purchases at the Gold Coast's[2] 'slave castle' ports of Cape Coast and Anomabu, before sailing onwards to the Americas. There *Nelly* would deliver its cargo of 200 slaves (less deaths *en voyage*) to St George's Harbour 'slave landing,' at the Caribbean island of Grenada.

At the age of 30 in 1777, Thomas Weeton was in his prime and at the zenith of his career as a competent master. The slave trade, also known as 'The Black Ivory Trade,' had become a principal source of income for Lancaster ship owners. By the year 1791, 14 brig-type snow vessels were engaged in the trade, forming the backbone of the Lancaster fleet.

The *Nelly* was owned by the Rawlinson family, an important family of ship owners in the City of Lancaster. The Rawlinson trading empire was established by two brothers, Abraham and Thomas Hutton Rawlinson, who were at the centre of a nexus of companies and organisations that included many ships. The brothers were Quakers, although unlike the reputation generally understood to be that of Quakers, they were very tough. However they did have the Quaker reputation of being plain and honest throughout their lives. Both brothers died during the 1780s.

1

According to a Log[3] for the privateer[4] brig, *Lively,* owned by Abraham and John Rawlinson, Captain Weeton had transferred his captaincy from *Nelly* to *Lively* during the American War of Independence. *Lively* carried a Letter of Marque,[5] which allowed Captain Weeton and his crew a lawful share of prize money, resulting from any successful engagements with the enemy. Being brave and enterprising, Captain Weeton took at least three prizes during his voyages, including *Perseverence* and *Prince of Austria.* On *Lively's* safe return to Lancaster, the ship's crew were greeted with many congratulations, and songs were sung in Captain Weeton's honour throughout Lancaster's streets. Even his home at the top of Church Street was subjected to repeated cheers.

Thomas Weeton was born in Lancaster in 1747, the second of three sons. Their father had farmed land as a tenant at Scale Hall, near Lancaster. Both parents died whilst their sons were very young. The eldest son, James, inherited a small estate at Sunderland, near Lancaster; the two youngest sons, Thomas and Edmund, were left destitute and taken to live with a sister of their mother. She was the wife of a Mr Gibson, an avaricious and parsimonious man of property, living at Birkland Barrow, near Kellet; about seven miles from Lancaster. Both brothers were immediately set to work by their aunt to nurse her many small children. Thomas soon tired of nursing and as soon as he was old enough he ran off to Lancaster and bound himself as an apprentice to the captain of a ship.

On his return from his first voyage, he visited his brothers. He found James living at a farm near Bolton Sand-side, with his uncle Jackson; Edmund was still in his previous occupation nursing the Gibson's children. Thomas took the opportunity to try to persuade Edmund to go to sea rather than to 'continue to drag somebody's brats about all day.' Not long after Thomas's visit, Edmund also ran away to Lancaster and like his brother, bound himself as an apprentice. From then onwards the two brothers continued seafaring for as long as they lived.

Thomas married Mary Rawlinson at St John's Parish Church, Preston, on 7 August 1774. She was a daughter of Richard Rawlinson, of Preston. The marriage produced four children. Edward was the first born. He died aged just three-and-a-half years in 1779. Next came Nelly, born 25th December 1776. She was named after her father's ship. Captain Weeton was *en voyage* in *Nelly* at the time of his daughter's birth. Next born was Margaret, born 1779; she lived for only a fortnight. Margaret and Edward died at about the same time. Nelly then became an only child until a fourth, Thomas Richard, was born 24th January 1781.

Mary Rawlinson was born in Preston in 1746. She was the second of three daughters, born to Richard and Mary Rawlinson. Elizabeth was the eldest, born c.1745; Margaret the youngest, born c.1750. Their father, a butcher by trade, was fortunate in having acquired the financial wherewithal to ensure that his three daughters received a good education. The sisters were additionally most fortunate in 'all being remarkably handsome.' Mary especially had a great desire to improve her mind and manners. She became lady's maid to a Miss Hoghton, sister to Sir Henry Hoghton (1728-95), sixth baronet, of Walton Hall, near Preston, who for 30 years represented the Borough of Preston as M.P. Lady Hoghton and Miss Rawlinson travelled extensively together over a period of twelve months to the various southern counties of England; including staying for some months at Sir Henry's London home.

Elizabeth married a Mr Thomas Ditchfield of Preston in 1766, a silk mercer and draper. Margaret married a Mr Wiggin of Wigan, a solicitor, in 1771. Mr Wiggin predeceased his wife, who then married a Mr Thomas Barton of Wigan, a retired saddler. On Mary's marriage to Thomas Weeton of Lancaster, she removed to Lancaster with her husband. From the time of Thomas and Mary's marriage 'they lived as happy a couple as any in existence', wrote Miss Weeton. She later described her father as 'generous, brave and enterprising, placing unbounded confidence in his wife.' She described her mother as 'industrious, prudent and faithful.'

By 1782 successes at sea had accumulated the colossal sum of £12,000 for Captain Weeton. He then decided to give up seafaring, but was persuaded by his employers to continue. In return they promised him that if he would go to sea once more, on his return he would find all his outstanding debts settled and his prize money awaiting him. He acquiesced and *Lively* set sail for the last time from Sunderland (Point), on 22nd March 1782, with a crew of 13 officers, 37 seamen and 4 apprentices. It was to be the final voyage for Captain Weeton and for about 10 of *Lively's* crew, who were killed or died at sea.

After many months news eventually reached Lancaster, that in an engagement with an American ship of superior strength, Captain Weeton had been mortally wounded. It was reported that whilst he was shouting orders through a trumpet to his men in the shrouds, 'the side of his face was took off by a chain shot.'[6] The American ship made off in a sinking state but *Lively* somehow remained afloat. His crew took him to nearby Jamaica, where he lived for a few days. He was buried there on 11 September 1782, aged 35 years. *Lively* never returned to Lancaster; it was sold in Jamaica.

Later reflecting on her father's death in her 'Retrospect', Miss Weeton wrote:

'He that liveth by the sword shall die by the sword.'[7] The warrior is not in the sight of God a man of honour and glory, whatever his fellow men may think. It is a dreadful life, a dreadful death; and such the Almighty deems it when he speaks to us in the same language. How glad I should be could I be assured that the universal Judge would pity those men who are educated in error and whose lives are destroyed in consequence.

As a result of her tragic loss, Mary Weeton was completely devastated; not only had she suffered the loss of her husband but she was also defrauded into losing the whole of her husband's prize money together with other property gained through his voyages. Soon afterwards she also suffered the loss of her own mother and a sister.

After making many applications to the Rawlinsons, she never received a single pound; nor did she receive any information regarding the manner in which her husband's property had been disposed[8] Such an accumulation of losses caused her health to become impaired, resulting in her suffering a 'deep depression of spirits.' Within a period of six months Mary Weeton had lost her husband, her own mother, her eldest sister Elizabeth and a fortune that consisted of her husband's prize money and other investments. The total value was considered by Mrs Weeton to be worth at least £12,000.

Nelly later recorded that the awful shock of her father's tragic death at sea was such as to 'shake her [mother's] reason.' On receiving the tragic news Mrs Weeton's children had been immediately conveyed to bed by a servant who informed Nelly of the calamitous loss the family had suffered. She awoke to see her mother sitting on the bed, weeping bitterly. 'Poor Nelly,' her mother said, 'you have no father now.'

Together with her two children, Mrs Weeton decided to seek a new life.

NOTES:

1. A 'snow' or 'snauw', pronounced 'snoo', was a two-masted brig-type vessel which carried square sails on both masts. In addition it had a smaller 'trysail', or 'snow-mast' immediately behind the main mast. This sail arrangement allowed a larger sail and more speed. It was typically the largest two-masted vessel around, employed both in the merchant service and the Navy.
2. The Gold Coast is now the nation of Ghana.
3. Log for the *Brig Lively 1782.* (Preston Record Office, Ref. DDX 2743/5546).
4. A privately equipped warship is referred to as a privateer and is granted a licence by the State in time of war to engage the enemy.
5. A 'Letter of Marque' is a State document authorising a private citizen to seek reprisals against enemy shipping. Used especially in the case of a privateer. Without the necessary Letter of Marque, such action was treated as piracy.
6. A chain shot is a missile fired from a cannon, consisting of two solid metal balls or half balls joined together by a chain. It was used in naval warfare to damage the enemy's rigging.
7. Refers to the words of Jesus paraphrased from Matthew's gospel: 'Put thy sword into its place: for they that take the sword shall perish with the sword'. (Matthew 26:52).
8. On the face of it, it would appear that Mrs Mary Weeton's claim of £12,000, on behalf of her husband, was spurious, or exaggerated. However, as the following pages reveal, Mrs Weeton's highly principled beliefs, would have made such an action anathema to her. Equally, it seems unlikely that the principled Rawlinson brothers would withhold lawfully earned money from one of their highly esteemed captains. Perhaps others were responsible for dealing with Captain Weeton's widow? Or perhaps there may have been a dispute about prize money? Without evidence coming to light, the truth may never be known. What is certain is that Mrs Weeton was a woman in a male dominated society, without the financial means to resort to law.

TWO

New pastures

Up Holland, near Wigan

May 1784 – July 1808

SOON AFTER THE death of her husband and also because of the
loss of her own mother, Mrs Mary Weeton decided to continue
with a plan she had previously discussed with her mother, who
had hoped to relocate to the ancient village of Up Holland, near
Wigan. Old Mrs Rawlinson had expressed a wish to spend her
final days in the place of her birth. She was the sister of an Up
Holland brewer, Randal Smith (then deceased). Mrs Weeton
also had a family connection with Up Holland through her sister
Margaret, whose second husband Thomas Barton of Wigan,
a saddler by trade, had decided on retirement to settle in Up
Holland. It was Margaret who informed her sister that 'both rents
and coals were much lower in Up Holland than in Lancaster.'
Together with her daughter, Nelly, aged seven, and three-year-
old son, Thomas, Mrs Weeton began her new life in Up Holland
in May 1784. There she rented a little cottage in Church Street.
Drawing on her eduction, experience and grounding in the social
graces, she soon became acquainted with the principal families in
Up Holland and neighbourhood.

Miss Weeton later described their cottage home as:

> A pretty cottage elevated from the road by a flight of steps to
> the front door. [There was] a kind of gallery across the front of
> the house, guarded on the open side by a row of white rails. At
> one end of the house was a little gate which opened into a pretty
> little garden on the side of a hill. The upper end contained an
> arbour of lilacs and roses, with a stone table and benches, round

6

where my mother has many a time entertained little tea-parties consisting of Mr Braithwaite, a clergyman, and his wife; Mr J. Clayton (brother to Sir Richard Clayton), likewise a clergyman, and his wife (who was sister to Mrs Braithwaite); the Rev R. Braithwaite, Captain Taylor, and his wife. The view from the cottage and garden was extensive, romantic, and beautiful.

Thomas attended Mr Braithwaite's nearby 'most excellent' school for boys, where he was a day scholar until his education was complete. Nelly did not attend school but was naturally an avid reader. She showed a natural aptitude for reading and scribbling rhymes. Nelly was taught by her mother and also by an usher from Mr Braithwaite's school who regularly attended the cottage to teach her writing, grammar, arithmetic and a little geography.

Both Nelly and Thomas were very happy in their cottage home but because of now severe financial constraints, Mrs Weeton became increasingly unhappy. Even with the strictest economy her little income from a very small estate at Sunderland, was insufficient to support the three of them. It was after four years residence in Up Holland, that Mrs Weeton was forced to increase her meagre income by starting a dame school.[1] Nelly was then 11 years old. For a small weekly fee Mrs Weeton gave an elementary education to the village children. Nelly herself was naturally bright but, unfortunately, her mother believed that she should be 'entirely ruined for any useful purpose in life if her inclinations for literature were indulged.' Whilst fond of arithmetic, Nelly 'burned to learn Latin, French, the Arts and the Sciences,' rather than spend the greater part of her day sewing, writing copies and washing dishes.

At this time Nelly's great joy was to greet her brother on his daily return from Mr Braithwaite's academy. The pair would then go into the cottage's garden to 'indulge in harmless children's frolics.' Nelly had only one doll but Thomas, being some four years younger, was rather more fond of it. Chalk and slate and quill and paper were Nelly's preferred indoor toys; for which she had a 'strong predilection,' Whilst indulging her preferences Nelly liked to tease her brother, until both usually collapsed in laughter.

7

In the summer evenings and during holidays they played together in the garden; in winter their amusements were much the same. What pleased one pleased the other and Mrs Weeton patiently indulged the pair's innocent amusement however troublesome it might be to herself. When it came to the composition of riddles, Nelly was invariably the victor. In answer Thomas would sport a little Latin, which was always impossible for Nelly.

When Thomas was away and her mother too busy to attend to her, Nelly turned to her only resource – reading and scribbling (either in chalk or with a quill). From the age of two years Nelly had been very fond of books, and greatly valued them as being her 'only companions.' Things began to change when Mrs Weeton commenced her school. From then onwards Nelly had companions in abundance during school hours but she was alone after five o'clock. At some point an agreement developed between brother and sister: When the weather was fine and they had permission to play in the garden, Nelly would join in her brother's boyish amusements, such as driving the hoop, sailing a ship (in a rain tub), running races and flying a kite. When the weather was cold or wet, Thomas would join in his sister's games such as visiting, nursing the doll, keeping school, reading, preaching, writing letters, composing prose enigmas and telling tales. Mrs Weeton did not allow her children to play with their village contemporaries.[2] Furthermore she zealously and rigidly instructed her children in 'every kind of religious duty and observance.'

Being firm and determined, Mary Weeton would 'never countenance the least impropriety of conduct.' She herself was 'correct to a high degree,' making hardly any allowance for those who were weaker in matters of conduct. Her anger was 'very dreadful' wrote Miss Weeton, 'not because it was loud, but because it was just. There was something awful in her looks that meanness or deceit could never appear before her, if she found any child deceitful.'

But for all that Mrs Weeton was loved too. When her pupils were obedient, industrious, generous and conciliatory towards each other, they had a full share of praise and caresses. Closely confined as Nelly was to her own studies, assisting her mother to teach, doing housework and 'taking in sewing for hire,' never at any time was she dissatisfied. Always she entered into 'all activities with continual alacrity.'

Religious conversations were initially received at the Weeton home from Mr Bannister (a clergyman) and then continued on Monday evenings at the home of a shoemaker. Miss Weeton described the religious instruction as one of strict formality:

> To avoid the censure of the Bishop of the Diocese, no prayers nor regular discourse were read. The room was divided into two portions; one for himself [Mr Bannister] and the Church Singers and the musicians, in number 10 or 12; the other for auditors. My brother, who was 7 years old, commenced learning the violin, was permitted to join the band. I sat in the auditory. Everyone present paid a penny for the use of the room, fire and candles. The meeting opened by one of the singers reading a versified psalm, with Mr B leaning on his violoncello, explaining and making remarks at the end of each verse.
>
> When it was read through, it was sung by all present. If there were (sic) sufficient time, one or two more were gone through, and then Mr B proceeded to ask the opinions of the band, each in succession, on some familiar and easy questions proposed the previous week from certain portions of scripture. Some, as may be supposed, replied with diffidence; others spoke well. Mr B then summed up altogether what had been said, and concluded by some remarks of his own, luminous and easily understood. The auditors were not expected to take a part in these discussions, but they received valuable instructions. About 20 generally attended. When a portion of scripture was given for the next week's consideration, the company separated, after singing a parting hymn. For my own part, no recreation was so agreeable to me as this. My mother had not the method of making religious instructions so interesting as Mr B had, for she taught wholly from books, and her children and pupils were required to get off by memory, chapters, catechisms and hymns, and if we said the words correctly, our task was done. But an equal portion of extempore instruction would have made repetitions tenfold more valuable.

At the age of fourteen, Thomas Weeton became articled to a solicitor, a Mr N. Grimshaw of Preston. Nelly was greatly saddened by the news and considered it to be 'interring him.' Now entirely without a companion; the 'promoter of mirth and frolic and stimulator of her studies' was gone. She visited each place where he used to be seen, in the knowledge that never would she see him again as before: his seat in church, his usual corner at home, his old clothes and books. Everything that had been his, reminded Nelly of the happy days that had fled; never to return:

> I revered and loved my mother, but I loved my brother a great deal better . . . It is all over now! My brother is happy – at least I hope so; and let me be thankful . . . I am but an insignificant individual; living unknown and neglected; and shall die unmourned. I am not of any consequence in the world. Great Power above, forgive my ingratitude.

Self pity then becomes apparent. Nelly was only too well aware that it was because of the particularly reclusive manner of her education, she had 'become averse to society.' When her mother encouraged her daughter to enter into social interaction, she became overwhelmed by shyness. Even beyond the age of 18 she would run upstairs to evade meeting an incidental caller at their home.

She later wrote that she never had a proper companion – a female one. Nor anyone of the opposite sex, other than her brother. The parents whose children were respectable were much too young and the girls of her own age – her mother's pupils – were 'so rudely and vulgarly taught at home.'

As Nelly grew up Mrs Weeton took great pains to cultivate an intimacy for her daughter with the daughters of the Revd R. Prescott,[3] Curate in charge at Up Holland Church. He was a clergyman of a 'handsome property.' He also esteemed Mrs Weeton highly; he too wished his daughters to be on terms of intimacy at his home. In obedience to their father's wishes they did so, and frequently invited Nelly to afternoons and even days with them. Unfortunately the sisters could not avoid showing Nelly that they considered being daughters of a clergyman as 'more superior in manners and in rank' to that of a schoolmistress;

although in Mrs Weeton's presence, they were never guilty of
such rudeness. Whenever Nelly complained of their rudeness
to her mother at home, she dismissed it as being wrong to take
offence where none is intended. Nelly's confidence was not
encouraged by her noticing that Revd Prescott's daughters were
'far superior' in manners than those she had been accustomed to.
As a result, her awkward timidity and their hauteur made visits
to the parsonage particularly disagreeable. Irksome hours passed
with the Misses Prescotts only made Nelly fonder of being alone,
sitting quietly in her brother's room with a book.

Mrs Weeton had a debilitating asthmatic complaint that
prevented her from assisting Nelly. As a result, the whole business
of running the home rested on her daughter. This included nine
hours a day at the dame school, cooking, cleaning, sewing and
nursing her mother. Both mother and daughter denied themselves
the necessaries of life in order to support Thomas at Preston.
Bread and potatoes were their principle diet. Butter, cream, sugar
and pastry, as well as butcher's meat, were rarities. Over time,
the confined life adversely affected Nelly's health, both physically
and mentally. She began to suffer a long lingering illness; for three
years she was in a very precarious state, to the point that she was
barely able to crawl.

From extreme parental care and tenderness, Mrs Weeton did
not let her daughter out of her sight until a doctor told her that her
life depended on her having more air and exercise. By degrees and
to the surprise of many, Nelly eventually recovered. 'It pleased the
Almighty that I should do so, for some good reason I hope,' she
wrote.

Before she was fully recovered, her mother's health, which
had always been delicate, began to decline rapidly. Her asthmatic
attack, exacerbated by the abusive language of one of her pupils,
hastened her end. She gradually became weaker and died on 5th
December, 1797. 'She quitted a life of sorrow for one, I hope, of
rest, at 51 years of age.' Nelly was not quite 21 years old when
her mother died. As a direct result of her mother's death she
then regarded herself as: 'An unprotected orphan' and with 'no
guardian on earth.' Revd Prescott had also died just three days

before Mrs Weeton, and within a few weeks his daughters left Up Holland to reside with their guardians. Feelings of isolation and vulnerability began to dominate Nelly's thoughts as she became forcibly aware that her brother was too young to assist her.

Four more years were to pass before Thomas would be free from his clerkship. This meant that his entire care had now become the responsibility of his sister. At the same time she realised that her income was too small to support both herself and her brother. Nevertheless Nelly set about fulfilling her mother's dying wish to continue running the dame school, while the small income from the Sunderland estate would support her brother until he was of age – and for two years afterwards:

> 'For, my dear Nelly [often repeated her mother], you know your brother is so situated he can earn nothing. And let him be as careful as he can, it will take our full income to support him. So you must let him have it until such time as he can maintain himself; which, is in two years after he is of age, if he is steady he may do, at which time it will be as little as he can do to let you have the whole whilst you remain unmarried; for if you do your duty, you will have dearly earned it. You are a good girl, and I have no doubt that you will do as I have requested.'

At the time of Mary Weeton's death, she was still in debt to her comfortably well-off sister, Margaret Barton. Margaret wasted no time in informing and requesting her niece to pay back the money owed to her by her mother. For her part, Nelly also wanted to pay off her mother's debt as quickly as possible, but her straitened circumstances made it very difficult to do so; although her aunt knew only too well of her niece's financial difficulties. Margaret Barton nevertheless pressed hard to be paid in full as soon as possible. It was a day of great rejoicing for Nelly when she finally paid her aunt the last half penny. She wrote: 'Unfeeling Aunt! You knew my circumstances, and should have given me a little more time.' The result of settling her mother's debt was that she had no choice but to starve herself for some two weeks. Daily she went without a dinner, and sometimes without supper; as for tea, she seldom drank any when alone.

For three years after her mother's death, Nelly became both 'feeble in mind and body.' Her frequent abstinences only served to increase her weakness. When she had food she could not eat it. What she did eat and drink 'came up again.' In time her health, very gradually did recover, but not before she accidentally received a violent blow to her ankle whilst playing with some little girls during a leisure hour. She bathed her ankle in rum and covered it with linen, but the bruise was too severe for such a remedy. One penny would have procured ointment but she had no money. For some months she suffered excruciating pain, and at one point the wound began to gather and stream with blood. Her Aunt Margaret paid her a rare visit and said: 'Why do you not get a poultice?' In response Nelly blushed and admitted that she had no money to buy a 'roll' with. Her aunt then lent her a penny. Unfortunately the result of the remedy being so long delayed, was that Nelly became confined for four months. During that time both she and her aunt considered that she might have to lose a leg, yet at no time did her aunt offer to procure medical assistance. Being childless in both her marriages, Margaret Barton 'had no earthly ties,' yet seldom found the time to visit her niece. Compared to Nelly's cousin, Anne (Nanny) Latham, living nearby, 'with a family to do everything for,' she considered her far more kind. Her cousin turned up as often as she could spare the time. 'Many a comfortable cup of tea should I have wanted had it not been for her.'

For a lengthy period of time Nelly went to bed with the idea that she 'might not rise up again to life,' even indicating at times, that she wished to die, and imagining that she might have 'lain undiscovered and putrid' for many days. As soon as she was well enough Nelly was invited by Mrs Braithwaite to spend evenings with her at The Priory.[4] It was during one such evening that Nelly felt an 'unusual sense of whirling' in her head, as if she was about to lose her senses. This was accompanied with palpitations to such an extent that Mrs Braithwaite insisted that one of her servants should accompany her home and stay the night with her. When sufficiently recovered, Nelly believed that her spirits and strength were low because of the 'want of society,' especially so outside of school hours. And yet after taking a walk one summer's evening about seven months after her mother's death, an appreciation for life was remembered whilst walking upstairs to take off her bonnet, and when every window in the house was open:

> The beauty of the evening tempted me to remain a long time at my room window. The prospect from it was extensive and pleasing; the children in the Church yard just beneath it were diverting themselves in many a harmless frolic; the people at a little distance were gathered together in small groups before their doors, enjoying the serenity of the evening; a clarinet played by some rustic sounded sweetly; the setting sun tinged the distant hills with a mild crimson; the windows of some scattered houses brilliantly reflected its sinking rays; everything seemed to rejoice in the perfect calm of the parting day. My heart swelled with gratitude to the Almighty Dispenser of Blessings! My soul was enraptured, my eyes filled with tears of pleasure! The shadows of night drew on; the hum of distant voices, the music, the peals of sportive laughter lessened on the ear. One object and then another vanished; a thick mist came on; every animate being seemed to be gone to rest – and I too, said I, will be gone, and in a twinkling was in bed fast asleep.

Over a period of time Nelly firmly believed that she had lost several of her 'genteel acquaintances' owing to the shabbiness of her dress, claiming that they were ashamed to be seen with her. But she could not afford to do better, being barely able to procure the necessities of life. Often, whilst weeping alone she mused that: 'I do it for my brother's sake, and he will reward me.' And therefore she thought it better that she should go about shabbily in a little village like Up Holland, rather than in a town like Preston, the location of Thomas's clerkship. Little did Nelly know that while she was wanting and needing pence, Thomas was spending sixpences and shillings.

In January 1802 Thomas Weeton's clerkship expired and he immediately left Preston for London. The three months he was there proved to be a traumatic time, not only for Thomas but also for Nelly. She does not spell out exactly what Thomas had experienced in London, but clues in her *Retrospect* suggest that

Thomas was becoming enmeshed in a 'vortex of vice.' To his credit, she stated 'twas well that he had resolution to quit when he did . . . and deserves some applause from it . . . he is sufficiently punished, poor dear fellow!'

Thomas returned from London to live with his sister for a few weeks, before settling in Wigan. It was there that he formed an attachment to a Miss Jane Scott, daughter of a cotton spinning factory owner. According to Nelly, Thomas had 'hastily and imprudently married [in 1803]; neither of them being able to command a farthing.' Miss Scott had married without the knowledge of friends, and Thomas had no house to take her to.

Nelly very kindly offered the happy couple her home and both arrived at Up Holland on the very day of the marriage. The financial arrangements for the couple's accommodation were decided by Thomas, 'at very ungenerous terms' for Nelly. She later wrote:

> The whole of our income was to go towards housekeeping; my furniture to fill the house; no servants to be kept; Mrs W. and me to do all the work. Nothing was said about me having any money allowed for cloaths (sic), so that I must have asked my brother for everything I wanted, and have appeared indebted to him for so much as a halfpennyworth of pins. I must have been a slave for them, for Mrs W was too indolent, too slow, and too little used to household work to have taken anything like a share in it.

A month later, Mrs Scott, Thomas's mother-in-law, sent 'a man and a horse' with a note requesting that the couple return on the horse. It was concluded best to comply with Mrs Scott's request and both returned to Wigan immediately. This left Nelly to live as a solitary person, once more.

One Saturday night Thomas returned to Up Holland and told his sister that Mrs Scott and her daughter had all concluded that 'it would be better I should not live with them; that such a kind of family was very unpleasant, causing the most unhappy dissensions.' At this news Nelly was devastated, as she remembered all that she had sacrificed on behalf of her brother: 'Abstinence from a necessary diet, rising early, sitting up late, depriving herself of almost every comfort,' was almost more than she could bear. Her heart was almost broken; especially so when she recalled sacrificing an offer of marriage, from a young man 'of great abilities and most excellent character.' At the time she had considered that her marriage would have been a great disappointment to her brother, who was then living in London:

> Had I told Mr M. my reasons for declining his offer, he would probably have made it again when he found out I was at liberty, but as he never knew, he probably thought it proceeded from dislike of him, and delicacy prevented my ever hinting anything on the subject to anyone. For the world I would not make a single advance. What a dreary prospect now presented itself. And as long as I do live, thought I, in this solitude – is there no hope?

For the next 18 months Nelly was unsettled. She considered various ways of improving her financial circumstances, but all were disapproved of by her Aunt Margaret, except for that of taking in lodgers. Finally, in opposition to their aunt, Thomas persuaded Nelly to leave Up Holland. She immediately set about making plans to do so, with the resolution 'never again to return to it unless to live in a very different manner to what I had lived'.

The earliest copy-letter (extant),[5] dated 25 October 1807, begins Volume 2 of Miss Weeton's copy-letter books. She was then in her 31st year. At the request of Mrs Braithwaite, Miss Weeton wrote to her daughter Anne, who was staying with friends at Clapham, London:

25 October 1807 (Up Holland). *To Miss Braithwaite:*

> And it came to pass that Mrs Braithwaite lifted up her voice one day and said, 'Oh Miss Weeton, will you write to Ann'(sic)? She returned for answer, 'Yes Ma'am, I will – I will if I can.' But afterwards she repented and wrote not.
>
> Again Mrs Braithwaite was urgent with her, and pressed her very much to write. And she was sore distressed, and knew not what to do; and turned the matter to and fro in her mind, whether she should write or not. But the spirit persuaded her and said, be not fearful; but be of good courage, and write.
>
> So she sat her down one Sunday after dinner and began, although she had nothing at all to say. For she had bought a

Flageolet a few days before, and it had turned her head; and she had nothing at all in it but demi ye semi quavers and crotchets. And she became agitated, and did puff her cheeks and shake her shoulders; for nothing *did run in her head* but folly.

Now whereas folly is exceedingly light, and doth shake the body to and fro like a feather if perchance it carrieth not ballast – nay, even if it doth, the ballast itself shall shake – how then can that which is light be composed of what is solid? Canst thou gather grapes of thorns, or figs of thistles? I trow not.

Can you then, my dear Miss Braithwaite, after *such* a preface, expect me to say anything worth the reading? My only hope is, that as it is a Lancashire letter, it may not be very unwelcome. And I will not be so unreasonable as to expect you to answer it, as your time must be a good deal taken up with other correspondents. I shall see the letters which came from you to the Abbey, or hear a part of them at least, and I will be contented.

In due course Anne did respond to Miss Weeton's letter and the pair continued to confide in each other by letter over many years.

Between November 1807 and July 1808, Miss Weeton corresponded with lengthy letters to Miss Chorley, a Liverpool friend. She was the daughter of a retired tanner. The family lived in Dale Street. Over the same period she also corresponded with Mrs Whitehead. She was the widowed daughter of the late curate-in-charge (Revd Richard Prescott) at Up Holland; then living in reduced circumstances in London.

On one occasion she corresponded with Mrs Edmondson, a Lancaster friend of her mother; also with Miss Bolton, a friend and a sister to Mr Robert Bolton of Wigan. However, whilst at Up Holland, her correspondence was largely with Miss Chorley and her brother, Thomas. She wrote at length, to both, between November 1807 and July 1808.

Serious consideration about relocation from Up Holland increasingly began to dominate Miss Weeton's thoughts. Various flexible plans concerning her move are revealed in the following four letters to both Miss Chorley and her brother:

10 June 1808 (Up Holland). *To Miss Chorley*:

The time draws near when I shall be leaving this place. In about a month I shall go to Leigh. My brother expects by that time to have got his new house, and he thought it would not be so pleasant to me to be there before, as I should be in all the bustle of moving, and he does not go into it than quite the end of the month. It suited me as well, too, to continue my school than the usual time of breaking up, and was not inconvenient to my tenant. This day three weeks I give up my school; in a week after, perhaps I may have settled my affairs; and then – farewell Holland.

By 1807, Thomas Weeton, at the age of 27, was settled in the little township of Leigh,[6] Lancashire. Through nothing less than dint of hard work and consistent persistence, he secured the bulk of the practice to be had in Leigh. Gradual progress, in terms of his increasing prosperity and status, encouraged by his demanding and socially-aspiring wife and sister-in-law (resident in the house), would eventually coalesce, to make him feel ashamed of his sister's humble status.

1 July 1808 (Up Holland). *To her Brother:*

In the midst of rubbage, lumber, furniture, dust, rags, cloathes, bottles, jars and boxes; and in the midst of hurry, sweat and bustle, I sit down to rest and to write (for in enjoying one, I can do the other), and to inform thee that I expect thee on Tuesday, and to tell thee of two or three other things, if I can tell where to begin first. But my head is so full of business, as well as my hands, that like as I was this morning when going to commence packing, I am almost at a stand, I hardly know where to begin, and find it rather difficult to methodise.

I have written to Meols[7] to procure lodgings. It will most certainly be a gratification to me, and I hope no inconvenience to you, if I go there for a few weeks before I visit you at Leigh.

8 July 1808 (Up Holland). *To Miss Chorley:*

I had the sale of my furniture on Tuesday and am now at Mrs Braithwaite's. My aunt has invited me to spend a few days with her on my return from Meols or Leigh.

I have been so busy for the last month that I have not had time, or even a thought of heaving a sigh at quitting a place I have resided in just 24 years. It is very strange! How shall be the last day, I can't tell. Is it philosophy, or apathy?

I have been most delightfully busy to-day. Oh Exercise! Thou banisher of sorrows! Thou art better than *Dr Solomon's Balm of Gilead*. Thou art a target to the soul, more impenetrable than steel to the body. The arrows of affliction or the shafts of sickness cannot injure those who are accompanied by thee.[8] 'Constant exercise is the best antidote for all human afflictions' shall be my motto when I keep a coach, or something to that purpose – 'How delightful is rest to the wearied labourer!' – this too I find, and just now sweetly experienced, whilst sitting at my ease at the writing table, after being on my legs from five o'clock this morning than six this evening.

13 July 1808 (Up Holland). *To her Brother:*

You will be at a loss to know where I am – whether at Holland or the Meols. I told you when you was at Holland, I should go to Mrs Braithwaite's as soon as I left my house there. I went, and – there I am now, at Mrs B's kind request, who wishes me to stay with her than Monday next; and then I go to my Aunt Barton's for the remaining few days, until I set out for Leigh.

It is clear from other correspondence to Miss Chorley, that Miss Weeton's brother had, reluctantly, been assisting his sister with applications for governess appointments at boarding schools. Other future employment possibilities were discussed within the family; such as her having a little school at Liverpool, or being engaged in the service of a 'private' family as a governess. In the event nothing positive came about, beyond Miss Weeton's own opinion that she should remove from Up Holland and stay in Liverpool to seek an employment opportunity there.

On Friday 22 July 1808, she removed to take up temporary residence with her brother and his family at Leigh. A month later, on 22 August, she left Leigh to proceed to her chosen destination – Liverpool – to become a 'guest' of the Chorley family, in Dale Street.

NOTES:

1. Before the 1870 Education Act many young children from the lower classes attended numerous private day schools, which provided cheap elementary education. Younger children attended dame schools run by older ladies, where for a few pence per week, they would be taught the rudiments of reading and sometimes writing as well. According to Miss Weeton, her mother had about 14 pupils in her school. Fees were 6 shillings a quarter.
2. It should be remembered that this was an age of deep-rooted polarisation of the classes. Mrs Weeton was far from being alone in not wanting her children to become influenced by their local contemporaries. At a later date Miss Weeton stated in correspondence that her mother had considered her pupils 'so rudely and vulgarly taught at home.'
3. Rev Richard Prescott, curate-in-charge (1767-97) at Up Holland Church. He was known as the 'galloping parson.' Evidently a man of substance, having several assistant curates during his incumbency, preferring instead the life of a country gentleman to that of a parish priest. He died December 1797.
4. Eight members of the Braithwaite family lived at 'The Priory.' It is located adjacent to Up Holland Church (now 'The Abbey'), on or near the site of a now demolished Benedictine Priory and only a very short distance from the Church Street home of the Weeton family.
5. According to Miss Weeton's own evidence, the first volume of her 'copy-letter' books began in the year 1805. It is now doubtful that Volume 1 will be discovered – if indeed it still exists?
6. In a Leigh directory for 1825, T. R. Weeton , Esq., is stated as living at Avenue Place, Leigh.
7. The flat and barren area of North Meols (pronounced 'Meels'), near Southport, became very popular through the sea-bathing craze from the early 1790s. There were no lodgings, except for the overcrowded homes of fishermen. Horse-drawn vehicles conveyed visitors to the beach.
8. 'Balm of Gilead' – the name is taken from a verse in the Old Testament Book of Jeremiah: 'Is there no balm in Gilead; is there no physician there?' why then is not the health of the daughter of my people recovered?' (Jer. 8:22). Samuel Solomon was born in Dublin, the year of his birth is uncertain. Eventually he relocated to Liverpool, where he started his quack medicine business. Of the many various concoctions, his 'Balm of Gilead' became the most famous and was advertised as a cure for all kinds of maladies. Solomon died in 1880.

THREE

A sea-port beckons

Liverpool

August 1808 – December 1809

MISS WEETON BEGAN her long journey from Leigh to Liverpool in the extreme heat of August 1808. She first walked with her brother to Winwick, near Warrington, before they parted company. There she caught the Warrington to Wigan stagecoach, calling for something to eat at the home of Mrs Scott (Thomas' mother-in-law), before embarking on the canal packet from Wigan for the nine hour journey to the bustling borough of Liverpool.

At the beginning of the 19th century, Liverpool was in its ascendancy, benefitting from the prosperity created by the 18th century African slave trade. Abolition of the trade in 1807 brought new opportunities through the import of linen yarn from Ireland and cotton from the American south for Lancashire's expanding mills. The population of Liverpool had risen from 5,000 in 1700 to 85,000 by 1801 and was still rising rapidly. It was to this up-and-coming vibrant seaport that Miss Weeton travelled.

On 31 August 1808, she wrote from Liverpool to her brother. The letter detailed her journey from Leigh to Liverpool and in addition chastised Thomas for his late rising. The result of which had meant her travelling in the heat of the day:

> I proceeded after you left me at the sign of the Swan,[1] three miles and a half on this side of Leigh; how I was overcome with the heat, all along of your late rising; how I got to Mrs Scott's [at Wigan] and dined there – very contrary to my first intention, which was to have assisted in consuming the product of the country at Holland; and how I found my Aunt and Uncle

[Barton] there, alive and hearty, and everybody else, for aught I know, in that land of health – and stupidity; how I left there next morning, all in the rain; and how it began to be fair soon after I got into the boat, and what an agreeable sail[2] I had.

Armed with a mental picture of what Liverpool would be like, she made her way to the Dale Street home of Mr and Mrs Chorley and their daughter. Miss Weeton realised that she would experience a great change in everyday living in a bustling seaport, so different from the small village community she had left behind. In February of that year, in a letter to Miss Chorley she had referred to her anticipated lifestyle changes between village and town life:

How delighted I feel as each day passes on, at the approach, or presence of Spring; at my consequent release from the torpid state to which Winter necessarily reduces me; and that the lengthening days and increasing warmth of the sun have just begun to enable me to put my head out of doors by daylight, and not, owl-like, to fly out only at dusk – But why talk to you of the pleasures of Spring? who, living in a town, know comparatively so little difference between one season and another. You might almost as well have winter all the year, when, even on the finest days you seldom see a furlong before you; whose prospect is generally bounded by high walls; who, instead of the 'music of the groves,' are compelled to hear little else than the rattle of carriages, carts, and wheel-barrows, the clack of horses, the din of mechanics; and whose most animating music is the screams of hawkers.

Well I am perfectly satisfied that you should enjoy the Orphean music of the streets, whilst I am so gratified by that of the fields and woods. What an amazing effect has habit! How greatly does it make one human creature differ from another, though wearing the same kind of form, possessing the same kind of soul. One prefers noise, another quiet; one exercise, another, inaction; one, like the ivy, clinging to every twig for protection; another, firm and independent as the oak; this, would be eternally wandering; that, scarce knows what it is, cased in walls, to see the light of heaven. Certainly, a great deal in the variety of our pursuits are not for the greater number of us employed in a very different manner to what our genius would lead us? The habits which education gives us when children, grow, with very few exceptions, into inclination in our riper years. You and I are in some measure examples of this. Though you can occasionally enjoy in a high degree the pleasures of the country, still, in general you prefer the bustle of a town. The calm of the country, after the novelty has ceased, grows into insipidity. The simplicity of the peasantry is soon discovered to be tiresome ignorance; and their wisdom little better than cunning. And you are glad to return to the conveniences and society of the town. So it is with me. The intelligent beings I meet with in large society, delight me beyond measure, but the noise of the crowd distracts me. The beautiful buildings, fine open streets, and elegant equipages, excite admiration; yet, when the novelty wears off, I wish for a more frequent sight of fields, groves, hills, and vales; and would sooner go into a hay meadow than the most crowded rout I could be invited to – because I have for so many years been accustomed to the country.

I thought of you today as I was enjoying a charming walk between twelve and two o'clock; such a one I think you would have liked, and I wished you with me. I passed Tower-hill[2], from whence the clearness of the air gave me such a delightful view of the country! The Welsh hills were uncommonly distinct, and the landscape in front of them, though so very level, and disfigured in some places by large patches of moss, was still infinitely pleasing. All around me, for some hundred miles in circumference, I had a variety of beautiful prospects. The air above me was so beautifully mingled with clouds of various shades, that that alone would have charmed me had there been nothing else to admire.

> *When I survey such thrilling scenes,*
> *Oh Thou the great First Cause!*
> *'My swelling soul denies the means*
> *To utter my applause."*

'How kind,' Miss Weeton explained, in a letter dated 10 September to her Aunt Barton, were the Chorley family towards her – even wishing her to stay the Winter. Mrs Chorley had suggested that Miss Weeton would be company for her daughter. In the event, it seems that she was determined not to overstay her welcome. She was all-too-aware that she was merely a 'guest' with the Chorley family, not a 'boarder.' A further letter to her

Aunt Barton dated 19 September, explained that she had been looking for lodgings at a 'white cottage close to the shore, about a mile from Liverpool.' It was located 'just below Kirkdale, and almost opposite to the Black-rock.'

She also kept her brother informed of her new lodgings; then despatched a further letter to her Aunt Barton, informing her of a new-found companion from Halifax, Yorkshire. Finally she described a dramatic rescue in a hurricane-strength gale in the River Mersey.

22 September 1808 (Liverpool). *To her Brother:*

I have taken lodgings near the shore in a most pleasing situation, just below Kirkdale, almost opposite the Black-rock. A man, his wife, and a little boy about six years old live at the house. From my room window I shall have a view of all the vessels coming in and going out of Liverpool (from which I shall be about one mile distant). I am to give 8 guineas a year, which Miss C. thinks exceedingly cheap. I am going on the 1st of October to stay that month, and then return again for a time to Mr C's. They are really kind, and strongly urge me to remain the winter with them. However, I shall like to have a home, and if not taken before Spring, as the people take in three or four genteel families during the bathing season; from one of which, a rich Quaker in Everton, Miss C. and I have this morning been making enquiries, and have received satisfactory information as to the character of the people of the house. Edward Smith is the man's name, a journeyman tobacconist. I like the situation most exceedingly, and hope I shall find things so comfortable as to be able to stay there.

15 October 1808 (Lodging at Beacon's Gutter, near Liverpool). *To her Aunt Barton:*

I came to my lodgings on the first of this month, and for so far as I can judge, I shall be very comfortable. A lady from Halifax, in Yorkshire, came a few days before I did, to stop a month. She was in rather a delicate state of health, but has recovered surprisingly, and I think is as stout as I am. Her husband is a great cotton manufacturer. He has been once to see her. She is a little younger than myself, and is a very lively, agreeable companion. I shall be sorry when she goes. It was by mere accident when Mrs H.

[Huntriss] came to these lodgings. It is almost close to the water's edge, and attracted their notice as being the most pleasantly and conveniently situated of any they saw, little more a mile from this end of Liverpool, not a quarter of a mile from the canal, and little more from Kirkdale.

Being so near the shore, and just at the mouth of the river, we are much exposed to the winds, and since I came here, have experienced a great deal of rough weather. For a few days at first, the weather was so warm and mild that Mrs H. and I frequently went and sat upon the banks for an hour or two at once, and spent most of our time out of doors. Since then, there has been one continued hurricane. Last Thursday night a storm began which continued the two following days. On Friday, several vessels were wrecked; one of them in our view. Mrs H. and I went into a bathing machine just opposite the vessel in distress, and whilst we stood sheltered from the violence of the wind, we saw it beat against the wind repeatedly. A crowd began to collect upon the shore within a few hundred yards of the ship. A reward was offered to any six or eight who would venture out in a boat to fetch the crew – for then the vessel lay quite down on one side, the waves dashing over the off side like drifting snow, and on the nearer side, washing over the decks and carrying away everything moveable. The men for a long time were busied in hacking at the masts, which at length fell overboard with a loud crash. A boat at length sett (sic) off, but could not reach the ship. A second time the force of the waves drove them back in spite of all their exertions. A man then boldly waded into the water till he was within hearing of the poor crew, and said something to them by means of a speaking trumpet. The boat then set off a third time, and fortunately reached the ship and took out the men, all except the mate and two black sailors, who bravely, or fool-hardily, staid in the vessel by themselves from ten in the morning than four in the afternoon. In a few minutes the crew were safely landed, and gave a shout which was heard as far as our cottage. The vessel was too high upon the rocks to sink, so that everyday since, she has been unloading, and yesterday was sold by auction on the shore for the benefit of the insurers; and to-day two fields adjoining this house are almost covered with Irish linen, which was part of her cargo, and which they have been washing in the gutter[3] that runs close by, to get out the salt water. She was just setting sail for the Brasils.

Relocation from Up Holland to Liverpool did not mean Miss Weeton relinquishing her duty as God parent to her nephew; as the following letter reveals.

1 November 1808 (Beacon[s] Gutter). *To her Nephew and Godchild, Master Henry Latham:*

Tell me how far you are advanced in your Arithmetic, whether you make any progress in Grammar, and whether you have begun to learn Geography yet. As to your writing, that I shall see by your letter. Tell me too, what books you have been reading in since Midsummer.

Give my love to Richard, and tell him that I shall expect to see a little of his writing at the bottom of your letter, just to tell me whether he goes to school; or if he does not, whether he ever does anything at his books at home. I could wish to be particularly attentive to his reading. And I dare say, you, my dear Henry, will give him every help in your power, if he will but pay attention to you. I hope he is not still the playful, idle boy he has been; merry tricks and active amusements are very right in proper play hours, but it is quite time for Richard to grow industrious and to attend to his books, or assist his mother, seven or eight hours every day. I have no occasion to say anything to on the subject of industry, for you was always as attentive as I could wish you; and you will have your reward for being so, in the pleasure you will always feel in the approbation of every one that knows you, which you will be sure to have so long as you continue to be a good boy as you have hitherto been. Richard has often promised me how good he would be. I hope he does not forget those promises, and then there needs not be a more engaging lad anywhere. I often think of him, and of you, and every one of you.

I am going in about ten days to Mr Chorley's again to stop – they say, than the first of April; but I say (though I cannot speak so plainly to them), that I like my present home so well that I would much rather stay here. They are indeed kind to me as it is possible for anybody to be, and urge me so much to stay with them, that I am afraid I should appear obstinately ungrateful were I still to refuse returning to them for a time. But not for long as they talk of; I will get back if I can for the first of January.

26

7 November 1808 (Beacon's Gutter), *To Mrs Braithwaite:*

The weather has not been altogether civil to me, for soon after I came here, I might have been Boreas himself, with one cheek, it was so puffed, and had you met me, you would have seen that cheek almost half a mile before you saw the other; but it would have been no easy matter to find my complaisant (sic) eye, it kept at such respectable distance. However, as I am a great advocate of equality, I sent for Mr Aranson [a dental surgeon], who extracted four teeth, and the operation soon reduced the great cheek to the level of its neighbour. Since that time, I have been in perfect good health, equally good spirits, and, (if you will believe me) in as good humour.

In the course of a week I shall return to Mr Chorley's to stay some time with them; and though to such kind friends, I shall be almost sorry to leave here, I spend my time so agreeably. I find employment or amusement in one way or another, the day through. My time has not yet hung heavily on my hands, notwithstanding I have only myself to attend to. This week I am going to be busy with the mantua maker for two or three days, that I may have something fit to appear in when I get to Mr C's; for Miss Chorley told me the other day that she could not for shame take me to Christ-Church, I had nothing fit to go in. But Christ's Church nowadays is not what the Church of Christ was formerly. He used to say, 'to the poor the Gospel is preached,' but now the age is grown more liberal, so that they pay their teachers. Of course, it is chiefly to the rich that the gospel is preached. 'The rich and the poor' do not 'meet together.' The poor go to pray – nobody knows where, and any scrubby fellow may instruct them. To be 'clothed in rags' was once a recommendation to the Church of Christ, but now the surest way of being denied entrance into it. Fashion in times of old could no more gain admittance into that Church, than a woman into a Turkish Mosque; but the present age are so little scrupulous, that Fashion, whatever garb she wears, is permitted; indeed, every pains taken to allure her to take her seat in Christ-Church. That Church is altogether *fashionable* – So, last Sunday I set out from here, to try if Saint Catherine would let me pray in her house; but Pleasure met me by the way in the shape of an Eastham Packet-boat, and Saint Catherine has not yet been put to the blush at my unfashionable appearance. Miss Winkley, a niece of Mrs Hawarden's of Wigan, with whom

I thought of going to Church, was just going to Eastham with a young gentleman to meet a sister of his, and invited me to be of the party. I went, and had a very agreeable sail indeed; for anybody may go in a packet boat. Mr Lucifer has not yet found it worth his while to tyrannize there, in the appearance of Fashion. He gains more converts by coming in the character of a bottle, a chicken, a ham, a veal pie, or a fiddle.

8 November 1808 (Beacon's Gutter). *To her Aunt Barton:*

This is a very retired situation, but pleasant and clean without, and quiet and comfortable within. I hope my Uncle and you will not take my word alone, but come for a week or two (or longer if your health permits), in the Summer, and see for yourselves whether I say more in its favour than the situation deserves. If you choose to bathe, you might undress in the house and walk into the water, the tide comes so neat. It was a very high tide about a fortnight ago, and it came close to the door; ships are going out or coming in almost every day; and brigs and boats are continually on the river. At low water I can frequently see people walking on the Black-rock; and anytime on the Cheshire shore, if the air is moderately clear.

I am at a very nice distance from Liverpool; about 2 miles from Castle Street. I have taken a walk every Saturday, and sometimes on other days, to make my markets and see Mr Chorley's. One night last week I went to the play with Edward Smith and his wife, and sat in the gallery. I got a front seat owing to Edward's great civility in getting in first and keeping it for me. *The Conscious Lovers*[4] was performed that night. I was much entertained, more so than I expected, and had a delightful walk home by moonlight.

14 November 1808 (Beacon's Gutter). *To her Brother:*

As I had not written to several of my correspondents for a long time, I have taken the opportunity of my present retirement to acquit myself of all my epistolary debts; and as my letters are often long, and I am not quite so quick at composition as you, each letter takes up a more considerable portion of my time than I choose to tell. And what takes up still more, I copy all my letters. It is an amusement to me to read them over again – again to recall former ideas, and incidents long past. But I must in some degree cease writing for two or three months unless to thee and my Aunt, if Mrs C. does not offer me the frequent indulgence of a fire in my room; which perhaps she will not think of, or not permit; and I shall not like to request It. If she does allow it me, it will remind me of Holland. A fire in my room on a cold winter's evening, was one of the great comforts I had during that long, dreary, solitary season; and many a snug sit have I had there, shut up in a box 7 feet by 9, with a bed, a chest of drawers, two chairs, and a wash-stand in it, (don't peep under the bed now!) with just spare room for myself and the fire, and a tea-tray put over the wash-stand to serve for a table. There have I sat, often and often, a voluntary prisoner from five or six o'clock in an evening till twelve, one, or two in the morning, before I got into bed; just as if I were the only human creature in existence.

Since I came here I have been very comfortable indeed. The unusual bustle I had been in, with as unusual a scene of a variety of human creatures to which I had been a spectator for three or four months, made me wish for a little rest and quiet, and here I enjoy it.

Betty Smith often goes on errands to Liverpool; and as her husband works there, I am frequently left quite alone, and by the perhaps that I get almost tired of my own company, she returns; and is very chearful and chatty, I find her no disagreeable companion. I have always sat with the family since Mrs Huntriss went, who only staid three weeks. I have been rather more than six. I contrive to prepare my meals at the time, and eat off the same table as I do. There are no neighbours very near, except the farmers about three or four hundred yards from hence; but they are a very rude, untaught family, and we seldom or never see them, except when we go for milk and butter. Very few people call here, so that we are as retired as possible. Betty is a second Mrs Weeton for being fond of bed in a morning, and as I do not like to come down before the fire is made, it is very often nine o'clock before either she or I make our appearance below stairs. Then we sit chatting over our breakfast for an hour, so that it is sometimes half past ten before we rise from it. Here is indolence and waste of time for you! You will have no occasion to wonder how it happens that I have not had time to write to you sooner, when so much of that time has been occupied in doing nothing. When two or three of the first hours of a day are thrown away in bed, or wasted at our meals, it throws the work of that day four or five hours back. I must give you no more lectures on the subject

29

of early rising until warmer days, when I can rise earlier myself; though indeed I should rise before so shamefully late an hour if I had a fire to come down to. I enjoyed my bed for a while, lying so long awake after daylight, but now I am beginning to get tired of it, and luckily, just as I am beginning to tire, I am going to Mr Chorley's, where they rise by seven.

Miss Weeton then abruptly changed the subject, to that of concern for her brother's apparent difficult financial circumstances in his growing business and profession as an attorney, by encouraging him not to lose hope:

I hope, my dear fellow, the losses thou wert apprehensive of are in a fairer way of being recovered than they were. Hope must not be dead within thee. Thou wilt do well yet, I am sure thou wilt, if thy health forsakes thee not. Take every care thou canst. And though business should be slack just now, something will turn up to support thee, if thou canst but wait with patience. Religion is such a consolation to a drooping spirit, that I could wish thou wouldest seek for comfort and chearfulness in it; for God never forsakes those who turn to him. I assure thee truly, my dear brother that often when my spirits have been low, I have found more real pleasure in reading the Psalms, and in Job[5] and a few others of the inspired writings, than in any other kind of amusement I could enter into. Let not thy spirit sink within thee. I am sure, Tom, I am sure, thou wilt do well, for thou dost not want diligence. God bless thee.

* * *

Late in the year of 1808, in addition to her letter writing, Miss Weeton began to write a 'Journal' which allowed her to record her private thoughts and feelings. The Journal also included observations on books she had read. Her journalistic musings additionally reveal a maturing understanding, rather than a hitherto idealistic one, of those in her circle she once held in very high esteem. (All 'Journal' entries are chronologically combined with her letters to correspondents).

* * *

[Journal, December 1808]:

What angry looks did I this evening receive from both Mrs and Miss Chorley, for merely asking so simple a question as whether they paid more for large oysters than small ones? The question was natural enough, considering the remark made but the moment before Mr Chorley, who, when his wife asked him why he had not bought some oysters for supper, said, he should have done so, but there were none in the market except those great dirty things, and he would not have them at any price. 'Why, no,' said Mrs Chorley. This made me conclude that the small ones, being considered the greater delicacy, would fetch a higher price. I suppose I was mistaken, for had my question been of a treasonable nature, I could not have been looked at with a greater degree of anger and indignation by the one, and contempt, by the other. My question remained unanswered, and the rude treatment I had received on so very *slight* an occasion, though not *uncommon,* was more than I could well bear. My heart swelled, my spirits sank – the tears flashed into my eyes; I covered them with my hand, as if the candle-light affected them, and fortunately – I think – I was unobserved. Had Mrs C. intended to have struck me dead, she could not have darted a more severe look at me; and had Miss C. meant to have annihilated me, she could not have looked with more contempt. They can make no allowances for me. How should *I* know anything about oysters, who have lived so very long in a place where they were never purchased, and very seldom seen? Mrs C. is an excellent cook, and I should like to know something of house-keeping, but the few questions I have ventured to ask on that subject, have either been unanswered, sneered at, or treated with so much ill-temper, that I dare ask no more. Had I the spirit of a dog, I should quit them. Thank Heaven I have elsewhere to go, where I should be far happier than I am here, and under obligation to no one, real or imputed. Here, should my spirit one day be roused to retort the frequent insults I meet with (though if I can command myself, it shall not), I should be charged with ingratitude. Under what obligation am I, whilst treated with so much contempt, ridicule, and ill-temper? They give me food and lodging, but they pay themselves again in the spleen they vent upon me. Miss C. in particular treats me in a manner scarcely to be endured. Mrs C. is very kind indeed in general; it is only sometimes that she treats me with rudeness; but one of her kind, benevolent looks sufficiently repays me. She is a fine old woman! She is more; she is a noble one! What expression there is in her whole appearance! What majesty and dignity! Oh, if she were but better tempered, there would scarcely exist her equal. She would have been an ornament to a throne. She seems as if she were born to command; and yet, if she were, how sadly has her destiny misplaced her. Instead of being the wife of an honest, simple, illiterate, good-tempered tanner, she should have been a Catherine, or an Elisabeth. I often think she is conscious of the infirmity of her temper. She appears to me to strive frequently to subdue its violence; and if she does (and I do think she does), she has great merit! She has a strong head and a warm heart; notwithstanding, she frequently makes me feel her indignation more forcibly (I think) than I deserve; yet one of her smiles is a cordial that dispels the gloom that her anger has caused; and when, on bidding her good night, she gives me an affectionate squeeze of the hand – which she sometimes does when in a good humour – I could call myself the most ungrateful of beings for ever indulging a moment's resentment, and resolve to bear with patience and humility whatever her anger may induce her to look or say; for at times, I feel as if I were all heart, and could bestow a very great portion of its esteem and affection upon her. Since, according to the human eye, she appears so greatly misplaced in this world, I could almost imagine that there was some probability in the doctrine of transmigration, and, that she must again make her appearance upon the stage of life in a character more suited to her abilities, for they are shining.

Her daughter inherits all her mother's violence of temper, without her strength of intellect or goodness of heart; for, if she had either, she would not insult the dependant, or tyrannize over the weak, without, without any intermission. I am no dependant, thank God for it! Yet she treats me as such, daily and almost hourly insulting me. And in so gross a manner! I have been under great obligations to her; but she has no firm principles. I have begun to find her friendship was mere caprice, and that it is turned into hatred – the most contemptuous hatred – I have been under great obligations to her, and I was not ungrateful. I have often defended her cause against censures; for indeed I have often had occasion. For I could not bear that a friend of mine should be ill spoken of in my hearing, and had almost quarrelled with my brother on her account – grievous indeed would that have been my dearest brother, my only loved friend, to have lost his esteem, would have been to have lost all I cared for in this world; and it shall never again be in danger of being over-balanced by straw – and it is no more than a straw – Then why do I suffer a straw to grieve me? I am weak and spiritless, or I should not – It pleases the Almighty to try us with trifling vexations at first, and if those do not humble us, to afflict us with greater. There is scarce an evening I go to bed, or a morning when I leave the room, that I do not pray for a humble mind, and resolve to bear with Christian patience the insults I have reason to expect that day. But is it a Christian's duty to bear the tyranny of a fellow creature without turning again? Without any reply, or any defence? If it is, a Christian's duty is hard to learn! Yet I do endeavour to learn it, so far as outward conduct goes. I seldom reply or retort. Sometimes the frailty of my nature or the violence of my resentment get the better, and I speak in all the bitterness of an anguished soul; at other times, it only flows in tears. Oh, Miss Chorley! You are to this house what Buonaparte (sic) is to Europe – a scourge – for good, I hope, to us, without any evil to yourself. May God forgive you. Your insolence to your parents, and the tyranny you are guilty of to all you have in your power, requires the prayers of all who feel it (and you have mine), and the particular forgiveness of Him who is pouring his benefits upon you every moment.

[Journal, December 1808]:

I had written little more than a page of the preceding thoughts on Sunday, after evening service, when as I was continuing them, Miss C. entered my room. What was her reason for coming in just then, I cannot tell. She had not done so for two or three weeks before; and such a condescension was very unexpected, and equally unwished for. I went to church with Mr and Mrs C. and their little granddaughter. Miss C. staid to lock the door after the servants, and did not come into Church than near half the service was over. Whether she had gone into my room in my absence, and read what I had in part written and incautiously left upon my dressing table, or whether she suspected that I was writing something against her, I cannot tell. She was conscious, I dare say, that she had given me reason. She asked what I was

33

writing. I hesitated to tell, for I did not choose to tell a falsehood, any more than the truth. 'Was it a letter?' 'No.' 'A Journal'? 'No.' 'Some work intended for publication.' 'No indeed.' 'What then is it?' said she, 'for I am determined to know' – at the same time endeavouring to read it, as I held the book half closed. I shut it. 'I replied, 'what right you have to insist upon seeing anything I write. I never ask you such questions, or pry into your affairs.' 'I am determined I will know by some means or other,' she said, 'or you will not write another line.' 'Very well,' said I, putting down my pen, 'if I don't write now, I can take some other opportunity.' 'Either let me see it, or read me one line; for I dare say it is something very satyrical (sic)! 'What makes you suppose so?' enquired I, looking steadily at her. 'Read me one line!' she replied, 'and convince me that it is not. It is something against me – or someone in this house, or you would not be so afraid of my seeing it.' 'Perhaps you have seen it,' rejoined I, 'and if so, I need not read it.' 'Only read me one line, or tell me what it is about, or I shall not stir out of this room.' 'I shall do neither,' I drily answered. 'I am not a mere machine, only to be moved by force. You have taken a wrong method; kindness will go a much greater way with me, Miss Chorley, than insult. You are much better acquainted with the latter than the former. It is very strange if I cannot write a few lines in a book, without being obliged to give an account of them,' I felt myself growing angry. Let me be cool, thought I, I won't give way to anger. 'So, Ma'am, if you please,' said I laughingly, 'please to walk out of my room.' 'I'll see what it is you have written first,' she said, attempting to take the book. 'Indeed you shan't,' I replied, taking hold of her hands. She laughed, and struggled to free them, still positively asserting that she would not leave the room than she knew what I had been writing. 'You oblige me to tell you, Miss C., that such curiosity is extremely impertinent. Were you a guest at my house, I should not treat you in the manner you do me. I can neither write a letter, nor receive one, but you must know to whom it is directed, and by what right?' I again recollected myself, and stopped to cool. 'Do you suppose,' she answered, 'that you shall do just what you like here? You may be plotting against the state for anything I know, and may bring us into trouble.' 'What nonsense! Do you suppose it likely?' 'Why, then,' she answered, 'do you not shew me what it is you are writing. Besides, we are answerable for your conduct.'

34

I stared – 'Answerable! to whom?' 'Let me see what it is you are writing,' she still continued; and she attempted again to get to the table where the book lay. We struggled, and I had almost got her out of the room, when, recollecting that I too was using force, I let her go, and seizing the book, ran out of the room and hid it. I durst not go downstairs lest she should discover the hiding place; and stood on the landing place. She continued in my room a long time. At length, being tired I suppose with waiting so long, she left it, and I took the first opportunity of taking the book back again into my room, and locking it up. And very carefully have I been ever since to keep my box locked; for one whose curiosity could lead them to such a length, I cannot be much injured though they were suspected of being capable of rummaging a box of a drawer to satisfy it. When at length we got into the parlour, she began in such a manner on the same subject, that Mrs Chorley was quite alarmed. 'Mary! Mary!' she cried, when she could be heard, 'what is the matter with you? Mary, you quite frighten me.' – for Miss Chorley was laughing so loud, and talking so fast, that there was no stopping her. 'Mary!' she again exclaimed, 'what is the matter with you. You are out of your senses.' – and she really appeared terrified. 'Do be calm, Mary, I beg of you.' She at length became calm, and I have heard no more on that subject; but for a fortnight before, and nearly the whole of the week following, she has treated me with almost one unvaried system of insult. I might not be a being of the same species with her. It is a long time since she answered my morning's salutation. I still persevere in saying 'Good morning,' but she only answers it with a nod of her head, or a cool 'How d'ye do' and very seldom speaks to me at other times, looking at me frequently with the utmost contempt; inveighing sometimes against African captains, sometimes against attorneys; and one day took occasion to say – 'So much for a pragmatical schoolmistress!' glancing an ill-tempered look at me. I laughed. What a littleness of mind! What a narrowness of heart! May she meet with better treatment than she bestows! – My father was an African captain; my brother is an attorney; and I have been a schoolmistress.

[Journal, December 1808]:

I went to bed this evening, as I have done many preceding ones since Miss C. began to treat me so differently to what she used to do, in exceedingly low spirits. I am very foolish to let trifles affect me so much – I cannot help it. I cried bitterly when I got into bed. I *had* flattered myself in the morning, that she was going to be better humoured again. I fancied the little she did say, was spoken with more kindness than usual – I was disappointed. Her former kindness had made me very partial to her. I cannot soon forget the favours I have received from her, though they only serve now to grieve me, since she who bestowed them is so much altered – with regard to me, at least. She had formed too high an opinion of me, probably, and now that she finds me frail and mortal, I cannot help venting the bitterness of her disappointment. I could very soon love her again, if she would be more kind – so I thought as I sat near her this morning, and she more good-humoured than usual. She was very silent all the way. I asked several questions, some of which were answered, and some not. When she wanted to cross the street, she pulled or pushed me rudely, without speaking; and not being always aware or her intention, I several times was in danger of stumbling, for she had hold of my arm. After calling on several friends (who were *not in*), we went into Willan's library. Two books, on a similar subject, were produced, but not belonging to each other, Miss C. was looking to see which was the right one. I advised her looking at the beginning of the different Vols. That she might compare them; for she was looking towards the middle, or conclusion. 'Do *you* look,' said she, throwing them to me with the most utmost scorn, and turning to a review which lay near. 'I did not mean to offend,' I said, half in tears, and drawing off my glove to do so as I was *ordered*. I was not quick enough. 'Why don't you look at them?' said she, glancing a look at me as if she would have knocked me down. – I put on my glove again. My spirit was roused. I spoke not, but turned to look at some other publications. She continued reading some time. At length she took one of the Vols. And we left the shop. 'What was the reason,' she enquired, 'that you would not look at the books I gave you'? The spirit of resentment still burned within me. I answered that I was little accustomed to so *much* temper and rudeness as she had for some time treated me with. That I did expect common civility. Kindness I would not ask for; perhaps I did not deserve it; but that unless I were degraded something below human, I *never would* submit to haughtiness, tyranny, and ill-temper. For

36

a *little* civility, I could do a *great deal*; I would have immediately complied with a request, but not with a *command*. 'You are a sad temper,' she replied. 'I never knew one more obstinate and perverse.' Little more was said during the remainder of our walk.

[Journal, December 1808]:

Miss C. went out this morning. She did not ask me to go with her, as she used to do when I was in high favour. However, I was in better company when left with Mr and Mrs Chorley. I was not sorry she did not ask me; but so marked a slight affected me. I told Mrs Chorley I would take a walk. I did so – alone. The passing objects served to dissipate the lowness of spirits, and I came back much more chearful (sic) than I set out. I determined to try what chearful looks would do, for I have lately been a good deal in the dismals. I exerted myself a little – indeed, a great deal, to try to talk, and Miss Chorley coming home in great spirits – though she never addressed herself to me – dinner passed over more agreeably than it often does. I wish Miss C. would take a walk every morning! It gives her spirits, and she is far more agreeable afterwards. Indeed, this is such a dark, dismal house, it is no wonder its inhabitants are infected with gloom. For my part, I shall be much rejoiced when the time comes that I can go back to Beacon's Gutter. My visit here shall not be much longer, when I can find a plausible pretext for shortening my visit – unless they alter greatly in their conduct towards me. I cannot all at once get the better of my respect and attachment for Miss C. If I could her marked contempt would not hurt me so. However, thank Heaven, I am in a fair way. I *was* under great obligation to her but her late conduct has almost cancelled them. The remembrance of them would revive in full force, were she again the affectionate friend she used to profess herself. – In how much better spirits have I been the greater part of this day than I have been for a long time. – What a *great* effect *trifles* have upon me. Some of these says I shall be going either crazy or mad, just as it may happen whether I am visited by a little prosperity, or adversity.

Every day I have more and more reason to admire and respect Mr Chorley. Such a good-tempered, honest-hearted fellow is not to be found in every house. I used to think meanly of him, and wonder that Mrs C. could think of marrying such an ugly, rude, simple creature as him. That he is still remarkably plain in his features and person, extremely blunt in his manners, and no strength of understanding, I still allow; but these are natural defects which he cannot help possessing; and his constant good humour and sincerity make me now cease to wonder that a Mrs C. would marry such a one.

About this time Miss Weeton began to show her natural business flair by entering the domestic property market, but at the same time displays naivety in her expectations from the motives and actions of others. It is perhaps timely to recall that she was brought up by that paragon of rectitude – her devout mother and dame school teacher. Mrs Weeton would 'never countenance the least impropriety of conduct.' Likewise, as a practising Christian, Miss Weeton lived her life as closely as possible to Christian precepts, which, because she trusted others implicitly, would unfortunately cost her dearly in years to come.

15 December 1808 (Liverpool – written from Dale Street). *To her Brother:*

Soon after I came to Liverpool I told Mr Chorley what sum I had in the bank and that it was only making 3 per cent; and requested him to inform me what would be the best method of laying it out, or how I might procure a Mortgage for it. 'Will you wait,' said he, 'a few weeks? Perhaps I may hear of something.' I did wait, and I was soon informed of a Corporation lease which I might have for £650 or £660 upon condition that the seller cleared all expensed of writings, &c. The Lease makes £57 pounds and 10 shillings a year. The property is in houses, 5 back, and one front one, situated in Roscoe Lane. The houses and the Lease are quite new. I have let them all together to a Mr Wm. M'Cartney, for 55 pounds clear money for 5 years. The Lease is so made, that I can at any time take the houses into my own hands, though Mr M. is obliged to fulfil the 5 years lease if I require. It reminds me of Mr Catterall's Memorandum on the back of a writing he shewed you, viz: Mr Clarke to be bound, but me loose.

As the houses makes near 9 per cent, I was glad of such an opportunity of increasing my income without sinking the principal; for I could at any time sell them, Mr Clements assures me, for more than I gave for them; which I would do, should I meet with some pretty little estate or land of inheritance.

My income will be about 60 pounds a year when the income tax is paid, which will be a very comfortable support for me. I have desired you would not mention this to my Aunt, and I now request you would not to anyone; for if Mrs W. knows, I am certain she cannot help telling her sisters; and so on, till my affairs will be as well known by others as myself.

I lead a very dull life here. I was far more chearful at my lodgings. I very often sit whole days without stirring, except just to move my chair, or fetch something out of my room; and so spiritless, that I scarcely speak a dozen sentences during the time. Miss Chorley is extremely ill-tempered with me. She has treated me with a degree of insolence which I can hardly for bear to resent. Indeed, I have sometimes resented it, though not one hundredth part of what I have been made to endure; and now she generally goes out a-walking or visiting without asking me to go with her, and takes very little notice of me when she is in the house, looking frequently at me in the most contemptuous manner. I assure thee, Tom, if it was not for Mr and Mrs Chorley's kindness, I would not stay another day in the house. I mean to go as soon as I well can. *Thou* shalt suffer no more from me, however, on her account. *She was* so very warm a friend!

I fancy she is tired of me; but why, then, was she so very urgent for me to stay the whole winter here? If I knew to say to Mrs Chorley, I would soon be gone. Blame must rest somewhere and I no more want to throw it upon her than to take it to myself – that my health suffers from so much confinement I can truly say, and for want of air – so that will do.

P.S. I yesterday told Mrs Chorley that I wished to go to my lodgings again, on the plea of ill-health, and have fixed to go on Wednesday next.

Direct for me to the care of Mrs Winkley, Princes Street. Miss Chorley still continues her insulting behaviour. You will almost rejoice at it, considering what has passed between you and me on her account. She hourly makes me feel my inferiority of birth, fortune, and talents, most painfully. She has made me miserable for near a month. I have fretted until I am almost deprived of sleep, and it has brought on a degree of languor and palpitation that has increased daily for some time. One so full of faults as I am, is best buried in the retirement of Beacon's Gutter – for, according to Miss Chorley, I am thoroughly contemptible.

3 January 1809 (Beacon's Gutter). *To Mrs Whitehead:*

I came here on the 18th of October [1808], to a small, white, shabby-looking house, close to the sea shore, called Beacon's Gutter (a fine elegant sounding name, is it not?). Here, though very retired, I am very happy, and comfortable. Edward Smith, his wife, and little boy (about 8 years old), compose the whole of the family, besides myself. Edward is in a tobacconist's warehouse, as a journeyman; his wife does nothing but take care of the house. In the summer they take in lodgers. They have, in general, very respectable families, otherwise it might be very unpleasant, as well as improper for me to remain, if *any* kind of people were taken in. Though only two miles from Liverpool, I am as retired here as possible, few people passing or coming in, and the weather preventing my going much out. In the Summer time it is very different. Betty is a very lively, chatty woman of seven and twenty, and not unpleasant company; and I promised Edward, that as soon as the days are a little longer, I will rise with him by daybreak, and assist him in working in his garden until he goes to the warehouse. It is a nice spot of ground, but much in want of cultivation, Now, whilst the days are short and the weather often preventing me from walking, I intend to have such a feast of reading! I have fasted a long time, but shall soon make it up. My brother promises to come to see me very soon. I informed him of many promises to come to see me very soon. I informed him of many particular instances of Miss Chorley's rudeness, and he is so much incensed, that he threatens purposely to insult her; but that he must not do – for the sake of her worthy parents – for the sake of her former favours – he must not do it.

I have often met with speculative opinions like yours, concerning the Plurality of Worlds.[6] I strongly incline to the belief. But do you suppose them as sinful as ours; and that a Saviour has suffered in each of them for the atonement of those sins? I can hardly go so far. Or that a soul who quits this world to undergo a further state of trial, is conscious of a second existence, a third, and so on, until it attains complete happiness or misery? Perhaps it may do all this, and yet not be conscious of having ever before existed; and if so, what a number of worlds we may have been in before we come here! In so *many* trials, surely the soul would be completely purified, and there would be no necessity for a hell. It is a *dangerous* doctrine; we might some of us be induced to sin to the utmost, as we should only have so many more lives for it.

No, no! If there are Plurality of Worlds, they are places of happiness, not of trial or misery.

I highly offended Miss Chorley one day by supposing that if she made another appearance in this world, she really does use servants as ill as any African captain could do the Negro slaves, only that she does not beat them. I was made to suffer sufficiently for sporting such an idea. I durst not speak for a long time on the most trifling subject, and I don't think I am forgiven yet.

11 January 1809 (Beacon's Gutter). *To her Brother:*

Miss M. Smith, Henry's second daughter, plays very well on the piano. I have heard her twice – not that *I* am the judge; others have told me so. I dined with them in Dale Street last Sunday. She played a good deal for me, and lent me a large music book – big! As a family Bible – which was lugged home that evening. I have been busy as possible these last two days copying a number of songs from it, as there are generally Notes with each, for the Flute as well as the Piano. Mrs Weeton will laugh as my being busy, but ever since I came home, I have contrived to be so. Last week I was *extensively bustled* in making a frock and petticoat for Mrs Smith's dog, Chloe. I have a cap and gipsy hat yet to add before his dress is complete. The dog is a *gentleman,* though he has got a lady's name and a lady's dress; but breeches are not quite so easy to cut out as petticoats; though when I can no longer laugh at him in his frock, I will set to making him trousers – He is the drollest object! as ugly a dog as ever was seen; just the size, and almost the shape and colour of a hare or rabbit at a distance. He had like to have been shot for one, one day. The *sportsman* would have had a valuable prize! The dog thought (I suppose) the gentleman was going to play with him when he pointed his gun at him, so galloped towards him, which *providentially* saved his life.

I have called once at Mr Chorley's since I ceased to reside with them; for I had no quarrel with Mr and Mrs Chorley. They had, at parting, in the kindest manner, requesting I would often call. Miss C. was astonishingly civil the day I called!

You did not, my dear Brother, comprehend entirely what I meant when I requested you not to tell any one what my income was. I did not it to be known that I had any increase at all. I wish you had been perfectly silent on the subject. However, it can't be helped; you meant no offence – but, my dear fellow, be more cautious in future.

13 January 1809 (Beacon's Gutter). *To her Aunt Barton:*

I am sorry Mr Ingold is giving up the house. Does he leave it before May? I have no objection to Winstanley, only I shall expect him to give ten guineas a year, and clear it. I am sure the house deserves it – and to take it upon the same conditions Mr Ingold did, viz: to keep and leave it in good repair as he finds it; to put up no kind of fixtures in the walls or window frames in the parlour; and to pay the rent regularly on the 1st of May and November.

Give my love to my Cousin's family, and tell Henry and Richard [Henry and Richard Latham] I am much pleased with their letter, and shall answer it by and by.

19 January 1809 (Beacon's Gutter). *To her Brother:*

Immediately on the receipt of your letter, I write to say that if any services of mine would be acceptable to you and Mrs Weeton in your present distressing situation, I shall most willingly do anything in my power to assist you. I am now an idle person, doing no good on earth; let me, if I can, be a consolation and a help to you. Poor sweet little suffering Angel! Heaven grant before this arrives he may be completely out of danger, and continue many, many years a blessing to you! Poor Tom! Tell him his Aunt Ellen is sorry, very sorry indeed that he should be so ill, and that she will either fetch him, or his father and mother shall bring him in a gig. He would be so delighted with the fine sights of Liverpool! Dear fellow! I hope his days are not so soon to be terminated.

28 January 1809 (Beacon's Gutter). *To Richard Jackson* (the defaulting tenant of a lately purchased Liverpool cottage):

Your letter of the 21st has so far influenced me to induce me to defer another week doing what I threatened; but no longer will it have any effect upon me. I again repeat, that unless your rent is paid before this day week, you may expect, and be *certain* of the consequences.

You say I am severe. Have I not reason? Not so much from my own experience (there has not yet been time), as from that of others who have suffered by you. The man who could be so dishonest as to trick one landlord out of his rent, and afterwards insultingly laugh in his face, is no very desirable tenant. If you cannot pay half a year's rent, I do not know how you will pay that of a whole year.

The times are hard, I will allow, but you would have felt them less so, had your character been more respectable. You would then have had more lenity shewn you. Your own relations, it appears, won't assist you; how then can you reasonably expect that I should?

You need not write again; it is only giving yourself unnecessary trouble, and wasting your time. If your rent is paid by next Saturday, it will be very well; if not, I shall not any longer defer writing to my brother, ordering him to proceed directly against you.

It seems that Miss Weeton's 'bark' was much worse than her 'bite.' Two years later she was still waiting for her rent and the tenant was still in possession.

6 February 1809 (Beacon's Gutter). *To her Brother:*

I begin now to enjoy the weather, for some days are very mild and fine. I have been, several mornings the last week, delving in the garden. Delving? Yes, *delving,* Tom; my pretty, delicate foot has been exalted, and stamped upon the spade many and many a time, with true feminine grace. But I need not describe it; you may imagine it all.

I go to Liverpool about once a week, when the weather permits, to call upon Mr Chorley's and Miss Winkley. What an uncommonly fine girl is Miss W. So sensible and so well informed. I think her quite a miracle, considering the sphere she moves in; such a jewel *should* be better sett. She has a strong desire to play on some musical instrument, to which she could sing, that is not too expensive. She has a pleasing voice and a good ear, and I have not the slightest doubt would soon learn. Miss W. says she knows, that considering her rank in life, music is an unfit accomplishment for her; but having a strong inclination, sufficient time, and being able to afford a *moderate* expence (sic), she cannot see the impropriety of her learning, as she is certain she should not neglect her duty for her amusement. I believe her, for I have seen different instances of her forbearance and prudence that have raised her highly in my esteem.

I am considering whether to continue my hair crop, or let it grow again. What says Miss C. Scott? She hears more of fashion than I do. I like it best as it is, but if out of fashion, it must conform.

[Journal, February 1809]:

I was so tranquil and happy before my brother came, but he is so affectionate, his manner is so endearing, that now he is gone again, I can do nothing but lament his absence, and wish myself with him. I have exerted myself to the utmost to be chearful all day, but cannot succeed entirely. I have been drawing, writing – anything to forget him. Oh dear! When he took leave today, my heart went with him. I almost wish I was boarded in Leigh, I should then see him and his family every day. I might have been there; he once expressed a desire that I would reside near him – I may yet. A few days will perhaps restore me to my former composure. I shall surely not relapse into discontent again. I have been very contented a great while; but for the present, am not a little unhinged – I wish I lived nearer to him. May blessings attend him wherever he goes!

2 March 1809 (Beacon's Gutter). *To Miss Catherine Braithwaite:*

Three letters have I written at three different periods to your family, not one of which has yet been thought worth an answer. One was sent from hence; the others, before I left Up Holland. Should a fourth meet with the same fate, I must give up all thoughts of corresponding with a family I very highly esteem. Perhaps the fault is mine; some passages in former letters may have appeared absurd and ridiculous; or I may have inadvertently offended. If I have offended, it has indeed been unintentional. If the flippancy of my manner or style has excited contempt, my desire to please must have been evident; for that reason, might in return have met with *some* notice. My turn of mind is so well known by every one in your house, that when I was requested to write, the kind of letter you would receive was easy to anticipate. Why then, if those letters would probably be unworthy of notice, was I desired to write? And why was I promised to be gratified by an answer? Was it only in the first instance to ridicule? And in the second to disappoint? Convince me that neither was your intention, by some mark of remembrance. I should have considered myself as honoured by Mrs Braithwaite's correspondence; as favoured by Miss B's. Since both of them have declined it, let me not, my dear Miss Catherine, imagine that I have sunk into contempt with every branch of your family.

The signs and tokens I receive from my Aunt Barton are extremely short and unsatisfactory. If you can, instil a few ideas

44

into her pen. Her head is not wanting, but they descend no farther than her mouth. She can talk very well; but that she can do as she sits rocking in her arm chair; it gives her no trouble. She will tell you, perhaps, how anxious she is for my welfare, but proofs of that anxiety are ever wanting when any degree of exertion is required. Let your pen speak instead of hers, if she cannot be prevailed upon to let her pen speak for itself.

Strange rumours have reached me from your little nook, that a certain gentleman in black[7] has as great a reason to carry a burning cheek in the streets and highways for his own transgressions, as ever he had in the preaching tub for those of others. Some people are said to do no good on earth. Now, if what I have heard is really so, certainly some good is done. Two are better than one,[8] the Scriptures themselves inform us· If one command is transgressed, two are fulfilled.[9] If fornication is committed, no *false* witness is borne.[10] And besides, he has *used* his *utmost endeavour* to obey that injunction – 'increase and multiply.'[11]

If Mr B. [Rev John Braithwaite] sees this (but you must not let him see it; I don't write to him, but only to you), if he *should* see this, I could just imagine how he would look, and what he would say. Drawing himself up with an intention of appearing with proper canonical dignity, with *such* a whimsical cast of countenance – between an intended frown and an involuntary smile – 'For shame! For shame! You are too bad for anything.'

You will wonder how I amuse myself. I assure you, time never moves too slowly with me. I find such a variety of employments, that the day is scarcely long enough. Sewing occupies a very small portion. It never was an amusement with me. I always consider it as work. I am a great deal in the garden, working – or according to my ideas, playing with the spade, the fork, and the rake, delving, planting potatoes, cabbages, and beans. I shall very soon learn to be as expeditious as Billy Holcroft. When my back aches with stooping, I rest against a rail, watching the vessels sail up and down the river; sometimes running down to the shore to have a more extensive view of them; then back again to my garden employ.

Whether others are affected as I am by the varying seasons, I know not. I could wish to retain Spring, Summer, and Autumn, but I would utterly exclude Winter. For, amongst other unpleasant effects of cold upon me, my heart is so frozen, so contracted, that

45

scarce a deed of charity, or one good warm hearty prayer, can escape me. In warm weather I am a thousand times more devout. Does it make any difference with you? Can you pray by your bed side in a morning or an evening, or silently breathe forth in the day time as pious a petition in frosty or stormy weather, as when the sun gives a genial glow of warmth? If most people are like myself in this respect, how devout must they be, who constantly inhabit warmer regions than this! How cold and indifferent, if not impious, those remove farther North!

I had a beautiful sight today, of near a hundred sail, most of them going out, many of them very large vessels. If so many can go out at once, surely Liverpool cannot be very injured by the abolition of the slave trade.

16 March 1809 (Beacon's Gutter). *To her Brother:*

You were a pretty while in writing, Master Tom, after you left me in the dismals – three whole weeks. I began to think you had forgot how to write, or that you had died on your way home, and no one had remembered to inform me; that you were ill, at least, or some of the family; that Tom perhaps had had a relapse and was dying; but that whatever happened, *I* was forgotten. I requested Edward to call at Mr T Smiths [her mother's cousin] almost every day; went several times myself; but still no tidings! I knew not whether to be alarmed or vexed. Now I know. What made you so long, Tom? If you had left Mrs Weeton behind you, instead of Miss, you would not have suffered three weeks to pass before you had written. Did I ever serve you so, after leaving you to go a long journey? If I did, you have taken your revenge and punished me sufficiently. In leaving me, you went to your wife and children; what consolation had I? If Mrs W. thinks an absence of three or four days so much, who has children, a mother, and sisters to chear (sic) her whilst you are away, how must I endure the deprivation of your society for three times that number of years? Who have neither mother, sisters, husband, nor children. All my affections are centred on you. I do not wish to boast of feeling more regard for you than any other sisters do for their brothers. I have no other love. But that affection must be proportionately greater when the number of objects are so very limited, when *all* is compromised in *one*. I expect more attention perhaps to be shewn to me than I ought – is it not a natural

46

consequence where there is no friend, no relation, no intimate at home? You have *many* to shew kindness to you, and always about you, I have but one, whom I seldom see – consider this, and make some allowance for me.

'I wish you had a husband or children of your own,' you will say, 'and then you would not teaze others so much with your pothering regards and complaints'! *I* do not wish it, I assure you. Never since you were married have I been so happy as since I came here. Days and weeks pass on so pleasantly to what they used to do, that I do not yet, and think I shall not, regret the change between last Year's change of abode and this. I should like to visit Holland sometimes, but not to live in it. My Aunt has very kindly invited me to come to see her soon, so I think I shall probably go in a month or six weeks.

Write soon, for fear of another scolding.

17 March 1809 (Beacon's Gutter). *To her Aunt Barton:*

You complain of my not writing often enough. It is pleasing to me to think that you wish to hear from me frequently, but does not the length of my letter atone for my not writing so often? Now, here is a letter, I am sure, long enough for four.

Would you wish them to be one fourth the length, if I sent one four times as often? If it is your wish I will comply, only it will put me to nonplus sometimes if I get into a long subject, for perhaps I may be in the middle of it at the end of my letter, and be obliged to finish with – to be concluded in my next, which will be a little awkward, you know. Whether it be better to have a little and often, or a great deal and seldom, I leave to your better judgement to determine – you have much the same quantity at the year's end. You may have it in *dribs* and *drabs* if you like it better; for though my letters are a little in the wholesale way, to oblige a friend, I can write as short a note as they could wish.

You give me a whole budget of news – I fear you will be little amused by what I write, for there is not one bit of news in it from beginning to end – let me see! – I'll invent some, no matter how unlikely: Mrs Chorley is in a family way, and is grown so good tempered in consequence, that the servants have the finest life of it in the world. Miss Chorley and Tom Smith are going to be married, as soon as the one gets rid of her asthmatic complaint, and the other rid of the old bachelor. Mr Chorley is quite a buck, and dashes away in his silk stockings, his Dickey [sham shirt] quizzing glass [single eye glass]. Mr Vause is a better man than a preacher, and his contemporary, Mr Martland, nick-named the Beauty of Holiness, is grown so attentive to his book, that he has quite forgot to admire the young ladies during Divine Service – alias the Beauties of Christ Church. And the Organ in that Church intends to cease roaring, as it is in danger of frightening away those who go to doze there.

18 April 1809 (Beacon's Gutter). *To Miss Catherine Braithwaite:*

If you knew, my dear Catherine, how delighted I was on the receipt of your flattering letter, you would be anxious to fulfil the promise you have made, of being a more punctual correspondent.

I saw Miss Broadhead a week ago. She is going to Rainford on the 13th inst. with Miss Molyneux, and me to go with her – I wonder why Reason and Inclination cannot always go together; they are then such pleasant company. One would think they were actuated by the spirit of contradiction, plague take 'em! For they seldom can agree. In the present instance, Inclination says, 'Go by all means, it will be an exceedingly pleasant visit; and I am sure you will meet with a welcome, for they are friendly, hospitable people, and you have been invited before.' Reason puts on a very serious face, as she generally does whenever consulted, and asks 'how can you think of such a thing? Troubling people you have very little acquaintance with, and who are under no obligation to you, and most probably never will be. Do you think they have not enough to do with their money, without spending it in the support of strangers? To indulge the wish of such a visit is extremely unreasonable.' Most convincingly spoken! – and yet – Oh dear! Inclination has such a good-tempered countenance, that for the soul of me I cannot help wishing to obey her. Whose advice I shall follow, must be determined in a day or two, for the time draws very near. If I could coax them both to be of the same mind now, how I should rejoice and sing.

When I do come amongst you, what a budget of news, scandal, &c. &c., shall I have to hear. Every mouth will be open to repeat something. You will be glad, no doubt, to have one amongst you to whom something will be new, whatever Solomon may say. Thank God! I am not as wise as Solomon, for I cannot comprehend everything at once. Sometimes new is continually presenting itself, which affords a continued succession of amusement, with a very slight mixture of vexation (I'll say nothing about Vanity).

You apologise for the badness of your writing. So would I too, if it did not occur to me that we seldom see people of genius write with a fine hand! There is something so mechanical in it. Beautiful writing costs so many hours in the attainment, that those who take much pleasure in it, must necessarily neglect some improvement of the mind whilst they employ so much time in flourishing the fingers.

Therefore I congratulate myself on writing so badly, and rejoice to think that I was so many years in learning – to write no better. It is a proof that the employment was uncongenial to my turn of mind; that I had a taste for something more exalted. *Great genius's* cannot attend to the minutiae of science.

Well done Vanity! Thou and I have long been friends, and we are not likely to separate yet I see.

During April 1809 Miss Weeton made a return visit to Up Holland and stayed with her Aunt and Uncle Barton. She also took the opportunity to visit her good friend Mrs Braithwaite at The Priory. A day or two later she travelled to Leigh with her Uncle on a single horse. There she visited her brother Thomas and his family before returning to Up Holland with her uncle. The following morning she walked to Appley Bridge (two miles from Up Holland) to catch the packet for the day's sail back to Liverpool.

21 April 1809 (Up Holland). *To her Brother:*

Up Holland looks so strange at the top of my letter, after having for some months dated from Beacon's Gutter. It looks as if it was scarcely right; as if I had made some mistake. The Liverpool post-man one day called at my Cousin Smith's with a letter for me. He looked over several before he perceived the right one. At last he found it, directed for Miss Weeton, Beacon's Gutter, to be left at Mr J Smith's, &c. 'Oh! Aye!' said he when he saw it, 'Miss Weeton, Bacon-Cutter, at Mr Smith's, Cheesemonger.' 'Bacon Cutter!' he again repeated in a tone of surprise, as if he thought it a very singular kind of employ, to be so particularly specified. As they really do sell a great-deal of bacon at that shop, as well as cheese, the drollery of the man's mistake caused a hearty laugh.

However, for a week or two I have ceased to be a Bacon-Cutter. I came here on Tuesday the 18th and would have written the next day, only my Uncle had some thoughts of going to Leigh tomorrow. I put off writing than he had determined about it. He and I have concluded to come over the Saturday following on a double horse [one person riding pillion], and spending the Sunday with you, if the weather permit.

Present my respectful compliments to Mrs W., my love and a few – no – a great many kisses to the little ones for me.

13 May 1809 (Beacon's Gutter). *To her Brother:*

You will think me long, my dear Brother, in writing to you. I deferred it until I arrived at home again, that I might give you a little more information than I could have done at Up Holland. I was nothing near so fatigued when I returned from Leigh, as I was on my arrival there. I got to my Uncle B's about one o'clock; at five that afternoon went to Mrs Braithwaite's, and danced from a little after six than ten; and was no more fatigued that evening or the following morning, than if I had no unusual exercise. How strange it is that I should be no more tired with my walk to Leigh, than I was in returning – but so it was.

Nothing occurred at Holland worth relating, excepting that I was often out to tea. I returned yesterday in the in the boat; had a very pleasant sail with six or seven passengers, who made themselves as agreeable as it was in their power. They were not what one calls genteel people, but they made up the deficiency by good humour, and making some attempts at elegance in their language, &c. I don't know but I feel more entertained when people assume what is not habitual to them, than when they really are what they wish to appear. Yesterday, in the midst of some fine sounding speech, a *becase* [because], or some such word, would force its way, and spoil all. I smiled at the sound, but was supposed to be entertained with the narration, and so gave no offence.

To see some such awkward dowdies that some men take a fancy to, and can think of spending their lives with! And to see some such nice women apparently totally neglected! Frequently excites my astonishment.

A young country girl, who from the account curiosity in a manner extorted from her, seemed to be without home and almost without habitation, was one who excited a good deal of attention. I was much hurt at the rudeness of two of the gentlemen, as well as some of the ladies, in asking questions about her affairs which she, from want of experience, knew not how to evade. She appeared to be in great affliction when she got into the boat, and continued quite dejected the greatest part of the way. She said she was from Richmond in Yorkshire; had been from thence to London. The family she was going to in Liverpool, did not expect her; and she knew nothing of the way to their house, or anything of the town. A gentleman in the boat offered to conduct her, and I suppose he did. It was recollected by several of the company, that she had eaten nothing all the day. Whether it was that she could not eat, or had nothing to eat, I cannot say. One of the company had offered her some pie, which she had declined taking, saying she had some meat in her bundle, but could not eat any then. I think more of the girl now than I did whilst with her, and blame myself severely for taking no further interest in her situation. It was not well to leave a simple, innocent girl of about twenty (as she appeared to be), to be conducted by a strange gentleman. The family she was going to are respectable; and I could have found them. A walk of five or six miles to one blest with the health and activity that I have, is nothing. The idea did not occur to me whilst I was in the boat. An elderly, good-tempered looking man, did his utmost to chear her spirits, and succeeded in raising a smile now and then; indeed, he kept us all on the smile most of the day; his raillery and jokes were conducted with real drollery, and generally well timed.

A gentleman – that is, a man with powdered hair, a good coat, well polished boots, &c. entered a few miles from Liverpool; and then I found out that this old man's dress was rather shabby, which I had not discovered before, though I had been upwards of seven hours in his company. I did not till then perceive that his hat and coat were old, his shoes dusty, and his stockings of old grey yarn. On making the discovery, I began to feel a little ashamed of my company. What silly creatures some of us are. Had he had a good coat on, I should have probably been proud of his notice; and if I had afterwards met him in the street and received a bow from him, should have been raised half an inch higher in my own estimation. Whereas now, I may possibly cross over to the other side of the street to avoid him – his coat I mean, (as Miss Scott used to do).

19 May 1809 (Beacon's Gutter). *To her Aunt Barton:*

I arrived again at my lodging's after a very pleasant sail down the canal, perfectly safe and sound both in body and mind, with a little less fat perhaps in the evening than I had set out with in the morning; for, whether inside or outside, I was almost half baked. The cook generally begins her operations by ten o'clock in the morning, frying bacon, eggs, beef steaks, potatoes, and mutton chops; roasting meat, warming pies, &c., and seldom finishes before 3 or 4 o'clock in the afternoon; for most people who go in the tail end of the packet seem to think that eating and drinking is the most delightful amusement of travelling. The generality of those who sail in the upper end seem to have very different ideas. They appear as if ashamed of such a piece of vulgarity as the indulging a propensity to eat; and just as one begins to think that they have learned to exist without eating, perhaps they bring forth a dainty bit of chicken, ham, or game; a pot of veal, or shrimps, or a little tart that will scarce be two mouthfuls, just to convince the rest of the company that they do eat sometimes. The perfumes of tobacco, spirits, and hot meat, which are often very plentiful in a conveyance of this kind, form a very cheap subsistence to some people; who, so far from requiring more food for the day than what they took at breakfast, frequently bestow a part of that meal upon the fishes with the greatest liberality, the various smells of the cabin being quite enough for them.

The company when I got into the boat, consisted of six or seven at the front end, who went all the way; eight others were all we took in. I wished to have seen a great many additional new faces, for that forms a great part of my amusement when travelling in this manner, but was not gratified. Some very odd faces are to be seen sometimes. Two old ladies got in a few miles from Liverpool. The very moment they could squat themselves on the cushion, they began to knit. One had a good hardly look, as if she had been stewed to make her keep. She looked more like a coddled gooseberry than anything else; her cheeks were very near the colour of one, and so were her eyes, not being a whit brighter. She had a most livid appearance, yet did not look too much out of health. They both affected a few girlish airs, which made me conclude them to be what some impertinent married ladies call – 'old maids,' which made me the more ready to ridicule them; for they had no title for such airs, except they laid a claim to antediluvian youth. A very nice old lady got in much about the same time, accompanied by almost as nice a young one; both of respectable appearance. The old one had rather an ill-tempered look, but fortunately she was very deaf, so she could not often be put out of her way by what she heard. A clergyman sailed with us five or six miles; he had that wolf-like keenness in his eyes, as if he knew which was the best method of taking tithe.

Many people have begun to bathe here. I have been dipping three days this week. I walk out of the house in my bathing dress.

23 May 1809 (Beacon's Gutter). *To Mrs Whitehead:*

On the 18th of last month I left Beacon's Gutter for Up Holland, and found that the place and its inhabitants very little altered since I left them last summer.

Perhaps you may have seen an account in the Papers of the death of Mrs Banks.[12] Sometime before I wrote to you last, I had heard she was pregnant, but believing, as many others did, that it would prove to be a dropsical complaint, I did not mention it. She had been married eleven or twelve years, I think, and had never been in the family way before. For several years past she had grown amazingly fat. When her pregnancy was announced, it occasioned great joy at Winstanley [Hall], and great preparations were made. It was determined upon that the child should positively be a son. Malt was procured for brewing ale, to be drunk when he came of age. The caps and other garments were all ordered, and made in the boyish forms; not so much as a *single one* for a girl. For the child and for Mrs B. upon the occasion, between 5 and £600 worth of linen were purchased, £400 worth of which came from London. Alterations were made in the house, partitions taken down, and rebuilt for the accommodation of a couple of nurses. Dr White from Manchester resided in the house upwards of three weeks before Mrs B's confinement. She had scarcely been allowed to stir during the whole time of her pregnancy, not so much as to reach a chair nor shut a door; nor to remove from one room to another without one or two assistants, for fear of a miscarriage – and yet all these preparations and all these precautions were of no avail! There is no making sure of anything on earth – After suffering a most severely painful time, a *son was born,* but heir only to the grave, for it was dead. The mother survived little more than a week – and died too; few more beloved or more lamented, she was so kind to her servants, so charitable to the poor. When living, the world said she was ambitious, proud, and ostentatious, but still confessed she was like a parent, as well as a mistress to her domestics; a most liberal benefactor to the needy; and affable to all. Mr Banks is in great affliction, for they had lived very happily together.

Holland is, if possible, more licentious and more scandalous than when I lived in it; such numbers of unmarried women have children, many of whom one would have thought had years, discretion, sense, and virtue to have guarded them. In two houses near together, there have been in each, a mother and daughter lying in, nearly at the same time; and one man (the notorious George Lyon[13]) reputed to be the father of all four! Mr Meyrick too, report strongly affirms, has been guilty, and is said to have seduced the servant girl of the house where he lives. He is so much disliked in many respects, that whether the report be true or false, people seem determined to believe it.

I was telling you in my last of Miss Chorley's conduct towards me whilst I was a guest at her father's house. Inconsistent woman! She would attempt now to make me believe that she has taken lodgings in the house I live in, on my account, that she may enjoy my society. She may have done it for her own convenience perhaps. Had she taken country lodgings elsewhere, she must probably have been without a companion to walk or converse with. She comes, she says, in July, to stay a fortnight! I know she does not come, for as that is just the busiest time of the bathing season, Mrs Smith says she is sure she cannot accommodate her; and she has only let the lodgings to Miss C. conditionally, as she does not choose to pay the full price of a bed-room and a parlour to herself; therefore, if a family should wish to engage them, Miss C. will have to give them up. Mrs S. Does not wish her to come, any more than I do; for I most either be a slave to her whims and humours, or we must quarrel, neither of which I should like.

Great alterations are made at Southport. A number of houses are built of various sizes for the accommodation of families; and a new inn. Many people of some consequence and fashion, I have resorted there the last two years. It is becoming a fashionable watering place.

54

A little while ago I had a very wild scheme in agitation, which was, to traverse Wales on foot; a mode of travelling I should prefer, were I ever so wealthy – but when I reflect on the many insults a female is liable to, if alone, I find it impracticable. My plan was, to get acquainted with some decent Welsh farmer's family and by their means to get acquainted with another; and so on, as long as the chain would last; and board with each family as long as I staid, and to dress in the plainest garments, I had that I might attract less notice. I must not think of putting such a scheme in practise. If I was a man, now! I could soon do it. A Miss Prescott of Leigh, a singular character, once travelled to the south of England that way, taking London in her rout, accompanied by a gentleman; which, as he was no way related, was worse than going alone, in the world's estimation. I am not quite so severe in my opinions, though I should not choose to do it myself.

[Journal, May 1809]:

When I came to Liverpool I expected to have found it filled with intelligent beings, imagining knowledge to be so generally diffused. I begin to discover that it contains as much proportionate ignorance as any little village in England, where perhaps the curate is the only intelligent man in it. How astonished am I daily to find so many more ignorant than myself, so few more knowing, considering as I have till now done, the great disparity of opportunities for acquiring knowledge between the inhabitants of so opulent a town as this, where science and literature make so great a noise, and the obscure individual of an obscure village, where such terms are scarcely ever heard, and their significance a mystery. Here, not one in ten can speak their native language tolerably; not more than one in twenty, correctly; and of these last, scarce one tenth can boast any greater literary acquirement than that of their grammar. I thought myself very ignorant when I came here, expecting to find so many wise, so many learned – I find them not – I need not be very proud to imagine myself a little superior in intellectual acquirements to most of those I meet with – and how does it happen that I am so? The disadvantages I thought I laboured under in the obscurity of my rank, and more particularly in that of my situation, I begin to perceive were directly the reverse. It gave me so much leisure, that I had more time for the improvement of my mind than the generality of people here. Where there were play-fellows, no toys, no amusements of any kind but such as I could find within myself, I had no other resource but reading and writing to fill up the solitary leisure. The people here do not seize the opportunities of improvement that so frequently occur – which they must wilfully reject – their ignorance is astonishing! It would almost appear as ignorance was taught, as if it were something to boast of.[14] Many intelligent tradesmen may be met with in Liverpool, but generally speaking, those of a similar rank in a little village are equally well informed.

14 June 1809 (Beacon's Gutter). *To her Brother:*

Every day I rejoice more and more that I have quitted Holland. If my aunt knew the many years of comfort the following her advice has deprived me of, she would no longer blame me for at last being so obstinate, as she terms it, to follow my own wishes. Neither is there any present appearance of my having done so, to my utter ruin, as she has often with much vehemence predicted. She is as a blighting wind. Not one chearing hope will bud that happens to be within reach of her influence.

I have been very ill ever since I wrote to you last, and though I have been ill indeed, it was such a comfort to have somebody in the house, that my sickness was almost a pleasure to me, when compared with the dreary, solitary, languishing, weary, agonized hours I have spent in that house at Holland. I have had an attack of my old complaint, a pain at my stomach, brought on by eating salad with a little vinegar, and drinking milk to it. The milk turned sour, and came up again black as ink; and from that time till within these two days I have scarcely been able to crawl. My appetite was quite gone. Last Saturday I ventured to get an Emetic at a Druggist's. I took it that afternoon, and got up an amazing quantity of yellow stuff, since which time I recovered rapidly.

Remember me affectionately to your little ones, respectfully to Mrs W., and believe me – your sister, as affectionate as ever, and grateful too, notwithstanding what sometimes passes between us.

17 July 1809 (Beacon's Gutter). *To her Brother:*

You and I, it seems, both wrote on the same day to the same purpose; you, to say you could not come, and I to say I could not receive you. I should indeed be very glad to have you here, but as I can command nothing but the room I sleep in, which is a present a mere closet, I cannot say when there would be room for you.

I wish you could have been here this week to have seen Mrs Siddons.[15] It will be too late now, for she finishes her career in Liverpool for this summer on Friday next. Henry Latham has been with me a fortnight, and one day last week he and I went to see her as Lady Macbeth. We got a very comfortable front seat in the gallery, and I was highly gratified. I have seen her before at Lancaster as Belvidera, but almost forgot her, it is so long ago. Much as I expected, my expectations were exceeded; particularly in that scene where Lady Macbeth is represented as walking in her sleep. The whole audience seemed wonder struck. I assure you I was. The witches, the thunder and lightning, the ghosts – had not even the *semblance* of anything terrible. Henry laughed at them as well as me. The witches seemed such a merry set; the ghosts so substantial – the theatre and the stage too light to give a sufficiently awful to lightning or the thunder (and that was not loud enough), that they must be weak indeed who are for one moment affected by them. We had a dismally dark walk home. It was eleven when we left the theatre. The glare of the house, with its lights, had so affected my eyes, that it was with difficulty I could distinguish my way. Luckily Henry could see better than me, and we got home very safely. We were a full hour in walking two miles and a half.

About ten days ago, I was drinking tea at Miss Dalrymple's. Miss Shaw from Lancaster is on a visit there – a puny, delicate little woman. Miss J. Lodge made one of the party – Tom, she is a very different woman to what I expected to have seen – I can't say that you ever described her to me; but one generally forms some kind of idea of a person one hears much of, and I had expected a very different woman – I can scarcely say what kind of one, either – perhaps a thin, light woman; small feminine features, and a fashionable, dashing exterior. 'Your brother was an admirer of Miss J. Lodge,' said Miss Dalrymple one day, when she had been telling me of her arrival in Liverpool. 'Yes,' I answered, 'but she cast him off.' Miss Dalrymple shook her head with doubtful kind of smile, but said no more. What she meant, I could not divine. Perhaps I spoke too freely, Tom, to say she cast thee off; but one may with more propriety say as much of a gentleman than of a lady. Perhaps Miss J. Lodge thought herself slighted in some way or other, and, too high spirited to shew herself hurt at it, affected an indifference she did not feel, and flirted with another effectually to hide her real sentiments. I fancied her chearfulness the evening I saw her, was put on. She talked of you, and made enquiries of Mrs Weeton's health with great composure – but – so far goes prejudice! I thought she seemed to take *pains* to appear perfectly at ease in her enquiries; neither to say too much nor so little as to give room for further thought in me. What was it that attracted you to Miss J. L.? What was it you most admired her for?

I rejoice in the recovery of your son – you positively will be breaking your neck some of these days. Tom, trudge on thy feet man; they cannot play thee such frisky tricks. Or if thou wilt ride, get such a tit [a small or poor horse] as Don Quixote bestrode, or a runt pony; but not a full blood hunter any more of thou meanest to tarry yet a little while with thy wife and children.

If I *am* altered, Tom, as yet in my manners, it is not to you or Mrs W. I am indebted for the improvement. What alteration there is yet, owing to an increase of chearfulness. My situation in every respect is amended. Even though I were a servant I should be better off than I was. All I now regret, is, that I staid in Holland so long. When with you last, I was more at ease because I was literally more at home than I had ever been before. My Uncle and Miss Dannett were with me – old acquaintances. Were I to be with you again, you would find me as before, after the first two or three says; for there is something peculiarly repellent in Mrs W's manner that would again throw a degree of reserve upon me. Many others notice that peculiarity in Mrs W. as well as myself. It is that, my dear Tom, more than anything, that has often prevented me joining the conversations at your house; and when I have opened my mouth, you have both appeared so alarmed lest I should exhibit some awkwardness in my expressions or manner, that it has thrown a degree of anxiety upon me that has made me exactly what you feared. Then Mrs W. has so much formality, that I momentarily felt apprehensive of forgetting some little ceremony, or transgressing some rule of etiquette, and have been thrilled into a two hours silence at a lift of her eyebrow, expressive of surprise at come impropriety or other I had been guilty of. Then she would so frequently glance some sarcastic expression at old maids, that I felt as if I were a constant theme of ridicule, and became almost motionless – almost speechless – for fear of exciting observations at my expense. I did not chose (sic) to retort. It may be a sign of abilities, but not of a Christian spirit. I am not easily roused; but when I am, I sometimes forget myself, and say what I would be glad to recall when calm again.

You say, 'You seemed to have lost something of that tarnish and to have less old-maidenly notions, in short, to be like other people in the more pleasant parts of their character.' I am certainly highly obliged for the latter part of that expression; and Mr Edward Smith and his wife, still more so; for it must be them who have worked the miracle. Had they not been in the house, I should have still less society than I had Holland, for I was then almost as often at Wigan as I have been this winter at Liverpool. Since I saw you in April, I have indeed mixed more in society a great deal. If you saw such a change then, great indeed will be your astonishment when you see me again. I shall be so wonderfully improved – and as to the old-maid, I may perhaps lose that title entirely before twelve months are over; not that I so much regard the man, but – to avoid the finger of contempt, the smile of ridicule. If it were not for that, I am too happy as I am to wish for any change. An old maid is a stock for everyone to laugh at. Every article of dress, every word, every movement is satirized. Boys play tricks upon them, and are applauded. Girls sneer at them, and are unreproved. – Upon my word, I think I will write an essay upon the pitiable state of old maids for some Magazine or Paper.

But I must make haste and do it,
> Whilst I can put,
>> Yours sincerely,
>>> Affectionate sister,
>>>> E.W. – to it.

[Journal, August 1809]:

I often think there is a great similarity of temper in Mrs Smith and myself. But surely, surely, I am not so bad. Whatever I may be naturally, I do hope the peevish selfishness of my temper is more effectually subdued than hers appears to be. For she is almost really past bearing with sometimes. Ever since I came, I have invariably submitted in silence to her ill-humours – three times very lately excepted. Perhaps she thinks she submits as much to me. I endeavour to put her as little out of the way as possible, making as little dirt, noise, or disturbance of any kind as I can. One cannot be quite automatons in a house. I may do many things perhaps which are inconvenient to her, that I am not conscious are so because she does not complain – for which she gives herself credit for her forbearance – but I often, very often reflect on what I do or say, lest something should escape me on that may displease her. Were she as cautious of displeasing me, she would, I think she would, be a great deal more obliging. For oh! She is indeed brutish, violent, and vulgar. She terrifies me so sometimes when she is brawling and hectoring over poor little Henry and his unfortunate father, that though she does not attack me in quite so violent a manner, I am momentarily in apprehension that my turn will be next. And so it would be if I ventured at such times to utter a word. My only refuge is in silence; and often do I pray that it may please the Almighty to subdue her tyrannical spirit ere her hour approaches. When she is in good humour (which she very often is), she is as pleasant and agreeable as so illiterate a woman can be; and I often forget all past grievances, and wonder at myself for being so frightened of her. She is hospitable and generous to her pecuniary injury – when she is in the humour. Yet there are times when she would scarcely give a child shelter from the inclemency of the weather, or a draught of water when requested. She is more afraid of her trouble than anything, and never thinks herself sufficiently paid for what she does, unless extravagant presents are made her – She is a compound of generosity and good-for-nothingness – just as the humour of the moment may actuate her.

7 August 1809 (Beacon's Gutter). *To Mrs Whitehead:*

I shall be writing to my Aunt Barton in a day or two, and through her means I can obtain the books you wish me for.[16] My Uncle and her are well acquainted in Wigan, and I dare say there are many friends who have preserved the works of an author they were personally acquainted with, and whose talents they valued and respected – even in that place of mental barrenness where ignorance and vulgarity are their boast, and literature has scarcely dawned; where it happens to appear, is so often treated with contemptuous neglect – yet I have often heard your father's talents spoken of in very high terms, and the few who had any taste were proud to boast that they had had such an author among them – my Aunt and Uncle Barton amongst that number.

I have been in danger of losing my brother, and his little boy too; the latter by a dangerous illness, and the former by a fall from his horse. He was riding from Wigan to Leigh in company with another gentleman, when a calf on the other side of the hedge, that was lying down, suddenly rose up and galloped away. My brother's horse was startled and sprang sideways, which threw him a little out of his seat, and in endeavouring to recover it, he accidentally spurred the horse in the flank. The animal set off at full gallop, and my brother was thrown over his head. Fortunately he fell rather flat, or his neck must have been broken. For some hours minutes he did not breathe, and was two full hours he came to himself. He is dreadfully bruised, but no bones broken. His knee was put out, but that was set whilst he remained motionless, and he has no recollection of it. He is now almost recovered.

You and I are at this moment pursuing exactly different plans. You, are leaving town; I, am going into it. Yet, like you, I can wonder how people can bear to live in a crowd. The society and not the situation tempt me; for I do not like the confined air and prospects of a town. I remain here than the end of September, and only to winter in Liverpool, with a widow and her daughters, the oldest of whom I am very partial to. I am to board with them. I could not think of quitting this place now, particularly that the weather promises to become more favourable than it has been for a long time. For many months there have been continual winds, cold and bleak in the extreme, and I began to think there never was anything else near the sea shore; but the people here tell me they never remember so cold a summer. This is indeed a beautiful day, and I fully enjoy it. I am sat writing at a bedroom window that overlooks the river, and often raise my head to look at the vessels, and see the people bathing – the latter is not the most delicate sight; but I am now so accustomed to it, that really I do not feel so much shocked as I ought to do. It appears to me as a mere thing of course, and I think no more now of the objects in the water, nor notice them any more I should passengers in the street. How much custom reconciles some people to – almost anything. Well! When I have dispatched this, I shall be in the most anxious pleasing expectation of the fulfilment of your promise – two whole sheets I think you say – containing – not one attempt at wisdom. I am glad of it – I hate to be always wise, for then wisdom, for want of a novelty, would lose its charms 'charm she ever so wisely.' I like mirth, and I am sure from you to be more than amused with 'silly tattle' as you call it – let me see it and judge for myself.

12 August 1809 (Beacon's Gutter). *To her Aunt Barton:*

I wonder whether Henry Latham has written to me. He promised me he would, soon after he got home. If he has not, tell him I expect in a week after this, to receive one from him. No pains are taken with Henry at school, in anything but writing and accounts; or else is he a great block-head, for he spells and reads shockingly. And in grammar he scarcely ever receives a lesson – about two or three in the half year – and I used to give one every day. He is a very good lad; it is a pity he should be so very countrified, clumpish, and awkward. Mr Smith's little boy here, who is three years younger, is ten times sharper than Henry. It is not his own fault; if he stays at home he will never be otherwise.

Perhaps by the time I write again, I shall have removed to my new dwelling. I came here on the first of October last year, and mean to leave about the same time as this. Miss Winkley has many young acquaintances, and I have no doubt but I spend my Winter agreeably. They live frugally, keeping no servant. Mrs Winkley is a great deal at the shop, and Miss Ann goes to school. Miss W. thinks of learning to play on the Pedal Harp this Winter, and as I begin to have some idea of music, we are in hopes to instruct ourselves. I have fought it out on the Flageolet without the least instruction, verbal or oral, and don't fear succeeding in some degree.

How is Miss Braithwaite? Miss Chorley gives me a very grievous account of her health – have you any hopes, my dear Aunt? I shall indeed rejoice if you have. Present my kindest, most affectionate remembrance to her and the family – they have given up writing to me, I suppose.

16 August 1809 (Beacon's Gutter). *To her Brother:*

My Uncle has been at Mr Tristram's of the Breck for two or three days, a fortnight or three weeks ago. He told me had got a stone for my Mother's grave, and asked what inscription we would have on it. I said I would enquire of you again, as you had given no direct answer to a former enquiry I made twelve months ago. I could wish, my dear Tom, to have it no longer neglected; and if you would, as soon as convenient, take a ride over Holland and give final orders concerning it, I shall be very glad. I once mentioned a few lines to you to put on the stone, but if you would only wish Name, Age, &c., why, let that only be put on. I leave it entirely to you. It is just two years since I first mentioned the subject to you before, and the lines I then proposed were these.

Let not my virtues be blazon'd here.
They are indelibly written in the hearts of my children,
And I am satisfied.
Neither let my weaknesses be hidden,
They will only cause a sigh for the frailty of humanity;
A sigh without a blush.
Those who knew me on earth had reason to rejoice that I existed,
But still greater reason have I to rejoice
That I ceased to exist.
A creature of many sorrows;
I now only find rest.

As I said before, so I repeat; you are at full liberty to choose, alter, or entirely reject what I have written.[17] For my own part, I only wish a plain, neat stone. My mother herself, could we ask her, would wish no more; she has often said it. When I die Tom, if you survive me, let no stone be placed over my grave on my account; nor my name put upon any that may have previously been placed there. If my friends cannot remember me without such a memento, let them forget me; it is of no consequence.

What an uncommonly wise fellow you are! What fine advice you can give! And how much it is needed, too! – as if I were not as capable of acting right, as you are of teaching me to do it. When you were going to marry, I set no terrors before you, gave you no sage advice, express'd no fears, anxieties, or sorrows about it, yet had far greater reason indeed than you will ever have. Of the few who have offered themselves to me, one esteemed and highly, yet felt no love; for another, I could have felt the warmest affection, but without esteem; a third, I neither esteemed nor loved – I have not met with one for whom I could feel both sentiments. But you need not fear any imprudence on my part; if I could guide myself at so early an age as when my mother died, surely I can now.

When I asked you what it was that attracted you to Miss J. Lodge, it was not that I meant she was in any deficient in my opinion. Far from it. I merely wished to know what particularly attracted you. So few men look at the qualities of the mind, when the exterior is plain – you need not have used so very contemptuous an expression as you have done, on so very slight an occasion – but I forgot myself; I had determined not to notice it. On first reading it, I was much hurt. I closed the letter, and let it lie untouched than I had to answer it – as I generally do when I meet with any unpleasant passage – in hopes to get the better of my resentment in a few days, and answer with composure, if not with chearfulness. Surely some merit is due for the intended forbearance, so don't scold, now. When you used to write in low spirits, did I ridicule you? Did I treat you with contempt? No! I invariably soothed and endeavoured to raise your spirits, and chear and comfort you as tenderly and affectionately as I could. Yet you used to write as often in a desponding way as ever I have done. Your sorrows existed then as much in 'your romantic imagination, which could suppose any unreal feelings and distresses in yourself, according to the Vapour and Sunshine of the moment as ever mine did – yet Tom, I did not accuse you. Neither did I ridicule, snear, or condemn. Reflect on the time when you were at Preston, and say if I did.

I did not *quiz* you, Tom, about your speedy recovery. I only wished to let you see I was not terrified to death about your danger; not that I felt it the less because I wrote chearfully. So then it is only what concerns you that I may be allowed to speak of with anxiety, sorrow, grief, fear, and alarm? Well then, to please thee, I will tell thee the truth. My chearfulness was affected; the other sentiments just mentioned, real, and very frequently felt on thy account.

I have been at Chester. Mrs Winkley and I have long talked of going there together. During our stay, we saw the Cathedral, the Bishop's Palace, and the Castle. The first and last were worth seeing. We rambled a great deal about the city walls, and you would have been entertained to have heard Mrs W's sagacious remarks and conjectures, though I was almost out of patience sometimes with the superabundance and frivolity of them. She reads a good deal, and has a remarkable retentive memory, but not strength of understanding sufficient to digest rationally what she reads. 'Well now, I dare say this was so and so; and that was in such a state once, &c. &c.' Then, as we returned home, she must tell the passengers where we had been, and why, and all we had seen, and gave such a minute description of things not worth mentioning. She is a very good-hearted, well-meaning woman too, and has been exceedingly kind to me; and if she would not talk so everlastingly, I should like her still better. I am going to board there this winter, and if an occurrence of yesterday is not soon cleared up to my satisfaction, I shall go sooner than I fixed. I would not cast suspicion on any one for slight grounds, so will wait a day or two; it 'exists perhaps in my own imagination.' I did intend to have remained there than the beginning of October.

Can you tell me, brother, which is considered as the best modern pronouncing Dictionary, at a moderate expence?

[Journal, August 1809]:

On Wednesday, the 22nd August, I was sent for by my Uncle Barton to go to Holland, to see my Aunt, who was dangerously ill. I went, though very ill myself at the time, and very unable and unfit to travel. The danger was over when I got there, though I found her very ill. She recovered very rapidly. I, too, gained strength, and wishing to see my brother's family before I quitted the neighbourhood, I walked over to Leigh one afternoon, and had scarcely sat down, when Mrs Weeton began, in a most irritating manner, to accuse me of ridiculous behaviour since my residence in Liverpool; in talking of the narrowness of my income; in saying I could not afford this and could not afford the other; and inducing people by that means to treat me with pity and contempt. I trembled, I felt myself turn paler than usual, I could scarcely hold the cup of tea I had taken. I attempted to defend myself, but I could not gain a hearing. I will subdue my resentment, thought I to myself, and speak calmly when she will let me speak. My brother came in, and for a minute interrupted the lecture by congratulations on my arrival. She began again – and then my brother began, and I found she had worked him up to the same violence with herself against me And all this mighty pother was owing to what I had said at Christopher Pennington's last summer, when I went to enquire the price of lodgings. I was there told they had generally twenty to twenty-five shillings a week for lodgings only. 'Dear me!' I said, 'I could not afford so much for a board and all included.' Some one had busily, or inadvertently, mentioned this again, so that Mrs W. had heard of it; and she, poor weak creature, was hurt that it should be supposed that Weeton's sister could not afford to pay so much for lodgings; and that if I had lived economically, it should rather be supposed to proceed from avarice than want of means to live otherwise. This appears to me ridiculous pride. I would wish to appear exactly as I am. I cannot bear puff. Mrs W. admires it much.

I know so well how much respect is paid to riches, and how little to merit without them, that I certainly would wish to appear poorer than I am, rather than richer, so that what little respect I do meet with, may be more evidently attributed to its real cause. This is a very different kind of conduct to what Mrs W. would wish me to pursue, and she persuaded my brother to think as she does. Mine is just as deceitful a conduct as that she pursues – deceit in any way is bad – which of the two is the worst? Yet I have not deceived much. I told the real state of my income when it was much less than it is, and I have endeavoured to keep its increase a secret. I have uttered no falsehood – Mrs W. did, for she has often represented it as much more than she knew it was. But of what consequence was it to anyone? It was never worth making a quarrel about. Mrs W., I suppose, thought it was, for she and my brother talked to me, *loudly* and *severely,* from tea-time that evening than half past ten – upwards of four hours. When I could have got a word in, my heart was so full, I was unable to speak. I cried violently; I could not help it; and the few efforts I did make, were violently suppressed by them both. They thumped with their hands on the table, and stamped with their feet, talking as loud and as quick as possible all the time. I was too humble, they said, and too open. The first laid me under the contempt; and the second, under the ridicule of everyone – All this is very probable; yet, if they had not told me of it in so unfeeling a manner, I might have lived in happy ignorance. Now – I feel every *appearance* of contempt or ridicule as premeditated, when perhaps it is quite unintentional, or perhaps fancied on my part.

What an unkind reception it was! Surely it was most unkind! Yet they will deny it. I know they will – I never received my brother so. He and Mrs W. might have let me spend the little time I went to spend, in peace. – The subject was renewed at breakfast the next morning, by Mrs W. My brother was much more calm than he had been the preceding evening, and frequently begged she would let the subject drop. When I spoke, she desired me to let her finish what she had to say. I listened until I began to think she never would have done. However, I sipped my tea with composure, except now and then sarcastically observing that, as she had requested my silence, she ought to have set the example – that I was tired of the subject and would rather hear her on a more entertaining one – and once enquired at what time she meant to finish, that I might know how much longer I had to sit as a hearer. I found these observations only served to lengthen the discourse, and I became totally silent, playing with the spoon, rattling the cup upon the saucer, or any other trick that might help to relieve the situation I was in. I was certainly in a provoking kind of humour. I was tired beyond anything with such an endless repetition of the same observation, over and over again, now and then have found some new fault to expatiate upon. My brother was as much tired as myself – almost; and after frequent requests that she would say no more on the subject, he was at length obliged to *insist* on her silence – She had still to conclude – he almost swore – at length she finished, and little more was said that day on the subject. I returned the day following. They walked with me part of the way. The old subject was again renewed, but in more mild terms, as I shewed no resentment nor attempted to defend myself. I could not leave my brother in anger. My heart was full enough at the thoughts of parting with him, and I determined not to say a word that should leave an unpleasant impression on his mind – I love him too well, and wish a return of that affection too sincerely. My conduct softened him – the humility he upbraided me for, only two days before, pleased now it was shewn to him! And yet in this instance, I felt convinced that I had less occasion to be so, than I had ever had in my life before. But had I still defended myself – been so tenacious of my opinions as both Mrs W. and he were of theirs, we must have quarrelled irreconcilably; and I determined, let him use me as he would, to bear with him. I could not, for the soul of me, I could not treat him as he did me. Mrs W. wou'd have died almost before she would make a concession, and my brother, good natured, excellent hearted fellow! is easily persuaded to think his wife is wisest, discreetest, best. It is right he should think so, and I would not for the universe attempt to persuade him to think otherwise, though *I suffer* for it; for jealous, as I have been told, of

67

his regard and affection for me, she tries every means to set him against me. She has failed hitherto, except for a short time, and she *never shall* succeed. My conduct has been, and shall continue to be, irreproachable, that she shall have nothing stronger than a straw to catch at. My brother, softened by my humility, my openness, and my tears – which I could not refrain – begged that I would consider what had been said, as meant in the most friendly affectionate manner. Mrs W., too, spoke kindly! – My resentment, which I had felt but not expressed, was completely subdued. I was rejoiced to the heart that I had made the first concessions, since they had had the desired effect, and eagerly took his proffered hand at parting. He affectionately hoped we parted friends? And he did look – as truly kind and affectionate as he spoke; his warm heart shone in his countenance. I squeezed his hand in affirmation of my unshaken regard – for I could not speak, my heart was too full. We then parted – and, *parted friends*.

16 September 1809 (Liverpool). *To her Aunt Barton:*

Perhaps you would expect to hear from me last Saturday, and I would have written then, had not my engagement with my brother and his party prevented me. Mrs Scott and Miss Margaret came to with my brother and Mrs Weeton, and were at an Inn, very comfortably and very cheaply accommodated; having meat and lodgings for 4/- [4 shillings] a day each. They had two good bed-rooms and a large carpeted drawing room to sit in. Both my brother and Mrs W. were very unwell whilst here; the sea air, my brother says, has always a very unpleasant effect upon him. He had a bowel complaint to a violent degree, and he was much weakened by it. Mrs W. is extremely delicate.

I dined and drank tea with them two days, and traversed the streets, or sat with them at their lodgings every day whilst they staid. They were here five days, and retuned last Wednesday.

Miss Winkley returns from Wigan on Tuesday next. I shall be very glad to see her. I am very comfortably fixed here indeed. Mrs Winkley is as attentive as she can be, and I hope I shall endeavour to deserve a continuance of her kindness.

2 October 1809 (Written from her new lodgings with the Winkley family at 19 Princes Street, Liverpool). *To her Brother:*

So stupified are my brains at this moment by the confined air and prospects of my present situation, that I begin to write to you with the expectation of not being able to find matter that will fill one fourth of my paper. The mere effort may perhaps cause ideas to flow. I will try and make one, since they will not flow without one. One kind of subject I am interdicted whom I might communicate my little mortifications and grievances, as well as the more pleasing occurrences of life; but I must touch only the brighter part of the picture, or not touch at all. But you ought to listen to the *fretful* tales of others, whilst you compel them to listen to yours.

Miss Winkley has twice been invited by Miss Hall and Miss Lancaster to tea, since my residence in the family, and no notice taken of me. On the arrival of a second invitation yesterday, my self-consequence, I must confess, was much mortified when I found I was not included. Miss H. and Miss L. called themselves upon Miss W. soon after the messenger had been, and repeated to Miss W. their invitation, and said they were going to a play. No invitation still to me, nor any apology for the omission, even by Miss Winkley. I thought *she* might have expressed something like a wish that I had been included in the party. She said not a word, nor on going out did she say good-bye. Perhaps, as being 7 or 8 years older than some of them, they might consider me as some restraint upon them. If Miss W. had been candid enough to have said as much, or made *any* plausible apology for her friend Miss H., I would very chearfully have accepted it. It was Miss Winkley's conduct that hurt me – for I received an invitation in which she had not been included, I should have been hurt at my friend's neglect of her, and have said as much; and on a second repetition of it, have taken further notice of it to Miss W. at least. And had I been on the intimate terms with my inviting friend Miss W. is with Miss Hall, I would have resented the insult to that friend. Mrs Winkley was more hurt than myself at her daughter's insulting behaviour, and threatened to be very severe with her on her return home. She had said nothing before Miss W. went, to try how she would proceed at the last; but when she went out and said not so much as good-bye to me, though she did to her mother, she was extremely hurt, and strove by every kind expression and soothing treatment to chear me. I begged in the most earnest manner I could, that Mrs W. would not be angry with her daughter, for I should then consider myself as a means of dissension between them, which would make me very unhappy. She would not promise, but did not say much to Miss W. on her return, for which I was very thankful indeed, for Miss W. might have disliked me more and more; for I am certain, from the cool though respectful manner in which she generally treats me, that she does not like me much. It is my misfortune, or my fault, I wish I could tell which, not to conciliate the regard of those I dwell with; at least, some of them. Mrs Winkley is very kind, and she and her daughter Ann both came to me to kiss me when I got into bed last night. I was very sorry they did not do the same to Miss W. and laughingly requested they would stretch out their necks a little further, if it were *only* half a yard, and salute her too, if it were too much trouble to walk round the other side of the bed. 'No!' said Mrs W., 'Betsy has displeased me.' I wish I had recalled that passage from Scripture – 'Let not the sun go down on thy wrath.' I would have quoted it; it would have had some influence, I am almost sure.

Our good cousin, Henry Smith, was married last week to a lady residing in Kirkdale. Mrs Chorley says she has her information from what may be termed good authority, that the lady (a widow) has £100 per ann. So the old fellow has got family and fortune, if there are neither youth nor beauty; and she may possess some portion of beauty for anything I know to the contrary. What a lucky old fellow! I wish with all my heart he may have met with a termagant! He deserves one for his villainous treatment of his first wife. And then perhaps he may get his punishment in this world – he must have it somewhere, and I wish no one so ill as to desire for them all their happiness in this world.

I have written myself into a more chearful humour, and I much rejoice that I have, for displeasure is a sensation of such an uncomfortable nature! Particularly when you either cannot, or do not, choose to give vent to it. When a person can rave or storm, it is certainly a very great relief to them, whatever it may be to those around them. Now, you can enjoy it, because you have somebody to storm over whom I can exert that privilege. – what a misfortune!!

I was at three places of Worship yesterday, Tom. The Church in the morning, the Presbyterian Chapel in the afternoon, and the Methodist meeting at night. What wilt thou say to me? If I had but room now, I would give thee some account of all three –

for want of room, thou wilt miss one of the finest satyrical (sic) descriptions ever penned by thy affectionate sister – E. Weeton.

28 October 1809 (Liverpool). *To her Aunt Barton:*

When you open this letter, I dare say it will be with an expectation to read a fine description of the rejoicings on Wednesday last [George III's Golden Jubilee]. What will be your disappointment when you scarce perceive a line on the subject? The newspapers will give you a much better account than any I can give – at least, a much longer and more exaggerated one than I should think proper. They will relate all the *beauties* of the Procession, and you will enjoy that as much, perhaps more, in the reading, as you would have done had you been a spectator. There was such a woeful want of music, that (to repeat a remark of Miss Braithwaite's yesterday), it looked more like a funeral procession than anything else. There were only two bands of music. There ought to have been one to each different company; had there been twenty, there would scarcely have been sufficient for such a length of procession. Taken altogether, it was ill-conducted. Immense crouds assembled and behaved extremely well, perfectly peaceable, and orderly.

15 November 1809 (Liverpool). *To her Brother:*

Not a day, scarcely an hour passes, my dear Tom, that I do not think of thee or conversing with thee. Many a little piece of information I wish for, which my partial heart makes me think I can obtain only from thee – When anything occurs – I will ask my brother, I say to myself, and he can tell me. If any subject peculiarly interests me, whether a mere flight of fancy of something on which the understanding may reason – I will mention it to my brother when I write to him, I still mentally repeat. Yet, when the times of writing arrives, many a question, and many a remark treasured in my memory for a week or two, escapes me. I sit down to write, and fill my paper without saying one half of what I had previously thought of too much interest to be forgotten. When I was at Holland, I used generally to have a slate in my bedroom on school days, and when any thought occurred that I was afraid to lose, I could have slipped out of the school for a few minutes, and noted it down, and have returned almost before I was missed. On Saturdays and Sundays, the slate was generally an appendage of the breakfast table. To sit reading and writing whilst I ate, was one of the greatest luxuries

I enjoyed. The morning's solitude was always agreeable to me. It was almost the only enjoyment I had, and, in leaving Holland, almost the only one of which I regret the loss. But it is amply made up to me. I want no other. At Beacon's Gutter, the slate was often my companion whilst I was delving in the garden. I had frequently the slate leaned up against the cop, to transcribe whatever I thought worth the trouble. A propensity to converse, is, I think, so natural to the human species without distinction of sex, that where there is little, or no opportunity of talking, most of those who are capable of it are apt to transcribe their thoughts, whether they are worth the trouble or not; and this, must have been the reason that I have always had such an itch for scribbling – the being almost unavoidably so much alone. The being taught to read and write has been the greatest comfort of my life, and its greatest blessing. What a happiness, too, that I was so fond of both! Had I had no resources within myself, I must have sought amusement in society; and where there was so little choice, I must have associated with an extremely illiterate, vulgar set. My ideas would have been confined, my language coarse, and my manners still more awkward than they are. You would then indeed have reason to blush for your sister. As it is, I begin to find so many my inferiors, that I flatter myself I in no way derogate from my brother's consequence in the world. The more I see of society, and the prouder I grow. I find not so many superiors as I expected I should when I left Up Holland – perhaps it is because it is because the class I have got amongst are rather below the middle station, than above it. Should I ever be enabled to rise a little higher, I may again become as humble in my own estimation as I used to be – but of rising in this world, there is no prospect; neither do I care about it. My chief delight is to learn, and to be with those who know how to teach. It is not often my lot to meet with living instructors; but there are plenty of the dead, and I am satisfied.

I often feel as if I were not in my proper sphere, as if I possessed talents that only want awakening – that are ready to bud, did they find the least encouragement, and – that will wither for want of it. I could, Tom, I think I could have been something greater, something better than I am, had not my natural genius been repressed, and – like the blighting winds to the rosebud – been shrivelled almost to nothing. Thou wilt smile at this as an effusion of vanity – I cannot help it – thou knowest not the ardour, the enthusiasm that often glows within me, almost beyond my power to conceal it. I cannot say to what my disposition would particularly lead me to – to what science I mean; for to science it very strongly inclines. For want of a proper guide, I first turn to one and then another. I cannot go regularly on in any, for want of a proper assortment of books. Why are not females permitted to study physic, divinity, astronomy, &c., &c., with their attendants, chemistry, botany, logic, mathematics, &c. To be sure the mere study is not prohibited, but the practise is in great measure. Who would employ a female physician? Who would listen to a female divine, except to ridicule? I could myself almost laugh at the idea. The more active employments on the stage often interests me strongly. When I read of battles by sea or land, how my heart beats to be with them! and a partaker of the danger. Some portion of this enthusiasm, I think, was instilled into us by my mother. I dare say thou rememberest the many evenings we have sat listening to her, as she recounted the deeds of a father whose manly, noble heart, and warlike achievements, she taught us to venerate. O Tom, what a mother too we had! Far above our praise. I frequently compare her with other mothers that I see, but seldom find her equal. What pains she took to instruct us in everything religious, moral, useful, and innocently amusing; often joining in our sports, as well as in our more serious occupations. Yet, to a stranger her manner appeared rather forbidding, rigid, and austere. She had the outward dignity and severity of a Cato,[18] accommodated by a heart as tender, affectionate, and benevolent as ever beat within a female breast. Surely I have been blest above the common lot of mortals, with such a father, such a mother, and such a brother! – A tide of ideas flow in upon me just now, I cannot repeat them; but thou canst think as well as me – on what is past, and what is present. – I am more serious than I intended, but I hope thou wilt not think me dull or melancholy. I write just as the thoughts occur. I scarcely know in one line how I shall treat the subject in the next; my heart expands as I write.

The idea with which I began this letter occurs again. Thou'lt let me finish it, wilt thou not? For, like as I compare my mother, so I compare thee – there may be a great many young men as intelligent as thou art, but I seldom, I know not that I ever, have the

73

luck to meet with them – It is well I do not, for I should certainly fall in love with some wise man or other, and what a woeful thing it would be! For, with all my vanity, I am not so vain as to suppose I should be admired in return; for mere understanding in a woman – even when accompanied by good temper, which is always the case – is often rather repellent than attractive when unattended by youth, beauty, and riches. Thinking as I always did of thee, Tom, and as I have lately begun to do of myself, what wonders we both must be; because thou knowest there are many with equal advantages, and even superior to either of us, that are much greater blockheads. We have both naturally an uncommon capacity, and application has finished what nature began.

> Well done! I've daubed it pretty thick,
> And filled with mortar 'stead of brick.

A few weeks ago I spoke to a Welsh harper, to bring his harp some evening, that Miss Winkley and I might hear the tone of it. He came, and we were much pleased with it, though not quite so much as we expected. The size of the instrument too, is rather unwieldy. He had one, he said, that he would sell to us for 7 guineas. We promised to let him know if we determined to have it, but have given up the intention. Since, I have heard a Pedal-harp, and the tone is so much richer than the Welsh harp we heard, that I was much more pleased with it. Something may be said for the instruments. The Pedal-harp was a good one of its kind; I don't think the other was. I cannot get to hear the Lute, the Lyre, or any other small instruments; and I should not like to purchase one unless I had heard it played upon. I have asked at one or two shops if they could sound them for me, but was answered that they could not play at all.

I was going to procure a guinea's worth of lessons on the Flageolet, but was told it was a pity I should learn on so simple an instrument; that there was one with two pipes which played two parts at once, that was much superior. I cannot say that I feel inclined to have two instruments so similar. I should certainly prefer the Pedal-harp to any other I ever heard, but shall take a little time to determine.

18 November 1809 (Liverpool). *To her Aunt Barton:*

I have heard nothing of you of such a great while, I begin to wonder what is become of you; what, if you have no news, you *should* find in your heart to write about something. Follow the *excellent* example I generally set you. I often enough fill my paper from beginning to end, with fifty lines in a page, and twenty or thirty words in a line, without so much as a sentence of news throughout the whole; my fertile genius, my exalted understanding, would scorn to be indebted for a whole letter to the news of the day – when the day afforded no news. I have had but one letter from you, I think, since I was at Holland, and that was by Ellen Sephton, with a promise (if I recollect right) to write again in a week or two – O faithless, faith

Mr Braithwaite would tell you I had been at Prescot. I was intending to give you a full, particular, and faithful account of my journey there; how I was entertained during my stay; how I walked back again; how I bore the extraordinary fatigue; and how I wonderfully escaped all the perils and dangers of the way – because there were none to encounter – but, waiting first to hear from you, all my wonderful, astonishing, extraordinary adventures have entirely slipped out of my noddle. Lack-a-day! What a loss you have had!

9 December 1809 (Liverpool) *To her Brother:*

Never was I so anxious to hear from you, my dear Tom, as I have been the whole of this week. I begun to fear your letter would not arrive than after my departure from Liverpool, which event I might expect to take place next Tuesday; and I wished to hear, that I might answer before I left, and inform you of the cause of my journey. I am going to be as companion to a Mrs Pedder, about six miles beyond Kendal, somewhere bordering, or not far from the Lakes. Mr Pedder (of whose family, near Preston, I have frequently heard you and my mother speak) has lately married a servant girl. He has taken her into retirement for a few years, until she becomes a little better fitted for the society he wishes hereafter to introduce her to, and has taken a little girl of eleven years old (by a former wife, I suppose), from school, intending to have her educated at home. I shall have to superintend her too, but as I am told she will have a maid, her education alone will employ me.

I was, with Miss Winkley, drinking tea at a Mr Nevett's, a bookseller in Castle Street, one evening a month or five weeks ago. A little before we left, Mrs Winkley came to accompany us home, and said she had just seen a Newspaper in the shop; and informing us what she had been reading, accidentally mentioned an advertisement for a Governess. When we got home, I asked the particulars of the Advertisement. She said she could not recollect but would enquire if I chose. We had a good deal of conversation about it that evening, and it was determined that I should enquire next day at the Publishers, who was the Advertiser. I did so, and was told that it was Mr Montgomery, Timber Merchant. I enquired further of a person who knew the family, what kind of people they were. I was told, highly respectable. They kept a carriage, and town and country houses.

I wrote to Mr Montgomery, imagining it was for himself he advertised; but several days elapsing, and receiving no answer, I began to give up the expectation of having any. At length, I received a note requesting I would call. I went at the time appointed, and he then informed me it was for a friend, not for himself he advertised. He had expected that friend in town that day, but as he had not arrived, he would let me know when he did, as he wished us to meet, that all responsibility for either party might be taken from him. More than a week passed, I think, before I heard again; and the time arriving for writing to you, I wrote without mentioning this subject, not wishing to do so until I felt some certainty, one way or the other, as possibly I might hear no more. In a few days after I had written to you, an elderly gentleman called at Mrs Winkley's shop, enquiring for me. She brought him down to the house. He had called in consequence of my application, he said, to Mr Montgomery, with whom he was intimately acquainted. His name was Barton. He lived at Walton, near Preston, and Mr Pedder had requested him to insert the Advertisement in a Liverpool paper. He related several circumstances respecting the family he wished to engage me for; said I should be treated as an equal by them, more as a companion to Mrs Pedder than as a governess to Miss P., to assist her in regulating the management of a family such as Mr P. wished his to be. He enquired what salary I should expect. I answered, thirty guineas.[19] He engaged me, and – I am going.

I leave here at 7 o'clock on Tuesday morning next, expect to arrive at Preston at 12, where Mr Barton and his niece (Miss Rhodes) will meet me, and conduct me to their house at Walton.

I shall stay there all night, and proceed the day following, under Mr Barton's protection, for the remainder of the journey.

I will write again in a week or two, my dear Tom, and relate any further particulars that may occur, and give you my address.

If the situation be an agreeable one, it will be a source of great profit and saving, with such an income as mine; and if not, I can at any time return. The family here express so much regret at parting with me, that I had the power to conciliate the affections of one, having never, as I remember, had any proof of it since my mother's death (except with children, and that made me so delighted with children's company). They are indeed kind, every one of them, and I shall ever think with pleasure, gratitude, and affection. How can I do otherwise? They treat me as a person of superior understanding.

I have given it out here that I am going to see Mrs Edmondson (from whom I have really had an invitation), and some other friends in the north, and that I expect to make a long visit; for should I find the situation uncomfortable, and be obliged to return soon, I should not wish anyone to know where I had been, or for why; and therefore, my dear Tom, I enjoin you to the strictest secrecy until I find how I am situated, and I will inform you when you are at liberty to tell, for if Mrs W. should tell her sisters, it is no longer a secret, I know. When you see my Aunt and Uncle Barton, you may inform them if you think proper; but – enjoin secrecy. I shall write to my aunt soon, but shall only tell them as I tell everyone else, referring them to you for the whole. Mrs Winkley and Mrs Chorley are the only people who know here. Mr C's should not have known, only I was obliged to refer Mr Montgomery to them for an account of my abilities, character, &c. What account they gave, I know not, but I was engaged immediately after.

Miss Chorley has requested my correspondence! Which I have declined. Mrs Chorley's, to the same effect, I could not, for she was always kind.

[Journal, December 1809]:

I have long wished that my brother should settle in some larger town than Leigh. He wished it too, but we neither of us can as yet fix on any plan to render it practicable. He assuredly possesses a certainty of supporting his family comfortably, but can do nothing more. He wished to save something for old age, when it comes upon him; something more to his children when he dies, than his blessing. But in Leigh he never will, I fear. There is not sufficient employ for him, though he has almost all the business there. To see him prosper is the darling wish of my heart, and I would sacrifice a good deal of my own comfort, if that would contribute to promote prosperity. When I heard of this Advertisement, the idea immediately struck me that if it were any person in or near Liverpool who advertised, I would endeavour to gain the situation. Perhaps it might be possible to influence them to favour my Brother for my sake, particularly if the gentleman were a man in power, or connected with those who were. When I heard it was a person residing in Kendal, I felt a severe check; but again being told it was Mr Pedder from Preston (a place my mother and brother were so fond of, and a place of such hope; Heaven grant I may not be disappointed! As it is very probable I may, I shall inform no one of my real motive for leaving such a comfortable home, When they know what kind of situation I am engaged in, the world will perhaps stare and wonder – Let them. If I accomplish my wish, I will then let the world know. Whether I do or not, I hope I shall never have cause to repent what I am about to do. Heaven's blessing be with me.

The following letter is the final one sent from Liverpool before Miss Weeton travelled to Ambleside, Westmoreland, to take up the position of Governess in the household of Mr E. Pedder of Dove's Nest. She left Liverpool by stagecoach on 12 December, 1809.

10 December 1809 (Liverpool). *To her Aunt Barton:*

As I am going a long journey on Tuesday next, the 12th inst., I wish to write to you before I go, to acquaint you with it. J. Latham would perhaps tell you where I was going to – Lancaster. I expect to stop some time; two or three, or four months perhaps. I shall write to my brother soon after I get to the end of my journey, and tell him how to direct me. I shall hope to hear from you in a few weeks, as my brother will, when you see him, tell you where to direct for me. I don't exactly know in what part of Lancaster Mrs Edmondson lives.

I have sent a bundle of old cloaths along with this. As my uncle is well acquainted with the abodes of age and poverty, he will easily find such as will accept them; and if you, my dear aunt, will send and bestow them, I shall consider myself much obliged to you.

There are – 2 pairs of cotton stockings – a bed gown – a pair of flannel petticoats – a brown chip bonnet – a pair of scissors – a pair of shoes – and a pair of stays.

The stays perhaps Miss Billingtons would accept; they would serve as a pattern to make others by; but do what you please with them.

I shall pay carriage on this to Wigan; will you bestow your charity on the bundles from thence to Holland?

NOTES:

1. The Swan Inn, Winwick, was a well-known stagecoach stop on the turnpike road (A49) between Chester and Kendal. It stands opposite the ancient Church of St Oswald, first mentioned in the Domesday Book (1086). The original Swan Inn was replaced in 1898 by the Swan Hotel.
2. The journey by canal passenger packet, inclusive of stops to pick-up passengers, averaged four miles an hour. Speed was maintained by the use of a couple of towing horses, usually jockeyed by scarlet-coated boys. When the wind was favourable, sails were used. Owing to the Canal's circuitous route, nine hours was taken up by the journey from Wigan to Liverpool. Miss Weeton would walk the two-and-a-half miles north from Up Holland to Appley Bridge to catch the packet. This form of transport, whilst much slower than the stagecoach, was far more comfortable and considerably cheaper.
3. A gutter or creek refers to a narrow inlet off the sea coast. Beacon's Gutter begins with an inland stream before reaching the River Mersey.
4. Sir Richard Steele (1672-1729), essayist, playwright and politician, was best known for his satirical, political and moral essays. His last and best complete comedy (in 1722) was *The Conscious Lovers,* remarkable because it included Steele's best ideas on life and character.
5. The Old Testament Book of Job is the story of a good man who suffered disaster. He lost all his children and his property; he also suffered from a repulsive disease. Job's friends adopted the traditional religious response by assuming that God rewards good and punishes evil. Job believed he did not deserve such punishment and instead challenged God; but in all of that Job did not lose his faith. In the end God responds, not to Job's questions, but to his faith.
6. The somewhat ambiguous expression 'Plurality of Worlds' suggests speculation concerning either 'Reincarnation,' the belief that following death some aspect of self or soul can be reborn in a new body (human or animal), or the Roman Catholic belief and doctrine of two distinctly separate places of 'Purgatory' and 'Heaven.' Purgatory is the place where the souls of the dead suffer for their sins, before being admitted to Heaven – God's dwelling place and the place of the blessed.
7. Miss Weeton is undoubtedly referring to Rev T. Meyrick, curate in charge at Up Holland (1802 until he resigned in 1821), a notorious character

of doubtful morality and who died 'unmourned.' (See also letter to Mrs Whitehead 23 May 1809).

8. Refers to: 'Two are better than one; because they have a good reward for their labour . . .' (Ecclesiastes 4:9).

9. Source unknown.

10. Source unknown.

11. Refers to: '. . . Be fruitful, and multiply, and replenish the earth, and subdue it . . .' (Genesis 1: 28).

12. 'Mrs Banks' refers to Anne Bankes, the first wife of Meyrick Bankes (1768-1827), of Winstanley Hall, Wigan. Mrs Bankes tragically died soon after her stillborn son. A report of her death appeared in the Liverpool Courier, Wednesday, 5th April, 1809: 'Same day in the 38th year of her age, greatly beloved and respected by all who knew her, and deeply regretted, Mrs Bankes daughter of Rev. Edmund Lally, and wife of Meyrick Bankes, Esq. of Winstanley Hall, near Wigan, late High Sheriff of this County.' The following year, Meyrick married Maria Elizabeth, daughter of Thomas Langford Brooke of Mere, Cheshire. Meyrick died in London in 1827. Maria Elizabeth survived him until 1850. He was buried at Up Holland Church, as are his wives and his two sons.

13. George Lyon (1761-1815) hanged at Lancaster, 22 April 1815, 'for robbery,' was more a footpad than an alleged highwayman. Lyon's burial in Up Holland Churchyard was watched by a crowd of 'several thousand people.' His grave lies a few yards from the grave of Mrs Mary Weeton and that of her sister, Mrs Margaret Barton.

14. It seems astonishing that Miss Weeton did not question the status quo that only one in four children of the poor received any kind of education.

15. Sarah Siddons (1755-1831), English actress. Considered by many to be England's greatest female tragedian. Her career was one long triumph; her final farewell was in 1812 as Lady Macbeth.

16. Referring to books by Rev J. Fawel (1754-1802), curate of All Saints Church, Wigan, 1780 to 1798, until he became incumbent at Up Holland, 1798 to 1802. He is the author of at least three works on divinity and also a poem. All were published in Wigan during his curacy at Wigan Parish Church. Miss Weeton received little assistance in her search for Fawel's books; although she did manage to secure one title many months later.

17. Thomas Weeton took full advantage of his sister's instruction that he should have 'full liberty to choose, alter or entirely reject' the suggested verse she had written. The actual inscription on the grave slab reads: 'Mary Weeton. Died 5th December 1797. Aged 51.' In the same grave also lie Miss Weeton's traducer, her cousin Latham and her husband; also a small child who died in 1864.

18. Marcus Porcius Cato (234-149 B.C.), 'The Elder' or 'the Censor,' Roman statesman and writer. Alternatively Marcus Porcius (95-46 B.C., 'The Younger,' surnamed Uticensis, great grandson of Cato the Elder, Roman statesman, soldier and Stoic philosopher.

19. It is a measure of Miss Weeton's confidence and boldness that at a time when the average annual salary of a schoolteacher rarely exceeded 23 guineas, she asked for and received 30 guineas.

FOUR

Pleasure and tragedy in Lakeland

Ambleside, Westmoreland

December 1809 – February 1811

MISS WEETON'S LONG and tiring journey from Liverpool to the 'charming seat' known as Dove's Nest, overlooking Windermere Lake, near Ambleside, was achieved through a combination of stagecoach, mail-coach and post-chaise. She arrived on 13th December 1809; the journey took two days.

The occupier of Dove's Nest, and Miss Weeton's first employer, was Edward Pedder, Esq., a member of the important Preston family of bankers, although Edward appeared not to have any active interest in the bank. In August 1809, when he lost his first wife, a Miss Shaw of Preston, he made a hurried Gretna Green marriage to a 17-year-old Preston dairy-maid. Mr Pedder was then about 34 years old. He took Dove's Nest on a seven year lease and advertised for a governess to undertake the education of his new wife and that of the child of his former marriage. His earnest desire was that his wife should confidently socialise within the upper echelons of Preston society.

Miss Weeton was received 'very politely' by Mr Pedder, whom she described as a 'good looking little man.' She was immediately 'taken' by Mrs Pedder, as a 'pretty woman' and she judged Mr Pedder's 10-year-old daughter, Mary Gertrude, to be 'a sad child.'

At first Mr Pedder treated Miss Weeton with courtesy and respect. She responded by considering him 'good natured, liberal, hospitable, with an unsuspicious nature.' Although later she began to notice that he had a propensity towards his 'bottle;' an omen that would later play a large part in his deterioration from an apparently civilised and courteous gentleman, to an unpredictable and violent brute.

Her first letter from Dove's Nest was to her brother, in which she gave a detailed account of her journey from Liverpool. She also tells of a humorous exchange in a Kendal bookshop before expressing her opinions about the personalities of her new-found acquaintances.

25 December 1809 (Dove's Nest). *To her Brother:*

My dear brother, I have no doubt, is very anxious to hear again from me; and I have been no less so, to give him every information in my power, as far as I have proceeded; but my situation is so very new to me, that I can scarcely recollect myself sufficiently to give you a clear account. A transition from an obscure street in Liverpool to an elevated situation near the head of Windermere lake, is enough to turn my brain a little. I could almost say with Nel, the cobbler's wife in the theatrical entertainment, 'Lord! is it I'?

The novelty of my situation begins to wear off a little. I begin to feel more at home, to grow more collected, and more and more pleased with those about me. For some days I knew not exactly what was required of me, or what degree of authority it would be proper for me to assume. I now discover what I have to do, and begin to form methodical plans for each day's employment; for, without method in the distribution of time, I never feel comfortable. Let wits and geniuses decry methodical arrangements as much as they please, as shackles on the intellect, the necessary employments and the intermediate amusements of existence can never, in my opinion, be well or agreeably conducted, without some regularity.

More will be necessary for me to undertake, I find, than I am almost competent to perform. Some days I have been in rather low spirits about it, thinking I was not equal to walk in the path I have stepped into; at other times I feel a little more encouraged, as I become better acquainted with the objects about me. It is not mere education in language, manners, books, and work I have to attend to, but to persist in the proper direction and management of the servants and the household. This, by degrees, I am beginning to think I shall attain; and, my dear Tom, if any rules of modern etiquette with which it is probable

I may be unacquainted, should occur to you or Mrs Weeton, I should really be obliged to you to write them down for me, particularly at the dinner or supper table. – I was at Kendal on Monday last, and enquiring of an old lady in a book-seller's shop, for a pamphlet on the art of carving, I observed she looked very odd, and seemed a good deal confused. 'No-o, Ma'am,' she hesitatingly answered, 'we have not got.' I repeated the question in two or three various ways, finding she either did not hear or understand me. 'Have you got any and books about cows?' she enquired of her husband. 'Cows!' thought I to myself, 'what is the woman rambling about?' 'Have you got any books,' I again enquired, 'that give directions for cutting up meat at the table when cooked?' 'Oh!' she said, and she smiled, 'I thought you wanted a book about cows and farriery, and was asking for a pamphlet on the art of calving!!!'

I left Liverpool on Tuesday, the 12th., and staid all night at Mr Barton's, at Walton. The next morning at 7 o'clock, he and I left Preston in the Mail, and arrived at Kendal soon after two that afternoon. We there, and then took a post-chaise to Mr Pedder's, of Dove-Nest, twelve miles from Kendal (and not six, as I told you before – I was misinformed). Dove-Nest is situated near the head of Windermere Lake, the lake extending only about 1 mile farther North than the house; we are within two or three hundred yards of it, and have a fine view. I really like my situation. At present, I am treated with a degree of respect and deference, which my conduct shall, if possible, continue deservedly to exact.

Until now, I have one way or another been fully engaged. I am now sitting up than midnight to write to you. On Sunday, Mr P. hired a chaise for Mr Barton and myself. He and Mrs P. rode in the curricle, followed by a servant. We proceeded to Grasmere Church, five or six miles from hence, but finding we were too late for the service we entered an Inn instead of the Church, and taking a little refreshment, we then drove on to Hawkshead, where we dined, and then returned home, having had a drive of about seventeen miles. The following day, as I have previously mentioned to you, we went to Kendal, Mr & Mrs Pedder in the curricle, and Mr B. and I in a chaise. Mr Barton returned home to Walton that day; the rest of us staid all night, returning to Dove-Nest the next afternoon. Since then I have been busily engaged in the schoolroom with Mrs and Miss P. Mrs Pedder is really a pretty woman; I may say handsome; and a most sweet temper. She seems to have an ardent desire to improve, and applies to her studies very closely indeed at present. I hope she will continue to do so, notwithstanding the trouble it gives me. Miss Pedder, poor child, has fits. Of these I was previously appraised, as well as of most necessary things for me to be acquainted with, before I was engaged.

There is a want of regularity in the house which I shall attempt to remove by insensible degrees.

I begin to understand Mr Pedder's character, with which I was previously unacquainted. Do you know anything of him, or Mr Barton? They both speak of you as being a young man well known in Preston. My being here, and the kind of situation I am in, will then probably not long remain a secret. What think you? – Write soon.

P.S. Another birth-day is very near.[1] A little revolution has happened to me since the last, with an increase rather than a diminution of happiness. Every birth-day I am permitted to see, may I see thee, my dear fellow, increasing in years and prosperity!"

Her next letter was sent to her loyal Liverpool friend, Miss Bessy Winkley, expounding in even greater detail than to her brother, about her journey from Liverpool. Additionally, she recounts her personal duties at Dove's Nest, and the circumstances that brought-about the hasty marriage of widowed Edward Pedder with his one-time dairy-maid. Miss Weeton also reports a conversation with a fellow coach passenger, revealing shrewd perception in her assessment of those whose talk belies their true circumstances and status.

28 December 1809 (Dove's Nest). *To Miss Winkley:*

When I left you, my dear Miss Winkley, on the morning of the 12th., I felt a degree of sorrow at the idea of parting with such kind friends, that was not entirely dissipated for many miles of my journey; and, if one ruling idea which has for years predominated, had not actuated me, I would not have left such an abode where I was so truly happy, for a long time to come – if permitted to stay. I could not expect to change for the better. I only hope the end for which I came hither may be accomplished, and then I shall not repent.

Just after I had got seated in the coach, and had taken leave of your Mother – who still lingered by the coach door than the horse began to move – a young gentleman came running, calling out to the coachman to stop. One moment later and he would have missed the coach, and I, a most agreeable companion. He had asked for a Lancaster coach, but when he got in, he accidentally heard from one of the passengers, that he was then going to Manchester. The names of the two towns have a great similarity of sound, and the person who had directed him had misunderstood him. However, he found out his mistake in time. He laughed heartily about it. Well was it for you, O Bessy Winkley, that you were not there (in the coach, I mean), or your inflammable heart would have been burnt entirely away, not so much as a bit of tinder left; for, O, he was the bonniest lad my e'en were ever *clapped on*. He was indeed one of the handsomest young men I ever saw. Luckily for me, he was too young for me, not more than one or two and twenty I dare say, so that though my heart bumped a little bit, it did not wish to leave me. We laughed and we talked than my throat was sore, for the coach makes such a pothering noise, I was obliged to bawl like a fisherwoman to be heard. The young man had a great deal of archness and waggery about him. He had been, perhaps was, in the army. He lived near Windermere, he said – the very place, O Bessy, I was going to! And yet, do you know, I have never seen him since that day; nor have I heard who he was, for I could not be rude enough to ask *him* any questions of the kind; neither did I say I was going any farther than Preston.

There was a nice old woman in the coach, who lived in Lancaster, and I obtained a good deal of information from her respecting the town, and some old friends in it.

An intelligent farmer became our companion for a part of the way. He appeared to be a man of great natural abilities, improved by reading, as will be evident to you when I tell you that he never once introduced himself of his own affairs or occupations into his conversation, ancient history and modern biography forming the chief subjects. – But vanity! Vanity! – thou art inseparable from man. He let us know that he went three or four times a year to Lord Derby's, and spent two or three nights there each time – with a significant kind of look, as if he would have us believe he was an acquaintance of his Lordship's, No! No! Mr Farmer, your garb and awkward address told tales. They said you were a tenant of his Lordship's, and went only to pay a quarterly rent to the steward; and that as you lived at some distance, you could not go and return the same day. You will not need to be told I had an agreeable ride to Preston. Mr Barton met me at an Inn there, and by his advice I got into another coach and rode down to Walton. Mr B's niece was exactly the person I expected to find, and had described to you, as an awkward, vulgar looking woman. Her features and figure are much against her. She might improve perhaps on a farther acquaintance. The house and everything about it indicates a degree of affluence which ought to be separated from anything vulgar. Mr B. is a widower with one child, a little girl at school. Don't smile now, *Mrs* Winkley, at this, and look knowing and significant. Mr Barton (as well as his niece, Miss Rhodes), must improve upon acquaintance before I could admire him. He and I are very different kind of people, our pursuits and our ideas as greatly opposite as those of any two beings can be; we should neither of us suit the other at all. His wisdom is all of this world, experimental, and useful; mine, of the brain, mere theory and speculation, and consequently good for little. If he wants a wife, he would wish one that could preside at the dining table, and superintend the kitchen – I can do neither of these well. I have yet to learn – what *am* I fit for? – not a wife. He loves a good dinner and his bottle. I despise both epicures and tipplers. He possesses in corporation what he wants in brain. You can vouch for my *deficiency* in the *one*; do I make it up in the other? I do not know what Mr Barton's profession or business is, farther than that he is steward to Mr P.

I had a tete-a-tete with Miss Rhodes the whole of the afternoon, and, going to bed soon after tea, saw nothing of Mr Barton from getting into the coach at Preston to go down to Walton, than next morning at half past six. At seven we got into the Mail which passes his door, and had a very stupid ride to Kendal, except what entertainment the prospects afforded. From Lancaster, there were no passengers besides ourselves. On entering the town, my anxious eyes surveyed every object in the expectation something I had known in my infancy, and I was not disappointed. I was much gratified at seeing the buildings, the market place, &c., just as I remembered them to be when a child – those places, at least, where the coach passed. The Mail stops so very short a time at any place, that I never got out until I arrived at Kendal, or took any refreshment. At Kendal we dined.

Mr Barton's ideas and mine are cast in such different molds (sic), that we were equally incapable of conversation. We did now and then squeeze out a word or two. The *man* did his *very best* to entertain me, and what could a *body* do more? But I was so amused with the approaching and the passing scenery, that I was very glad to be silent.

From Kendal, we set out in a post-chaise, and arrived at Dove Nest about four o'clock. The house is situated upon a hill a few hundred yards above Windermere, with a still higher hill behind it; and on ascending it in the chaise, I felt some degree of alarm. Mr B. had got out. I preferred riding up, because of the wetness of the ground; but so steep was the road, that if the horses had slipped ever so little, they would have been precipitated all together into the lake, there being not so much as a wall or bank to have prevented us. I got up safe, however, and was very politely received.

Mr and Mrs Pedder were seated at their wine after dinner, Mrs P. dressed in a pink muslin, with a very becoming head dress of the same. At supper we had two servants in livery attending, and some display of plate, silver nutcrackers, &c., and some things of which poor ignorant I knew not the use. I felt a little awkward, but as you may suppose, strove not to let it appear. I now feel much more at home, and quite comfortable. For more than a week I was far otherwise, not knowing exactly what was expected from me. I am now better acquainted with the task I have undertaken, and find it both an easy and agreeable one. Mr and Mrs Pedder treat me in a most pleasing, flattering manner. So far from making me feel any dependence, I am treated with so much deference, that I must endeavour to be cautious lest I thoughtlessly assume too much. Mr P. is very good tempered in general, a little passionate sometimes. Mrs P. is a most sweet tempered woman, and of a disposition upright and amiable in the extreme. I have had some instances of it that have delighted and astonished me. I am fortunate to have such a one under my care, for she is my pupil as well as Miss Pedder. The latter is not a pleasing child; far otherwise. Her fits, I think, have an effect upon her disposition. She has them very frequently, sometimes five in a day; seldom a whole day without. I don't feel so much alarmed with them as I expected. I have frequently to hold her in them. They seldom last five minutes.

I have to attend to the direction of the House, the table, &c., as well as literary studies; to assist in entertaining company in the parlour; and give directions to the servants. I am studying the art of carving, and learning, as far as books will teach me, as well as giving instructions. Mr P. has a most excellent library.

Mrs Pedder was a dairy maid at Darwen-Bank, Mr P's house near Preston, when he fell in love with her. Her father heard of the connexion and fearing his daughter might be seduced, sent her home. He lives near-by here. Mr P. followed her, took her off to Gretna Green and married her. They lived some some time at Darwen-Bank, and then took this house, where he intends to live retired than his wife (every way worthy her present rank, in my opinion), is fit to appear in the presence of his relations; and her improvement is so rapid, her application so close, and her disposition and understanding so superior, that a little time will make her all he wishes. He is a lucky fellow to have hit upon such a one. She is not eighteen yet. She expresses herself as much pleased with me, and satisfied with my attentions; and Mr Barton told me, Mr Pedder did the same. – How gratifying!

Mr P. is a very little man of about 34. He first married a Miss Shaw of Preston, by whom he had this little girl, now ten years old. Mrs P. is almost my height, and very pretty, I may say handsome woman. The pleasing expression of her countenance, more than her beauty, pleases me.

I have written you a long letter. I hope it will atone for the length of time I have been in sending it. 'Will they be able to read it?' enquired Mrs P. with a smile just now as she looked over – not that she looked at what I wrote – 'I hope so,' I replied, 'though it would require good eyes, and some quickness of apprehension.'

I have received my cloaths. I find by the direction, they had lain some time at Preston.

18 January 1810 (Dove's Nest). *To Mrs Chorley:*

With a considerable degree of diffidence, I begin to write to my dear and respected Mrs Chorley, scarcely knowing in what manner to commence a correspondence so flattering to myself, but which, from the peculiarity of my situation, will perhaps not be so agreeable to you; nor can I make it so communicative as

I might wish to make it. Perhaps, at one time or other, I may be enabled to repeat a few leading circumstances respecting the family, but it will require caution to avoid saying too much. I must recollect that it is not amongst my own family I dwell, consequently I am not at liberty to relate family occurrences; but if I can make it up to you by occasionally giving you little stories of the neighbouring families, I shall consider myself as at full liberty to do so.

I certainly may think myself wonderfully fortunate in getting into such a family, all circumstances considered; for, previously knowing that Mr Pedder had married his servant, I might have expected to have met with the one, a low-lived libertine, and the other, an exalted piece of arrogant vulgarity. I can assure you with truth, that I am very fond of Mrs Pedder. She has many virtues that make her more than equal to the rank to which she is raised – *in my opinion.* Miss Chorley perhaps will smile at this, for she thinks no qualities of the mind, no dignity of character, can compensate for the want of high birth. Miss Chorley's opinions are of this world, and will be annihilated with it. – Whenever Miss C. sees death as near as I think I have seen it, she will see the vanities of this life with very different eyes than those with which she contemplates them – and when the change in her opinion takes place, in whatever state I may then exist, may I be conscious of it! It would give me such delight! *Superior* even to the pain she has frequently inflicted; and she has wounded me to the very soul. She has made me feel *most bitterly* how much it was possible for one human being to afflict the mind of another. – Forgive this, my dear, respected Mrs Chorley. I will be more cautious in future. Miss C. too, will *some time* forgive it. – I wish I could as easily forget, as forgive – but I can at least be silent.

Mrs Pedder's father is a respectable farmer, four or five miles from here.[2] He has another daughter and a son. Mrs P., his youngest daughter, not contented at home, after much entreaty prevailed with her father to let her go to service. She went to an aunt in Preston, who immediately procured her the Dairy-maid's place at Mr Pedder's, of Darwen-Bank, a few miles from hence. It was the opinion of her fellow servants when she first went, that she would never be able to do the work; for, said they, 'Look at her hands, they are too white, and too soft; she has never been used to such work; besides, she is a deal too young, she'll never stay.' (She was scarcely seventeen; she is not eighteen yet). She was too pretty a girl to remain long unnoticed by Mr Pedder. He soon fell in love with her. Her father got to hear of it, and had her home. He knew too much of the world to expect Mr P. meant honourably, and prudently took her out of the reach of dishonour. Mr P. followed her, and with her father's consent, took her to Gretna Green. They returned for a few days to Darwen-Bank, and then came to the house they now reside in, which they have taken for a term of seven years.

Mr P. is a good looking little man of 33 or 34. His natural disposition is good but worked a little by the usual dissipation of a military life. He is good natured, liberal, hospitable, and unsuspicious, he is what most people would call a good husband – he would be a better if he were less fond of the bottle. This makes my situation less agreeable than it would otherwise be, though indeed I have no personal complaint. I am treated in a most pleasing, respectful manner.

I found on my arrival here, an establishment of five servants (two men and three maids), a curricle, four or five horses, five or six dogs, a cow, two pigs, and a whole host of rats, too many to be counted. The dogs one day chose to have a little sport to themselves, and worried about 30 sheep, for which offence the ringleaders were tried, condemned, and executed; besides which, ample compensation was made to the owners. Two dogs were left, too quiet and good tempered to be any guard to the house.

There is a report here that the house and grounds about it are haunted. Old Benson,[3] the builder and late owner of it, a great miser, is supposed to have hid a considerable sum of money somewhere about the house; and (as is usual on such occasions), cannot rest, his spirit being seen, as the servants say, in various forms at several places near the house. He has not been seen in it, but makes strange noises all over it sometimes. One night, about two o'clock, I was awoke with a noise like some one opening my room window and letting it down again with great violence; so much so, as to shake the whole room and the bed I lay in. I looked towards the window, but saw nothing. The noise was still continued, and very loud. I lay, as you may suppose, in great fear, but hoping every moment to hear Mr P. or some of the servants stir. The hope was in vain! Not a creature stirred. They must be robbers, thought I, attempting to get into the house; but what fools they must be to make such a noise. I'll get up and see, however, since nobody else will stir. I had lain above an hour, the noises being continued all the time, and the whole house shaking with the commotion. With fear and trembling, I walked to the window, determining not to be murdered in bed, or without the utmost resistance. I opened it and looked out. All was in perfect quiet; not a creature, not so much as a *soul,* to be seen. I shut it again, and as I stood for some time near it, the noise seemed to proceed from Mrs P's room on my right hand, as if she were opening and shutting the drawers in it. I heard very distinctly, as I thought, some one walking in her room. Dear me! Thought I, if Mrs P. could not sleep herself, she need not have disturbed others with such noises. I got into bed heartily vexed, but much less frightened than when I got out. I lay listening for above an hour longer. The chairs in Mrs P's room seemed to be carried from one part of it to the other, and sometimes as if the whole chest of drawers were dragged over the floor at once. The windows rattled! the bed shook! – This is the oddest fancy! I still thought, when at length I heard a scream – not *very* loud, but enough to convince me that the previous noise, loud and dreadful as it was entirely caused – by rats!!! So I composed myself, and soon fell into a profound sleep. Next morning we made mutual enquiries of what we had heard the preceding night. Mr P. said the noise began before one o'clock, and continued than five. I asked him if he were not alarmed. He was, indeed, he answered. 'And what did you do, Sir? Did you get up?' 'No,' said he laughingly, blushing at the same time like a damask rose; and I discovered that the *great* – the *little* coward, I mean – had put his head under the bed cloaths, and clung to his wife for protection! Perspiring with fear for four hours together. – Heaven help me from such a husband!

The servants laughed at my idea of rats. I determined, however, to make an investigation. The loft immediately under the roof, I was told, was perfectly dark, and no stairs into it. I got a ladder, and a candle; *accompanied* by Mrs P., and *followed* by the tittering domestics, I set out on my rat-hunting expedition. Mounting the ladder, I ascended through a square hole left in the flooring, and soon discovered by the heaps of ----- dirt, that there must be rats, immense both in numbers and size. The boards of the floor were laid loosely on, and not nailed, so that the rats in running over and under them, not only shook, but moved them considerably. They were laid over another in various directions, and not in the parallel state in which they had originally laid. We have heard them frequently since, but never so loud as on that dreadful *night*. Perhaps I was considered by them as – a scare crow. They must have had a grand battle that night, though I saw no slain.

There are many characters here worth observation. S. Coleridge, the conductor of a new and valued publication entitled 'The Friend' resides only a few miles hence.[4]

I have been some time in writing this letter, Mrs Chorley. A real want of time must be my excuse, for, though I have very little to do, Mr and Mrs P. require my society when not engaged in instruction, and I must steal time from sleep when I write, as I cannot rise early in a morning, and sit without a fire at this time of the year. In the Summer I shall have time enough. Remember me to Miss Chorley, and with every sentiment of respect, I conclude.

[Journal, January 1810]:

The comforts of which I have deprived myself in coming here, and the vexations that occur sometimes during the hours of instruction with a child of such a strange temper to instruct, would almost induce me to give up my present situation, did not the consideration which brought me here, still retain me. O Brother! Sometime thou wilt know perhaps the deprivations I have undergone for thy sake, and that thy attentions have not been such as to compensate them. For thy sake I have wanted food and fire, and have gone about in rags; have spent the flower of my youth in obscurity, deserted, and neglected; and now, when God has blessed me with a competence, have given up its comforts to promote the interest in the world. Should I fail in this desire, should I not succeed! – what will recompense me? – God perhaps will bless me for the thought that was in my heart; and if I am rewarded in heaven – I am rewarded indeed! I will be patient – I will be resigned, and – with the help of the Power around me, I will persevere.

28 January 1810 (Dove's Nest). *To her Brother:*

I was very anxious for thy letter, my dear Tom. I wished to know what thou wouldst say respecting the step I have taken, and what Mrs Weeton would say, and I am pleased to find you neither of you express any disapprobation; which I expected from Mrs W. – she has said so much on the subject before. As to thee, my dear fellow, when left to thyself, there are few actions of my life thou wouldst censure, I know.

I am not now anxious for secrecy, as I find I am not likely to quit here very soon; but, had I found it necessary to have returned in a month or two, I should not have liked my Liverpool or Holland acquaintances to have known where I had been. This reason I gave you before; and do you, then, think it such a foolish one?

You will have seen my Aunt and Uncle Barton by this time. What say they? I will write to my Aunt very soon; but tell what she says, for she will perhaps be a long time before she answers me. I wonder whether the expence of postage will be any consideration with her?

By this time I hope Mrs Weeton has got over her confinement, and is doing well. As thy family encreases (sic), Tom, so I hope will thy prosperity. I drank thy health on thy birthday (the 24th.) [Thomas Weeton's 29th birthday]. So did Mr and Mrs Pedder.

The weather has been unusually warm for the season, If it is everywhere as it has been here, and must be unhealthy for every one; the little frost we have had, is gone again, and was by no means so severe whilst it lasted, as the papers say it has been in the south of England. The local situation of this house is generally allowed by the surrounding inhabitants to be peculiary warm. It fronts to the south, having in prospect nearly the whole of Windermere. A hill rises immediately behind it. It is sheltered on the East and the West by hills, and a good deal of coppice wood, almost the only wood now left. The natives say the country is nothing like so beautiful as it was twenty or thirty years ago, the timber has been so much cut.[5] In addition to the sheltered situation of the house, Mr P. keeps such warm fires, that nothing (scarcely) can surpass the domestic comfort I enjoy. I have known, Tom, so many wants in my life-time, and that of necessity, fire, amongst the rest, that you can have no idea how much I enjoy life – much more, I am convinced, than the affluent who never knew the wants that money can supply.

My good, i.e. my luxurious living, has give me such a pimpled face! I fear when the spots are gone, I shall have a mask of purple complete. It can't be helped. I never was a beauty, and sure enough I grow uglier every day. There must be *little* evils, thou knowest, to counterbalance every *great* good – thyself, for example – a wife is a *great* good, everyone allows, but there often follows a train of *little* evils at the heels of that great good.

Alack a day! I have almost filled my paper, and I really have a great deal to tell thee. Dear me! I wish I could carry thee about with me, and then I could talk enough to thee, surely. The distance between us is now great, thou sayest. What difference will it make? We saw not each other so often when we were nearer.

Mr Green,[6] an artist, lives in Ambleside. He keeps an exhibition of views of the lakes in water colours. I went with Mrs Pedder a few days ago to see some of them. They are well done, in my opinion. He is said to have improved much since he came to reside here 7 or 8 years ago. He is employed all the summer in taking sketches, and all the winter in finishing them. He is indefatigable; a singular kind of man. Some time or other *I* may give you a sketch of *him.*

I have just received a letter from Miss Winkley. She says my cousin Latham called there a week or two ago, and gives a curious and laughable account of the various enquiries she made respecting me. Do go over to Holland, Tom, if you have not been, and hear what my aunt says. My cousin asked if I were gone to be a lady's maid. Waiting maids don't visit their mistresses. I visit with Mrs P., and have been noticed in a pleasing manner by those who visit here. I have had several little journeys with them in a chaise, and am promised more in the Spring, but those, I hope, will be either pedestrian or equestrian, for there is no seeing the country out of a chair [an open chaise]. Mr and Mrs Pedder are in London in two or three months. Mr P. once said he would take me with them, but I rather expect he will change that intention. It would be better, I think, that I should remain house-keeper; they are not well fixed with servants.

29 January 1810 (Dove's Nest). *To her Aunt Barton:*

Expecting that my brother would have informed you some time ago of the place of my present residence, I have not been so early as indeed I ought to have been, in writing to you, I thought, when you knew through him all the particulars of my journey here, my reason for coming, and fixing in so agreeable a situation as I am now in, and the advantages of it, you would be quite at ease respecting me. From what Miss Winkley says in a letter I received from her yesterday, my cousin Latham has made many enquiries, and talked much of your uneasiness in not knowing where I was. Why did you not ask my brother at once? He would have informed you of everything. My uncle might have seen him at Wigan, or have written by Holcroft; and I had requested you to enquire of him.

It was not kind of you, my dear aunt, to raise such talk about me; until you had known by means of my brother how I was fixed, it would have been as well to have been silent. Have you not had proof enough of my conduct ever since my mother's death, that I was not likely to act very imprudently? For, if I could conduct myself so as to be a credit rather than a discredit to my friends at that early age, surely I may escape the *premature* imputation of imprudence now.[7] Let me act wrong first, and then blame me.

I have hitherto had great reason to rejoice that I left Holland, for I have since made my income more than twice what it was; first, by selling advantageously out of the funds, and next, by a fortunate purchase, for which I can at any time receive more than I gave. In addition to which, I am now kept, and receiving a handsome salary, without undergoing half the slavery I used to do. If I can but give satisfaction here, I may, in a few years, save sufficient to purchase a tolerable estate; and by the time I am no longer wanted here, may have an income to support me handsomely. Should my talents prove insufficient for my situation, I shall but be where I was. Mrs Winkley has frequently repeated that she would at any moment receive me again. Miss Winkley has often said she hoped I should not like my situation, that I might return to them again; and both Mrs Winkley and she offered to keep me without paying board if I would but stay with them. They were kind to me indeed, beyond everything I ever met with since my mother was taken from me. Mrs Winkley used to call me her daughter, and treated me like one. And nothing but the hope of advantage to myself, and perhaps to my brother, would have induced me to leave such a happy home. Here, too, I meet with kindness, am treated with very great respect by the family and their acquaintances, and shall strive to the utmost to deserve a continuance of it. You said, my dear Aunt, that when I left Holland, I was going to utter ruin, and many other expressions, violent and bitter in the extreme. Has your unkind prophecy yet come true? I never did deserve them, and never shall. I *may* be reduced to want, but never, I hope, by any glaring imprudence of my own.

I have desired my brother will inform you immediately of all you want to know – and which you might have known long ago, with *very little* trouble.

It was uncertain, in my opinion, whether I should suit Mr P. when I arrived here, and therefore I did not wish it to be known, by mere acquaintances, where I had been had I returned soon. This was my only reason for attempting to keep the *motive* of my departure from Liverpool a secret. I informed my brother of every particular a day or two before I left, and requested he would likewise tell you; for I was really so busy the last fortnight of my stay in Liverpool, I had not time to write to you. My departure was rather sudden at the last. I had scarcely time to eat or sleep.

Several of my Liverpool acquaintances, on leaving them, requested my correspondence. If I do my duty here, I shall have little time to write; but to my brother, and to you, my dear aunt, notwithstanding I am a little hurt at the noise that has been made, I will always find time to write, if you will answer in return, and hope the next letter you receive from me will be a more entertaining one than this.

Mrs Chorley told me when I was taking leave of her, that Miss Braithwaite, in a letter to her, had requested I would write. If Miss B. will first write to me, I will promise to take some notice of it; but she must not any more expect repeated letters from me, treated with neglect, which, in my opinion, is next to contempt. How is she? And how are all the family? Present my respects to them all. I often think of them. I highly regard the whole family, the four eldest daughters in particular. I will pay for one year's schooling for Richard [Latham] if Mr Braithwaite will take him, provided Henry continues going constantly. If only one of the boys goes, their father may afford to pay for one; but if both are sent, I will engage to pay for Richard for one year. You have the means in your hands, and I shall be obliged to you to settle with Mr Braithwaite at each half year out of the rents you will receive for me; and let him be entered immediately. If both boys continue to go constantly, I may perhaps pay for more than one year, but that will depend on their being regularly sent.

What say my Uncle and you on the politics of the time? Since I left you, I have been so little amongst politicians, and have heard so little of politics, that I have almost forgot what opinion I was of, on the subject. My Uncle, you, and I, used to have an argument. Battles have been fought and kings deposed, and I have been in perfect ignorance. Tranquility in my bosom, and peace in my habitation, I had almost forgot the political world and all its commotions. Since I came here, I have regularly seen the newspapers, and again interest myself in the affairs of the wicked world.

Do you ever hear anything of Miss Davenport? As long as that girl lives I shall feel an interest in her fate. She has been cruelly used by a depraved aunt, a designing villain and a censorious world.

The following three letters (to her Brother, to Miss Winkley and to Mrs Chorley) graphically explain the horrific circumstances of the death of Miss Mary Gertrude Pedder. Miss Weeton also vividly illustrates Pedder's drunken and depraved actions over his daughter's body, prior to the funeral.

25 February 1810 (Dove's Nest). *To her Brother:*

My poor afflicted Brother! [See also letter to Miss Winkley, dated 25th February 1810].

But all is now well, I hope, and comfort again gleaming over thee. Thee and thy family suffer heavily – have suffered, let me say, for the worst is surely over by this. Write again as soon as thou canst – my heart palpitates – my fears are surely greater than there is any occasion for – but Tom! my mind is at this moment enervated by a *most awful* Catastrophe.

I have to present thee with calamity, for affliction –

Not for more than I can just now think of, would I that the last eight or nine days should again return, if they must bring all their train of awful, afflictive events with them.

Brother – Miss Pedder is – burnt to death!

I will relate to thee as circumstantially as I can how it happened. On Friday morning, the 16th. inst., Mrs P. & I went into the larder to give orders to the cook about dinner. We left Miss P. sitting down in the parlour window, as I had requested her to do whilst we were out. She had just complained of being overheated. The fire was certainly extremely warm, and I had

97

been obliged to remove farther from it. Miss P. was remarkably fond of fire, and I had, only the day but one before, strictly prohibited her going within a certain distance of it. Thinking, poor unfortunate girl, that she would take the opportunity whilst we were out, of indulging herself in her usual propensity of standing as near the fire as she liked, notwithstanding she was over-heated by it, she left her seat the moment we went out of the room, and went to the fire.

I strictly believe we had been absent one whole minute – so, brother, have I sworn before the Coroner – when I heard a scream. I ran instantly. I heard her scream again, and opening the parlour door, met her running towards it, the flames higher than her head.

What a sight it was! Without the loss of a moment, I flew into the servants' hall for the ironing blanket – it was washing week, and I recollected seeing it there. Mrs Pedder's screams had brought all the servants together. I threw the blanket to the nurse, who was trying to extinguish the flames with her apron. Whilst she rolling her in the blanket, I ran again into the butler's pantry and servants' hall, to find some water to throw upon her, and cool the burning flesh. I could find no liquid of any kind. I returned to find someone who knew where it might be found. The blanket lay on the floor in the lobby, beside the suffering child, the servants having nearly put out the fire. I seized it again, to extinguish the glowing tinder of her remaining clothes, but the nurse's extraordinary exertions had completely extinguished the blaze.

Mr Pedder despatched the footman for a surgeon to Ambleside. The child was led into the hall, with her head like a glowing cinder; but that was soon extinguished, and she did not appear to be so much burnt as to endanger her life. You may suppose how little we thought of the danger, whilst, as we were cutting and tearing off the remains, the very small remains of her clothes, we were consulting whether she would be marked. 'Oh! Miss Weeton,' she several times repeated, 'shall I die?' 'No, my love, that you wont,' I answered. Indeed, so I thought; so we all thought.

By way of cheering her, I was going to rally her on the sooty face – when the change, the total change of her countenance, shocked me beyond description. I ran screaming for oil, for water, for any thing I could get. The consternation was still such, nothing for a short time could be procured. At length a small phial of hair oil was mentioned. Mrs P. & I ran into her room for it, whilst we sent the dairy-man for the milk and cream he could get. I anointed her with the oil as far as it would go. And then we all busied ourselves in pouring the milk upon her, she, poor girl, standing all the time quite naked, and so patient!

She complained not – except of her legs – but neither screamed, cried, or moaned. She was almost past feeling, that was the reason. Her legs seemed to give her some pain, and the dear child took the linen we had dipped in the milk, and rung out the milk upon her legs herself, as busily as any of us – Who would have thought of death?

She begged several times that we would let her sit. We durst not for some time comply, lest the skin and flesh should stick to those who held her. Her thighs, legs, and arms, were shockingly burnt indeed. The skin hung from her poor trembling limbs like shreds of paper, We durst not move her until the surgeon's arrival, but kept her standing, except for a very short time, thinking every minute, ten.

The Surgeon was gone to a lying-in woman; but whilst the messenger was sent for him, an apprentice came and brought a bottle of something, with which she was well anointed. I then led her by the hand (for her hands were not burnt), and she walked upstairs and stepped into bed herself. Shreds of linen soaked in what the young man had brought, were placed on every part, and for about an hour she lay tolerably still, enveloped in a sheet oiled, her night cap oiled, and then covered with blankets – she complained of being so cold. She was then seized with fits – I had hold of her hands to keep her from pulling the skin, which she frequently attempted to do – How terrified I was. She had three without intermission. They were not strong – I thought her dying – we all thought so – it was one of nature's last efforts.

She recovered for a time. Whilst the nurse and everyone else were procuring everything that they could think of to give her ease, I discovered her feet to be cold as stone. I set to rubbing one foot, whilst the cook rubbed the other. Someone else heated a piece of flannel. Whilst that was in applying, I ran downstairs and got a bottle of moderately hot water and held it to her feet a long time. She lay in a very feeble state, just able to answer the few questions we asked her. She said she was very well; had no pain; her fits had taken away the remaining strength and sensation she had till then left. At last the Surgeon arrived. She was again uncovered, and anointed, and long strips of linen rolled entirely over each leg, her body, her arms, and neck. The Surgeon asked how the accident happened. She said her brat [apron] caught fire as she stood warming herself. The accident happened between eleven and twelve in the morning; by this time it was nearly three. Mr P. requested he might send for a physician. The surgeon said he did not think there was the least danger, yet, if it would afford Mr P. the least satisfaction, he would wish him to do so. Dr Cassels was sent for, and arrived about six in the evening.

Before his arrival I perceived Miss Pedder to be more and more feeble, but as no one apprehended danger, I would not instil what might prove unnecessary fears. Still, I thought the symptoms alarming – her feet continuing as cold as death; her hands had become as cold as her feet; her eyes dim; her breathing very short. She still knew those about her. Between five and six, I was called down to make tea in the parlour for Mr Dawes (a clergyman), and the surgeon. Whilst I was absent, Miss Pedder had three fits more like the former – it was enough!

When Dr Cassels came, he instantly perceives that there was no pulsation; breath alone was left. Poor Scrambler (the surgeon, clever young man), was thunderstruck. Neither he nor any other person in the house thought Miss P's life was in danger, except myself, who had said nothing. The nurse and I sat up with her all night. The two doctors sat in the parlour below, coming up occasionally. The rest of the family were prevailed on to go to bed. Mustard plasters and bottles of warm water were applied to the feet; frequent drafts of ether, brandy and water, and wine, were administered. They were of no avail! I went almost every half hour to acquaint Mr and Mrs P. how she was – there was yet a kind of hope. About three o'clock in the morning, as I was kneeling by the bed, praying for the soul – if mortal prayers can have any effect – she breathed audibly. I expected every gasp to be her last, for my hopes had long vanished. Alarmed, I crept gently downstairs to the doctors. They followed me up. We found her better again, but in a complete stupor – she merely breathed. About five, each succeeding respiration was evidently shorter than the last. I fetched the doctors again, and, at their desire, called up Mr and Mrs Pedder. We stood round the bed in the utmost silence, listening to every breath – she went so gently, brother, we knew not which breath was the last. She died before six.

From the time she caught fire until it was completely extinguished, I firmly believe, was not more than five minutes. This is the opinion of us all – not speaking in the usual way of exaggeration, but with the utmost minuteness. – How short the space between life and death! Her body was very little burnt, scarcely scorched on the breast, stomach, or belly; her back scorched in various places; her neck; under her chin; her ear and left side of her face and nose a good deal burnt. Her legs and arms were by much the worst. That the fire occasioned her death, is without; but in my opinion, literally speaking she was not burnt to death. A child nowadays previously afflicted with fits, would, I think, have recovered from such a burning.

I helped to lay her out, brother! – was the chief witness before the coroner when the inquest was taken. These things try the fortitude of such as are unaccustomed to such afflictive scenes, severely.

I listened with such intense anxiety for so many hours to every breath, every motion of the unfortunate girl whilst she did live, that, when I am in the room where she died, I imagine I hear her breathe, and move, and cannot think it fancy, until I convince myself by looking at the bed.

The house is so remarkably infested with rats, that whilst the body remained in it, people were obliged to sit constantly in the room, night and day, lest the body should be injured by them. I took my turn last night (Tuesday). On Wednesday, about twelve at noon, the funeral left Dove's-Nest, and was expected to arrive at Preston about four the next afternoon. Mr P. and his brother James, and Mr Barton, attended all the way. Several gentlemen attended a little beyond Kendal. Mrs Pedder and the nurse, too, are gone. Mr P. would insist upon it. Mrs P. was distressed at the idea of going, beyond anything. Mr P. thinks this event will reconcile him to his father. So it might, had he gone alone, but his brother and Mr Barton are of the opinion that her presence will render it more difficult – not through any fault of hers, but the old gentleman will not acknowledge her all at once. I am grieved for Mrs P. She suffers greatly. She is not the happier for being exalted.

I do not wonder, Brother, at the unhappiness of Mr Pedder's former marriage. No woman anything better than an automaton, could submit to all his humours. He is scarcely ever sober, and often out of temper, except when drinking and singing with workmen and servants. Whilst the dead body of his child lay in the house, he was drinking, morning or evening, with any person who called in the kitchen. He could even attempt to excite laughter in the room of death itself, and make that room the scene of several quarrels with his wife, without the slightest reason. The afternoon before the corpse was taken away, thinking perhaps he should be accused of want of feeling, he went, completely drunk, into the room where the body lay, and worked himself up into almost a complete frenzy; lying down by the side of the coffin, getting astride of it, pulling and mawling the body, till the servants attending durst stay no longer in the room, expecting every moment he would have it out of the coffin. They were in an agony of horror. He opened the mouth repeatedly, kissing it and declaring she was not dead; calling her to speak to him, bewailing the loss of an heir to that part of his property he had it in his power to leave. All this, brother, was feigned sorrow. He felt a little, I will allow, but real grief acts not in this manner. The whole of his previous conduct showed too evidently that he thought more of the expense of the funeral than the loss of his child. He would not afford the nurse even decent mourning – she whose great exertions prevented immediate death, whose hands were severely burnt in the service rendered to his child. He is not always careful. He is mean at one time, and lavish at another. He would throw away guineas, and would stoop to gather pence.

Mr P. has ever been civil to me, and respectful. Soon after Miss Pedder's death he desired me to stay to be a companion to his wife. She, very affectionately and earnestly desired the same; but some expressions in my absence, which I have been told, have hurt me extremely. 'Had it not been for Miss Weeton and Mrs Pedder, the child would have been living now,' he said. Whose fault is that? Has he not been the means of bringing us both here?

This, among other unfeeling speeches, he uttered to Mrs P. She was deeply hurt. – So this is the reward we have for our exertions. We did all we could to save the child. His repentance is oft as great as his fault. He will think differently when he returns, – 'Miss Weeton said she would pay for her mourning herself; he

102

wished she would.' – You need be in no fear on that head, Mr Pedder. I do not grudge it, if you do

I was very fond of the child. She was, in general, peculiarly affectionate – sometimes most excessively perverse, worse than any child I ever had to manage, except Susanah Meek – but this was only sometimes. We spent many an hour together without other society, often conversing very seriously. She had an understanding beyond her years, but deeply tinged with cunning. Yet, notwithstanding, I have lost a valuable and endearing companion.

By the time Mr P. returns, I shall be more cool. He was drunk when he said what he did. I will calmly and seriously ask him if my presence is disagreeable to him. The expence of keeping me is, I have no doubt, the great consideration, though he will in one day sometimes idly lavish twenty guineas; then, repenting of his folly, will save it by his meanness. It is a pity he should be so inconsistent. It prevents his being so much respected as he ought, even by his drinking companions, the workmen. He is killing himself – unless he reforms, he cannot live long. His treatment of me has, until the present instance, been really flattering and respectful. Mrs P. I am very fond of. I could really wish to stay, notwithstanding Mr P's. usual irregular conduct. Wherever I go, I must expect some unpleasant circumstances. – I speak freely to you, my dear brother. I would not relate these family occurrences to any one.

My way of life here is very retired indeed, no ladies of any rank visiting Mrs P., and she not choosing on Mr P's. account, to visit with those who do not rank as high as his friends in Preston. Mr P. scarcely ever goes out into company, and has but little that is respectable at home. Three or four gentlemen visit here sometimes, who really are respectable, though not quite of equal rank with Mr P. I wish he would take a little more pains to cultivate an intimacy with them; he might in time be weaned from his bad habits – he almost lives in the kitchen.

I shall be hearing from you soon, dear brother? For the last ten days or a fortnight, I have been so anxious to hear from you, dreading some bad account when you deferred writing so long. I woke in much agitation one night, ten or twelve days ago, thinking I saw you vomit blood for a long time. How glad I was to find it nothing but a dream.

103

25 February 1810 (Dove's Nest). *To Miss Winkley*:

Oh, Miss Winkley, were I to relate to you the distressing scenes I have lately witnessed, your feeling heart would sympathise, and almost chill with horror. Mr Pedder is a strange man! Miss Winkley, if you knew the sorrow that person must undergo who marries above herself, you would never be ambitious to marry out of your own rank; people call it doing well; they are most egregiously mistaken. Let the husband be ever so kind, it cannot compensate for the numberless mortifications a woman so raised must endure. Those married people have the greatest chance of being happy whose original rank was most nearly equal.

I have often thought of you lately and of the prospect before you. Surely Smith's attachment to you has been long, firm, and disinterested; but in such a case, do not be entirely led by advice; consult your own heart only.[8]

My stay here is, I now think, rather uncertain, though Mr Barton said this week that Mr P's friends were very desirous that I should remain. Mrs Pedder has earnestly requested me to stay. Mr P. hoped that I would not leave, but stay to be company for his wife. But Mr P. is so fond of wine, is so constantly intoxicated, that my residence here is peculiarly unpleasant. I want for no comfort nor any attention. Mrs P. Can confer, and Mr P. is as kind as his daily habits will permit – I know not what to do – I will consider about it, and not decide hastily; you and your kind mother are the first persons I would wish to be with, if my stay here is improper. Mrs Pedder so earnestly begged of me to stay to be a companion to her, that it would grieve me to leave her – when Mr P. returns, I will have a little serious conversation with him. And I shall then be able to decide.

I have had a sad broken out face since I came here. I have had another boil on my face very near the former, only a little nearer the ear. I neither lanced, not poulticed it, but when ripe, let out the matter with a needle, and then washed it with a little cold water. I think the mark will disappear very soon. The one Dr Marwood lanced, will leave a small mark like a seam.

The servants here are very superstitious; they say they are sure there will be another death in the house before long. An eagle was seen in the wood directly behind the house, either the day Miss Pedder was burnt, or the day she died; I think, the latter;

and the body did not stiffen, as is usual, particularly the head and face, though perfectly cold

Saturday morning [February 24th]:

Last night I received a most afflicting account from my brother of the state of his family. I wondered he was so long in writing; but the wonder ceases now. The three children have all been ill; two, dangerously. The fatigue of attending on them brought Mrs Weeton into a Pleurisy, and from that into premature labour. The child lived three days in continued convulsions, and then died; and Mrs Weeton is in a state almost too shocking to describe – most probably dead by this time. Such an account does my brother give! I wonder how the poor fellow exerted himself so far as to write at all! You may have some idea of the state of the house, my dear Miss Winkley, when I inform you, two Miss Scotts are there, two nurses, and two servants.

Dr Guest of Leigh is so offended that my brother should, in his great distress, send for Dr Caunce from Wigan, he has refused to attend any longer!!! – Can such a man be human? My brother calls him a Devil – I do not wonder at it.

Such a palpitation have I all over me, I can scarcely stand – I dread some further calamity – my mind is weakened at present – I must exert myself.

14 March 1810 (Dove's Nest). *To Mrs Chorley:*

My dear and respected Mrs Chorley would hear from Miss Winkley of the dreadful accident that happened here a few weeks ago, the recollection of which, and the grief it has occasioned throughout the family, is yet of too recent a nature to diminish the effects of such a heart-rending shock.

Mr Pedder attended the funeral to Preston, taking Mrs Pedder with him, in the hope this afflictive event would soften the heart of his father, and bring on a reconciliation. The old gentleman was cordial enough to his son, offering him a bed at his own house, but when informed he had brought his wife, he did not say another word, never once enquiring after, or taking the slightest notice of her. I was in hopes, from the length of their stay, that a complete reconciliation had taken place, and was a good deal disappointed, when, on their return, I found it only partial; however, as the old gentleman is friendly with his son, a little time will effect the rest, I have no doubt.

Mr Pedder had, on his marriage, given up Darwen Bank, intending to let it; he now intends to keep Doves-Nest as a summer retreat, and reside at Darwen Bank in the Winter. So near a residence to Preston must, I think, unavoidably bring on some intercourse with Mr Pedder's friends there; and when they know Mrs P. better, they cannot help respecting her, and feeling surprised and rejoiced that their son has done so well. She takes lessons almost every day in the different branches of instruction I am capable of bestowing. I was apprehensive the loss of one pupil might be thought to preclude any necessity for my remaining here; but Mrs P. has earnestly requested my stay, and he says all Mr P's friends in Preston say that by all means he must continue me in his house; and so he says himself; it is therefore most probable I may remain some time; they have given orders for the fitting up a bed-room at Darwen-Bank, where we expect to be by the conclusion of summer.

Mr P. has got a boat now fitting up, and intends in a few weeks to have it on the lake. I am promised many excursions by land and water in the course of the summer; hitherto I have led a very sedentary, retired kind of life, my time a good deal occupied, or unavoidably sauntered away. Mr P. likes us to sit a long time with him after dinner.

P.S. As I find I have a little more time than I expected to have before the post day, which is four times a week, I will write a few more lines, though I have little to give you worth the trouble of reading.

I have seen many accounts in the newspapers of the severity of the weather in the south; we are so sheltered by hills, we feel little of its inclemency. I never recollect so warm a Winter, and from all accounts the weather has not been so cold as usual; the highest hills in our view have not been always covered with snow. Last Winter the Lake was frozen over so that carts passed frequently upon it; this winter its edges have scarcely been fringed with ice, and that only for a few days. Again, Good bye.

3 April 1810 (Dove's Nest). *To Miss Winkley:*

I am really sorry that you felt hurt at my not writing sooner than I did when I wrote last; my time now, you know, is not my own. I have many duties to perform that almost wholly occupy it; neither could I suppose you wished me to write soon, or often, when you so *very unwillingly* consented to correspond at all. After perceiving so much reluctance on your part, I should have ceased to urge you, had I deemed you 'a trifling correspondent' or thought the time spent in writing to you 'might be more agreeably employed.' I did not think so then; I do not think so still. Indeed, my valued friend, I do not; but you must make some allowance for me; though my time is far from slavishly occupied, yet I have very little to myself uninterrupted, except what I steal from sleep at night, or in the morning. I have little time for reading, little for writing, less for music, and none at all for drawing. How do you spend the day? Perhaps you will enquire. When Miss Pedder was living, she was continually with me, and the care of her, and instructing Mrs P., left me very little leisure. Since we lost the poor child, my duties are in some degree increased; the principal care and direction of the house have devolved to me, and a part of the sewing: these avocations occupy my time in a morning until Mrs P. comes down, who is seldom early. Then her instruction occupies me several hours; by the time that is concluded, and we have had a walk, tea time arrives, and the evening is often spent in cards, or sewing. When it happens to be cards, it is a most serious mortification to me. I often think how much more agreeably those might be spent in writing to – some such *trifling* correspondent – as you. But Mrs P. is so affectionate, that I do not wish to prevent her an innocent gratification by any great appearance of reluctance to play with her.

I sometimes speak of the waste of time, and have hinted how profitably it would be spent in reading; this, I think, is a little check, or otherwise, I fear much more time would be spent in cards. I wish she were less fond of them; the passion may decrease in a little time, with a little gentle persuasion. If I could but once prevail upon her to read for amusement, she would soon grow less fond of cards or any other idle relaxation by which time is thrown away. She is very young yet, and by frequent mild appeals to her reason, against her inclination, she may by and bye assume strength of mind sufficient to conquer the one, by means of the other, when they cannot be reconciled. She is really amiable, and I consider it as my duty to contribute to her amusement in a certain degree, however much I may dislike that which she prefers.

Some unpleasant circumstances to which I alluded in my last letter have ceased to impress my mind with disgust, and are almost forgotten. Domestic uneasiness will occur in almost every family; they grieve me for an hour or two, and pass away. Some disagreeable incidents which made me feel very uncomfortable at first, I have now got used to, and make little impression. I *could* be as contented, as happy, as mortal ought to be, if those uneasy, malicious relations of mine at Holland would but let me. – Oh, Miss Winkley, they have used me most cruelly! Perhaps you may have heard the reports they have raised. That they have come from my Aunt I am convinced, and my cousin has helped to spread them; my brother, too! – he, for whom I have done, have suffered so much; for whose happiness I have sacrificed so greatly, for whom I spent my best years in drudgery, seclusion, and want; he too – takes sides with my Aunt against me. Well! I shall be out of the way of them all some time or other, and when it is too late, they will repent of the severity of their conduct towards me. Thinking and feeling as I now do, their astonishing injustice to me will prevent me ever attempting to see any of them again.

I little thought when I last saw them, that I had taken such a *long* farewell! May they repent and be happy! happier than they strove to make me. I did think, Miss Winkley – I did flatter myself, that I had ever acted with such cautious prudence, that even a breath of slander could not have been raised against me; and yet somebody in Holland has said, when I left you in December last, that I was gone off with a gentleman, nobody knew where. – This implies a conduct the most flagrant a woman can be guilty of.

That I left Liverpool, and, at Preston did put myself under the protection of a respected elderly gentleman, is true enough. I thought it more prudent to be escorted hither by Mr P's steward than to come so long a journey alone – but in the *manner* in which the report is spread, my fame is wounded, perhaps for ever!

You, and your kind mother, advised me not to make any secret of my departure; my only reason was, that if I should prove incompetent to the situation I was entering upon, and be obliged to return soon, I should not wish mere acquaintances to know that I had failed; it might prevent others engaging me, should I wish to try again. When I was last at Leigh, my brother severely reproved me for being too open; now, with greater severity, I am accused of being too close; then, he said I was too humble, now – too irritable. How must I act to please him? Whatever I do, or whatever I say, is wrong.

His present severity is owing to a letter I wrote my aunt some weeks ago; she had talked of great distress at not knowing where I was, and made a public talk about it. Why did she not know? She preferred *talking* of her great distress, I suppose. Such *wordy* misery deserves nothing but contempt; if her grief had been real, she would soon have written to my brother; she might then so soon, so easily, have been relieved from her *dreadful* unhappiness. What *she* has said, has been the *sole* cause of such a report, I am convinced. I know her so well! When my aunt so treated my brother, I defended *him* – he – joins with her against *me*! Am I not hardly dealt with, Miss Winkley?

My brother tells me the whole report without offering one word of consolation; any uninterested person would imagine he believes all he relates. Innocent as I am, still, such a report cannot fail to distress me greatly; he must think so, and should have offered something kind and affectionate, to sweeten the bitter pill.

7 April 1810 (Dove's Nest). *To Miss Winkley:*

I suppose the box which I received last night, was on its way at the time you would receive my enquiry respecting it. I wish I had written sooner, and then you would not only have been enabled to forward the little presents to Holland much sooner than I can possibly, but have seen something which would really have recompensed you for the trouble you have, and would have had; you would have seen a packet of letters – four sheets of paper very closely written, and completely filled – that would have entertained and gratified you exceedingly.

One of the articles sent to me, is a small satin-wood box, with divisions for four balls of cotton. The lid, which is a slide, Mrs Whitehead has ornamented herself; it is really beautiful, and, to me, quite novel. On the middle of the lid is a very elegant, though very small, group of flowers, formed with coloured papers, cut so neatly and with such minuteness, that each flower, leaf, vein, and stem, are perfectly distinct; one leaf being placed separately over the other in each flower, gives the appearance of reality, much more than you *generally* meet with in flowers that are drawn. It is raised like embossed work; the stems are almost as fine as hair; the veins to the leaves are cut in the nicest manner in brown paper, and gummed over the leaf; it certainly is at the same time, a little

109

and a great, curiosity. I hope to have the pleasure of shewing it to you some time or other.

For my cousin Latham's two eldest boys, Mrs W. has sent a red morocco purse, and a small printed book, *her own* composition; the subject adapted to boyish taste and capacity, entitled 'Orlando Herbert, or the Runaway.' Should my Cousin Latham happen to call upon you before long, as *perhaps* she may, tell her of these presents, if you please, for I shan't send them immediately, for probably I may inclose a letter or two to some acquaintances in Holland; I am yet undecided, but I think there is one or two of its inhabitants who would plead my cause, were I to appeal to them. What do you think of such a step? The people I mean are Mr Braithwaite's and Mr Dannett's. Sometimes I think I will let the report die away unnoticed, as being, like its propagators, unworthy of notice; at other times, I think that whether such a report gain much ground or not, my silence may be construed into a tacit acknowledgment of guilt; and not only for my own sake, but for the *good* of *others*, such slanderous tongues should be severely reprobated, and put a stop to, if not from a sense of wrong, at least from fear of the consequences to themselves.

I have not yet answered my brother's letter; I will consider in what kind of style to compose it. If I could but see him, I could soon bring him to treat his sister with unprejudiced affection; but, to my *letters,* there is, I think, a spirit at his elbow that gives a dingy cast to the greatest part of what I say.

I often think of you – at the house, I was, for almost the first time during the preceding twelve years, possessed of – a mother, and a sister; and let me not forget that other addition to a mother's comfort, the animated Ann; remember me affectionately to her.

P.S. I have several times lately had some delightful excursions on the lake, and have much wished that I could have had you one of the party. Mr Pedder has two boats – a small sail boat, and a large one.

A few weeks ago, he, Mrs P. and myself, walked to the ferry, where there is an Inn on the edge of the lake, delightfully situated, about nine miles from here; the weather was *peculiarly* favourable, and I would not have missed such a romantic walk, to have rode in the most elegant carriage in the universe. I was so sailing mad, whilst there, that once or twice when Mr and Mrs P. were more inclined to indulge by the fire, Joe (the footman), and I, took the boat ourselves, he at one oar, and myself at the other, for several miles down the lake; and one morning, Joe being otherwise employed, I went in a small row boat round one of the islands alone. At this early part of the year, there is no company, or you may suppose I should not have done *anything* that would attract the gaze of spectators; no houses are near the Inn, and the family are well known to Mrs Pedder. We were there near three days, and *sailed* home, a distance of five or six miles on the water, Mrs P. and I taking one oar in turn, a boatman being employed at the other.

Mr P. is the most timid character I think I ever met with for a man; simple as is the art of rowing, and smooth as is the water in general, I do not think he dare venture to row himself, or venture on the water alone; he has two boats, one a very handsome one, just purchased, yet I think they will accommodate his friends and his servants much oftener than himself. Mrs P. and myself have had two or three little aquatic excursions, accompanied only by a rower; to-day (Sunday) we are going down to Bowness (opposite the ferry) in the new boat, the second time of our being in it. We shall go with sails; for my own part, I think a small row boat much more pleasant. The large boat will cost above 50 guineas; its original cost was more than 80; it had scarcely been on the water before Mr P. purchased it of its original owner.

You *must* write me a very long letter; *you know,* you may find time if you will do – as does.

Your affectionate friend E. Weeton – rise early.

13 April 1810 (Dove's Nest). *To her Brother.*

Your last letter, my dear Brother, had been long and anxiously looked for. Glad indeed was I when your last letter did arrive, to find that the children were got well again, and that Mrs Weeton was in an apparently sure, though slow, way of recovery.

You speak rather slightingly of your indisposition, fearful perhaps of giving an uneasiness you cannot soon dissipate. Some questions and observations in the different letters I have written to you since I came here, I should like to have your answers to, and comments upon; but perhaps the letters are lost, and you have forgot them; they are not of *very* great importance.

I often think, brother, if you had Mr Pedder's fortune, how much you would enjoy it, and what a different use you would make of it. This little Nest of Harmony, as its name seems to indicate, would just suit you, though not so large as your own house; but as to that, it would be very easy to enlarge it at the back. There are 30 acres of land belonging; a kitchen garden close by the kitchen door; a flower garden a little distance from the house, a short, but pretty walk leading to it; There is an arbour in it,[9] exactly like that in the garden belonging to Mr Lee's house opposite the parsonage of Holland. On the wall inside, is written with a pencil – 'Adam Walker was delighted here, June 24th 1807.' Underneath, to explain who that Adam Walker was, is written – 'The celebrated experimental philosopher.' I have laughed at this inscription, for it is not said *how* delighted, or with what; with the prospect of course; a wag like you would give it some other meaning. Whether Adam Walker[10] wrote his own *celebration* or no, is not known. It is very probable; and in that single word, has *celebrated* his own vanity.

There is a patatoe garden, separated from the flower garden by a high hedge. If this place belonged to thee, I would advise thee to keep out of the potatoe ground, if potatoes have really that wonderfully miraculous fruitful quality, ascribed to them in Sir John Carr's 'Stranger in Ireland.' The rulers of this family have not yet resided here long enough to have experimented the effects of eating potatoes; and, for anything I can see, seem inclined to wait until their own are ready.

Mr P. gives a hundred a year for the house and land. Estates here let and sell amazingly high; almost as big, and some places higher, than the same extent of ground would do in the more populous neighbourhood in Lancashire, without considering the Quality of the land, which is universally very poor. The beauty of the situation is the attraction; water, wood, and hills, so delightfully and majestically mingled! These draw the opulent from populous flat countries. The intrinsic value of the land is not the object, and perhaps in time the land may be much enriched by agriculture; for, in my opinion, it has hitherto been much neglected. The ground might be improved, I think, unless it is here as a fisherman once informed me at the Meols [near Southport], when I remarked the barrenness of the ground. 'They had no manure,' he said. Why it would not answer as well there to *pay* people for *making* and collecting it, as it does in other places, I am not knowing enough to discover; unless it is that they are not so *ingenious* there as in *most* other places in the world, and don't know how to make it.

I think, my dear fellow, if you had coolly and unprejudiced, perused my letter to my aunt, you would not have joined *with* her *against* me. I am convinced you would not. Reflect a while on what I there said; take each assertion separately, and prove or disprove as you think just. Do you think I *dared* to assert *to* my aunt, expressions which she never used? I must have effrontery indeed! Such, brother, as you never knew your sister guilty of before; and, if true, which I assure you they were, it required no *peculiar* share of irritability to resent. A milder temper than mine would express more loudly a degree of resentment that the event has proved is strongly called for. What is your opinion of the authors of this calumny?

Write as soon as you can, and tell me all you know and think upon it. If one sheet won't contain all you have to say, write two or three – if it won't trespass too much upon your time.

18 April 1810 (Dove's Nest). *To Mrs Whitehead:*

The attention you have ever shewn, have ever gratified; and the last instances of remembrance I have received from you, have contributed greatly to chear a sinking heart. Your box, and its highly valued contents have safely arrived; with real delight have I surveyed, and shewn those intended for me; the others I will send, directed for Mrs Smith, in a few weeks, and she will give my cousin L. what are intended for her. How pleased they will all be! They used to be so with the little messages I have conveyed from you to them.

I wish Miss Chorley, and some others I know in Liverpool, had held the same opinions in dress that you do. I should then have escaped some severe insults and mortifications. I do admire a neat, plain style of dress, even in the rich, and much more in those whose incomes are limited. Cards, too, I am no great friend to; and have been thought a person of no consequence in a tea party, because I did not assist to make up a quadrille table. Expecting, when I went to Liverpool, to reside there for some time, I determined to begin as I wished to continue; and I do think it a shocking waste of time to spend several evenings every week in cards. Miss Chorley was passionately fond of them, and treated me with the utmost contempt because she could not induce me to play. I used to think this very unkind, for I never censured the passion for cards in her, but merely said, I was not partial to them.

I am sorry to find a growing inclination in Mrs P. for them. I have hitherto thought it my duty to sacrifice my own inclinations to a certain degree, until we have at length to spend every evening (Sundays excepted) in cards. How to act, I know not; I have several times represented how much more profitably our evenings might be passed in reading, writing letters to each other, &c. &c.; but for literature, Mrs P. has not the least taste. Her common lessons she submits to as a task, with very great reluctance; and were I to say much on the subject, I am afraid she would reject them altogether. She is very ignorant, and does not seem to possess the slightest wish to emerge from it. Some days she takes lessons, and some days none. I endeavour to make them as alluring as I can, and as easy. How would you act in a similar situation? Play cards for three hours every evening, under the consideration that it is my duty to contribute to the amusement of those who support, and treat me kindly? Or decline them in the idea of encouraging a sad waste of time, that would otherwise *perhaps* be better employed. I say *perhaps*, for she has little activity of mind or body; but still, I think those hours can hardly be worse employed. What do you think? She treats me so kindly, that I would gladly do great violence to my own inclination, if I thought at the same time I was doing my duty to her and Mr Pedder.

Would you were here, and could wear 'The invisible ring' I have read of; what a feast of books you might have. Mr P., like many of the wealthy, possesses a library of little real use. He himself reads little, so that the shelves make a display of knowledge he possesses not; many a volume, I dare say, has never been opened. The collection is numerous, valuable, and well selected. How rich I would be in books if I had all in Mr P's library that have never been read. There are a great many costly works with fine engravings; these, too would suit you – but why set you a-longing?

When a little impatient myself, at the grievous ignorance I have unavoidably been always kept in, my consolation has ever been – well! A time will come when the soul will be unfettered by the body, and the wisdom of the earth will appear completely ridiculous in comparison to what I shall then know. So I can only say to you – have a little patience, and more than all contained in the books I have ever seen, will be yours. *Perhaps* that same somebody, who composes with so much genius, will not suffer you to wait *so long*, but put you into possession of a *useful* library, whilst you can read with mortal eyes.

I am very comfortable, and could be still more so, if my Holland *friends* would but let me. – *Talking* to you has enlivened me considerably. A few weeks will obliterate nearly all unpleasant reflection, and I shall be as merry and as ready to laugh as ever. I wish I were a little more of the philosopher. I am often in one extreme, most frequently in the merry one. Mrs P. and I often shake our sides, notwithstanding I tell her of the *horrid* vulgarity – I set the example, and then amuse myself with reprobating her for following it; she laughs again! An untowardly slut.

[Journal, latter part of April 1810]:

My spirits are very low, quite sunk. My heart is sad, and in a continual palpitation, from which it has seldom been free since my brother gave me so distressing an account of the sickly state of his family. I am now a little relieved on that account; but, ever from that time, one distressing event after another has succeeded with so much rapidity, that it has kept me in a state of continual agitation. I could weep continually – I must get the better of this dejection. It is weak, very weak, to give way to it so much – and, by the help of that Cherishing Power who has hitherto supported me, I shall, in the event, I trust, rise above every evil, every affliction. And oh! If it be Thy Will, change the hearts of some of the inhabitants, that so they may experience mercy from thee.

A want of consistency in the conduct of any person, however insignificant they may appear in the scale of society, has greater influence on the comfort of those around them, than can easily be conceived on a slight view; but when that person, as a master of a family, possesses some degree of consequence, what misery will preponderate should he lean to the wrong side! Self, and *self alone*, is the powerful principle with the master of this house. From selfish motives alone did he marry. He considered not the happiness of her to whom he united himself – or he would not use her as he does. A great deal of money has been spent in his education – yet, what a wretched one he has received. Naturally well disposed, but with a weak head, a public school, the University, the Army, were not the places to set the heart right, and to strengthen an understanding, which, well directed, was certainly capable of great improvement.

From a boy he has been too easily led; any one that would take pains, might allure him into vicious company and vicious habits, both of which he has entered deeply into. From a boy he has received wrong ideas of the character of a gentleman; of the value of riches; of the sacrifices due to society. He seems to think a gentleman is one who has many dependants, whom he may use and abuse as he pleases; at one time lavishly bestowing upon them spirits or any other liquid that intoxicates, to the serious injury of themselves and families; at others, withholding from them wages they have hardly earned, and are justly their due. Money he is ever unwilling to part with. He bestows none charitably, except where he can put his name to a subscription list. His tradesmen's bills are not punctually settled; and when they are paid, it is so grudgingly, that an honest man would almost as soon be unpaid. He thinks he does enough for his wife by feeding and clothing her. She has, at this time, been weeks, almost months, begging money from him to pay the washerwoman, and cannot get it. She may be said to live in splendid misery.

The world thinks her fortunate in having married a man whose rank and fortune are so much superior to her own. How much is the world mistaken! Had she married a man of her own rank, she would at least not have been, as she often is now – pennyless. She would have been, what now she is not – *mistress* of her house. She has not even power to order the necessary provisions into the house. Mr P. is master, mistress, housekeeper. He will sometimes order such quantities of perishable household articles, that one half are sometimes wasted; at the same time, the money thrown away he would grudge to bestow in useful charity. The provisions he orders into the house are not paid for immediately. Of them, therefore, he is lavish, whilst of the money honestly due for them, he is meanly sparing. What strange inconsistency! Tradesmen's bills must be paid some time; why then not as well pay them soon after they are due, as defer for so long when there is never a want of money to pay them with; it is only lying by in the bureau doing no good.

He will grudge his wife a decent gown at the very time he is squandering 20, 30, 40, 50 or 60 guineas at once on a hobby horse, of no use to any living creature but himself; and even he gets tired of one hobby horse after another, before he has had them many weeks in his possession. *I am only kept here for ostentation,* not out of real kindness to his wife. I was a sort of hobby for a time. He is now grown tired of me, and I verily believe grudges the expence of keeping me. Whether I am to be discarded, as many a hobby has been before me, I know not. This I know, he treats me unjustly, tyrannically, and meanly in the extreme. If this accords with his idea of a gentleman, he has a very different idea to what I have of the term. For some time I was really handsomely treated; and though I despised him for his meanness and ill-treatment of others, I had not experienced it towards myself. My turn is now come, and nothing but gratitude for past civilities, with a high regard for Mrs P's uniform conduct towards me, which has ever been delicately respectful, prevents my resenting in a high tone the indignities I have lately received. How much longer I can support a passive character, I know not. I am often in fear lest the conduct I always advise Mrs P. to pursue, should not likewise be followed by myself. Let me yet keep in view the motive which brought me here – the hope of doing something which may advance my brother's interest in the world – the hope that the friends I make for myself, may eventually prove valuable ones to him. When my spirits are sunk to a very low pitch; when the punishment of any error I may be guilty of is heaped upon me in tenfold proportion to my desert; when I am threatened to be turned out, because a look only has given offence; and when I forget, in my own selfish affliction, any motive that can induce me to bear it with patience, how my spirits rise when the idea of a brother's advantage again occurs! Again I resolve to bear with apparent calmness, however I may weep in private. It would be a pity, I repeat to myself, that I should have suffered so many deprivations for such a length of time, and in a fit of vexation, let it all go for nothing. NO! NO! I will persevere still – be humble, be patient, be submissive, be anything but vicious. I will be as faithful to those I serve as it is in my power to be; and comfort myself in the hope, that in serving the world, I may at the same time serve the Power we universally venerate.

It almost would seem as if Mr P. ill-used those most whom he most regarded. Mrs P. suffers much more than I do. What a tyrant he is to her! He seems to think that by lording it over two or three women, he increases his own consequence; and the more we submit, the worse he grows. Mrs P. has often told me that she has been strongly advised never to let him abuse her without making resistance. I have often advised submission. She says she is told by those who have known him long, that the more a person submits to him, or seems afraid of him, the oftener he exerts the power he finds he has over them; and that when a strong resistance is made, when his violent passion meets with proportionate resentment of is treated with contempt, he in turn will become afraid of those he would oppress. Still, I advise *her* from pursuing such conduct. I say it is a disgrace to the dignity of the female character for any woman to strive to become master in her husband's house, or to make her husband afraid of her. It is an equal disgrace to a man, so to submit. So she thinks too, provided a medium kind of conduct could be observed. But that is impossible; nothing will do but either the most abject slavery to his will, or the making him submit to hers. *He* knows no medium between the tyrant and the slave. Acting according to the advice others have given her, Mrs P. has at different times resented strongly his shamefully abusive language, and when she could no longer endure, has, two or three times, quitted his house and fled to her father's. Though I highly disapprove such conduct, I do not wonder at it. It is scarcely possible for human nature not to be maddened by the cruel language he makes use of. What a miserable house it is when such quarrels take place! And of late they have been very frequent.

I shall almost be a convert to Mrs P's advisers and their opinions – that it will be more for the whole household not to submit to all his humours – and yet I am very unwilling to either give, or take, such advice. Whenever Mr P. is in one of his violent passions, I earnestly beg of Mrs P. not to answer again, but to be quiet and as patient as she can. She has lately frequently endeavoured to do so; but what would please most men, seems to have no effect upon him. She trembles, she weeps, she submits – and he daily grows more and more tyrannical. He appears to be often visited by a strong compunction, though he makes no confession of the kind (he is too mean-spirited), and seems to think a ride in the curricle, or on horseback, will make atonement to his wife for his ill-treatment. Generally, the day after a violent quarrel, he proposes a journey somewhere or other, and just as the report of these sad doings is noised in the neighbourhood, they are seen riding out together, apparently amicable and happy. Mr P. when in good humour, is as much in the other extreme; he is not many degrees removed from a complete fool.

11 May 1810 (Dove's Nest). *To Miss Winkley:*

There are several things in my drawers, my dear friend, which would be useful to me now, if you would be useful to me now, if you would take the trouble of sending them. Little expecting to wear black so soon after I left you, I brought nothing of the kind with me; and there are several things which might be worn to save better. What I have now is too good for every day, and if I had known a little while ago that we were to wear crape (sic) six months, I would have troubled you a little sooner; had we worn it only the usual time, three months, what I have would have lasted very well. I do not wish to buy new again if I can help it.

Inclosed with this you will find the necessary keys for the three long drawers: in the bottom are a black Chambray gown, a silk petticoat, a cambric muslin petticoat and a blue flannel bathing dress; in the middle drawer is some black lace net, wrapped in a piece of black mode, and a black silk work bag with some crape and a blue duffel coat, which will be very useful when sailing. There are some patterns for fancy work; I am not quite sure whether they are in a work bag in the bottom, or middle drawer, or bound up with the last new *Lady's Magazine* in the top drawer; if they are, I shall be obliged to you to take them out and send them in the bundle.

Perhaps I may be at Allonby when you travel northwards; we go next week, and Mr Pedder proposes staying a fortnight. Allonby is in Cumberland, not far from Maryport. I can't say I propose to myself much pleasure in the journey. I wish I may be left at home; the few excursions I have had here, have ever been embittered by some untoward accident. Mr P. is so difficult to please, that he is not an agreeable travelling companion.

The season is now commencing for visits to the lakes; a few have already been, and I suppose we shall have many accidental visitors at Doves-Nest during the summer; a gentleman was here last week, staying five or six days; he is a clergyman,[11] and resides in Lancaster. I cannot say I ever met with a man I thought so agreeable; the great difference between a governess and a clergyman of family and fortune, made me cautious of being in his company more than I could help, lest my heart should involuntarily form an attachment that might cause me years of unhappiness. I never did before feel such a sentiment, as I did whilst he was here; as I still yet do. I avoided him as much as I could without appearing singular, during his stay. I was as reserved as possible, lest he should perceive my sentiments; for, of all things, Miss Winkley, I should dread to deserve the imputation of an indelicacy so great as that of shewing a regard for a man who had not previously endeavoured to excite it. I am glad he is gone, and not likely to come again in a hurry. All I have now to do, is to forget him as soon as I can, which I hope I have the power to do. I wish Mr P. were more amiable in my opinion, and then the contrast would not have been so striking. It was the great difference between them, that first attracted my attention, and I am grieved it was excited. – I am very open, very unreserved to you, my dear Miss Winkley; I place a confidence you will not abuse; I know no one else to whom I could have spoken on such a subject. I could not have done it to my brother – I could not do it here, though I am really fond of Mrs P.

Mr and Mrs P., myself and Mr ----- sailed down to Newby Bridge one day, the opposite and lowest end of the lake from here; we had a very pleasant sail there, but there came on so strong a wind as we were returning after dinner, that was exactly against us, that after tacking above thirty times in two miles, we were obliged at eleven o'clock at night, to put in at Bowness, and stay there all night. We were very comfortably accommodated, for which we were in part indebted to Mr -----'s attention; had it not been for him, we must have fended for ourselves, for Mr P. has no idea of being attentive to women, even at an Inn.

We had a very pleasant sail home in the morning; Mr ----- left us that day. Mr P. told us his friend was almost in tears at leaving. I wonder at it, for he had two or three times been most rudely treated by Mr P. – but he knows Mr Pedder's value in many respects, and therefore bears with him. If Mr P. were always so ill-tempered as he is often so much otherwise, that those who know him, may bear with the evil for the sake of the good.

25 May 1810 (Allonby). *To Mrs Chorley:*

On the 18th inst., Mr and Mrs Pedder and myself left Doves-Nest for Allonby, a watering place in Cumberland, near Maryport;

all three travelled in the Curricle. We stopped at Keswick on our way, two nights. I never before saw any place I so much admired, as the vale of Keswick, and its lake.

Hutton, our guide, and the keeper of a second-rate Museum, is a very intelligent man; he is very clever as a Mineralogist and Botanist, but not so absorbed in science as to prevent his being a most entertaining travelling companion to any one; he related many anecdotes, and his descriptions of the scenery are correct and sufficiently diffuse, without being either dry or tedious. He is a grandfather, and quite of a plain, farmer-like appearance.

We visited both Museums: Crosthwaite, the original proprietor of the principal one, is lately dead [Mr P. Crosthwaite was Admiral at Keswick Regatta and Keeper of the Museum at Keswick]; his son and successor appears to me a mere drone; the father was said to be very clever.

My letters are always very long, I can seldom find in my heart to leave a shred of unscrawled paper; in this, adding another instance to the many of which Miss Chorley has so often accused me, of that mean, contemptible, parsimonious disposition, that can *give* nothing, not even a bit of blank paper. The papers give a sad account of the tumultuous disposition of *some* of the inhabitants of Liverpool who have attended the theatre since it opened. I have often observed a weak disposition in many of the inhabitants of that place, to emulate London follies; one would think such disgraceful scenes as have lately so often stained the London Chronicles, would have been an example for the Liverpool people to have shunned rather than to have imitated. The good sense of the majority of the inhabitants, will I hope soon put a stop to such despicable proceedings.

I am afraid you will scarcely be able to read this cross writing[12] – a little more and I will have done. I have never yet heard from my aunt Barton, or any other person in Holland. I mean to write to her once more the next week, and if I still remain unnoticed, I shall trouble her no more; her constant indisposition might be some excuse for her, but it does not excuse my uncle.

June 10th: Last night we arrived at Doves-Nest after spending near a month at Allonby very agreeably. As soon as I recovered from my indisposition, I bathed and am now very well, though I must have an attack of my old bilious complaint, I fear, before summer is over.

4 June 1810 (Dove's Nest). *To Mrs Edmondson* (of Lancaster):

Perhaps you may have heard from some of your Preston friends that I am now at Mr E. Pedder's of Doves-Nest, near Ambleside, and in what capacity. I do not look upon my present situation as likely to be a permanent one; Mr P. is such an odd-tempered man, that it really is not easy to bear with him. With Mrs P. I could live all the days of my life, and for her sake submit to a great deal which only a sense of her kindness, which never ceases, could oblige me to do. You will smile, perhaps, at my talking in this high strain of Mrs P's kindness and condescension – she, who was nothing but a dairy maid. See Mrs Pedder, then – judge which she most deserves; respect for what she is, or the humiliating consideration of what she was.

So attached am I to this beautiful country, that should I quit my present residence, I think I should endeavour to fix my abode at some farm house near here, with a wish to live and die there. I admire this country exceedingly, and if my time were my own, would ramble the country over; would traverse the vales, glide over the surface of the lakes, and run up the hills like a mountain sheep – here, I could live a life of seclusion, and scarce heave a sigh for society for six months out of twelve; heart-cheering society would draw me from self in the cold months – at least, draw me into converse with my own species a little more. Is it not strange that so mean a principle should predominate so very very strongly with human nature? I could follow on this subject to a great length, but – it as a letter, and not an essay I am writing.

Do you know Mr Saul of Lancaster, a clergyman? He paid a visit to Mr Pedder a little while ago, and staid near a week. Mrs P. and myself were highly pleased with him; he appeared to me what we think a clergyman ought to be, a good man, without being too rigid, or too relax in his principles and conduct. For my part, I was so apprehensive lest I should admire him too much, that I avoided him as much as possible. 'David,' we are told, 'was the man after God's own heart.' I was sadly frightened lest I should be made to acknowledge that for my part, I liked Saul better – which would have been very wicked, you know; besides, how dreadful it would have been to have suffered my heart to leave me, without getting another in its place; so, with much ado, I kept it.

14 June 1810 (Dove's Nest). *To her Aunt Barton:*

It is a very long time since I wrote to you, and have yet received no answer. If this letter too remains unnoticed, I must desist from troubling you any more, and try to forget that there ever was a friend or relation dear to me in Holland. I would act towards you with all the respect and affection I so warmly feel, but I have often purposely repressed those feelings, lest you should suspect me of motives too contemptible to be owned by any person of an independent spirit. It is *this* sentiment which has ever made me act with much less apparent regard towards you than I really felt; it is *this* which prevents me writing more than letter for letter, since I left you; it is a conduct, the natural result of such sentiment, that has given you offence. I am grieved that it has done so, but, my dear Aunt, I cannot alter my conduct – I will be affectionate, tender, and kind towards you, but in return, you must be each of these to me.

I am just returned from a journey into Cumberland. Mr P. keeps a curricle and a pair of fine horses, and we three went in it to Allonby. Who do you think I saw at Allonby, getting out, and in, to a stagecoach that arrives there every day? Mr Saul of Orrel-post! [a small hamlet near Up Holland]. The coach stays so short a time, I had not an opportunity of speaking to him. Mr and Mrs Watmough of Liverpool, formerly of Wigan, I saw there one day. A blacksmith in the village was the magnet that attracted them. I did not speak to them, as I never had the slightest acquaintance with them. Mrs W. pretended to the landlord that she was well acquainted with Mr Pedder's family in Preston. As they did not come into our apartments, Mrs Watmough had no opportunity of claiming Mr P's acquaintance. He heard her say, as he passed a window where she sat, 'Ay! I could loik t'be e' yond bote.' – pointing to a fishing smack at sea, Liverpool has had no effect on her Lingo, it seems; nor the dead horse with the large protuberance on its back that Mrs Bolton gave you such a laughable account of.

1 July 1810 (Dove's Nest). *To her Brother:*

You are in a fairer way for heaven than I am, brother; your daily vexations will in time wean you from the pleasures of this world, and make you look for the happiness in store for you in another; you will soon, I hope, live such a Christian life, as will prepare you for the death of a Christian. – as for me, I grow daily more fond of life; I think more of the present and less of the future than I used to do. Had I died soon after my mother did, there would have been some chance of happiness for me – to be sure, my present comforts are a good deal damped by the unhappy temper of the master of this house; having little disposition for rational amusement himself, the day is wearisome to him; fretful and peevish, he cannot bear to see others more chearful than he is; if he is good-tempered for a whole day, we are as much surprised as pleased; if for several days together, it is quite a wonder. He makes us all fear him, but no one loves or esteems him, except his wife, and I really think she does, notwithstanding he so often treats her with so little feeling and kindness. If he had but common sense with his ill-humour, it would be more bearable; but he is very weak; he knows no medium between the tyrant and the slave. He is, himself, frequently as abject abroad as he is despotic at home. He wears two faces; often good-humoured to a degree of folly in company, in his own immediate domestic circle, silence occasioned by fear hovers o'er his table; at one time extravagant in the extreme in his own pleasures, at another meanly penurious of those of others. Generally deceitful, and just as ready to utter a falsehood as a truth, I never know to believe him; he has lately used me with a good deal of indignity, but Mrs P's treatment of me is so much the reverse of his, that I feel anxious to remain, and I always keep as much out of his sight as possible.

During the summer, we shall be very liable to visitors, which will ameliorate my condition in a considerable degree; in their presence he treats me with respect, and even good-humour; in the presence of his guests, I dare venture to converse, or even support an opinion, though it should not exactly accord with his; when without company, the least motion, or even a look – though without meaning – has excited rancour. I in general see little of him, except at dinner; when in one of ill-humours, if Mrs P. and I simply look at each other, he flies into a rage, and says we are laughing at him; he feels himself contemptible, and it makes him continually suspicious of Mrs P. as well as me.

And ought, then, so cruel a report to die away unnoticed? Well! I am content; the foul slander may follow me through this world – it can reach no further – for, as to your saying no one did for a moment suppose me capable of wrong, that cannot be, my dear fellow, where a slander makes a *noise*, and excites *thousands* of enquiries. Had you given me this consolation along with the intelligence, it might have had some effect – it is too late now – it has sunk too deep, though I do begin to recover. I have had two fevers; they were not very severe, and did not last long. I was very ill for near a week whilst at Allonby.

I do wish you could be here with your rod and line; perhaps your presence would induce me to join in the cruel sport; at present, I can take no pleasure in it. I too could wish to see your little ones; I often speak of them and oftener think of them.

8 July 1810 (Dove's Nest). *To Mrs Whitehead:*

Who is the poet you allude to in a former letter, who resided near Holland, or not very far from it?

Richard Latham will be delighted with his little book, I told him, in my letter to his brother, that it was your composition. It is a very good one. Why are you so diffident that you cannot ask the publishers for the remuneration you deserve? You are not fit to wade through the mud of this world.

When I left Holland, my cousin L. said 'There would be one less in the nest now, and there would be more room for her.' – alluding to her expectations from my Aunt Barton.[13] My cousin mistakes me – she is perfectly welcome to all my aunt can bestow upon her. Should my aunt entirely overlook me in her will, I shall never for a moment grudge her of any addition she may receive by that means. Had I ever been influenced by interested motives, I should have acted very differently to what I have done. On my cousin, however, I have revenged myself in a way that pleases me. I have sent her second boy to school to Mr Braithwaite; the eldest has gone there for some time.

8 July 1810 (Dove's Nest). *To Miss Winkley:*

My dear Miss Winkley will think me long in writing to her. I have had so little time for writing to my friends lately, that I have been obliged to commission the man who milks the cows, and who lives in the house, to call me up at five o'clock every morning for some weeks past, that I may dedicate two or three hours to the writing of letters before the rest of the family are stirring; for, as I write very long ones in general, and take copies of them all, it frequently takes three, and sometimes four mornings to each letter.

I have now nearly acquitted all my epistolary debts, and shall be able, for the next two or three weeks, to enjoy the early morning hours in a walk or with a book. Indeed, my eyes require a little respite, for sitting down to write almost as soon as I was out of bed, they are become much inflamed, and I have been obliged to remain a little longer in bed this morning than usual, that I might be able to write to you to-day whilst left to myself, as Mr and Mrs P., and two ladies, strangers, are just set out on a two days excursion to Keswick. I feel so comfortable just now whilst writing to you, in the certainty of beginning and being able to finish perfectly undisturbed, and in the writing to one to whom I can speak without reserve, that I sincerely prefer this moment's employment, to the going any journey where Mr P. makes one of the party. His father was of the opinion when I first came here, that I should never stay. If that father but knew the virtues of his yet unacknowledged daughter-in-law, he would soon discover what it was that induced me to bear the insulting language of his son without resentment.

I was very ill whilst at Allonby, in some degree owing to a previous depression of spirits, and the fatigue of travelling, but chiefly owing to Mr P's not permitting me to breakfast before he did. I rose at seven, and could not conveniently do without it than near eleven, and had therefore presumed, two or three times, to order my own breakfast in at nine, Mrs P. taking some time with me. He would permit it no longer; and, to revenge himself, kept us waiting than past eleven o'clock for several days after. My stomach could not bear such a long abstinence, particularly as I do not eat supper. Since my recovery, I have been allowed to breakfast when I please.

Miss Rhodes, and Miss Barton (whom she calls her niece), have been with us three weeks. She is a sensible woman, and a very nice housekeeper for her uncle. From what she says, she is about 27; I should have thought her older. Her face is much marked with the small-pox, so that she appears five or six years older. She dresses with much neatness. Mr Barton was only married a few years, and had no children by his wife; the little girl who is now here, is a natural daughter, whose mother died in giving birth to her. Mrs P. says he has many other natural children, boys as well as girls, but he notices only this. Her father doats on her, and I dare say, at his death will leave her all the property he has.

Since Miss Rhodes came, a party was made up to go on the top of Fairfield, a high mountain a few miles from here. I made one; we were fifteen in number, besides four men who attended and carried provisions, &c. Mrs Pedder, Miss Rhodes, Miss Barton, and myself, left home soon after five o'clock in the morning, in a cart, Mr Pedder on a pony, and the footman on an ass. We stopped to breakfast at a Mr Scambler's, in Ambleside, two miles from here, where the rest of the party joined us. Soon after six, we proceed, the ladies in carts, the gentlemen on foot – Mr Pedder and Mr Partridge, senior, excepted. We travelled up a very steep, and a very rocky, rugged road, for five or six miles. Were you to see such a road, you would be astonished how any horse could drag a load up it, for such a length of way; it is one continued steep, without any respite for the poor animals. Fearless as I in general am, I could not divest myself of some anxiety, until we arrived at the place where we should each be obliged to trust to our own feet alone. The other ladies screamed several times, expecting to be overturned, or precipitated backwards. No accident, however, happened.

When arrived at the extremity of Scandale, from whence we were to *begin* to ascend, we alighted from our vehicles, and proceeded on foot. The provisions were taken out of the carts and placed upon the ass, which had been brought for the purpose. We were, altogether, as odd a group as ever were assembled. Our companion, the ass, afforded us much entertainment. Mr Partridge, junior, by way of announcing our arrival at the foot of the mountain, blew a horn he had brought with him. He is a very conceited, pedantic, though clever young man, and appeared to fancy he blew with *so much* grace! Though he made it sound as like the braying of an ass as ever I heard. The ass mistook the sound as proceeding from a fellow creature in reality, and set up such a tremendous bray that every echo in the mountains resounded. Our laughter was scarcely less loud on hearing such a comical reply; peal succeeded peal for some time. Mr P. jun., though he could not help joining in the laugh, was not a little disconcerted at being so *egregiously* mistaken by the animal; this added still more to our mirth.

After labouring up the steep for an hour or two, over moss and rocks, we at length reached the summit. We immediately began to search for a convenient resting-place where we could sit and make our repast, and finding a very snug one where we were sheltered from the bitter cold wind, we all sat down upon the ground, and enjoyed a hearty meal of veal, ham, chicken, gooseberry pies, bread, cheese, butter, hung leg of mutton, wine, porter, rum, brandy, and bitters. When our hunger was appeased, we began to stroll about and enjoy the extensive prospect. We had several prospect glasses, and the air was very clear. I was much pleased, though awed, by the tremendous rocks and precipices in various directions. I crept to the edge of several of them; but of one in particular, when I found myself seated upon its projecting point, and a direct perpendicular descent on every side but one, of many hundred yards, the sheep and the cattle beneath scarcely visible, such a degree of terror overpowered me, I durst no longer behold it. I closed my eyes, and laying flat down upon a surface just large enough to contain me, I remained a considerable time before I dared rise and make a retreat.

The mountain is shaped very like a horse shoe; we ascended at one end, and descended at the other, making a circuit of eight or ten miles at least; some say, twelve.

In descending, one or two of the party who had not provided nails in the soles of their shoes to make their footing firm, were obliged to sit down frequently, and descend by sliding; the mountain heath and moss glaze the shoes in such a manner when without nails, it is impossible to stand, much less to walk with safety where the ground is not perfectly level.

At the foot of Fairfield, we again ascended our *carriage,* and arrived in Ambleside about five o'clock, and concluded the evening at Scambler's. I have never in my life enjoyed a more agreeable excursion; such a scramble exactly suited me. To me, there is little pleasure in a straight forward walk on level ground. A fine, noble, lofty, rugged mountain, has far more charms for me than a fine, formal, artificial walk in a garden or pleasure-ground.

Early in April last, I wrote to Mr M'Cartney,[14] to inform him of my present place of residence, and how to remit the half year's rents. I have never heard from him. I mean to write again soon. If I should hear nothing, do you think Mrs Winkley would object to requesting him to send the money soon, and instead of giving me a draft on the Kendal Bank as I desired, send it in one and two pound notes, by the Mail, with his own name indorsed on

128

the back of each as several of the last I received, were rather objectcd to.

I am sorry you are disappointed in your wish of travelling this way; you would have been so much gratified.

[Journal, July 1810]:

When I begin to enumerate the works I have read since I came to Doves-Nest, I feel surprised that I should have read so few, and that the greater part of those few should have been of the Novel species, a kind of composition which, though I do not altogether condemn, I am not the greatest friend to. Some works of that kind, I highly approve, but taken collectively, they are a dangerous, fascinating kind of amusement, and destroy all relish for useful, instructive studies.

[Journal, late July 1810]:

On a reperusal of many of my letters, there appears some strange contradictions in the sentiments. I write as I think at the moment; but present circumstances have frequently a strong influence on my opinions, and, to an observer ignorant of the cause of the apparent fluctuations of ideas, I must appear extremely capricious and unsettled. I could make a satisfactory explanation of each seeming change of opinion, and say why I write so differently at one time, to the expressions made use of at another. But it is not worth while, for these Vols. will probably never fall into the hands of those who might peruse them, or be read with the attention necessary to discover any contradictions of the kind, if they do.

What I have related as facts, are truly such. The manner of the describing entirely on who was the correspondent, not chusing to relate to every one *all* the causes of such effects, but only attributing in part. I never in the most trivial circumstance, attempted to deceive or mislead. Prudence sometimes suggested that it would be improper to discover all the truth to the friend or acquaintance I addressed. I was only careful not in the slightest degree to misrepresent.

If these letters should ever be read by other eyes than my own, with any degree of attention, the reader will easily discover the motives which induced me to utter sentiments at one time so apparently opposite to those expressed at another. In the moment of strong feeling, I think, speak, and write, what my cooler judgement afterwards condemns.

[Journal, early August 1810]:

Surely of all men in existence, Mr P. ranks amongst the strangest! – He who so debases himself by the company he keeps – by his almost continual intoxication – by the violence of a tyrannical temper – by a meanness in every action contemptible beyond everything! That he, who is neither a half-wit, nor physically mad, can see neither the folly, the impropriety, nor the violence and wickedness of his hourly conduct, is indeed most strange! – I have wondered and wondered again, why he should treat the wife he has endured so much from his friends for, so much more unkindly than the commonest servant in the house – but so it is. She whom, after all I really believe he is as fond of as is in his nature to be of any creature besides himself.

A mixture of cowardice, meanness, and extreme selfishness are the only reasons I can discover for such a behaviour to a worthy woman. If anything has displeased him, however innocent his wife may be of having caused the vexation, he seldom fails to wreak his vengeance upon her – for this laudable reason – she is a victim fastened to the stake – she must endure whatever he chooses to inflict. She has no help for herself; she cannot escape – the laws of the realm prevent that. 'A servant,' as he said one day, 'must not be spoken harshly to, for they can quit you when please,' – What a sorry motive! What a contemptible reason for using a servant well. Pity that so good an effect should not be produced by a better cause. A wife , I suppose, may be treated in any way, according to the whim of the moment, because – she is tied by the law, and cannot quit you when she pleases.

Several times when after a journey she has been fatigued and really very ill, owing to the motion of the carriage, which she can never bear without being sick, he has obliged her to sit at table during supper, because he does not like to eat alone. She has begged, she has supplicated, that she might be permitted to go to bed; her pale face, her depressed spirits and debilitated frame, her pitiable looks, all sufficiently indicating how greatly she wanted rest, if nothing more. – Inhuman wretch! – he still insisted on her remaining than he had finished supper; and still farther to shew the peevishness of his temper, he has taken up a book or a newspaper, and read to himself the whole time, not uttering a word to her while, except in bitterness and rancour of his heart at her requesting she might go to bed; cursing her for her d------d tempers. – Often and often has he treated her thus; and though she does sometimes strongly resent his cruelties, yet in general, she bears with astonishing, admirable patience.

She will never ruin him; she is too just, too good a wife, to do that. At the very time he bought an ass out of frolic, for which he gave five guineas; saddle, &c., two more; at the very time a boat was building for him, on which he was going to expend between two and three hundred guineas, he could abuse his wife in the most virulent manner for giving five shillings to a poor man who had lost two cows out of three, and who had a family of five or six to support; again repeating, she would ruin him. He needs be in little fear of that; he keeps her too poor. If he is ruined, he will ruin himself. She has as little power, as the will.

One day he ran out of the parlour, and almost without assigning a cause, instantly struck her, because he had overheard her desire the servant boy to go to Ambleside for a bottle of blacking. Perhaps he has been calculating the immense expence of his boat as he sat over his wine, and his heart smote him for his extravagance; so, on hearing Mrs P's order, determined to save something towards it in blacking. – For a fortnight after, not a pair of shoes could be cleaned. At length, a cheap receipt was procured, and again we have polished shoes – for I had been obliged to *grease* mine!

For some time, we have been very little at church indeed. Mr P. has subscribed ten guineas for a set of etchings of landscapes of the lakes; and for two or three pairs of views taken of Dove's-Nest and the scenery opposite.[15] he will probably pay ten or fifteen more. – How the man who cannot afford the expence of a conveyance of six miles journey to church once a week, can afford to squander so much on drawings, I know not. The servants are allowed to spend the Sunday in any way they chuse; to go to church, or to stay at home,. The consequence is, they seldom or never go.

One day last week, Mrs P. ordered the ass to be saddled, and rode backwards and forwards in front of the house. I stood a spectator, highly amused, as well as Mrs P. Mr P., who had been sitting a long time over his wine, on hearing us laugh, came out, and stood near where I did. I remarked to him that the saddle was too small for a grown-up person to ride upon, and that it was only long enough for a girl (Mrs P. was obliged to sit upon the ridge of it). Mr P. said the saddle was big enough for the ass; and as it had been ordered and made purposely for it, it was not my place to find fault with it; adding, in a great rage, that he looked upon what I said as an insult; that I took a great deal too much upon me; and that if I was not more cautious in what I said, he and I should part very soon. He then bounced back towards the house.

Mrs P. and I were struck with astonishment, little imagining that what I said, and the laughing manner in which it was uttered, could have raised any degree of resentment. No insult was meant. I knew not till then that *he* had ordered the saddle, little imagining, weak as he is, that he would have ordered such a one; for, though it was intended for an ass, it was at the same time intended for Mrs P. to ride upon; and when she sat at her ease, she sat upon the back of the animal, behind the saddle.

Before he got into the house, I said, "Sir, I am ready to go at any time. I will never stay anywhere, an unwelcome inmate; for, of this I am certain, no person could possibly take fewer liberties than I do."

He said, I did take many liberties, which did not belong to me.

"Then, why, Sir, did you never tell me before? I am unconscious of having taken the least liberty that could be taken as such; but if you will point them out to me, I will try to be more cautious."

Did I suppose, he answered, that he should tell me particulars. I might easily find out that I did take a great deal upon me; but I must not expect that he should submit to me.

"But, Sir, if you will not tell me what part of my conduct gives offence, I may err again and again, and be ignorant all the time that I am doing wrong."

I am still left in ignorance as to what part of my conduct gives offence. However, to make sure of avoiding every cause of error, I have since done nothing that I was not asked to do; the consequence is, I lead a sad life, for I am not required to do much. I scarcely stir from my seat from morning than night, employing my time in sewing for the family or myself, writing and reading when I have nothing else to do; for were I to be walking often in the garden or elsewhere, I might occasionally meet with Mr P., who might discover something or other to excite his displeasure.

132

By keeping out of his sight, I run less risk, and since I cannot please, may at least have the pleasure of being forgotten, and be at peace whilst passing so much time in solitude and inaction.

As Mr P's violence had annihilated all idea of amusement for the evening, Mrs P. quitted the ass, and retired with me into the parlour. I gave vent to a considerable degree of resentment, for my spirit was roused. Mrs P. endeavoured to allay it – she was awkwardly situated – she could say but little – he who had offended me, was her husband. I begged of her to acquaint me with what part of my conduct Mr P. was displeased. She said she could not inform me; he had not mentioned it to her. I requested she would ask him in the morning, when his passion was cooled. She promised she would. Next morning, I enquired what had been the result of her enquiries. She said nothing had been said on the subject – and no farther information could I obtain.

When I reflect with calmness, I can easily discover that there is a considerable portion of ingratitude in what I have been saying of Mr P., for though he is sometimes most grossly insulting, he is frequently much otherwise. I may say, that on an average, for one uncomfortable hour, I pass four in peace so far concerns his conduct towards me; and though, when he does begin to express his anger, he makes use of tones, gestures, and language approximating much more to the blackguard than the gentleman, yet, such violence to gentle feelings does not occur every day. – Let me endeavour in every point of view.

15 August 1810 (Dove's Nest). *To her Brother:*

H-m! and so you can propose, my dear, inconsistent, brother, that we should answer each other alternatively at the end of every fortnight; now, when I half seriously suggested that we should write on the first of the month – You! – that could so often keep me in a most cruel suspense of three, four, five, nay even six weeks! Whose dilatory answers induced me to think that I should be thankful could I be sure of hearing from you only once in two months. However, I will try you, and again be the first to be punctual; but – beware of the least infringement on what is now your own proposal, for – if you exceed the time, I will just as far o'erstep the limits of your boundaries, as you do those of mine; that is, if, instead of answering me at the end of fifteen days, you make it eighteen, I likewise will stretch as many

133

days beyond you, and make them twenty one; so, I again repeat – beware!

Thy letter is so affectionate, too, that tears of the sincerest gratitude and pleasure rise to my eyes – heaven bless and prosper thee. Thy picture of domestic comfort too, is sweetly drawn; may it last long. Mrs Weeton would indeed rejoice in thee, if she were witness to the violence of temper I am almost daily spectator of; it makes even those who do not personally suffer, more than uncomfortable. I should soon turn tell-tale, if I had thee to talk to. I can tell no tales here, for I have no society, male nor female, so I am prevented the temptation. We do see company sometimes, but it is very seldom; and as Mrs P. and I generally sit in a small breakfast parlour, the few who do call, I seldom see. Now and then we go to an afternoon party at one of three houses where we visit, the inhabitants of which are in a middle class of life, not more elegant in their manners than Dr Guest's of Leigh. Mr P. is so much amongst the workmen, he cares for little other society, and takes no pains to get Mrs P. introduced, seldom even taking her in a walk. The consequence is, she becomes spiritless as a poor humble creature can be, and takes little pleasure in anything; her lessons are almost given up, and the next thing may be, that Mr P. will consider me as of so little use, that I may be dismissed.

On the 25th of July, there was a Regatta held at the Ferry Inn, opposite the large island, five of six miles below Dove's Nest. The nestlings fled with canvas wings to view the sports; the entertainments were nothing near so grand as the name imports, and as I expected, consisting merely in a succession of boat-races, foot-races, and wrestling. Mr P's new boat had not then arrived; the Rover, in which we went, won the race for second-sized boats, and very unexpectedly; but Mr Pedder's sailor is a very clever young man; the other competitors were left far, very far, behind. You must not suppose that Mr and Mrs P. or myself were in the boat during the sailing match. Col Bolton, of Liverpool (now residing in a most elegant house bordering the lake) had a beautiful barge rowed by six men, dressed in white, the ladies in which, twelve or fourteen in number, sat under a square canopy. A great number of boats of all sizes were on the water. A fine large, stately sailing boat of Col Bolton's has invariably gained the prize for several years, to the great mortification of Mr Wilson, whose boat of larger size, has generally been put in competition with it. Mr Curwen [a local principal landowner] was so hurt at being so completely beaten, that he has given up the contest entirely, and all his boats are on sale.

There is to be another Regatta on the 27th of this month, to be held at Water-head, just above Mr Pedder's, when Mr P. means to try his new boat, which is just completed; against Col Bolton and Mr Wilson. A very numerous company are expected to be assembled upon the occasion; if you write in due time, perhaps I may give you a full account of the entertainment; if you do not, some other correspondent may receive it, and I shall not like to write the same description twice. It is said the second Regatta is to be much more grand than the first; it may very easily be made so, for the first savoured much more of blackguardism than of elegance.

13 August 1810 (Dove's Nest). *To Miss Winkley:*

I could wish to have your advice, my dear Miss Winkley, respecting the cloth coat I wore last Winter, which, if you remember, I had cleaned in Liverpool. One day, to preserve it from the rain, I put over it a new Scotch plaid of Mr Pedder's, and the dye of it has stained the coat in such a manner that I cannot wear it again as it is; it must be dyed some dark colour; what do you think of dark bottle green?

I am almost out of the world here, so far as regards fashion, seeing and hearing less than I used to do at Holland; for Mrs P. and I have no female acquaintances except a village surgeon's wife, and an acquaintance of hers, both of them as plain in their dress, and knowing as little about fashion as can be. At present I wear a grey sarsenet bonnet, and short mantle or fly, worked with black chenille; but we go out little, that my coat may serve well enough for the Winter, if decently dyed. I should like to have it done in Liverpool, and made up again by Miss Marwood, if she continues the business. She will be married soon, I suppose.

I have been thinking of getting a riding habit, but have so little occasion to go on horse-back, that if any other travelling dress is considered as equally, or perhaps more, genteel, I don't know but it would suit me better, as being more generally useful.

If my coat can be made to look well again, perhaps I may make it serve for the present; for if Mr Pedder remains here during the Winter, I shall scarcely have occasion to put on any thing of the kind twice in the month, we go out so *very* little.

5 September 1810 (Dove's Nest). *To Mrs Chorley:*

When I first came here, I was surprised to find such a general degree of civilization amongst the inhabitants of the lowest class, much more so than I have in general found in the poorer natives of Lancashire; nor are they anything near so depraved. A reason may easily be given for such a striking difference. In the first place, so much travelling through the country softens the rude manners of the people very much; they lose their simplicity, indeed, but in its stead they find intelligence; and if they do not go out into the world (as it is generally expressed), the world comes to them, and this country, being far from populous, prevents that depravity that is ever found amongst crowds.

Since the beauties of the country have attracted such general notice, I am told the characters of its natives have undergone a considerable alteration. Thirty years ago, if a stranger had lost his way, or stood in need of refreshment when no Inn was near, if he could but find a house, he was sure to meet with a welcome reception from its inhabitants: the best food, the best bed – perhaps their only one – was ever at his service; and when he left them, as much provision as he could carry was given to him, without the least expectation of return; and thus a man might have travelled from house to house, day after day. It has been no uncommon thing for them even to furnish him with clothes and money. But since there has been such an influx of travellers, who have carried profusion with them wherever they went, wealth has flowed into the country; genuine hospitality is seldom met with, for avarice and rapacity have too generally supplied the place.

The inhabitants of Westmoreland are a handsome race of people; everywhere, in almost every face, you may meet with the lily and the rose. Lancashire used to be famed for its witches, but since it has become such a manufacturing county, most of the witches have been smoked out, and taken refuge further north.

The shepherds of the mountains still retain in a great degree, their primitive simplicity and ignorance, and the wiser inhabitants of the vallies often amuse themselves by relating some ridiculous tale or other of them. The Borrowdale shepherds are ignorant to a proverb. (Borrowdale is in Cumberland). It is said of one of them, that as he was one day returning from driving his sheep over a mountain, he saw something on the ground

1. Up Holland Village, 1815. From an original painting by Charles Towne (1763-1840). *Courtesy of Museum of Wigan Life, Wigan Council.*

2. Up Holland Parish Church of St Thomas The Martyr, c.1900. Founded 1307 by Robert de Holland. Soon after 1318 the church became a Benedictine priory, and the final Benedictine priory in England before the Reformation. The building on the right (now Up Holland Conservative Club), was once the Parsonage. *Courtesy of Wigan Archives and Local Studies.*

3. 'The Priory', Up Holland, c.1910. The home of Revd and Mrs John Braithwaite and their six children in the early years of the 19th century. It was "the place of good humour and careless untidiness," declared Miss Weeton. It stands but a short distance from the site of the cottage home of Mrs Mary Weeton and her two children. 'The Priory' is now named 'The Abbey' and is in private ownership. *Courtesy of Wigan Archives and Local Studies.*

4. Church Street, Up Holland, c.1920. The three storeys building on the left (now demolished) was known as 'School House,' where Mrs Mary Weeton began a dame school to teach the village children. *Courtesy of Wigan Archives and Local Studies.*

5. Dean Wood, Up Holland, c.1895. The place where Miss Weeton and her brother, Thomas, spent many happy hours of childhood. See poem critique: A Ramble in Dean Wood. (Appendix VIII). *Courtesy of Wigan Archives and Local Studies.*

6. William Yates's Map of Lancashire, 1786. Showing the villages and towns to which Miss Weeton walked from Up Holland: To Wigan, Leigh, St. Helens (Parr Hall), Prescot and Appley Bridge. Originally reproduced at 1 inch to 1 mile. *Courtesy of Lancashire Record Office.*

Four Yates
Bartons
Brinsop
Grundy House
Chen Moor
Rainsworth
Earl Balcarres
Park
Aspull
Bark Hill
Bradshaw Hall
Hall
Win Yate
Sindle Hall
Engine
WIGAN
Whirley
Kirk Hay
Pennington Hall
West Houghton
Chequer Bent
Over Hulton
Ince
Ince Hall
Hindley Hall
C E
W. Houghton Chapel
Win Hulton Esqr
Hulton Hall
Smithy Green
Holt Esqr
T B
D C
Castlehill
H i n d l e y
Darcey Hillock
Baglane
W. Sprowd
Old Hall
Amber
P C
Hollins
C E
Chov
Mofs Side
Wood
Low
Rottenron
West Leigh
Hen Bridge
Bein Mofs
Low Green
Platt Bridge
Coal Pits
Hindley Green
Pickley Green
Atherton
Ralph Peters
D
R
E
Bickershaw Hall
D
Atherton Park
Atherton Hall
Brim Hall
Bamferlong
Abram Hall
Dever
Parfonage
Atherton Esqr
Tildfl
A b r a m
Coal Pits
Fire
L E I G H
Dam
Edge Green
Lightshaw Hall
J. Hilton Esqr
Bedford
Makersfield
late E. Byrom Esqr
Byrom Hall
Mofley
Pennington Hall
Morley Hall
P C
Golborn
Pennington
Hopcarr Hall
Haydock Lodge
Lonsten Chap
Lately Common
Light Oak Mill
P. Legh Esqr
L o w t o n
Landside
Wiswall
Berry Lane
Golborn Park
The P. Legh Esqr
Kenyon
Brofeley Hall
Fowley Common
Culcheth
Culcheth Hall
Mofs
N E W T O N
C E
Barons Mill
Newton Park
Kenyon Hall
Heath Lane
Wigshaw
Jno. Trafford Esqr
Holcroft Hall
C E
New Church
W. Banks Esqr
Old Hay
New Bar
Ferret Hall
Little Town
Reat Houfe
C r o f t
Highfield Hall
Southworth
Pefurlong
Glafsbrook Mofs
W i n w i c k
Hall
W. Hornby
Middleton
Croft Eaves
D C
Rifley Chapel
Old Hall
Caufe Bridge
R
Arbury
Highfield Spaw
Noggin Hillock
New Hall
H u l m e
H o u g h t o n
R i f l e y
Gra
Dallam Mofs
Dallum
T B
Ferry Shed
Rifley Mofs

7. Map of the environs of Liverpool, 1768, by William Yates and George Perry. Beacon's Gutter was the location of a white cottage on the edge of the River Mersey, Kirkdale, where Miss Weeton lodged from September 1808 to December 1809. *Courtesy of Liverpool Record Office, Liverpool Libraries.*

8. The Mersey at Liverpool, c.1835, drawn by W. H. Bartlett. *Courtesy of Liverpool Record Office, Liverpool Libraries.*

9. Liverpool Theatre, 1825. Drawn by James Brierley. Also known as the Theatre Royal, it was located in Williamson Square. The Theatre Royal was the venue for Miss Weeton in November 1808 and July 1809. The building was demolished in the 1970s. *Courtesy of Liverpool Record Office, Liverpool Libraries.*

THEATRE-ROYAL.

Mrs. SIDDONS, for a Fortnight only.

Messrs. LEWIS and KNIGHT most respectfully beg leave to assure the Patrons of the Theatre, and the Public in general, that they were not inattentive to the repeated wishes and inquiries, conveyed last Season through the Box-Office Keeper and other channels, concerning such Theatrical Performers of Eminence as they had not then the satisfaction to have engaged, in particular respecting that UNRIVALLED TRAGEDIAN Mrs. SIDDONS. The Managers have now the honour to announce, that they have this Season succeeded in prevailing on this celebrated Actress again to visit this Theatre for the above period; during which she will perform ten Nights, and no more.

MRS. SIDDONS'S THIRD NIGHT.

This present WEDNESDAY, JULY 12, their Majesties' Servants will perform the Tragedy of

MACBETH.

Duncan.................Mr. MUSGRAVE,
Malcolm.................Mr. POWELL,
Macbeth.................Mr. RAE,
Macduff.................Mr. GRANT,
Banquo.................Mr. JONES,
Fleance......Master HOWELL,
Lenox.................Mr. WRIGHT,
Ross.................Mr. TERRY,
Siward.................Mr. D. GRANT,
Seyton...........Mr. HOWELL,
1st Officer.............Mr. MORETON,
2d Officer...Mr. WOODWARD,
Physician.....Mr. HOLLINGSWORTH,
Speaking Witches, Mr. ROMER, Mr. TURPIN, and Mrs. TAYLEURE.
Hecate......Mr. TAYLEURE,
Lady Macbeth............Mrs. SIDDONS,
Gentlewoman...Mrs. GRANT.
The Vocal Parts by Messrs. Andrews, D'Arcy, M'Farland, Msdms. Garrick, Turpin, Moreton, Parker, Grant, and Misses Larkman and Grant,

After which, the favourite Farce of

BON TON.

Lord Miniken.................Mr. JONES,
Sir John Trotley.............Mr. ROMER,
Davy.................Mr. SIMMONS,
Lady Minikin.............Mrs. TURPIN,
Tittup.................Miss GRANT.

N. B. In order that the strictest impartiality may be observed in the letting of the places for the Boxes, the Public are respectfully informed, that during Mrs. SIDDONS's Engagement they are to be taken with Tickets at the Box-Office only, from Ten to Three o'clock, the day preceding the Performance, and not before.

Boxes 4s. 6d.—Upper Boxes 4s.—Pit 3s.—Gallery 1s.
Days of Performing are Monday, Tuesday, Wednesday, Thursday, and Friday.

10. An advertisement from the *Liverpool Courier,* dated Wednesday, July 12th, 1809. Accompanied by her nephew, Henry Latham, Miss Weeton, went to see 'that unrivalled tragedian' Mrs Siddons, in 'Macbeth,' at the Theatre Royal. *Courtesy of Liverpool Record Office, Liverpool Libraries.*

11. Castle Street, Liverpool, 1786, drawn by W. G. Herdman. Its appearance would have changed little by 1808, when Miss Weeton and Miss Winkley drank tea together at Mr Nevett's Castle Street bookshop. *Courtesy of Liverpool Record Office, Liverpool Libraries.*

that glistened. He approached pretty near to examine what it was. It was about the size and shape of a small turnip, perfectly bright, and very oddly spotted. It had a long tale. He concluded it was something alive, but what was his terror when he heard it distinctly and repeatedly pronounce the words, tick him, tack him, tick him, tack him!! Terrified lest it *should take* him, he took to his heels, and ran for some miles until he got to a cottage. He there told his wonderful tale. The people of the house sent messengers various ways to fetch the inhabitants of all the hamlets within a few miles round. When arrived, they proceeded in a body, armed with large sticks, to put to death this before unheard of creature. When they reached the spot, they likewise heard it cry, tick-him, tack-him!! Expecting that the creature would be instantly flying at some of them, without loss of time they began to pelt it with large stones, and when they durst approach near enough, completed its destruction with their sticks – not knowing, poor simple fellows, than some time after, that they had taken all this pains to demolish – a handsome gold watch!

The hills and mountains present a singular sight to a stranger, they are so intersected with high walls, even to their very summits. It spoils the beauty of them; they resemble maps traced with the boundary lines of different provinces; walls six feet high, built only of loose stones, round, angular, or any other shape, are frequently seen rising in a direct line *up* the steepest hills in every direction. It must have taken an immense labour though probably built at different periods. Many of the houses in this country are built in the same manner, of stones unformed by the chisel, of all sizes, and without mortar or any other cement whatever, the inside of the walls being plastered. Of course, they are very damp, particularly on the weather side, there being nothing to prevent the driving in of rain or snow. The people are hardy and healthy, and accustomed from their infancy to such dwellings. How they bear in Winter, with so little fire, I know not. The luxurious, and consequently tender, weakly, and delicate inhabitants of most parts of Lancashire, would think themselves as miserable in such houses. These people are contented, and even comfortable, because they never knew anything better.

The great and noble Skiddaw, which is amongst mountains what Dr Johnson was amongst authors, is, I am sorry to say, is going to be enclosed; the tracing of it with walls, and dividing it into portions will greatly deface it. It will be majestic still, but twill be majesty without beauty. The Bishop of Landaff, who resides about two miles from here, has been the occasion of it. A considerable portion of it belongs to him, and will be much more valuable to him enclosed, than if it remained a common. He means to plant it.

When I was at Keswick, I admired the stupendous beauty of the mountains so much, that I shall scarcely think it being clothed with wood any additional ornament to it. The Bishop is a clever, sensible man, with an uncommon share of penetration and foresight. He purchased a great deal of land in various parts of the county, before it was so dear as it is now – for at present it sells exorbitantly high, merely on account of the romantic beauty of the country. The land he purchased, is said to be strictly worth ten times the sum at the present period, to that he gave some years ago. He has been a great speculator. Most of his speculating days are nearly over, for he has attained a good age, and his health begins to fail. He has (six) daughters, all unmarried, the youngest of whom, I have been told, is five or six and twenty; two sons, one a Colonel, and married – the other – nothing, for the Bishop can make nothing of him. He is not accused of depravity, but will settle to nothing. His father destined him for the Church, but the son will not consent, and has been for some time at home, the father not knowing what to do with him, for he is too old for the navy, and almost the army.

Great part of the Bishop's income was left to him by a young gentleman to whom he was tutor (three thousand a year), which at his death devolves to his eldest son, so that his other children will be very humbly provided for. He saves as much as he can out of his annual income. To increase his property, he proposed, about twenty years ago, the draining of Windermere, a considerable part belonging to him. He expected to gain some hundred acres by it. It was found to be practicable, as I was informed, but the expense of doing it would have greatly exceeded the advantages, and it was given up. Though such a plan would have increased the landed estates of a few individuals, it would have materially injured the generality of the inhabitants of the county, for the beauty of Windermere is one great attraction for tourists, and the wealthy settlers who have built handsome houses on its margin, would soon quit it in disgust, when only an insignificant river rolls where once spread so noble a lake; the land would consequently decrease in value, and the natives become as poor as they were thirty or forty years ago. Perhaps the Bishop foresaw all this, and that the increase of land would not compensate for the decrease of rents.

5 September 1810 (Dove's Nest). *To her Aunt Barton:*

The time fast is approaching when I expect to see my brother, if he comes at all. I will therefore prepare my promised letter some days beforehand, that it may be ready for him to take on his return. In a letter I received from him about a month ago, he will not be able to come. Dear me! Cannot he stir without his wife? I wish, with all my heart, she may stay at home, and he come without her, for there is no pleasure with them both together, they have so much gabble about their own affairs, and Mrs W. is so consequential, and so full of fuss! Nobody else can get a word in. When my brother is without his wife, there is some chance of a little general conversation.

We have had such a continuance of wet, stormy weather for the last six or seven weeks, that the hay harvest is not yet completely got in. The manner of mowing and making hay differs materially from the method pursued in Lancashire. Their scythes are much longer, nearly half as much longer; by this means they mow the same quantity of ground in much less time than they would in Lancashire, and with much less labour, standing almost upright to their work, and sweeping down almost twice as much grass at once. I have observed that they do not cut so close to the ground, and of course they must have less hay, if they have more after-grass. The Westmoreland haymakers laugh at the Lancashire for the foolish trouble they give themselves in overworking their hay; these people begin to spread it out about ten in the morning, with their hands only, using no hay forks only for loading or unloading; they let it lie than afternoon, without turning, making it into small cocks out of the spread hay, which, they say, turns it sufficiently, and that the cocks take much less time in making than if they first rowed it, and afterwards made it up; and that the hay is as well made, and as soon. The farmers here make their butter from cream alone, churning no milk with it; of course they have a great quantity of skim milk, which goes all of it to the pigs, most of them having no market for it, living often in very lonely situations,

Mrs Jackson, of Liverpool (Mrs Jas. Hawarden's daughter), used to do so, and her neighbours thought her shamefully extravagant. To be sure, she often gave new milk to the pigs, and the cream was used without being churned.

In Westmoreland, there are great numbers of pigs kept, a quantity of hams and bacon exported, and a good deal of butter. In a county where the thinly scattered towns leave room for a great number of farms, and markets often at a great distance, they must do something with their produce. I do not think these farmers are anything near so industrious and managing as those in most parts of Lancashire; their ground is very poor, and they take little pains to improve it. They complain, as do the North-Meols people, of the want of manure; they are too idle, and too proud, to collect what there is, not considering, unthankful people, that the least of God's blessings ought not to be wasted, but made the most of, be it ever such a *dirty blessing*.

Many of the farmers live on their own estates, and as it is less trouble to get rich by dint of saving than by industry, they are content to follow the former plan, rather than be at the trouble of combining both. What money they receive, is generally hoarded; they have little occasion to spend it usefully, and few temptations to do it idly. Each farmer has on his own estate, his own wool, which forms great part of the clothing of himself and family; his own oaten and wheaten bread, potatoes, butter, milk, eggs, cheese, bacon, hams, mutton, and sometimes veal. There is nothing, I think, I should like better than farming, if I did but understand it, particularly if it was on my own estate, and I had no rent to pay; but I should not like to be a farmer where the markets are so far off.

Butter is never more than 16 ounces to the pound in this neighbourhood; it is seldom higher than fourteen pence a pound. Mr Pedder has it the year round at a shilling; new milk a penny, and three half-pence a quart. Most other things are quite as dear as they are in Lancashire.

I received Henry Latham's letter a few days ago, and am much pleased with it; he writes a very fine hand. I shewed it to Mrs Pedder, and she praised it highly; she thought it quite a beautiful hand.

There have been a great number of travellers this summer to the lakes, some very great folks amongst them; amongst others,

Lord Castlereagh,[16] of whom the newspapers say, he comes as much with the intention of visiting the sheep as the country.

The Prince of Orange passed through Ambleside two or three weeks ago; report says he is destined to marry the Princess Charlotte of Wales.[17] He has a house in Oxford, where he is receiving his education. The inhabitants of Doves-Nest see none of these fine folks; the house is too far from the road; we only hear of them.

I am obliged to you for your invitation, but Mr Pedder's going to Preston for the Winter is so uncertain, that perhaps it may be a very long time before I see you, unless I were to leave here entirely. Neither should I wish to come, until I know who is the author of so scandalous a report as was raised against me in Holland on my leaving Liverpool. There has been too much of the malicious work in Holland; many an innocent young woman has lost her character, and someone should exert themselves to put a stop to it. I for one will do all in my power, and like a second Hampden,[18] will, out of a private wrong, endeavour to work a public good, though I may injure myself in the arduous task.

During the summer, for several years lately there has been one or two entertainments held on the lake and its banks, called a Regatta. They were first begun by Mr Curwen, who has a beautiful island on the lake, of about thirty acres in extent, and a handsome circular house upon it.[19] Since he entirely quitted this neighbourhood, a sailing club consisting of four or five young men of fortune, have conducted the annual Regattas. There was one on the 25th of July last, and another on the 27th of August following. The first held at the ferry house, near the island, I was much pleased with. There was one footrace in the water; several stakes were, at certain distances, driven into the ground where the water was about three feet deep; several deep holes were made, purposely that the runner, plunging unexpectedly in, might and get a ducking. It was laughable indeed, for there was no danger.

The second Regatta was expected to have been more splendid still, in consequence of which, Mr Pedder invited a number of friends. We were sadly disappointed; it was one of the most blackguard things ever conducted. After a rowing match or two, which began the entertainment, there followed a footrace by four men. Two of them ran without shirts; one had breeches on, the other only drawers, very thin calico, without gallaces [braces]. Expecting they would burst or come off, the ladies durst not view the race, and turned away from the sight. And well it was that they did, for during the race, and with the exertion of running, the drawers did actually burst, and the man cried out as he run – "O Lord! O Lord! I cannot keep my tackle in, G—d d—n it! I cannot keep my tackle in."

The ladies, disgusted, every one left the ground; there were many of Fashion and of rank; amongst others, Lady Diana Fleming, and her daughter Lady Fleming, and the Bishop of Landaff's daughters; several carriages, barouches, curricles; but all trooped off. Wrestling and leaping occupied the remainder of the day, we were told. The principal conductor was much to blame in suffering the men to run with so little clothing; it was a gross insult to every woman there, and there was a much greater number assembled on that day, than there was at the preceding Regatta; of elegant, well-bred women, I mean.

September 11. My brother does not come, I find. I feel disappointed, for I should like to have seen him.

14 September 1810 (Dove's Nest). *To her Nephew, Henry Latham:*

I have no doubt it will be a gratification to you, and I assure you it is one to me, to say that I am very much pleased to observe the improvement you have made in writing. Continue a little longer to make equal progress, and you will write a very fine hand indeed. *Great praise* is due to those whose method of teaching enables you to improve so quickly; and a great deal belongs to you, too, my dear boy, for taking so much pains; for let your teacher be ever so clever, if you were careless, he could be of little service.

You don't tell me what progress you make in Grammar or Geography, or how far you are in Arithmetic. I am afraid you have made no great progress in the two first. In accompts I dare say you go on fast. Geography is not taught, I think, to day scholars at your school; and English Grammar, I fear, they take little trouble with. If so, it is not you that must be blamed; for you must be a wonderful genius if you could teach yourself; to speak and write English well is a great acquisition; though a man may get a good living without it. You spell very well indeed; in that you are much improved. And in the grammatical part, your letter is only defective in a very few places. I will tell you where, for if you are not told your faults, Henry, you know, you will never mend them.

You say – 'my aunt and uncle *says.*' It should be – my aunt and uncle *say*, – Aunt and uncle being plural, must have a plural verb; *says* is singular, *say* plural. In another place you say, 'the family are all well, and *begs* to be remembered, &c.' – It should be *beg*, for the same reason before given. Again – 'Miss Taylor and her brother *has*,' should have been written *have*, for the same reason.

A few misspelt words I will mention. – 'Cousen,' should be cousin; 'Whishes' – wishes; 'give *there* compliments,' should be – give *their*, &c.; as this last word must be used when we speak of persons or things; the other means yonder, or in that place. 'I am *sorrow*,' ought to be 'I am *sorry.*' '*Is self*' must be written himself. These are all, Henry, worth notice, and very few for a boy like you. The diction is good, and the sense of the letter well expressed.

Does your father intend to continue you another year at school? If he does, I will pay for you one year more. Let me know when you write again, as I shall wish to hear from you before Christmas.

We have had a sad accident here. One morning last week (Sept. 5th), a young man was found drowned where Mr Pedder moors his boats, a few yards from the water's edge. We cannot tell how it happened, as no one was present. There is great reason to fear he did it intentionally. He is said to be a native of Ormskirk, of the name of Toothill,[20] only son to a dissenting minister there, of good property, and traveller for a gentleman in Manchester, whose name is Brown.

When Mr Pedder's boatman returned from breakfast about 9 o'clock, a little row boat which they had left fast to a stake, was drifted to some distance, and a hat lay in the water near it, scarcely wet. This gave rise to a suspicion that some one had fallen out of the boat into the water, in attempting to go to examine a beautiful pleasure boat of Mr P's that lay about 20 yards off shore, and that it had overset, being very small and unsteady, and in unskilful hands, very dangerous. A search was immediately begun, but it was more than an hour before he was found, not ten yards from the shore, in about 7 feet of water. He might have saved himself, even if he could not swim, had he tried to do so.

I was present when he was brought up. It was a shocking sight. The surgeon told me afterwards that he was one of the finest formed young men he ever saw. He said there was an incision on both sides of his neck, as if he had attempted to cut his throat. His heart had failed him, I suppose. A razor was, that day he drowned, discovered in his bed. He had only come from Kendal the night before, and his master said he had no business anywhere in the immediate precincts of the lake. He had written to his master to come on such a fine day, for that he was so unwell, he could get no further. When his master found he had left Kendal, he followed to Ambleside on the very evening of the day he was drowned. By this, it seems as if he had intended it some days previously. Mr Brown could not, he said, assign any reason why the young man should be guilty of so wicked an action. Oh, my dear Henry! Do you never be guilty of any deed which may make you dread to meet with any man on earth. – But I do not fear you; I feel confident you will ever act honestly by every one.

Your affectionate cousin,
E. Weeton.

* My cousin [Latham] wrote to request the loan of a sum of money (£20), for twelve months, larding her letter with a great deal of flattery and cant.

15 September 1810 (Dove's Nest). *To her Brother:*

I feel rather disappointed that you do not come to the Assizes, for I was in hopes, after your business there was over, that you could have spared me two or three whole days here, and I had been planning how we would dispose of them, if the weather permitted.

The day, or evening, of your arrival, we would have walked to Ambleside, a beautiful road from here of about two miles. I would have introduced you to Mr Green, who keeps an exhibition of drawings (all his own) in that village, where you might have been amused for two or three hours; for he has a very great number, two rooms being kept open for the purpose. He draws well, in water colours only. He charges excessively high for them; a large size, such as might be contained in the frames of your and Mrs Weeton's portraits, he asks 20 guineas the pair. He gets a great deal by shewing his landscapes at one shilling each visitor. By that means, and selling drawings now and then, he supports his family, which are very numerous.

He is a great oddity. If you had paid him a visit without being previously prepared, I should have expected to have seen you struggling with all your might to restrain a violent inclination to laugh; and perhaps, after all, unsuccessful. How I should have been entertained to have seen you and him together! I was planning a few days ago whether to give you a few previous hints of his singular manner, or not, considering which would have been most amusing to myself. – How mischievously you have disappointed me!

Green is a man of good size, rather inclining to corpulent, and good, solid, thick legs. His eyes are black and somewhat small, and he does peep so queerly with them! His eyes both look one way, to be sure, but I can seldom catch them looking straight forward. A stranger that was addressed by him, would imagine he was talking to someone else; or if no other person was in the room, would stare about him, wondering what the fellow was talking to. Green talks a good deal in an inflated style, and always looks sideways at the object he is speaking to; when he looks directly forward, it is at some piece of furniture or other inanimate object, still talking all the while. I have often much ado to keep my countenance when I hear and see him, though really the man means well; and Oh! He does load one with such great big thumping, barefaced, compliments; bestowing a pretty decent one upon himself now and then.

Just imagine him standing by the side of you, with his hands crossed before him in a Miss Mollyish style, his intended bow half a courtesy, his fat arms and legs assisting, as in duty bound; his side glances at you every ten seconds, while he softly, sweetly, and insinuatingly informs you – 'that he has made the arts his peculiar study for the last eight years,' and that he flatters himself, by his unremitting study he has greatly contributed to their improvement; that he came to Ambleside for that purpose ('tis a great big lie – he came solely to get a living for himself and family, but he is too proud to acknowledge this), and hopes the time has been employed with equal advantage to the arts and to himself.

This is his general speech to strangers; the word arts, and artist, he is particularly fond of. He is high and proud to a degree, yet he was originally a drawing master in Manchester, and his wife a player. He certainly draws well – but, he needs no trumpeter.

He has very great merit in many respects. He is indefatigably industrious, and by his own labour alone in drawing, supports a wife, six children, and two servants, in a respectable style. He is very sober too, and bears a good moral character; and he is laughable, but not contemptible. Mrs G. is a very respectable kind of woman.

Mr P. is going to his brother James's, a general reconciliation having taken place. – Oh, I wish you could come by that time, or before, why, even defer it than Spring, for the days will become so short, so cold, and so misty, that the scenery will lose more than half its beauty.

My paying for my own mourning is nothing to the many instances of Mr P's meanness to myself and others – even to his wife – which I could relate; yet such a complete hypocrite is he, that none but those who reside a considerable time in the house, can perceive it. Such consummate hypocrisy, such contemptible meanness, I never witnessed on any other.

I am scarcely permitted either to speak or stir in his presence; nor ever to maintain any opinion different to his own. When in a violent passion (which is but too frequent), on the most trifling occasions he will sometimes beat and turn his wife out of doors. Twice she has run away to her father's – oh! Brother, and then, such a house! Mr P. roaring drunk and swearing horribly, and making all the men about the house drunk. I have thought at such times, I really could not bear to stay any longer, particularly when he has been in his violent passions with me, which has occurred six or seven times. As he at one time found fault with almost everything I did, I have ceased to do anything I am not asked to do. The consequence is, I have almost all my time to myself, as I do little else than sew for Mr and Mrs P. will have Mrs P. take such an active part in the house, that she has little time for my instruction; and as my assistance in domestic concerns has not been required for 3 or 4 months back, I sit a great deal alone, chiefly employed at my needle. Whether Mr P. means to keep me thus idle, or to dismiss me, I know not. Mrs P's gentle and kind treatment of me makes me very comfortable, for in general, I see little of Mr P, except at dinner.

Don't say anything of my cousin's letter or application to me, to my aunt; she would only get scolded, and I have said enough.

9 October 1810 (Dove's Nest). *To Mr and Mrs Green:*

A few conscientious scruples have induced Miss Weeton to hesitate a little in complying with Mr and Mrs Green's flattering request to undertake so serious a charge as that of the religious superintendence of their little son; for, a few months, or so at most, a few years, may remove her to such a distance, that she might never hear of him again.

If M and Mrs Green think the duties of a Sponsor extend not so far, but are merely temporary, Miss W., will with pleasure comply, and wait on them at the appointed hour on Thursday next."

———

Books lately read:

A Journal of a Tour to the Hebrides with Dr Johnson, by James Boswell, Esq.

J. Boswell does appear so wonderfully simple, so surprisingly ingenious, that I cannot but smile as I read his work. He sometimes represents himself in so ridiculous a point of view, that he would be almost contemptible if his openness and the absence of anything like deceit, did not operate greatly in his favour. Most men would be much injured by such a friend. Dr J. has not been greatly benefitted. But he only looked to the present, using Boswell as a temporary convenience, and thinking him too insignificant to affect his fame in future – such men are only to be despised as enemies; it is their friendship that is dangerous.

Lord Chesterfield's Letters to his Son. 4 vols.

It has been said of these letters that they inculcate an attention to the exterior graces of person and manners, so strongly and so repeatedly, as if their author was convinced that the cultivation of the mind was of inferior importance. The reader who thoroughly peruses the work will, I think, discover a satisfactory reason for it. The boy, as he grew up, shewed a great deal of timidity, and his awkward and reserved manner was a natural consequence; which was a thousand times more difficult to remove, than it was to instruct him in literature. In books, he made a considerable progress; there was little occasion for anything to be said on that subject; and those books, and able masters, together inculcated everything necessary on the subjects of morality and religion;

and these lessons *he had daily*. The only instruction left for the father to give, was such as we find in his letters; and as the youth was destined for a public character, the graces of oratory, ease of deportment, and elegances of person and dress, were absolutely necessary to his advancement in life. These, as he grew up, were all he wanted; therefore, they were so frequently the subjects of his father's letters.

The first and 2*d*. Vols appear to me unexceptionable. Of the others, I cannot say so much; there is a degree of libertinism expressed, and almost enforced, in many parts of them, which incurs the strongest censure. Lord C. must be very short sighted indeed if he could not foresee that if such sentiments were generally acted upon, society would be in a most miserable state! If women are to be generally and systematically encouraged to be unfaithful to their husbands, what man in his senses would marry? And when matrimony is treated with contempt by the men throughout a whole nation, the women who have not an opportunity of marrying will, by those very men, be *forced* to do worse, where inclination did not seduce them; and then, what myriads of miserable creatures would crawl about upon the earth.

14 October 1810 (Dove's Nest). *To Miss Winkley:*

What a great deal of trouble you and your mother have on my account, my dear Miss Winkley, with that shaffling fellow, M'Cartney. I did think, when Mr Clements gave him such a recommendation for honesty, industry, and sobriety, that I was well off indeed in having such an one to intrust with the collection of my rents. When I first saw him, which was at your house, I formed a very mean opinion of him indeed, but still considered that I must be wrong, when such a respectable man as Mr Clements spoke well of him, and Mr Banning[21] patronised him.

His selling his houses, is in the way of his business; he builds them but to sell; still, I do not like him, and a man so utterly void of all punctuality, never prosper; for, as it is justly said, 'punctuality is the very soul of business.' And in my opinion, it is the want of it, which is so general in Liverpool, that ruins so many of its tradesmen.

I have been examining an agreement drawn up by Mr Clements between Mr M'Cartney and myself, at the time I purchased the houses, in which M'Cartney is bound to take the houses for 5 years, paying me an annual sum of £55 clear of any deduction whatever, except for income tax; the windows to be left in perfect repair whenever I take the premises into my own hands. The houses ought to have been completely finished when I bought them; for, by an inadvertent confession, when I saw him at your house, he cleared, he said, more than £200 by the bargain; he then mentioned the chimnies, and said they would not cost more than 20s, in doing; to this sum I agreed, though I ought not to have done it, for he is tied by the agreement to pay and clear everything except income tax. If, when he pays you, he deducts a year's income tax, ask him whether he himself has paid it to the collector, for, if he cannot prove that he has, and should become unable, perhaps I may have it to pay again.

Your mother had done right in desiring the tenants not to pay any more rents to Mr M'Cartney. She has a disagreeable, troublesome task to perform for me, but perhaps when rid of M'Cartney, it might be easier to her if she would undertake it. His agreeing to collect the rents, indeed the *whole* agreement, signed by us both, was *entirely* his own doing; and If he could at any time have made more rent than he paid me, he had full liberty to do so for his own profit.

How is your own heart? You told me a tale some time ago of a certain swain, but I have heard no more; is he forever excluded?

15 October 1810 (Dove's Nest). *To her Brother:*

Pray, master Tom, do you mean to quiz my style of writing when you say – 'A long letter I could soon write in the above *much ado about nothing style*, which only after all tells you – I am writing to you.' – If you do, Sir, let me tell you, that from you I would rather have *much ado about nothing*, than no ado at all, and that I only do as I would be done by.

You are grown such a mere matter-of-fact man, that you appear quite out of your element when writing – at least, making the *attempt* to write – on any subject more exalted than – the shop! Pshaw! – such mere men of business, they may do very well at home, but barely none of 'em for my companions. They are just like those women who are nothing but shirt-and-pudding makers – as if neither men nor women could well perform their domestic concerns at one time, and raise themselves above them at another.

149

I always feel a degree of disgust at the man who can say, when speaking of female attainments, 'If she can make a shirt and a good pudding, it is enough.' – What a narrow minded epicure he must be! She must be of very narrow capacity indeed who cannot both attend to domestic affairs with a competent knowledge and care, and to the more exalted attainments of the mind. The kitchen should be kept in the kitchen, and never introduced into the parlour except at eating hours – and not be the sole subject, even then. There are certainly many people whose understandings are so confined wither by nature, education, or unavoidable habits, that they can never stir without taking their homes abroad with them, being truly *always at home*, wherever they are.

For a mind almost altogether immersed in business, it would be next to a prodigy if it could be entirely divested of it just when it wishes; yet there is something noble in striving to shake off the usual business occasionally – and, dwelling on this idea, my heart turns towards thee, my dear brother, to thank thee for thy endeavours to please. They never fail, I assure thee. Any ridicule I may thoughtlessly scatter, is not meant to wound, but only to amuse – perhaps tinged with a latent desire to excite a little admiration at my talents. As it is only directed to a brother, he will rather be gratified than hurt by it, I hope. – Hm-m-m, I tell thee what, Tom, thou never praisest me now; or if thou dost, it is bestowed so delicately, that my craving, gross capacity, does not discover it. (If this strong bait will not do, I do not know what will – aside). I shall be obliged to tell thee wherein my excellence consist. – Let me consider. I cannot discover them myself *all* at once – only because there are so many of them, take notice; they are not difficult to find, I *assure* thee. – What, then, does it stand in need of *assurance*? Indeed, a considerable share of *assurance* is requisite, openly, and directly, to blazon one's own virtues; and as *that* is not one of my excellencies, the quizzical humour may turn a key if it will, and unlock them.

Whenever thou canst bestow upon me the epithet of romantic, thou always dost! I acknowledge thou hast experienced some extraordinary instances from me of a romantic spirit, as thou callest it. But Mr P. is not a character to excite the slightest mark of romantic generosity. I had been here so short a time when Miss P. died, that I had no comprehension of the thorough meanness of his character. I never expected he would suffer me to pay for my mourning. He did not particularize what I was to order, and I ordered it at a venture, thinking, if he would not allow the whole, he would allow something *decent*. He *may* do it yet, for he has never said a single word on the subject, though he knows I have paid for it. Should he offer to pay for any part, I shall not refuse it. So that thou art greatly mistaken, Tom, when thou sneerest contemptuously at my 'fine spun romantic ideas.' And when thou still farthest observes, in allusion to me – 'Romantic ideas carried beyond the pale of common sense, are ridiculous,' – couldst thou not use more gentle language, when thou seest occasion for censure? An arrow *without* a barb would make a wound severe enough, even were it really necessary; in the present case, it is not.

I wrote immediately on the receipt of your last letter – which I fear you have not received, as I have neither heard from you nor seen you. I informed you in that letter that Mr and Mrs P. left here on the 3rd inst. To visit his father and brother; that their going to Darwen Bank for the Winter will be settled during their present visit; but that it was my opinion they would remain here.

I have had two or three long walks now since they went; one day, between 19 and 20 miles; the day before, and after, about 12 each. The weather is still exquisitely beautiful, and appears settled. I have been sat some time this afternoon upon a little hill that fronts the house, and overlooks the lake, amusing myself with my Flageolet. Oh, how I did wish that you could have accompanied me with your flute; and it is such a heavenly day, too! Oh, if you could but afford both money and time, and come, you would be so delighted.[22]

Mr Green, the artist, requested me to stand Godmother for his child on Thursday last (the 11th inst.). I consented, and spent a most agreeable day. In the evening we had a dance. A Mr Lewis, an historic painter from London, came for a few weeks on a jaunt of pleasure, played on the piano for us. Mr G. has again promised me the pencilled sketches of Dove's Nest. When I get, I should like to send them to you to copy.

Mr M'Cartney shaffles and wades from time to time. If it should be necessary to use the law against him, can you undertake the business, by employing some agent in Liverpool?

Tell Tom, and Catherine, and Jane, that I often think of them, and love them very dearly. I have a great mind to write Tom a little letter before long. Father could read it for him – at his age I could read writing myself, and make a legible scrawl. How does Tom read? Does he appear fond of his books? He will be seven years old, won't he, the 6th of next month. I will remember to drink his health on his birthday.

A fortnight ago I was very near quitting Mr P. This place is as much like a lunatic asylum as a residence for rational creatures, when he is at home. It is settled, however, that I remain. I believe he really wishes me to stay. Mrs P does decidedly. I love her dearly.

Remember me respectfully to Mrs Weeton.

18 October 1810 (Dove's Nest). *To Mrs Whitehead:*

L. Forster is deficient in his accounts to the Collector of Taxes, to such an amount – above £1000 – that he has absconded. I am sorry for his family. It is indolence, and that alone, that has occasioned his distress. He had neglected collecting Income Tax, &c., year after year, until it has become impossible to obtain it. I sincerely think he was an honest man, and had a good heart and an easy temper; but he wanted activity, energy, and punctuality in the common affairs of life.

Your slight touches of a few branches of the Royal Family, are interesting. I have often felt surprised that so little should be said of the Princess C. of W. Had her talents been of the commonest order, I should have thought the Editors of newspapers would have been ready at every opportunity to have flattered as much as they could. I had concluded our prospects of a future sovereign were not very great; I am glad there is some appearance of my being mistaken.

I was mistaken when I told you I thought Mrs P. was in a way to increase the family; there is no prospect of it.

Your domestic pictures are always interesting. Do not call them dull and dry; they may, perhaps, be to you 'as a tale twice told,' to experience the incidents and then to relate them; but remember, I have them with all the charms of novelty. Be kind enough, then, still to entertain me with them, and do not forget to give me the 'history of your *hobby* the garret,' as you playfully term it, and which you have promised.

Since my mother's death, my brother has bestowed the strongest disapprobation on every literary attempt, until, sunk in indifference, I dare no longer shew him anything, and am now too dispirited to attempt any other composition than that of a letter. Notwithstanding my itch for scribbling, I could be competent to the cares of a family, owing to my mother's excellent management in my education; but I do not appear to be destined to preside in one – at present, as useless a creature as is in existence – and recurring again to your suggestion, I can do no good with my pen; besides, there are books enow already on every subject, without my adding to the number. If all the volumes which are scattered over the world, were collected together, there would be a sufficient quantity to build a Babel.

During Mr and Mrs P's absence, I spent two days with Mrs P's father; or, I may rather say, with her sister, for he goes to work every day. When I see the house she was brought up in, more unfinished than any farm house I ever saw – the loneliness of its situation, the strange mixture of simplicity and good sense, honesty and ignorance, that characterises the only parent Mrs P. has had from infancy, I do think her the most astonishing woman I ever knew. Unimproved by reading or experience, she has ideas of the world and of polite life I cannot imagine how she has come by; an ease of manner in herself, which until the last 12 months she never witnessed in another. Her observation is remarkably quick – the only method by which she is inclined to improve. Her talents are sufficient for anything, had she but application; but indeed, she meets with no encouragement from Mr P. He is no genius himself. I am often as much surprised at his ignorance, considering the very liberal education he has had, as at her knowledge.

Mrs P. has a brother and sister. The brother is just apprenticed to a country house-carpenter; the sister keeps her father's house, working in the fields, on the peat; moss, or her father's house, as occasion requires. – What a difference in the situation of the two sisters! The one with her father wishes much to emerge from her present obscurity; but her father, an honest, warm-hearted, affectionate parent, sensibly says 'there is more happiness in his humble situation, than where there is more bustle, shew, and finery; he thinks his eldest daughter might do just as well, or better, in marrying a farmer, as the youngest has done in marrying a gentleman. 'People,' he says, 'do not always do well that marry so much above them, for they only get despised and abused by their fine new relations; and the wealthy husband or wife had need to be very kind, to render their poor partner barely comfortable.'

Tomorrow (19th) or the day following, the family are expected home. They will have been absent not quite 3 weeks. I have enjoyed their absence as an opportunity for many a long scribble, I shall enjoy their return as a release from solitude.

11 to 15 November 1810 (Dove's Nest). *To her Brother:*

I have waited to hear from Miss Winkley before I answered your last letter. I have not yet heard, so begin to write to you, as perhaps before I finish, I may receive some kind of intelligence. I am afraid the money is not paid by M'Cartney or she would have written.

I think I informed you that Mr and Mrs P. were in Preston when I wrote last; they were absent upwards of 3 weeks. Whilst they were away, I spent two days at Holms-Head, the farm where Mrs P's father lives upon. It is 4 miles from here. The first day, Miss Robinson took me to Coniston, to shew me the lake; going and returning was 12 miles. We returned to dinner after a most agreeable walk. The next morning we set out at 8 o'clock, intending to ramble 3 or 4 miles; but one object and then another drew me on, until at length I and my companion had arrived at the foot of Langdale Pikes, two lofty heads of a mountain, that may be seen as far as Lancaster, or farther in clear weather. I could not think of returning without mounting to the top, which, after a long scramble, we at length accomplished, and I thought myself well repaid for the trouble; indeed, the ruggedness and steepness of the ascent and descent were to me one half the inducement, for I dearly love a scramble. Had the day not been on the decline, and that we had to return to Dove-Nest that evening, I could scarcely have persuaded myself to return without traversing the summit, until I had a peep into Borrowdale, which was, or at least appeared to be, about 2 or 3 miles farther – but – it would not do to be wandering among rocks and mountains in the evening at that season of the year.

We got back to Holms head to a 5 o'clock dinner, and having eaten nothing for 9 hours, you may imagine how abstinence and the keen mountain air had sharpened our appetites. I really thought I should never have had enough. It was wonderful I had not felt faint with fatigue and hunger; it was not the case. When we were satisfied, we set off by moonlight for Dove's Nest; we had been, in all, about 20 miles that day, and that length of way in a mountain excursion is much more fatiguing than the same extent on level ground. I don't know when I spent two such delightful days.

The next day (Sunday) we walked to Grasmere Church, 6 miles each way. Miss R. staid 2 or 3 days with me; the rest of the time I was entirely alone, spending the time chiefly in reading and writing letters, until I had brought on an almost perpetual head-ache; it has been quite well ever since Mr and Mrs P. came home, for I have little opportunity of reading when they are here; there is such frequent interruption, and to enjoy a book, I must be in perfect quiet.

I was beginning to be tired of such perpetual solitude when they arrived, and was sincerely glad to see them. They are going again about Christmas, to the christening of Mr J. Pedder's little boy. They mean to stay a fortnight. I shall again be left at home, so Tom, there will be no chance of my seeing you for this long, long while, I don't know when, unless I leave here; and really, I am so very little service, I am expecting Mr P. will be having a terrible uproar some day with Mrs P. for having entirely given up her studies, and then the consequence will be – my dismissal; for, rather than apply to books, she would probably consent to part with me, for she cannot bear books, nor even to *hear* one read. I should, as I have told you before, be sorry to leave; nor does she appear to think of it. Indeed, she says so. I am only afraid Mr P. will think it too great an expence to keep me here, for nothing but a companion to his wife.

I feel myself in a writing humour, and as I have entirely filled one large half sheet, I will, for once, put thee to the expence of a double letter [postage paid by the recipient]; had I thought, when I begun, that I should have scribbled so much, I would not have cut the sheet, and then I might, with a safe conscience, have informed the Post-master that it was only a 'single sheet.'

Since Mr P's return from Preston, he has in general been in better humour that he was for some time before – he is certainly very odd. I always advise Mrs P. to quietness and submission when he is in one of his strange humours; a kind of advice she is sometimes unwilling to take, but in general I think it has some effect. Submission has certainly less effect upon him than it has upon some men, for, where he finds he can tyrannize, he will. Were I to tell you how he sometimes treats his wife, your blood would almost boil; yet, before his Preston friends, he appears so doatingly fond, so lavish of his money upon her! He will, there, force cloaths and ornaments upon her, which when he gets home he is continually reproaching her with. He will sometimes scarcely let her wear a decent gown for a length of time; then, if any acquaintance of his accidentally sees her in a shabby dress, he will storm at her for wearing it. One day he will scold us both for sitting in the same room with him – 'for he has never a moment to himself.' We leave the room quietly, and go to another; in less than half an hour, we hear the bell ringing violently. We know what we are to expect. Mrs P. is sent for, and asked what the devil she and I left the room, for; did we think he should allow fire and candles in two rooms; if Miss W. gave herself those airs, Mrs P. should not. I creep off to bed, and Mrs P., determining not to stay there to be scolded for two or three hours together, attempts to leave the room. He forcibly detains her in it, by locking the door, and gives full scope to his causeless anger; sometimes, after forcibly keeping her in the room, he will forcibly put her out – once out of the doors into the rain, at 11 o'clock at night, where she was obliged to stay near an hour, he fastening every door. Then, next morning, after one of these violent storms, he will often be so over kind, so perfectly good humoured!

There is a *sad* defect in his temper, for I am sure he is fond of his wife; yet it must be a selfish fondness, or he would seek her happiness along with his own. He keeps a curricle and 3 horses. Mrs P. is fond of riding, yet, because he is not fond of it, he will not let her ride scarce once in a month; she must walk, or stay at home; consequently she stays at home, for she is unable to walk far, owing to a pain in her left side, which she is often teased with. She grows pale and thin. It seems to be Mrs P's greatest pleasure to ride on horse-back attended by her husband, for, like the spaniel, she loves the very hand that strikes her; yet I do not remember that they have rode together 5 times since I came. To hear his abusive language to his wife is very distressing; he has got into the habit of it, I think. However, it is the only unpleasant part of my situation; and I do fully enjoy all the other comforts, many of which I never knew before I came here.

156

21 November 1810 (Dove's Nest). *To Miss Winkley:*

I can write but a short letter, for just now I am altogether agitation and fret; that same agreeable Mr ---- [Saul] I once mentioned before, from Lancaster, is here again. I wish he were either less agreeable, or would take himself away; his presence is too much for me, I shall be downright ill if he stays much longer. I do most sincerely wish him gone.

I am too humble, too insignificant, too ignorant, and too poor to excite any attention from him. Such a man should not go loose; he should either marry, or be confined, for he is calculated to win characters ten times more exalted than I am, and almost ten thousand of them. He is so like my brother in mind, but superior to him in disposition and figure – These sentiments ought to have been kept within my bosom. I *earnestly* beg of you to keep the secret *better than I have done.*

The wine that I have at your house, would be better used whilst it is good; let me, therefore, beg Mrs Winkley's acceptance of it. I thought of it when I left you. But was apprehensive I might have to return soon, and my finances were such as required economy, so that I might have wanted it. As I hear nothing of quitting my present situation, I am desirous the wine should not spoil for want using, and request your mother will take it all and use it as she pleases.

P.S. Burn this letter, my dear friend, as soon as possible; let *no one* see it. (Mr S. left on the 24th).

28 December 1810 (Dove's Nest). *To her Brother:*

How often do I wish that I could see you for a few weeks. I could tell you much that would exceed the limits of a letter – perhaps when Mr and Mrs P. go to Preston in the Spring, I may get a seat with them as far as there, if they go in a chaise – not that I think there is any chance of it either, for they always take such a load of luggage with them, when they go from home – perhaps I may come soon enough, for Mr P., when he is in one of his violent fits of passion, often threatens to turn me out so he does with his wife, or the servants. I am not worse treated then others; often better; but still I feel very uncomfortable when he talks in such a style. Were any person a spectator or a hearer my bitterest enemy, still, if they spoke as their conscience dictates, I am certain they must say that there was scarcely the shadow of an error in my conduct, when I am so found fault with.

He will sometimes, as we sit after dinner, introduce some observations on Politics, History, Geography, and still more frequently on other subjects, almost too trifling to entertain *even a woman*. His memory is rather treacherous, and if I should unfortunately hold a different opinion to his, or appear to discover any incorrectness in his statement of facts or incidents, he does not forget it for the remainder of that day; and after he has stormed at me in the parlour, will walk into the kitchen and tell the servants that 'Miss Weeton may appear to know more than he, but! – he knows better!' Which sound argument is enforced by a flourish of the arm, and a thwack with thumb and middle finger.

If I listen to him in a kind of submissive silence, not venturing to speak lest I should give offence, he will attack me in high style for disrespect and ill-behaviour in not conversing with him; in short, in some humours, there is no pleasing him, and these humours will often hold for a week or a fortnight at once without intermission – if no visitors arrive; for then, whilst they stay, he is exactly the opposite character to what I have been describing; you would be astonished to see him act two parts so different. When any acquaintance is here, he treats me with a degree of deference and respect too much for him to offer, or me to receive, my situation considered.

Have you any chance of putting out the money to interest when M'Cartney has paid it? If it would be more easy to procure a bond or a mortgage for £80 or £100, let me know. Mrs Winkley has £25 of mine, for which she pays interest. I have only a note without stamp for it; by giving her proper notice, I might add that sum to what you will have, and then next half year's income may likewise be added to it, which, altogether, if no extraordinary expence has been incurred, will arrive to something more than £100.

I have sometimes thought, if a little estate could be purchased some time or other on moderate terms, and I could sell my houses without loss, I should like to sell the one and buy the other; for, if I had not quite money enough, part of the estate might be mortgaged until I had saved enough to redeem it; and then, if in an agreeable situation, it might be a retreat to me a few years hence, for I am sure I could manage a milk farm, and should you meet with anything of the kind in the course of two or three years, let me know. If I did not like to live at it, I could let it.

I am much better than I was when I wrote last. My appetite has not quite returned, and my nerves are not the steadiest, as perhaps you may discover by my writing, but quite well enough to walk out every day if the weather would but permit me. We have had dreadful storms of wind lately, and one night last week, some very loud thunder, and for many weeks a great deal of rain.

4 February 1811 (Dove's Nest). *To Miss Winkley:*

Only yesterday morning was I pleasing myself with the idea that if I lived than the next Winter, I should return to you. – How vain to plan for the future, in a world so uncertain. – and how wicked, too, if done with any idea that we can accomplish our eager hopes. – Last night, when the papers arrived, I was grieved indeed to see so melancholy a circumstance announced as there met my eye; and so shortly, too, after hearing from you!

The disappointment of my hopes is nothing when compared to your loss. – I can feel for you, for I have been in a similar situation. Your friends – for I hope you will find many – will bestow every comfort and assistance you may need; and if I can add to the number, hesitate not a moment to ask any help I can afford you.

I am afraid to ask any intrusive question, but when you can exert yourself to write me, and if you then think proper to confide your plans for the future, if I can render any assistance, I shall indeed be glad to do all in my power. If I cannot be of service, I shall still be anxious to hear of you and from you. Do not, my dear friend, be long ere you write to me. After a few days are past, I shall anxiously look for every post, until I hear something of you. My other corresponding friends neglect me greatly, and what can be the reason, I cannot imagine. I wrote to Mrs Chorley early in September last, and have never received any answer or heard a single word of them from anyone else. They may some of them be dead, too, for anything I know. I think I will write to Mrs C. again in a day or two; if her silence is mere neglect, I shall not trouble her any farther.

It is five weeks since I wrote to my brother, expecting an almost immediate answer from him – and no intelligence from thence either! After having for the last 3 weeks looked with eager hope for the arrival of every post, I now begin to dread it, lest it should bring some evil tidings. If no misfortune has befallen him or his family, he is reprehensible indeed!

I have my little grievances, too, you see, my dear Miss W., and am just now fretful enough to magnify them into afflictions; but my nerves are sadly weakened; an involuntary attachment, and the struggle to conquer it, though a successful one, has had a much more powerful effect than I could have imagined; added to which, the unhappy temper of the master of this house, the continual quarrels in which he involves himself with his domestics and acquaintances, his brutal conduct towards his poor suffering wife, and his tyrannical treatment of me, have had such an effect on my health and spirits, that if I have any value for my life, I must endure it no longer, and am quitting Mr P's house about the middle of next month.

I propose boarding with some respectable family in Ambleside, or near it, for the next 6 or 8 months, that I may recruit my spirits and my health by an intelligent society and the pure air of the country, and then to return amongst you in Lancashire for the winter. In a few days I shall know, I expect, at whose house I can be accommodated, and when I write to you again, can inform you more at large of my particulars. At present, my plan is not quite fixed.

Ambleside is a village, beautifully situated, and many respectable, opulent, and genteel people inhabit the surrounding neighbourhood. I have been requested to commence a school, for there is not *one* decent one in the place. I am very certain it would answer, either as a day school, a boarding school, or both, but could wish to be at full liberty for the whole of the ensuing; and if my rents do not fail me, and I have no pecuniary losses, I would rather not engage in it at all.

Where are the two Miss Sproston's? If they are unfixed, It would be a most desirable situation for them; and if they would take me in as a boarder, I should be glad to be with them. – *It is possible* that I may undertake the charge myself. I shall decide in a few weeks – or – I may engage in another family, should an opportunity occur. If my brother would but write to tell me how my money matters are going on, and if from his accounts I was likely to become a serious loser, I should decide at once. I have desired him, if he is fortunate in getting all that is due to me, to place it out to interest; and, as the larger sum, the better will be the security I can obtain, I could wish you to keep the money you have received for me, until you hear from me again, by which time, I shall know what sum my brother can put out, and whether that will be wanted; if not, it can then be remitted to me.

Mr and Mrs Pedder have this morning set off for Preston, to stay a week or ten days. I shall spend the *lucid* interval in writing to a few friends; in reading; and with two families who have invited me to come frequently to see them.

When you say to anyone that I am leaving my present residence, so not say for why, if I publish my complaints, it will subject me to Mr Pedder's resentment, or to some remarks from my own acquaintances; and the less said, the better. If necessary, I shall certainly defend myself; and you would be astonished were I to describe the scenes I have witnessed here.

Remember me very affectionately to your sister, who I hope will be a comfort to you, and you to her.

Yours sincerely and affectionately,

E. Weeton.

Thomas Weeton's 'persuasive' professional services were brought to bear on Miss Weeton's agent, Mr M'Cartney, resulting in accrued back rent on her Liverpool cottage property being paid. This enabled Miss Weeton to escape 'the unhappy temper of the master of the house.' She vacated Dove's Nest early in 1811. The next seven months were spent in and around Ambleside, where she received warm hospitality in the home of William Green, the ever-industrious and prolific Lakeland artist and engraver. Mr Green, was a family man who had sole responsibility for feeding his growing brood of eventually ten children. It was in the Green's Ambleside home that Miss Weeton rediscovered the lost liberty she had once enjoyed before relocating from Liverpool.

Whilst in the Ambleside area she also included a stay at Harrowslack, with a Mr Roberts until October. Leaving Ambleside, she moved south to stay for two weeks with Mr Edmondson at Lancaster. (By that time Mrs Edmondson, the once very good loyal friend of Mrs Mary Weeton, had died). After her stay, she travelled to Liverpool, where she stayed for two weeks in order to 'settle some pecuniary affairs,' before staying for six weeks with her brother and his family at Leigh. Finally, before returning to Liverpool to stay with Miss Bessy Winkley, she called to see her Uncle and Aunt Barton at Up Holland.

As for the Pedders, they duly vacated Dove's Nest at the expiry of the lease in 1816.

Writing at a much later date (in November 1812), to Mrs Green at Ambleside, Miss Weeton said:

> Never during the whole course of my life did I spend so many happy months in succession as those I passed amongst you from the time I left Mr Pedder, to the time I quitted your lovely country altogether; it was certainly a most romantic kind of life there; but, as I knew that in all human probability, it could only last for the Summer, I determined to pursue the bent of my inclination whilst I was at liberty to do so. – Liberty! Oh, how sweet thou art! I never knew thee till I found thee on the banks of Winandermere (sic); and in leaving that noble lake, I quitted thee likewise. I have lived almost altogether for others; whilst amongst you for the last 7 months, I ventured to live for myself alone, and do not now look back upon that period with regret, except that it is for ever fled!

It was whilst staying with Miss Bessy Winkley, in Liverpool, that Miss Weeton finally got to the bottom of who was responsible for questioning her honour. That person had imaginatively made the most of the fact that she had 'gone off with a gentleman' and 'nobody knew where.' The tale had lost nothing in its telling; especially amongst those closest to her. Even worse, as a result of that embellished tale, she had discovered herself to be in the midst of what had been a subsequent and deliberate attempt to embitter her Aunt and Uncle Barton against her. She was shocked to learn that the perpetrators were none other than her brother and his wife; her cousin Latham being the principal villain of the piece. It was on a Liverpool street, during the month of May 1812, that she accidentally met her cousin:

> I met my cousin Latham one day in Liverpool, 6 or 7 weeks before I left. She looked at me, with all the assumed indifference possible. At first, I did not appear to notice it; after asking how

my aunt was, I inquired why she had never written? 'I do-n't know,' she drawled in answer. 'Don't know!' I said; 'you must have heard some reason for it; has she sent no message now?' 'N-o,' was all the answer, and she turned her head another way. 'And did you not intend to call on me to-day?' 'I know not; happen I should.' 'Happen'! I repeated, in excessive anger, 'happen! there has been some strange mischief-making among you, and I should not wonder if you as busy as any of them.'

I waited to hear no more. I was so much affected by this little incident, that I could not forbear tears, even in the street – to think of my cousin's insolence! After this, I gave up any further idea of seeking a reconciliation, and Mrs Price [future mother-in-law to Miss Bessy Winkley] said she rejoiced at it; for that I had not had half spirit enough, and that if I did not wait till they sought me, I should deserve all she was sure they would make me suffer.

Despite now having an income to keep her comfortable, Miss Weeton increasingly became ill-at-ease with her inactivity. In a letter to Miss Ann Winkley, the sister whose friendship she most valued and who had recently departed to take up the position of governess to an important Dublin family, Miss Weeton explained that she was 'on the point of engaging to instruct the children of a lady in Yorkshire.' But that would not be until the end of June 1812:

> I shall there be too much engaged to have leisure to think with regret on those who seem so willingly to forget me; and indeed I have so long lived a life of industry that I know not how to live in indolence; my conscience, too, reproaches me almost hourly for wasting my time so wickedly; and what a sad account should I give, if asked what good I had done for the last 5 years.

And finally added:

> I think I talked of visiting Isle-of-Man when you were here; I still think of doing so in May, and to remain about a month; perhaps longer if I don't go into Yorkshire.

True to Miss Weeton's industrious character and her desire for adventure, before taking up a position in July with the important Armitage family near Huddersfield, she visited the Isle-of-Man in May 1812.

NOTES:

1. Both Miss Weeton and Dorothy Wordsworth (sister of William) then living at nearby Allan Bank, were both born on Christmas Day. Miss Weeton (1776), Dorothy Wordsworth (1771). It is doubtful they ever met, yet both ladies were prolific journal writers and both adored and loved a brother.
2. Mrs Pedder's father's surname name was Robinson. The farm on which he and his elder daughter did all the work, was called Holms Farm.
3. Dorothy Wordsworth mentions Mr Benson a number of times in her Journal, and often admired the situation of Dove's Nest.
4. Samuel Taylor Coleridge (1772-1834), poet and philosopher. Having left his family with Southey at Keswick, he was then dependent on Wordsworth's charity at Allan Bank. 'The Friend' was a weekly paper, which achieved only 27 issues.
5. Dorothy Wordsworth remarked: 'I came home at the foot of our own hill under Loughrigg. They are making sad ravages in the Woods. Benson's wood is going, and the woods above the River' (*Dorothy Wordsworth's Journal, Thursday, March 4th 1802).*
6. William Green (1760-1823), water-colour painter and engraver, born Manchester, settled in Ambleside. Exhibited at the Royal Academy in the years 1797, 1798 and 1801. Also exhibited his work at Manchester and Ambleside.
7. Following a visit to Liverpool, Miss Weeton learned that her cousin Latham had been enthusiastically circulating the rumour that she had 'gone off with a gentleman in a coach;' a scandalous imputation which had lost nothing in the telling.
8. Mr Smith did not forget Miss Weeton's sage-like comments. Years later, a fugitive from her husband's cruelty, the then ex-governess found sanctuary with the Smiths.
9. Felicia Dorothea Hemans (1793-1835), poet. In one of her letters whilst staying at Dove's Nest, wrote: 'I am writing to you from an old-fashioned alcove in the little garden, round which the sweet-briar and the rose tree have completely run wild.'
10. Adam Walker (1731?-1821), author and inventor. Self educated, born at Patterdale in Westmorland, became a travelling lecturer of physics, employed at Eton and Winchester, published tracts on ventilation and notes of his lectures. He refers to Dove's Nest in his *Remarks made on a Tour from London to the Lakes of Westmoreland and Cumberland* (1792).
11. Rev Thomas Saul, M.A. Saul was the incumbent of St John's Church, Chapel Street, Lancaster, 1807; also the non-resident incumbent of St James, Whitechapel, Beacon Fell, Lancashire, 1808-13. (See also letter to Mrs Edmondson dated 4 June 1810).
12. It was customary to save on postage and to reduce the use of paper, by writing at right-angles over an already completed page.
13. Miss Weeton did not benefit from her aunt's will, although her brother Thomas was a legatee. Mrs Margaret Barton died 25 September 1813.
14. After much delay, the services of brother Thomas were brought to bear in order to persuade Mr M'Cartney to pay up.
15. No drawing, painting or engraving, of Dove's Nest, by William Green, has been traced, despite Miss Weeton having witnessed them in progress at Mr Green's studio.

16. Lord Castlereagh (1769-1822), Minister of War and Foreign Secretary.
17. Believed to refer to Princess Charlotte Augusta (1796-1817), only child of George, Prince of Wales (later George IV). Engaged to William Prince of Orange 1813; angered her father by breaking off her engagement 1814. She married another prince, Prince Leopold of Sax-Coburg-Saalfield in May 1816. Died in childbirth, 19 November 1817.
18. John Hampton (1594-1643). English statesman. In 1629 he became imprisoned for refusing to contribute to a forced loan, but his fame rests on his refusal to pay Charles I's imposed duty for 'Ship-Money'. He refused to pay the tax and finally won his case
19. 'And that great house! Mercy upon us! If it *could* be concealed, it *would* be well for all who are pained to see the pleasantest of earthly spots deformed by man. But it *cannot* be covered.' *(Dorothy Wordsworth's Journal, 8th June 1802).*
20. Refers to the son of Rev John Toothill (1760-1839), minister of Rainford Congregational Church, near St Helens: 'September 5 [1810], Mr. Abr[aham] Toothill (only son of the Rev. J. T., of Rainford, Lancashire), travelling for a respectable house in Manchester, lost his life, as supposed by accident, in one of the lakes of Westmoreland. He was a young man of serious and amiable character, having just attained the age of 21. A Bible was found in his pocket. His remains were interred at Rainford.' *(Evangelical Magazine, 1810).*
21. Mr Banning was the Postmaster of Liverpool. He speculated in small cottage buildings.
22. Thomas Weeton's income at that time was about £200 a year.

FIVE

Sojourn on the 'Isle of Refuge'

Isle-of-Man

23 May – 5 July 1812

As PLANNED, ON Saturday 23 May, 1812, Miss Weeton embarked from Liverpool for the morning sail to the Isle-of-Man. The ship made little progress and was so becalmed that by 4 o'clock the same day, passengers had the 'comfort' of being informed that the ship was then further away from the Island than when it set out. The rising tide was beginning to make the ship drift eastward, forcing the captain to drop anchor for some two or three hours. Meanwhile, weary with doing nothing, Miss Weeton read two newspapers from cover to cover, traversed the deck backwards and forwards and finally took out her flageolet. As she began to play she was soon surrounded with a crowd, making her feel distinctly uncomfortable. Her comfort was not improved when a 'rough-faced' fellow produced a cracked flute to accompany her in attempting several duets. Unfortunately, lack of comfort was to be her lot until after the ship finally arrived at Douglas harbour between nine and ten the next morning.

Two days after arriving on the island, she wrote to Bessy Winkley at Liverpool, now newly married as Mrs Price, but it was to her very close friend, Ann Winkley, now employed in Ireland, that she wrote a fascinating 10,000 words travelogue, which she began on 15 June and concluded 5 July 1812:

25 May 1812 (Douglas). *To Mrs Price:*

      The day I left you (23rd) was so calm, that after we were beyond the rock [Black-rock, Liverpool], we did not see advance 2 miles an hour. I was amused with seeing a species of what I think were star-fish, swimming about, alternately closing and expanding like a bag. They are only seen in very smooth water. Porpoises, too, here and there made their appearance, a sign, sailors say, of approaching storm. We made so little progress till after midnight, that I had not the slightest inclination to sickness, and felt so hungry that I began to be alarmed at the deplorable decrease of my sea-store; for, at 4 o'clock on Saturday afternoon, we had the comfort of being told that we were farther off the Isle than when we set out, and there was a dead calm, that the rising tide was drifting us far to the Eastward; therefore, to prevent our progress the wrong way, the captain cast anchor, where we remained for two or three hours.

Weary with doing nothing, I read over the *whole* of 2 newspapers, traversed the deck, and at last unpacked my box, and took out my flageolet; but I soon found that, like a street-fiddler, I got such a crowd about me, as made me feel quite uncomfortable. A rough-faced fellow, a journey-man saddler I suppose from what he said, produced a cracked flute; and, would you suppose it, he and I attempted several duetts (sic). Oh, how you – No! not you, for you are not much given to laughing; but oh, how some people that I know would have laughed to have seen such a contrasted pair, piping and fluting duetts! I shall have many a *solo* laugh when I think of it. I hope I shall never be taken with a sudden fit of laughter in the streets here, should the recollection rush all at once upon me; for, if I am, the people will think I am crazy; or, if I hang down my head to hide my grinning face, the most charitable construction they can put upon it will be, that I am ill of the gripes. The man behaved as civilly as it was in his power to do; but his exterior bespoke him as a blackguard of no high degree. Our fellow travellers were all as civil as they could be; but there was a want of that delicacy and gentleness of manner which attends a cultivated and refined understanding.

I don't know that I ever was in such company before; towards ten at night, one or two of them frequently requested we women would go to bed, really intending to be considerate and kind. My companion looked at me and smiled; I knew what that meant; these men never thought of leaving the cabin whilst we got into bed, and as there was but one cabin, the men and women must all herd together. I gave a hint to the captain, who likewise gave a hint to the fellows (for they were not gentlemen). When we were got into bed, they came down into the cabin, and a sweet scene of riotous mirth ensued, and void of any indelicacy, for which we were obliged, but too noisy to admit of any possibility of sleeping before two o'clock next morning. About 4, the vessel began to roll a little, and the wind rising, the ropes and sails rattling, made me feel apprehensive that we were going to have a storm. At 7, I could lie no longer, I heaved incessantly; the quantity of bile that came up, would have shocked any one to see. Ill as I was, I was thankful for it. I might well be ill whilst I was in Liverpool, with such a load upon my stomach, for I think I am not guilty of the slightest exaggeration when I say that there was above a pint of pure bile.

Between 9 & 10 on Sunday morning, we were moored in Douglas harbour; the custom-house officers were not very strict on their search, for which I was not sorry, merely because it saved me a little trouble, for I had nothing to fear. In going to bed, I had slackened my cloaths, but had not taken them off, and in a totally unlaced, inpinned state, I was obliged to crawl through the streets, to the Inn, being perfectly unable to dress myself. I wrapped my coat round me, and threw my shawl over it; my hair uncombed, uncurled, my face wan, and eyes sunken, I presented no very beautiful picture. I remained at the inn that day, and till after breakfast the next, and recruited tolerably; but oh, such a filthy Inn throughout, I never saw! The house was good, and wanted nothing but cleanliness to make it respectable; I fancy it was one of the lower orders of houses. However, it must have served me, had it been worse. I dined with the family and a few of their friends, on a fine turkey, a fowl, asparagus, and potatoes, and paid only a shilling.

I will not expect you to write to me unless you should have anything necessary to communicate; and probably I shall not write again whilst I stay. When a month has elapsed from the time I left you, you may daily expect me.

15 June – concluded 5 July 1812 (Douglas, Isle of Man). *To Miss Ann Winkley:*

It was my wish to have answered your last letter the moment I received it; for I found you had dwelt too strongly on one or two passages of mine.

Though I have *appeared* to neglect you, I have incessantly thought of you, and the unhappiness which I have caused you, my intention was, to prepare you for the evils which *might* happen; not to afflict you in reality. When I last wrote to you, it was certainly under a very unpleasant impression; my own suffering pressed heavily upon my spirits; and the gloom that overclouded me, gave a tinge to everything; I thought the excuses your sister made, when I urged her to write to you, were trivial, and I was much more hurt that I am sure I had any reason to be.

And now, my young friend, to present you with something more lively – to mingle sweets with bitters – the gay with the grave – and narrative with precept, I will give you some account of my journey here; for I am at this moment in Douglas. The week after Mr and Mrs Price had removed to Copperas Hill, I prepared for my travels; and on Saturday morning, about 10 o'clock, May 23rd I left Liverpool in the *Brilliant*. For three hours before I landed, I was extremely ill, and scarcely able to crawl out of the cabin when the vessel arrived at the pier. I went to a public house for that day; for, being Sunday, it was an awkward and improper day to inquire for lodgings; though, indeed, I did make an attempt in the afternoon, accompanied by a young married man who lodged at the house; notwithstanding I was unsuccessful, I was really rejoiced to find that the people had such a veneration for the day, as to think it improper to take in a lodger, or that I should apply.

I contented myself as well as I could, in the dirty, uncomfortable house I was in, until next morning, when I set out alone. I rambled along the streets until I found the stationer's shop, from whence the Douglas newspaper was issued, which I had seen the day before. I enquired for the lodgings he had advertised; I was directed to them; those, and several others were engaged. One house was occupied by a barber, who told me that though his rooms were taken, such a one would perhaps be vacant. As I was a total stranger to every one, an old soldier, who was shaving, offered to go with me, and, escorted by him I knocked at two doors, but they were not 'opened to me.' I did not knock at the 3rd house in vain; the door was opened, the people civil and respectable, the house spacious and convenient, and my accommodation in every respect as comfortable as I could wish. I agreed to lodge and dine with the family for 12s a week, finding everything else myself. This was all settled by 10 o'clock in the morning, that same hour which for 3 days together had been propitious for me.

I was very anxious to see Mrs Dodson, formerly Mrs W. Singleton of Wigan, with whom, when she was Miss Prescott, I had spent so many agreeable hours in Up Holland. I was no sooner, therefore settled, than faint and weakly as I still was from the violent sea sickness I had undergone, I dressed and set out to call upon Mrs Dodson. As I proceeded, I was a good deal surprised to find the streets so narrow and intricate; they are one continued zig-zag; I never saw a town so ill-built, nor altogether so shabby and dirty. The best houses, with very few exceptions, are in an almost total want of whitewash, paper, and paint; and so mingled with little, dirty huts, as to present the most opposite ideas from those of cleanliness, comfort, or symmetry. The tradesmen's signs in any town, in my opinion, present the quickest and most just idea of the general taste and degree of opulence of the inhabitants; and here, they are strikingly mean; and the combination of trades in the same person, rather singular.

But I rather mean to give you an account of *my* peregrinations, than of the Island, which you may find in print. I will go on to tell you that I was received by Mrs Dodson in as pleasing a manner as I could wish. It was a happy thing for her that Mr Prescott settled her fortune upon her and her children, or otherwise she would at this moment have been a beggar; for Mr W. Singleton's embarrassed circumstances drove him to this *Isle of refuge* for the *unfortunate* and the *unprincipled*; for it literally swarms with English vagabonds.[1] Mrs W. S's income was near £400 a year; a very comfortable support for the family; and better to be in a sort of voluntary exile here, with her husband and children, than to live in England, and her husband perhaps spending his days in a prison.

Mr W. S. has been dead 2 or 3 years, leaving his widow with 3 daughters and a son. About 12 months ago, she married a Mr Dodson, a Manchester gentleman, who had seen richer days, but who now had absolutely nothing. His manners were elegant, his conversation was intelligent; but his habits had been dissipated. *He* wanted a home, and in Mrs Singleton's house he found one; *she* was pleased with his manners, and, far removed from all her friends, felt the want of an adviser and a companion. In hopes to obtain both, she married him; exactly 3 weeks from the day they married – he died!!! His constitution had been greatly injured by former dissipation, and 2 days sickness carried him off.

Mrs Dodson's friends, and those of her first husband, were greatly displeased at so imprudent a marriage, and rejoiced at Mr D's death. It was an afflictive event for her; but she did not meet with one to soothe or console her. Her relations in England wish her to return, but she says she is settled here, and can educate her children at much less expence than elsewhere, and shall therefore remain for some years at least. She has a governess for her girls, a Miss Maddocks, to whom she gives only £12 a year! Mrs Dodson keeps only 2 women servants, no carriages, and very little company.

There are many very pretty houses in the neighbourhood of Douglas; and indeed, all over the Island. I have nearly walked round it, and think myself amply repaid for the fatigue I have undergone, by the pleasure I have experienced in viewing so romantic a country.

A promontory, called Douglas-Head, commands a fine view of the town, harbour, and some distant mountains; and when I am not inclined to take a long walk, I amuse myself with ascending here, where I can arrive in 20 minutes any time from my lodgings. For 2 or 3 days after my arrival, I took only short walks, to reconnoitre the country and the people. The want, the almost total want of wood, except a few ornamental plantations, gives the country a very bleak and naked appearance; for a day or two, I thought there had been nothing but broom hedges, which, being nearly in full flower, have a gaudy and flaring appearance. I have since observed many other kinds of fences; some are of earth and sods entirely; and it's no uncommon thing to see people walking upon the fences, which are quite broad enough, and path-worn. Walls prevail everywhere, particularly on the hills and mountains, and certainly as far from being ornamental, as a fence can be; 7d a yard is the price now usually paid to wall-builders; whether that is cheaper than making green fences, I do not know. The land is generally well cultivated; much better, I think than in the North of England. Here, is very little waste land that can be made use of; and the commons are not so extensive as in many parts of England, where the ground is similar in extent and surface. The industry becoming prevalent here, is chiefly owing to the English farmers, who have settled in the Island; and the Manks, discovered the utility of the English method of agriculture, are by degrees universally adopting it; so much corn in the Isle, that they are enabled to export a great deal, and can raise all the common necessaries of life without foreign aid.

Nothing is allowed to be imported, but for the consumption of the islanders; not for the purposes of trade, of which there is very little; of course, no merchants of any consequence. The imports, if consumed on the Island, are duty-free; which makes tea, wine, sugar, salt many other things extremely cheap. Tea, which we procure in England for 8s., is here 5s. p. lb. Strangers are frequently charged 6s.; but it is invariably the rule here to impose upon the ignorant. Wine may be had at 2s. 4d. p. bottle; 3s. is, I think the highest price; at the best hand it may be had at 24s. p. Doz^n. Brown sugar of the middle price, $6^1/_2$d. lb.; brown paper loaf 9d. Do. Rum 2s. 6d. a bottle; salt 5d. For 14 lb. Bread is quite as dear as in England; wearing apparel of all kinds dearer, except coarse woollens. Butchers meat and vegetables no cheaper; and rents of land, or houses, extremely high. No land taxes, window-money, or poor's rates are levied; which are considerations of value. The rents, on an average, may be nearly as they are in Wigan, and the country around it. To compensate for the want of poor rates, a collection is made in the churches every Sunday morning, between the sermon and concluding prayer.

Eggs are from 28 to 36 for a shilling; poultry is very cheap; fish is moderate, not cheap as might be expected, herrings excepted; the season for which will commence in about a fortnight, and continue for several months. This fishery is the principal support of the Manks;[2] and the coasts of the Island during the time is as complete a scene of bustle as can be imagined. During this period, the interior is nearly deserted by the men, and as few of the women left as can be helped. Douglas, and all the little sea-ports are in one continued state of hurry and drunkenness. I should like to have seen a specimen of all this, and the little one-masted boats going out, and returning every day, but I cannot stay so long, for I must be in Yorkshire the 2nd week in July, if possible; and I have only allowed myself a fortnight to prepare, after I return to Liverpool. I am again wandering from my own

172

little adventures, and telling you that, which I dare say you may meet with in many a publication.

The first long walk I took, was on the 28th, after my arrival. When I had been on Douglas-Head one day, I had seen some mountains at a distance, and this day I set out with the intention of ascending the highest, if it were not too far. By paying strict attention to a map which I purchased, I have had very little occasion to ask any questions respecting roads, distances, or other places. I took my guide in my hand, and wanted no other. In this, and in all my walks, I have ever been without a companion; I prefer being alone; I can then stop, go on, sit down, proceed, turn to the right or to the left, as my fancy may prompt, without restraint; and, even if it were probable I could find a *proper* companion who would with pleasure accompany me 12, 15, 20, or 30 miles a day, still, her taste would not perhaps assimilate in most respects with my own, and we should teaze each other – I, in listening to conversation which did not interest me, and, she, in attending to observation to which she was indifferent. But, as it is extremely unlikely I should find one who would take such long walks, and give way to my taste, wishes, and curiosity in every thing, I choose to go alone, in places unfrequented by those of my own species, that my thoughts, as well as my feet, may ramble without restraint; when I enter towns, and crowds, I do then like to have a companion; but when the wonders of nature alone occupy me, when my soul is filled with admiration and rapture at scenes of rural beauty, or mountainous grandeur, I never wish for company of one earthly being, save that of my brother, for whom it is in vain to sigh . . . Oh, Ann, how the thought of him makes my heart ache! Once, so affectionate, so noble! Now, so led by a malicious, envious, mischief-making! . . . but no matter.

On my way to Greeva (the name of the mountain), I passed by Kirk-Braddon, about 2 miles from Douglas; it stands at a distance from any house, and almost buried in trees. As I got a glimpse of it from the road, I thought it looked beautifully. This stands as a Church should do; retired from the haunts of business, or thoughtless levity; the remains of the departed here rest in peace, and a kind of sacred solitude reigns perpetually. I remained some time in the Church-yard after I went into it, and quitted it with sentiments of religious awe. Four miles farther,

173

and I arrived at the foot of Greeva, which projects nearly into the Peel-road. I asked a girl, who stood at the door of a little hut, if I might be permitted to pass that way? She instantly complied, and showed me through the garden, from whence I began directly to ascend the rocks, which were very steep. I might have ascended a much less difficult way, but this was nearer; and walls, and rocks, are slight impediments to me. When arrived at the top, I could see nearly round the Island: east, west, and south, the view was clear, and fine. Snafield,[3] the highest mountain in the Island, impeded the view to the north. A number of sheep and a few goats (the only ones I have seen here), were feeding around me; and an old man and young woman were gathering furze for firing, and carrying it down the mountain on their backs; the young woman was without shoes or stockings, and her feet bled very much; it grieved me to see it; often did she sit down to rest from her burthen, and the tears in her eyes evinced the pains she felt. The poor women in the Island seldom wear shoes or stockings, whilst the men seldom go without them; why there should be such apparent injustice or partiality, I know not; I see it every day. I sat some time on the top of the mountain, and saw distinctly the Scotch and Irish coasts.

When I descended the mountain, the same girl who had so civily let me pass through her garden, even taking down some stones that I might the more easily get over the wall at the back, met me as I returned, and said she was glad to see me again, for she thought I was lost, and had climbed ever so high up the rocks to find me, but could see nothing of me; and expressed some surprise when I told her I had been to the summit of the hill. It is no very common thing, I suppose, to see strangers go up the mountains, particularly a decently dressed female, alone.

I returned home, highly pleased with my walk, which was about 13 miles; the few people I had met with, either took no notice of me, or spoke civilly; which gave me more confidence, as I confess my first walks were not without considerable apprehensions, lest I should meet with insult, as I was so totally unaccompanied; but to me, the country people, as well as others, have been altogether as civil as I could wish, sometimes entering into conversation, which I generally encouraged, that I might gain all the information I could. In return for my questions respecting the roads, gentlemen's houses, &c., I was sure to be questioned in turn. I never met with a more inquisitive, prying set of people in my life! Where did I come from? How long had I been in the Island? When did I mean to return? Where was I going? Were questions asked by every one. Sometimes I answered, and sometimes civilly evaded their inquiries; for, though I thought their curiosity impertinent, I saw they meant not to be rude; and as they were ignorant that they were guilty of any impropriety, I should have been wrong to have answered them with ill-humour. Many of them spoke to me in Manks, and when they found that I did not understand them, would then address me in English; few of them, indeed, none, that do not understand English (which I think is principally, If not spoken in the Manks towns; but in the hamlets, and scattered houses, the native language is most prevalent). The natives adhere with great tenacity to their original language, and will speak nothing else if they can help it, frequently refusing to answer strangers in any other. I have met with some instances of this, and felt somewhat chagrined at their rudeness and stupidity, when I have wished for a little information. The schools that are established all over the Island, teach only English; and that, only, is spoken in them, so that probably in 20 or 30 years, the Manks language will be almost obsolete. There is a school in Douglas on the Lancastrian plan,[4] lately established; I was as much surprised, as pleased, to see so good a building erected for the purpose, for there is scarcely another instance of so much public spirit.

My next long walk was on the 30th to Kirk-Santon, on the road to Castletown; it was rather an uninteresting road, and served only to give me a farther idea of the nature of that part of the country, which, as far as I went, is the least fertile of any. As I seldom go directly on without swerving occasionally from the road, to ascend some eminence for a better view, my walks are often unnecessarily, though pleasingly, lengthened; and this, which was only in a direct road, going and returning, 12 miles, I stretched into 16.

Encouraged by the little fatigue I felt after these walks, I meditated others of greater lengths; and, on June 1st, going up to Douglas-Head to take a view of the country, I concluded upon going to Laxey, 8 miles distant, the road to which I could plainly see. I accordingly set out after dinner; some scenes along the road are very pretty for the first 4 miles. Kirk Conchan and the village

175

near it have a rural romantic effect at this season of the year; some boys were, or more correctly, ringing a bell for a funeral, when I passed; as few of the churches have any steeple, the bell is hung just above the roof, and the rope hangs outside the wall into the church-yard. When I first heard the odd manner in which this bell was jingled, and saw the children in the church yard from between the trees, I really thought they were making use of the church-bell, instead of a frying pan, to ring a swarm of bees into a hive; for it had exactly that kind of sound, and had I not asked a boy who sat on the road-side, should have thought so to this moment. How careful should travellers be of making conjectures, and of taking for reality, what only appears to be very probable.

I walked on, laughing heartily at the idea; the country for the remaining 4 miles, was very uninteresting, for want of wood; but as a compensation, I was overtaken by a *most agreeable fellow pedestrian* . . . an old Irishman, with a sack on his back! He made several attempts to converse with me, which I rather shyly answered at first, wishing to be rid of him; but when I perceived that there was not another human being anywhere in sight, I began to examine him with more attention. He was old, and rather infirm, and I was confident I could overpower him, should he attempt to rob me; at any rate, I can run five times as fast, thought I. Thus *wisely* reflecting, I became *amazingly* courageous, and began to talk with him. He told me he had walked that day from Ramsey to Douglas (16 miles) and was then returning! A long way, Ann, for an old man between 60 and 70, was it not? He then asked me what o'clock it was? I did not quite like this question, as it appeared as if he wanted to know whether I had a watch. I said I did not know; perhaps it was 4 o'clock. Then the usual questions of, where did I come from, &c? succeeded. If I would tell him, he said, where I lived in Douglas, he would call and see me. I could have laughed at this, for I saw the drift of it; he had, in a sly kind of way, been wanting to beg of me. As there was no shaking him off, let me stop, or walk at what pace I would, I gave him to understand I had no money. Then, like a true Irishman, he would call to see me, for the respect he had for such a nice young woman. I *seemed* to be much pleased, but I was leaving Douglas soon . . . the cunning old fellow. Accidentally, I recollected that I had $2^1/_2$d., and giving it to him for a glass of ale at Laxey, made a decided stop, sitting down by the road side that I might get rid of him. He had not the impudence to sit down too; but, as he went, often stopped and turned. I watched him quite out of sight before I proceeded.

Laxey is a beautiful little vale, and scattered village; the houses are poor, but in fine weather, they have altogether a romantic, picturesque appearance. The vale is long, and narrow; high hills rising steeply on each side, and terminated at the upper extremity by Snafield, the highest mountain in the Island. Cottages, huts, gardens, orchards, and little patches of corn and meadow-land, ornament the view for 2 or 3 miles in length, whilst in front, the bay, surrounded with 30 or 40 fishermen's boats, gives an animated finish to the picture. I walked half a mile up the vale, and returned, highly gratified. I had scarcely quitted Laxey, when the old Irishman again made his appearance out of a hut by the road side, to repeat his thanks for the money I had given him. Certainly, I must never be quit of this fellow! thought I; however, he did not follow me.

About half way home, I met a decent-looking woman, who, civilly bidding me 'good-even,' encouraged me to ask a few questions respecting the different places within view. She was a pedestrian traveller, pedlar, and fortune-teller, and had a good deal of sly drollery. She offered to tell me my fortune. I laughed, and told her I dared not venture; for she could only tell me that I must die a miserable old maid. She would *fain* have persuaded me to the contrary, but could not succeed. We cordially bid each other good-bye, and parted. Had we both been walking the same way, I might have drawn from her many an entertaining anecdote. I have since wished I had suffered her to exert her talent in prediction; the future recollection of such an adventure would have entertained me so much – but alas! I cast the *silver* opportunity away, and – if I choose it, may live in sorrow that I did so all my days. Foolish creature that I was! when the *hope* of a husband, and a fine coach, might have cheered me even to my last moments, thus ridiculously to have lost all chance of the wretches' last resource! Goosecap! Noodle! Ninny hammer! No name too bad for me!

I did not again take any long walk till the 5th of June, the intervening time being taken up in short rambles of 3, 4, or 5 miles around Douglas; and in dining and drinking tea with Mrs

Dodson, who has taken a great deal of notice of me indeed. I had seen little of her since her first marriage; previous to that time, we saw each other almost daily for several years. The sight of each other now, bring again for recollection 'the days that are gone,' and we have many a long conversation. Mrs D. Is quite the gentle-woman; yet, there is something in her manner most strikingly peculiar; in my opinion, she will retain her life longer than her senses, although she is at present as perfectly clear in idea as ever she was. She has vanity to a most astonishing degree, and it would scarcely be possible to flatter her too grossly; but as I really am partial to her, and value her health of mind more than her favour, I am particularly cautious not to feed a vanity that strongly wants a check; she is almost as often guilty of praising herself as is Mrs Edwards.[5] It shewed an extreme weakness, which requires many a valuable trait besides to palliate. She has invited me to spend some weeks with her, next summer but one, if all be well; and urges me often to fix near her in Douglas; nay, has even offered me to live with her; and as she knows how tenacious I am in receiving obligations, has proposed such moderate terms for board as she knows I could easily comply with.

This last offer must be a profound secret, my dear Ann; for, as I am engaged to Mr Armitage, I must fulfil it. Should it so happen that I cannot stay in Yorkshire, I am to inform Mrs D., and then, if convenient to them both, come and stay with her. Such an offer has filled me with sentiments of the warmest gratitude; the more unkind my brother's family is, the greater friendship do I meet with from others. Mrs D. one day said that I was a dangerous character to be near Mrs Weeton; for that my virtues and my talents were so much superior, that my brother would continually be drawing comparisons to her disadvantage. In transcribing this high compliment, my dear Ann, I am guilty of the vanity of which I accuse others. I am weak as the weakest, and have not even the sense to hide it! Mrs D. meant it kindly, and to reconcile me to the estrangement under which I now suffer.

You will scarcely credit me when I tell you that on the 5th of June, I walked 35 miles. I left home at half past nine, with an intention to go to Castletown, and as much farther as I could walk. So as to get well home, I put my map, memorandum book, 3 boiled eggs, and a crust of bread into a work-bag; and, thus prepared, sallied forth. I met with nothing worth observation until I arrived near Castletown, which I think is by much the prettiest town on the Island. I walked slowly through it, passing by the castle, an ancient-looking building; a few soldiers were scattered in groups here and there, and gave the place a rather martial appearance. The streets are wide, and more cleanly that either of the other three principal towns; and the good houses that are in it, are seen to more advantage than they are in Douglas, Ramsay, or Peel. I walked 2 or 3 miles beyond Castletown, to a rising ground that commanded an extensive view; and, springing upon a high copse by the road side, where I seated myself, I had the double pleasure of satisfying my appetite, and feasting my eyes. Then, retracing a part of the road, I turned towards Peel, thinking I would only go a little way, just to have a more extended view. I saw an old woman on the road behind me, knitting; I walked slowly, that she might overtake me, for I wanted to have a little chat with her, and to ask her a few questions respecting the country. She was very communicative, and we went sociably on till we arrived at some cottages, where she stopped and bid me a 'good day.' I have ever found women, when I, as a stranger addressed to them, civil, humane, and hospitable, both here and in the north of England, (I have travelled no where else); but of men, I cannot say so; frequently, when I, or other females, have passed them, have I seen their sneers, or heard their rude remarks. Mungo Park[6] makes some observation in his travels, that, from men he frequently met with unkindness, but from women, never; *they* protected, nursed, or fed him, whenever he wanted assistance; whilst from men his life was frequently endangered.

I will go a little further, and a little further, just to that pretty house, or to the top of that high road,' I frequently repeated to myself, until I had had got full 5 miles beyond Castletown. To return, or go through Peel, would be equally 15 or 16 miles. I stood hesitating for some time what to do. I looked at my watch, and found that it was half past 4 o'clock! I confess I was a little alarmed, but there was no time for delay, I turned towards Peel, over a mountain road the old woman had shewn me; preferring that to the high-road, because it was in fact a much *lower* one; and I wanted scenery and prospect, not caring for the additional fatigue. Often and often, as I went on, did I turn to feast my eyes on the beauties spread out at my feet. The view was serenely clear; England, Ireland, Scotland, and Wales were all perfectly distinct; some Irish mountains appeared so near, I fancied I could row myself to them in an open boat; they were of a deep purple, tinged with the declining sun; and did look most beautifully! I could distinctly mark the mountains in Cumberland and Westmoreland; Skiddaw, Saddleback, Helvellyn, Coniston, and several others. I felt a pleasure in looking at them, for *there* had *my* feet trodden, and some of my happiest days been spent! To stand as I did, upon an island, and in one half hour see three kingdoms and a principality, is no common view.

Numbers of men were on the mountains as I passed, cutting turf; many of them, when they saw me, ceased working, and stood to gaze; others sat down. I did not feel quite comfortable. Should they insult me, I thought, I have only my own temerity to blame. However, they did not utter a single word. A lonely female, dressed as I was, I dare say they never saw such in such a place; for I had on a small slouch straw hat, a grey stuff jacket, and a petticoat; a white net bag in one hand, and a parasol in the other; and in their eyes, I dare say I made rather a singular figure. I got into Peel at 6 o'clock, having in my way down the mountains, and along the vales, seen many a lovely little cultivated patch of earth, and romantic lonely little hut on the sides of the hills, the streamlets running wildly at the bottom, over their rocky beds. There is a simple grandeur and beauty in such scenes that infuses a greater portion of enthusiasm within me than I can express. I admire! I wonder! I adore! Oh Ann! If you knew the pleasure I feel in running wild among such scenery, you would not wonder at my temerity, or at my undergoing so much fatigue to obtain the gratification.

The ruins of an ancient castle at Peel are worth seeing; and the view of them from the pier-head, and of the harbour, vessels, and town, are very fine. The town is, of itself, insignificant, and poor; it looks best at a distance. When I was on the pier-head at Peel, I had walked 25 miles, and had still 10 to go. The Tynwald mount, from whence all the Manx laws are promulgated, is about 4 miles from Peel, near to the road I had to go; it is only a small, circular mound of earth, with 3 rows of earthen steps, and derives all its consequence from the above circumstance.

I now became rather footsore, and for the remaining 6 miles, was more anxious to get home than to survey the beauties a setting sun displayed. I arrived there at half past 9, having been just 12 hours away. If you can get a map, you will see that I made quite a circuit of the southern part of the Island; a tolerable journey, even for a horse.

I was so tired, I could hardly undress myself for bed, where I immediately went on getting into the house. Mrs Allen (my landlady) laughed heartily at me. 'Now really,' said she, 'if anybody had obliged you to go such a journey, you would have thought it the greatest hardship that ever was. Lord help you! I see you are almost killed; why, you'll never be able to get up tomorrow.' I joined her in the laugh, and begged she would send me up some tea, for I had not tasted since 2 o'clock. I was obliged to lie down between each cup, and almost between each mouthful of bread & butter.

Next day, I was well enough, only a little stiff and footsore. I rested that and the succeeding one, and on Monday, the 8th., set forward on another expedition. I had been told that the northern part of the Island was much more beautiful than the southern. I mentioned my wish of seeing it, and my intention of taking lodgings at Ramsay for a week, to Mrs Dodson, who advised my going to Mrs St. George's, of West-Kella, in preference. Miss Maddocks gave me a letter of introduction to her mother, and I went, and staid there till Friday the 12th. In going, I went by St. John's, Kirk Michael, Bishop's-Court, and Balaff, near 22 miles; the mountain road is only about 16. The second 8 miles of the way led along a deep vale, which was very pretty, though the view was confined. I have observed, that bare as the Island is of wood, wherever there is a cluster of huts, there is always a plantation of trees amongst them, so that they appear almost embosomed in trees. I several times sat down by the road side, to note in my memorandum book any observation or idea which I thought would be worth transcribing to you; for I had the road to myself nearly all the way.

To give you a satisfactory account of Mr & Mrs St. George, would be to write a little history. Mrs St. George is a most unfortunate, imprudent woman! She was educated in a convent in France; and in England, married a man in Shropshire, by whom she had 9 children. Her friends were so displeased at her marrying a protestant, that, until her husband's death, they would never notice her; then, being in indigent circumstances, a wealthy uncle became a friend.

Some inconsistencies of conduct on her part, displeased him a second time; and, becoming attached to a Mr St. George, he and she, with all or most of her children, came over to this Island, where, after some time, they were married. Mr St. George boasted of himself as a man of a great family, and allied to nobility; a gentleman really of that family, happening to be in Douglas, and hearing of this, investigated the matter, and he was proved to be a complete imposter! It is said he has been a candle-snuffer at the Dublin theatre, and afterwards enlisted as a common soldier; that he deserted, and fled hither, not daring to return any more. His real name is Rickey, but, as he married under an assumed one, Mrs St. George is living with a man – not her husband – not worth a halfpenny – not possessed of either virtue or talents – and, too idle to earn a livelihood!!! Her eldest daughter is governess to Mrs Dodson's children; 3 or 4 boys are in England; and 4 girls are with her at West-Kella. She keeps a school, but everything wears the appearance of distress. What will become of her, I cannot tell. I fear she is wavering and unsteady; and her attachment to an idle fellow, will be the ruin of the whole family. Mr St. George is younger than his wife; I dare say 10 years; and in my opinion, only stays with her so long as she can keep him. She has an annuity of £50, which she wants to dispose of for her life. I hope she may not succeed in selling it, for, if she should, I fear he will get hold of the money, and disappear. If she is wise enough to keep her family from starving.

West-Kella as a pretty-looking farm house, with a good garden and orchard. The day after I got there, I took a very short walk, being too stiff and foot-sore to take a long one. From Primrose Hill, I had a very pleasing view; the country behind, and to the right and left, was more mountainous; in front, spacious; the sea spreading far and wide. The mornings I spent, whilst I staid, in reading a manuscript translation from the French, by Mrs St. G., and of which she wanted my opinion, as she had some thoughts of publishing it. It is an account of the suffering of the Princess Royale of France, whilst in prison, after the decapitation of her parents; and entitled 'Irma,' is represented as a Persian tale. Mrs St. George is really a pleasing, well-informed woman; but as she has now placed herself, it is dangerous to speculate; and in publishing this work, it would be a great risk. The expense of printing an edition will cost £200, she says; for the London

182

booksellers will not run the risk themselves, and it is very uncertain that it will sell; still, she seems bent on trying it I dared not give her any encouragement; the risk is too great; yet the work has considerable merit. It is rather too literal a translation, which, in a work in the Persian style of writing, is a great fault; in Mrs St. George's, there is great want of amplification and embellishment to make it sufficiently Eastern.

On the 19th., I walked, after dinner, to Ramsay, $4^1/_2$ miles from W.Kella; and as I had a great wish to see where Mrs Askins (Miss Chorley's friend) lived, I inquired for her cottage, and found it; it was beyond Ramsay from W.Kella, near a mile. I went to within 50 yards of it, but did not call upon Mrs A., though when I saw her in Liverpool last October, she desired I would, if ever I came to the Island; and even talked of introducing me to the Bishop's family. Still, I felt diffident; I had a great desire to see her, yet could not assume resolution to knock at her door. I lingered about the house some time; then, sitting down upon a high bank, just hid from view, I surveyed with delight the fine bay of Ramsey, still thinking of Mrs A., and peeping over the bank every now and then, to catch another glimpse of her cottage. She is a most elegant woman, tall, handsome, dignified, affable. She is not now young, having children grown up. I got home at 8 o'clock in the evening, after walking 13 miles.

The next afternoon, I ascended a mountain not far distant; the view from it was new, and pleasing. After tea, Mr & Mrs St. George went with me again to the same mountain, to shew me a famous well on the top, which they had heard of, but had never seen. A countryman, of whom they were asking where to find it, offered to go with us; and, as we laboured up the mountain side, told us many a superstitious, wonderful tale. The well which we went to see, is shallow, and merely remarkable for curing violent diseases of the eyes; it was first discovered, our guide told us, by a blind man, many, many years ago; perhaps 2 or 300; who dreamed that on such a mountain in the Isle of Man, was a well, where, if he would wash, he should recover his sight. He left his dwelling place (I think in Ireland), came, and saw.

The following afternoon, I left West-Kella, for Douglas, accompanied by Mr & Mrs St. George. We walked over the mountains. Mrs St. George entertained me with many an anecdote of what she had seen in France, in England, and knew of the families in this Island. As to Mr St. George, he is a surely nonentity; handsome, but far from well-bred. I stopped, and took tea with them at a Mr Woods, 3 miles from Douglas; after tea, Mrs St. George came on and slept with me, as she had to breakfast at a friend's house in Douglas next morning, from whence she went back to Mr Wood's to stay a few days.

The very long walk I had taken on the 5th. and the repeated ones just after, with so little intermission, caused blisters on my feet, and prevented them healing; and after I returned from W.Kella, I was obliged to rest a few days, amusing myself with short walks, writing, and visiting Mrs Dodson, where, for the last 3 weeks I have spent almost half my time; she is extremely kind to me, and urges me to spend more time with her than is altogether convenient, as I wished to have seen a few places yet, that my frequent visits to her have prevented.

To find my society so much courted, is highly grateful to me; particularly after being treated at Leigh and at Holland as if I were a creature deserving every punishment that contempt and violence could inflict; and at best forgotten, than thought of. Were I to tell you, my dear Ann, how flatteringly I am treated, how highly complimented, by Mrs D. And her acquaintances; how chearful, agreeable, intelligent, or humorous they profess to think me; you would justly condemn my excess of vanity. It was always my wish to please; but till I left Holland, I never so easily succeeded as I appear to have done since. Your sister sometimes says that never poor creature was so harassingly situated as I was, or a lot cast amongst such a strange-tempered set of mortals; for my Aunt Barton, Mrs Braithwaite, Mrs Weeton, and Miss Chorley, are all notoriously ill-tempered, proud, and over-bearing. Since I left Up Holland, I have seen more of the world, care for it less, know better how to please, and am ten times more happy.

I set out on the 16th. with a design of walking to the top of Snafield, if the unusual coldness of the day, and lowering aspect of the sky, would permit. I often hesitated as I went – looked around me – meditated to return; yet still my feet carried me onward. A sort of irresistible impulse impelled me; perhaps, thought I, to my destruction, for mists are floating thickly round; but as the time of my departure is very near, I may not have another day to spare. When I had got about 6 miles from Douglas, I was in the midst of a dreary moor, terminated by mountains, over which the sun strongly gleamed every now and then. My heart ached at the sight of so barren a prospect, and with uncertainty whether to proceed; but curiosity surmounted caution, and I went on, apparently the only human being within view. The passing clouds flew over swiftly, and light and darkness alternatively covered the face of nature. There was a wildness in the scene and the state of the air that impressed an idea of woe and desolation. The wind blew furiously, whistling sharply amongst the furze, sometimes moaning amongst the rocks like the voice of a human in distress. It was a day to impress gloom, awe, and dread, and I felt as if I were the miserable creature doomed to experience it, with only now and then a bright ray of hope. I felt a sort of melancholy pleasure in the contemplation, as I walked on over a mountain road. Snafield, at length, reared his lofty head, and when I was about a mile from his summit, the road terminated, and I had to walk over peat-bog and swamp, wet and slippery to a degree. When I had passed over this, I was soon at the top; the wind was here a complete tempest, roaring most loudly; my slender figure could not bear up against it. I attempted to walk over a heap of stone piled on the highest point, but was blown down instantly. Determined that the wind should not entirely conquer me, I crept over on my hands and knees, though with great difficulty, and then added my mite to the heap, by placing a stone on the top, the wind urging me forward so impetuously, that I was nearly precipitated down the side, which was extremely steep; with difficulty I faced about, and returned to the heap of stones. I stood for a few minutes to view the prospect; the sea was in view all round, but no land beyond.

The surrounding country had a mistiness upon it, that obscured its beauty though it did not hide its features. I looked up and saw a large black cloud hang over me, one end of which I could almost touch! Terrified lest I should be enveloped in fog, I ran down with the utmost speed, my senses and my breath almost battered out of me with the wind, and my fright not at all contributing to restore them. Nearly at the bottom, I saw the skeleton of a sheep. And I too, may die here, thought I, if I cannot get away before the cloud settles; for it is cold enough to starve me totally, and I am so far from any human habitation, that I shall soon be lost. And, thinking how uncomfortable that it would be to lie dead in such a place, unburied, my cloaths battered off my body by the winds, my flesh pecked off by sea gulls, and my naked bones bleached by the weather till they were as white as those of the sheep, I heaved a sigh! . . . when, such is the mutability of my disposition, I burst out into a loud laugh at the charming picture my imagination had drawn. For some paces, I had been so busied with it, I had forgot the cloud, the mist, and my own danger; but now, looking up, I saw it had all passed away. Other clouds were fast approaching, and some of them might settle, so I walked homewards, and arrived safely, feeling as little fatigue after a walk of 20 miles, as if I had scarcely walked four.

On the 19th., I had sat at home all morning, and part of the afternoon, reading, and writing to you, when, at 4 o'clock, I heard the *Friends* would sail that evening at 7. The summons was sudden, as I did not expect it to sail till the 20th. However, I took a hasty leave of Mrs Dodson and Mrs Singleton's, and prepared as fast as I could for my exit. I sent to the washerwomen for cloaths she ought to have sent home the day before; and the stupid woman would not let me have them till she had finished ironing them! Four times did I send without effect, and the distance was almost half a mile. The vessel, I heard, was moving from the pier! You may suppose what a trepidation I was in; but, as expressions of anger or vexation could be of no service, I quietly sat myself down, and at least to be patient. At last, the cloaths were brought and, hastily locking them into my box, I hurried down to the pier. The vessel was off!!

I wanted to hire a boat; the men said they would not go for less than 5s. 'Very well then,' I answered, 'I shall not go,' and was returning, when they said they would take me for 2s. I got into the boat; the sea rolled awfully, and the *Friends* alternatively mounted, and then sunk, almost out of sight, sailing at a furious rate. I found it would be impossible to reach it; the boat I was in could never live in such a sea, so I ordered the men to turn about, and I again landed in Douglas. I was convinced the men must know they could not reach the vessel when they took me into the boat, and I would therefore only give them 1s., with which they were obliged to be contented. They made the attempt, merely by way of getting something for a drink, but were almost as much disappointed as myself.

186

June 21st.

I am now, my dear Ann, closing my adventures here, as I have taken a place in the *Duchess*, which sails tonight (Sunday), so I have only been detained 2 days.

I am much pleased with my visit to the Island; it will afford me a fund of entertaining reflection in many a lonely hour, and a subject for conversation in society. The renewal of my acquaintance with Mrs Dodson has been highly gratifying, and in every point of view I rejoice that I came. I have received a great deal of pleasure, and have not bought it dearly. £7 will include every expence of my journey, travelling, lodging, eating, and servants.

I shall not soon again, perhaps, have an opportunity of rambling in a country rich and romantic; and I shall feel a degree of regret at taking a final leave of this beautiful Isle; for, most likely I shall not come again. I shall often think of the times when I sat on the rocks at Douglas-Head, the air calm and clear, the mountains, vales, scattered huts, farm houses, gentlemen's country seats, spread wide and far; on one hand the town encircling the bay; on the other, the sea spread out to a great distance beneath my feet, the waves dashing unceasingly against the rocks, and bounded far, almost as the eye could see, by English mountains – many a yawning chasm in the rocks, the sea-gulls hovering over them, and the fishing boats rocking on the water – altogether form a noble view. The hours I have spent here, my thoughts expanded with the prospect; and, free and unrestrained as the air I breathed, I was happy as mortal could be.

Were there any lakes here, this Island would be a paradise, but the streams descend so rapidly from the mountains, all the way to the sea, that they cannot form any, nor any rivers of consequence; many a noisy little rivulet runs down the glens; and many a little thatched hut is scattered along the banks, which, though they look beautifully romantic just now, must be wretched habitations in winter; for, being built with uncemented stone, the wind and rain must beat through a thousand crevices. The poor natives have one advantage here; the proximity of the sea air, whilst it renders the summers more cool, makes the winters less severe, the snow melting soon after it falls; and the frost is of shorter duration, and less intensity, than in most parts of England. They shelter themselves from the storms, by building most of their huts just under the mountains; which are, many of them, cultivated to their summits. The people can have as much turf[7] as they please, for the labour of getting it; which is a great blessing where coals are so dear. An attempt is now making, for the first time, to procure coals near Peel, a seam having lately been discovered there; it is yet uncertain whether it is sufficient to afford the proprietors any hope of success.

The laws are very mild here, and seldom enforced in capital offences; even murder goes unpunished!! To the credit of the people, it is seldom committed; but 4 or 5 instances within 10 or 15 years, of which there were sufficient proof, were unnoticed by the laws. Yesterday, as a very uncommon thing, two women were publicly whipped in the market for theft; petty thefts are very frequent; house-breaking seldom, or never heard of, or highway robbery. Frauds and imposition of all kinds are practised to a great extent by the majority of the people and litigious lawsuits are perpetually carrying on, in which the unwary stranger suffers most severely; for the knavish indeed must that foreigner be, who can outwit a Manksman; yet the English, or Irish, have only to thank themselves for it; for, much to their discredit, the Manks have only been their pupils, and have paid dearly for their learning. A few, and but a few, 'retain their integrity to the last.' Happy are they, for they will meet with a joyful reward.

Liverpool: July 5th:

My rambles are now, my dear Ann, completed for the present; and my rambling account of them. If they afford you entertainment, I shall be delighted; for, in proportion as I contribute to the innocent enjoyment of others, so do I feel happy.

My walks during my residence in the Island, have been many and long. I have set down in a concise journal the number of miles I walked whilst in it, rather setting down too little than too much; and I find they amount to at least 203.

You will have received your sister's letter before you receive this; we are afraid to give you the expence of postage, and therefore wait, to send our letters by private hand to Dublin. I have been quite anxious that your sister should send her letter, even by post, rather than delay it any longer, as it is long since you heard from her; at last she has sent it, and my dear girl's heart will, in a day or two from the present moment, be relieved from a little load of anxiety, which I fear has possessed it some time.

I am leaving Liverpool on Friday next (July 19th), and have, ever since my return, been extremely busy. After I am settled in my new habitation, I shall give your sister my address; and as soon as she informs you, I hope you will write to me.

Miss Weeton duly arrived back in Liverpool on 22 June, only to learn of the sudden death the previous day, of her old friend, Rev John Braithwaite, of The Priory, Up Holland. At which news she despatched a short note to his bereaved daughter, Charlotte, before completing her letter to Ann Winkley, in Ireland.

Five days later she set off eastwards over the Pennines – to take up a position as governess once again.

NOTES:

1. William Stout (1665-1752), social historian, said of the Isle-of-Man: "Many goe there to dwell who are reduced to strates here by extravlgance here or other misfortunes, who are safe there from any prosecution of the laws of England for any debts contracted here, or other misdemeaneures committed in England of Ireland."
2. 'Life to man, and death to fish' was once a common Manx proverb.
3. Snaefell.
4. Joseph Lancaster (1778-1838) instituted a scheme of monitorial supervision in schools. By Miss Weeton referring to the school on the 'Lancastrian' plan indicates her interest in popular education.
5. The sister of Mrs Price, of whom Miss Weeton had little good to say.
6. Mungo Park, a Scottish country doctor, left England for Senegambia on the trade ship *Endeavour*, to arrive at the Africa coast on 4th June 1795. His expedition lasted for two years. He published an account of his mission: *Travels into the Interior Districts of Africa* (1799).
7. Peat-turf – attempts to bring coal to the island had proved far too expensive.

SIX

Spare the rod and spoil the child

Honley, near Huddersfield

July 1812 – June 1814

In 1812 Miss Weeton was aged 36 and in her prime. From the age of seven she had lived for 24 years in the rural atmosphere of village life in Up Holland before spending almost 18 months in the busy sea-port of Liverpool. The hustle and bustle of Liverpool, together with her subsequent 14 months employment as governess to both the daughter and the young, but illiterate second wife of moody Edward Pedder at Dove's Nest, Ambleside, Westmorland, greatly improved Miss Weeton's self-confidence.

When the back rent that had accrued on her cottage property in Liverpool had been paid, she was able to leave the Pedder household without first seeking another position. By May 1812, with sufficient rent income to keep herself comfortable, she became increasingly ill-at-ease with inactivity and visited the Isle of Man before taking up a further position as a governess east of The Pennines. While on the island, she had combined an exhilarating six weeks of walking and climbing with visiting acquaintances. Suitably refreshed, Miss Weeton was ready and eager to take on the new challenge awaiting her at High Royd, Honley, near Huddersfield.

The village of Honley had a population of 2,529 souls together with so many donkeys employed by the weavers to transport cloth, that it was commonly acknowledged that the village contained more donkeys than people.

One of the oldest families in the district, the Armitages, had lived in the area since the 14th century. In addition to occupying the usual public offices, the Armitages had become prosperous as 'clothiers' and also through 'coal-getting.' The family's good fortunes had culminated with the famous Justice Armitage. George Armitage ("Th' Justice"), had been born at High Royd in 1738, and had meted out justice during very difficult and dangerous times.

By the summer of 1812, the districts around Huddersfield were still suffering the destructive effects of Luddite activities; the Armitage family had not escaped its violent repercussions. Mr George Armitage had recently vacated High Royd in favour of his eldest son, Joseph Armitage, J.P., D.L., Deputy Lieutenant of the West Riding. It was Joseph who would become Miss Weeton's new employer.

Indifferent to the Luddite disturbances that had been taking place throughout Lancashire, Cheshire and Yorkshire since the early part of 1812, Miss Weeton left Liverpool on 10 July 1812, travelling by stagecoach via Manchester to Huddersfield. After a short time of adjustment, her first letter was addressed to Bessy Price.

At that time it appears the newly-appointed governess was at a loss for correspondents. To give Bessy the opportunity to pay postage on a 'double sheet' of paper, would be a way of testing her friendship.

(Undated) July 1812 (High Royd). *To Bessy Price:*

I had a very pleasant ride to Manchester the day I left you, for I soon got the seat by the coachman, who was very communicative, and described every object or place worth notice. After dinner at Manchester, I took a walk; chance led me to the old Church, and through the College-yard; from thence I walked down a road which led to a large building. I went up to it, and found it was a Lying-in Hospital. 'It won't do for me to seen here,' thought I, and I turned away. Presently I saw a road which I imagined would take me back another way into the town. I went up it, I was stopped by a wall, which totally prevented any further progress; and, looking up at an inscription, I found I was at the back door of the aforesaid Hospital! I was both diverted and vexed at the accident. 'Chance! Thou hast too much to do here,' said I, 'thou needest not have brought me, for I have nothing to give thee.'

If any person who had a slight acquaintance with me had been passing by just then, and seen me walk up to both doors, they would certainly have thought I intended to gain admittance, and might so have reported it to some persons elsewhere – at Leigh for instance, at Wigan, or Holland.

The next morning was wet, and I was obliged to travel inside the coach, in consequence of which I was very sickly all the way, and for two or three days after I got here, was very unwell indeed, owing to the fatigue and sickness. Had I walked all the way in two days, I should not have been so ill; want of air affects me materially.

High-royd is a country house, four miles from Huddersfield; it stands on very high ground, and will be much exposed to the storms and cold of Winter; but, as Mr Armitage has plenty of coals on his own estate, only a few hundred yards off, we shall have fire enough; and I rejoice exceedingly thereat.

He and his wife are young people, not 30 yet, I dare say, either of them. Mr A. is engaged in the woollen trade, has a handsome fortune of his own, and had another with his wife, though their parents are all living; at whose death, I suppose, they will have considerably more. They have no carriage, no in-door man-servant; there are four women servants. They kept a man till lately, but as Mr Armitage's house at Lockwood was one of the first that was attacked by the Luddites a few months ago, he has not ventured since to keep a man in his house, as many gentlemen have been betrayed by their servants, who have been discovered to be of the Luddite party. Mr A. has but lately come to this house; he had only just got well settled in it, when I arrived. His father had long wanted him to come to it, but his wife and he objected to so very retired a situation. However, the affair at Lockwood (3 miles distant), and the threats of his father to leave the estate out of the family if he did not come to it now, induced him to comply; the house and lands, all together are a very pretty present from the old gentleman; but the situation is too retired for a young man who has any relish for society. There has been a good deal of company since I came; but, though I dine or drink tea with them, I am obliged to leave the room so immediately after I have swallowed it, that I may truly be said to see little of them.

My time is totally taken up with the children; from 7 o'clock in the morning, till half past 7, or 8 at night. I cannot lie any longer than 6 o'clock in a morning; and, if I have anything to do for myself, in sewing, writing, &c., I must rise sooner. At 7, I go into the nursery, to hear the children their prayers, and remain with them till after they have breakfasted, when I go out with them whilst they play; and am often so cold, that I join in their sports, to warm myself. About half past 8, I breakfast with Mr & Mrs Armitage, and then return again to the children till 9, when we go into the school-room till 12. We then bustle on our bonnets, &c., for play, or a short walk. At One, we bustle them off again, to dress for dinner, to which we sit down at a quarter past; the children always dine with their parents. By the time dinner is well over, it is 2 o'clock, when we go into school, and remain till 5. Whilst I am at tea in the parlour, the children eat their suppers in the nursery. I then go to them, and remain with them till 7, either walking out of doors, or playing within, as the weather may permit. I then hear their prayers, and see them washed; at half past 7, they are generally in bed.

Mrs Armitage conducts her house in so excellent a manner, that we are as punctual as the clock. I never have to wait of any one; and I take care that no one shall have to wait of me. It is the same with all in the house; breakfast, dinner, tea, or supper, are always within five minutes of the appointed time. The only thing I feel inclined to grumble at, is the being obliged to attend the children at play in a morning, as they are only in the yard. I should voluntarily choose to do it sometimes but the nursery maid, I should think, would be sufficient in general; however, I get a little air, and it will render me less subject to take colds; it will do me good, though I don't like it.

The children, though well ordered by their parents, when out of their sight are as unruly, noisy, insolent, quarrelsome, and ill-tempered a set, as I ever met with. I am beginning to get them to pay some respect to my mandates, and perhaps by and bye, I may to my requests; but I assure you, I have had, and still have, a tough task to perform; and if Mr & Mrs Armitage had not given me every authority, in the most liberal manner, I must have despaired of doing any good. A few days ago, I felt a necessity of proceeding to some very severe methods; certain, almost, at the same time, I should meet the displeasure of Mr & Mrs A. in consequence, when they came to be informed; but how great was my satisfaction, when they expressed their approbation of the method and severity of punishment which I had inflicted. It has given me spirits to proceed with tenfold more confidence, and a greater desire to please them, than before. The little creatures are very affectionate to me already; and of the three younger ones, I think I can make something. Miss A., the eldest, is the bad sheep that infects the flock: punishment or reward make no lasting impression; I fear she is naturally depraved. Though 7 years of age,[1] she has no ideas of common modesty; it is a wrong thing in parents to inure children to be stript entirely in the nursery, whilst washing. I am endeavouring to correct this, by degrees, as no innovation must be made suddenly that affects the mistress of the house or the servants.

I have begun to teach the children to dance; and a sweet boy of 5 years old,[2] to write; and he does both, admirably. Their instruction, and sewing for Mrs A., keep me very busy the whole of school-time; I begin again to know the value of minutes, and to be very careful to waste none of them.

Give my love to Ann when you write; and in your letter to me, let me have every information respecting her worth your trouble.

18 August 1812 (High Royd). *To Mrs Dodson,* Douglas, Isle of Man:

Feeling myself comfortably settled in my new abode, I shall attempt to give you some account of my proceedings since I quitted you. You will sometimes find that I relate little events in my letters, with extreme minuteness. I will tell you why I do so, as I know you like to have a reason for everything. Great events seldom occur in common life; and where an epistolary correspondence is frequent, trifles are not accurately delineated, they sink to nothing. To me, the everyday pleasures and anxieties in the domestic life of my friends, have an interest at all times; and I relate my own little affairs, in hopes to draw forth a similar communication from them.

I had not left your shores above an hour, when I grew very sickly, and for many hours, was extremely ill; so much so, that when I arrived in Liverpool, I could not walk home, and was obliged to get a coach. That voyage of only 24 hours, had reduced me almost to a skeleton; the difference in my size and strength, between the day I left you and that of my arrival in Liverpool, was really astonishing, and I was more than a week before I recovered either strength or spirits.

194

Be kind enough to tell Mrs Singleton, that I forwarded the potted lobster by the canal as soon as I could get it out of the Custom-house, the day after I landed.

What troubles and turmoils people bring themselves into, by burthening themselves with children! Mr and Mrs A. might have kept their carriage, had they only the root and stem of the tree to have supported; but they have foolishly contrived to increase, and multiply, so many branches, that they must deny themselves many a gratification, in order to provide those branches with leaves. A fortnight ago, the eldest of six children completed her seventh year; and another will, I suppose, make its entrance into this comical bustling world by Christmas. I don't suppose the parents are either of them more than thirty, so they may have at least a dozen children yet, in addition to the present number. Heaven help them![3] though indeed they don't seem to want it; I may rather crave it for myself, if I stay amongst them, for I am quite busy enough as it is; you don't know how much you are indebted for this scrawl; it has been almost the work of a week, my leisure moments are so very limited.

The children appear to have been allowed full liberty to a riotous degree; yet Mrs A. seems to expect that I shall now, speedily, bring them into the exactest order . . . the task is a most arduous one! The eldest, a girl, is of that strange kind of temper, that she will purposely do the very thing that she thinks will excite most displeasure. I often wish that I could exchange her for one of yours. Of this girl, I shall never reap any credit, I fear; but the 2d, a boy, not six yet, will evince to his friends whether or no I possess any talents in the education of children. He is a fine little fellow, and understands, with great quickness, every thing I attempt to teach him. I have begun to instruct him in writing, and the elements of grammar and arithmetic; and they all learn to dance. I have four under my care.

Mr and Mrs A. are pleasant and easy in their temper and manners, and make my situation as comfortable as such a one can be; for it is rather an awkward one for a female of any reflection or feeling. A governess is almost shut out of society; not choosing to associate with servants, and not being treated as an equal by the heads of the house or their visitors, she must possess some fortitude and strength of mind to render herself tranquil or happy; but indeed, the master or mistress of a house, if they have any goodness of heart, would take pains to prevent her feeling her inferiority. For my part, I have no cause of just complaint; but I know some that are treated in a most mortifying manner.

When I was last in Liverpool, I had great reason to regret that I had never learned French; for, if I had only understood that in addition to my other attainments, I could have had a situation where I should have received a salary of a hundred a year, in a family of distinction. I could have obtained a situation in Westmoreland, in a wealthy family there, had I only been acquainted with that language. My Mother used to think it a very useless acquisition to the generality of Englishwomen. She had no idea how great a loss my ignorance of it would one day be to me; for she never thought of my leaving Holland, but to live with my brother; upon this, she always calculated . . . how short and ill-judging is human foresight.

Huddersfield, from which I am only 4 miles distant, has been the principal scene of riot, depredation, and alarm. Mr Armitage's house was the first, or one of the first, that was attacked a few months ago. He then resided at Lockwood, still nearer Huddersfield, and he and Mrs Armitage were shot at, and stones thrown in at the windows one night, as they lay in bed. They were obliged, in consequence of this, to be constantly guarded by a party of military, until they could quit the house to come to High-royd, where they have resided about 3 months, unmolested. Since I came here; he was shot at, and blinded in consequence, but not killed. I have heard of no other sanguinary or riotous event lately; and, for my own part, feel no alarm. I care little what becomes of me; all I wish is, that when I am tried at the great day, I may not be found wanting; and when my days on earth are terminated, it will make little difference whether my life has been long or short.[4]

28 August 1812 (High Royd). *To Miss C. Braithwaite:*

I am beginning to write to you in a very melancholy mood. I hope I shall not infect you, but that my own spirits may be exhilarated by the mental exertion; for I have often found writing to have that effect. Will you permit me to give vent a little to my present feelings? The mighty crime that has estranged me from an aunt and a brother, still remains unknown to me; and that I can so easily be forgotten by them, so strangely treated on such slight grounds (for slight they must be, or I should be conscious of the offence), is a matter of continual astonishment, and continual conjecture. The unfeeling may accuse me of folly in permitting the ill-treatment I cannot avoid, to make so deep an impression – it is easy for those to do so, who have some relatives to cling to, some one who can sympathise when they suffer; but let them be deprived of all, and then hear what they would say. Had I any domestic ties, the unkindness of those without doors would only mortify me for a short time; but having none in whom I can confide, none to whom I can speak my griefs, I dwell upon one depressing subject altogether, having nothing to divert my attention from it. Write to me before long, and tell me how my aunt's health is, and any Holland news you can collect; and particularly how all are at the Abbey, for I have not yet learnt the agreeable qualification of forgetting old friends.

With Mrs Dodson, I was unusually talkative; the sight of each other brought in a torrent of ideas, and the days that were gone again flitted before us. You would have been diverted to have heard what a gabble we raised whenever we met; and lest one should have a greater share of the beforementioned elegantly termed gabble than the other, we occasionally repeated – 'now it's my turn.' Mrs D. Is just the same kind of women that Miss Prescott was; she does not even look older, I think. She fancies herself very thin!!! And very nimble!!! Oh dear, oh dear, I should be just as sorry to walk 10 miles with her, as she would with me. I would certainly prefer talking with her 10 hours, for she lets me give vent to all my odd whims and saucy speeches, and seems entertained with them; which is encouragement to go on . . . Not so, Mrs T. Weeton. She, on such occasions, would look wondrous wise! – or wondrous sour! Not being capable of understanding me, and thinking what I said was either very silly or very insulting. When I have been at Leigh, poor Tom and I have suddenly become chop-fallen many a time in the midst of a hearty laugh, when we found, by Mrs Weeton's dignified looks, that we were not better than a couple of fools. Heaven help us! When I keep a carriage, I will not have an owl for my crest, for there is no wisdom in mere gravity.

Mrs D.'s 3 girls are fine children; her boy, in mind and manners, is quite an unlicked cub, though a great favourite with mamma. Mr Singleton gave me a most satyrical account of many of the exiles in the Island; I was highly entertained with it, though it left an unpleasant impression. I would have taken down his anecdotes in my memorandum book, if I could have found any other title for them but that of 'The Scandalous chronicle.' There are a strange set of beings in that Island, particularly in, and about Douglas; it is the wicked world, and nothing but the wicked world, in miniature. Mr Allen, at whose house I lodged, called Douglas, Botany Bay, and the strangers, convicts.

Douglas is a nasty, dirty, filthy, scrubby, mean, pitiful (help me out with some more pretty epithets, for mine are exhausted), ill-built town.

I have begun a correspondence with Mrs Dodson, a little reluctantly I confess, as thinking I should not now have much time for writing; but she would insist upon it.

I am going, next week, to commence head-house-keeper for three weeks, as Mrs A. is going with a party to South-Port, near Ormskirk; they have a house to themselves. Mr A. will only go for a few days, as business must be attended to.

Let me again request you to write soon. I wish to know how you all are; I hope, better than when I last heard. And scold me heartily if you think proper, for the contrast between the beginning, and a paragraph near the conclusion of this letter; for indeed, I think myself reprehensible in giving vent to my thoughts and ideas on both subjects.

15 to 30 October 1812 (High Royd House). *To Miss Winkley* at F. French's Esq., Sopwell-Hall, Roscrea, Ireland.

You can scarcely imagine, my dear Ann, how much I was rejoiced at the receipt of your letter; more particularly so, as it was the only one I had then received since I came into Yorkshire. I was beginning to be most seriously angry at your sister's neglect, when, the other day, I received her first letter; and such an one, that it banished almost all my displeasure.

It gives me great pleasure to find that you like your situation better than you did; and I hope that you will even like it better still; for I really am very desirous that you should remain in it. You will be so much benefitted and improved by it; the advantages you will obtain, will far outbalance the mortifications you endure to gain them. You were in danger of becoming a vain, selfish, indolent character; you will now, I think, secure to yourself the opposite virtues – humility, benevolence, and industry. The pains which you say Mrs French takes with you, is a great kindness in her, and I hope she will, in return, receive a part of the benefit as well as yourself; which she certainly will if you stay with her. But how do you manage, Ann, to go through a course of reading? For really, I find it almost as much as I can do, to keep my clothes in repair, and write to my correspondents, besides reading a newspaper now and then. I had pleased myself with the idea, that when I came here, I should have an opportunity to teach myself music and drawing; that airy castle, however, is vanished, as I am never a moment free from the children, from 7 o'clock in the morning, till half past 7 at night. I don't complain of this; it is no more than my duty; but certainly a governess is more a prisoner than any servant in the house.[5]

Last week, we were in danger of being deprived of a very good master, father, and husband, in Mr Armitage, by a fall from a horse; but providentially he has recovered surprisingly. No limbs are broken, but he was in a senseless state for some hours, that his revival was scarcely expected.

The children have really made a very great progress since my arrival, in their books; but as Mr A. leaves all domestic management to his wife, and she never examines the children, I sometimes feel myself suspected of a neglect, of which I am certainly left at liberty to be guilty during school hours, but of which I never can, or will be guilty. There are some people with whom we cannot soon become friends at the first interview. The former seems to be the case with Mrs Armitage and me; the idea of receiving wages, and being, in truth, a servant, keeps my spirit down, and throws a degree of reserve over me, which I sometimes think has a correspondant effect on Mrs A.; and perhaps it is my own fault that she has hitherto treated me in a manner less open than I could wish. How should she know what is the cause of my reserve? For, that it should proceed from diffidence, would be the last thing she would suspect in a woman of 35.

8 December 1812 (High Royd). *To Miss C. Braithwaite:*

Oh dear, Catherine! If it had not been to convince you that I am yet in this land of wool-packs, and likely to continue in it, I don't know when I should have written to you. Really, that was an unfortunate piece of news which you heard in the jangling village of Up Holland – 'that I had returned to Liverpool.' 1st., because it was a f-i-b; and 2dly, because it obliges me to tell you so, after I had resolved, and determined, and concluded, upon letting my pen lie still and sleep for 3 or 4 months this winter.

That my uncle calls me unfeeling and undutiful, surprises me still more, when he knew my intention of engaging again as a governess; and both he and my aunt approved it. My uncle is, indeed, much to be pitied; for he has little comfort. My aunt is not able to attend to him in those little offices that compose enjoyment of domestic life; nor will she keep a decent servant to do the work of the house, or trust to her if she had one. She consequently does many things herself, totally unfit for a person suffering as she does, and increases her illness and my uncle's misery, along with her own. Often has he expressed a wish that I should live with them, and my heart has beat with fear less my aunt should agree to it, and make the proposal, as I thought myself bound to do what my mother had said, and was apprehensive I should be obliged to tell them why I rejected it. The proposal was never made whilst I lived in Holland, and I therefore never told them, nor anyone else in that village, that my mother had desired I never would live with them. My having promised my mother never to do so, would prevent my ever offering to go to them, if no other reasons withheld me.

Frequently when I have nursed my aunt, and been several hours with her, have I been suffered to go home to my tea, and requested to return again as soon as it was over. Once or twice I staid to make my uncle's tea, sat by whilst he drank it, and was not asked to taste, and went home to make my own. When my brother has been a guest at my house, he has often dined with my uncle, whilst I have dined alone. Feeling so much the want friends and comforts in my own house, how I have enjoyed the sight of the happy family at yours! It was to me, certainly, as a picture only; but of a most delightful kind; and when I have spent an evening with you, and returned home, it was like quitting light for darkness. How has my heart ached to bid you good-night, and enter my own dismal, dreary dwelling, of which Darkness and Solitude seemed to have taken possession. This may account to you for my conduct once at Mr Snape's. You know not how bitterly I felt the contrast between that gay party – surrounded by mothers, brothers, and sisters, enjoying health, affluence, and chearfulness; and myself, who had not one of these. I could have refrained from so violent a fit of crying had it not been for the music and dancing; but my depressed spirits could not bear the sound of music and mirth. I shall never forget that day, and am sorry I ever went, or so conducted myself – I could not help it!

I am too comfortable here, my dear Catherine, to have any thoughts of leaving, and have no reason to suppose that my employers are dissatisfied. I love my pupils, and receive many an affectionate embrace from them; it must be an advantageous offer indeed, that would now induce me to leave them.

Write soon. If I do not answer soon, be assured it proceeds from real business, and not from indolence or forgetfulness.

22 December 1812 (High Royd). *To Mrs Price:*

There has been a report in Holland that I had left Yorkshire, and returned to Liverpool; somebody makes themselves busy. I am not likely to leave, that I know of, for I am very comfortable and contented. I begin to like Mrs A. much better than I did, and have no want, but – want of time, which is no great evil. Mrs A. is really a nice woman, and the genteelest woman I have seen since I came to Yorkshire. The manners and dress of the people here are much inferior to those of the same rank in Liverpool; appearances here are not so much attended to as there. I believe I have been thought quite dashing.

I am sometimes invited with Mr and Mrs A. to Mr Armitage's senior, to tea and supper; excepting this, I am totally excluded all society out of the house; and have little but that of the children within. The old gentleman's family consist of himself, his wife, and one daughter,[6] a little younger than myself; two women servants, and a boy in livery. He is a justice of the Peace; his residence is about 200 yards hence.

There is a something like selfishness in Mrs A. that prevents her feeling warmly for anyone. She is a good wife, a good mother, and a good mistress, but she does not seem to carry her heart with her; or, if she does, it is devoid of melting pity; she is not one of whom I should like to make a confidential friend. Mrs Armitage senior has presented me with a new scarlet stuff gown, in which you may suppose I look very glowing. She is a very generous, charitable, hospitable woman; and when I tell you that all that family are kind hearted, you will suppose that I am very partial to them.

This part of Yorkshire seems to be principally inhabited by manufacturers and farmers; a plodding, money-getting, good kind of people; even everything in this house is conducted with tradesman-like regularity and bustle; no sitting after breakfast or dinner, as we used to do at Mr Pedders. I generally rise from table with some of the meal in my mouth. Yet I like the family far better than Mr P's; no quarrelling, rioting, or drunkenness here, that used, when I was at Dove-Nest, to terrify me so. Here, I know what I have to do, there I never did.

I could smile with contempt at my brother's accusations of my fretfulness and dictating spirit. He and Mrs W. scold me by the hour; and when I attempt to justify myself, will not allow me to say a word. Mrs W. seems to have conceived a most violent hatred against me, and has left no arts untried to bring about a lasting separation between my brother and me. She has been years in effecting it, but has succeeded at last; may Heaven forgive her!

14 January 1813 (High Royd). *To Miss C. Braithwaite:*

I commissioned Mr Leece, a clerk in Mr Bird's office, Castle Ditch, to receive my rents for me, and it has been a very culpable neglect in him not to have applied for them long ago. I have written to him upon the subject since I received your letter.

The inhabitants of this part of Yorkshire have had very anxious hearts lately, in consequence of the assizes at York; and their uneasiness will be some time yet before it is dissipated; for the numbers of turbulent people that must still remain, will have a burning spirit within them for some time. Though Mr and Mrs A. are extremely cautious in what they say on the subject, I can discover that they feel very serious uneasiness respecting the Luddites; and, they may well! Having been fired at in their bed, and an intimate acquaintance (Mr Horsfall)[7] murdered, their terror will be some time ere it subsides. Even since the assizes commenced, Mr Radcliffe's house has been fired into, I have just heard, by some unknown hand. He has been a most active magistrate, and by his means, principally, have the ringleaders been discovered and apprehended. He received, a short time ago, several anonymous letters, threatening his life if the men then in York were executed; these threats did not in the slightest degree intimidate him from proceeding with the utmost activity, and I hope he will not suffer in consequence of so dauntless a spirit. Mr A's father is a magistrate, and between him and Mr R., there is great intimacy, owing to which I hear a great deal of him.

26 January 1813 (High Royd). *To Miss Ann Winkley:*

I wish that my employers were more frequent observers of my exertions, as I have never, since I came here, received the slightest acknowledgement of the improvement of my pupils. It appears like a tacit degree of dissatisfaction with me; and when I do labour hard indeed, till my spirits sink with the daily anxiety and exertion of mind, and the excessive confinement I am kept in injures my health, it is really mortifying to be left to suppose that my services are considered as inadequate to the situation I hold.

As Mr and Mrs A. never examine into the progress their children make, except in a very trifling manner, they are totally unacquainted with a great part of what their children learn. A weekly account which I render every Saturday, and which is totally my own doing, Is listened to with greater indifference than I could wish; and the children's education has never, that I recollect, been a subject of conversation since my arrival. For anything the parents might know, I might teach the children to be Deists, or Atheists; or, what is almost worse, might never teach them anything like religion at all. 'Why does God make lions?' said George one day, 'when they do nothing but kill and eat us, or anything else they can catch?' (George has often an idea of the superior excellence of mankind in general, and of his own in particular). 'If flies could speak, George,' I answered, 'they would say, why does God make little children, who do nothing else but kill us for sport'?

When I arrived, the two eldest could read but few words of 3 or 4 letters; the third,[8] words of only 2; and the fourth[9] has his alphabet to learn; they did not appear to have received the slightest verbal instruction! I never met with children of such vacant minds, considering the natural quickness of their capacities; and so indulged, that they seemed not to know what obedience was. I have had, and have even yet, a hard task to bring them under any degree of subordination; but the worst, I think, is over, though I am still obliged to correct and punish much more frequently than I could wish. Now they begin to want more books, and I mentioned, the other week, a few such as

I could wish them to have. Mr A. made objections to all, without proposing any others in their stead.[10] The expence seems to be an object, and I am surprised at it; for those who choose to keep a governess, should not be afraid of a few shillings in books, and I did not exceed in my proposal, ten or twelve shillings. I was so much hurt at the cavilling manner in which Mr A's objections were made, that I really meditated leaving their house next Summer. I said nothing, but perhaps my countenance and manner expressed a part of my displeasure, for Mr and Mrs A. have been more conciliatory their manner for the last few days, and I feel more comfortable; this evening he has been telling me he expected a few books from London for the children. I had mentally determined that I would myself purchase a few, and lend them to my pupils.

I really will begin to talk of everything I teach the children – of the trouble they give me – how often I repeat the same thing, before it is remembered – and boast of my continued exertions for their improvement; for it will, I believe, be necessary to my own consequence to do so.

My aunt and brother have begun to make a little stir about me, and have taken some pains to obtain my address from Miss C. Braithwaite. What they will do when they know where I am, I don't know; or what they will say for themselves, should they write. I assure you I dread hearing from them. Should I receive a letter with my aunt's or my brother's writing upon it, I shall be almost too nervous to open it.

There has been dreadful execution at York amongst the Luddites the last fortnight; no less than 17 have been hung! It was a necessary severity, and the threats of those who have been liberated, has spread considerable uneasiness in this neighbourhood; for I am in the centre of the mischief that has been committed by these mistaken people.[11]

Mr Forster of Up Holland will, I hope, have paid his rent by this, as I should be sorry to proceed to any extremity with him. The other tenant deserves no mercy; and yet he is so poor, that all he is worth would not pay half a year's rent. I have long tried to get him away, but cannot even buy him out, having offered to give him half a year's rent.[12]

At about this time Miss Weeton continued in haphazard fashion, to add to the list of books she had read. Due to her onerous undertakings at High Royd, it is doubtful that she would have been in a position to read books to any extent, whilst employed there. It is more likely that she had already read the books and written notes about them earlier, before entering them into her Journal at a later date:

A Satyrical view of London, by J. Corry. 1 Vol.
The above vol. Is a tolerable production; it treats principally of Fashion, Beaux, Belles, London Tradesmen, Quack Doctors, Lawyers, Parsons, &c. &c. &c.

Windermere: a novel in 2 Vols.
This is below mediocrity; the title induced me to read it; and with the title I am satisfied – and disappointed.

Letters on Mythology addressed to a Lady, by R. Morgan. 1 Vol.
A humourous (sic) and entertaining production, written in a light and easy style, to make it palatable to a lady's taste.

Lessons of a Governess to her pupils by Madame de Sillery-Brulart (formerly Countess de Genlis). 3 Vols.
For further remarks, see page 11th.

Lake of Killarney, by A. M. Porter. 3 Vols.
Rose de Blaguere, a foundling, is the heroine of the tale. Mr Clermont the hero. Mr O.Neil and has maiden sister bring up Rose, whom they found left at their door and who eventually proves to be the daughter of the haughty Countess Dunallan by a first and private marriage.

Ellinor, or the World as it is, by M. A. Hanway. 4 Vols.
An Entertaining production, written in a light, easy style.

The Royal Sufferer, or Intrigues at the close of the 18th Century, by J. Agg. 3 Vols.
[No comment on this book].

The Cottagers of Glenburnie, by Miss Hamilton. 1 Vol.
A little tale tending to shew the folly of adhering to old customs merely because they have been habitual for many generations, particularly the Scottish tenacity, indolence, and want of cleanliness in their houses and about their farms. The tale is told in such a manner as scarcely to offend even a Scotchman, and very probably have some influence in effecting a reformation.

The Mysterious Gentleman Farmer, by J. Corry. 3 Vols.

There is nothing in this novel, or in the author's Satyrical View of London, that would induce me to waste my time again in perusal of any other of his works. This may probably be worth five guineas at Minerva Press; the author may earn a little money; fame is out of the question in such caterpillar productions. [The Minerva Press produced a long series of sentimental novels in the early part of the century].

An Essay on Old Maids. 3 Vols.

Has my approbation, although, or because, I am an Old Maid. What is the public opinion – but shall take the first opportunity to discover.

9 February 1813 (High Royd). *To Mrs Dodson,* I-o-Man:

I can give you nothing entertaining here in regard to myself; were I to tell you how I live, it would be the dullest account of the dullest life ever dragged on by mortal. I want for nothing, in the common acceptation of the word; but I go on in that monotonous tenor, in which there is no enjoyment; happily, however, for me, I can derive amusement from the oddity of my own thoughts, and have many a hearty solo laugh.

I am very sensible of want of elegance so glaringly observable in some parts of my letter; but if you will only permit me to make fine speeches, you'll have a wond'rous few of them! Besides, there's no drollery in them; and a little low humour, I should imagine, is better than blank paper. If you don't think so, what must be done? For, as to plain every-day chit-chat, I was never in the way of it, and am unacquainted even with the theory. I know nothing of my neighbours, good or bad – as to fashion, I might as well be blind and deaf for what I either see or hear; visits, balls, plays, concerts, card-parties, equipages, scandal, tempest, war, trade, and all the other epithets of busy, bustling life, are to me as words without meaning; my own ideas must either entertain me, or I must be in a most dismal predicament! whether they entertain my correspondents or not. I read very seldom indeed; having, in the first place, but very little time for it, my own sewing and letter-writing occupying most of my leisure hours; and in the 2d place, Mr and Mrs A. having never offered to lend me any books except an Encyclopedia,[13] which is not an every-day kind of reading. High-royd is at such a great distance from any other house, that

Mr and Mrs A. can have little or no company in Winter. Mrs A. is now in immediate expectation of bringing an increase to her family. I never was in a house where there was a bustle of the kind; and whether or no I shall be expected to perform a part, I cannot tell; not a word has been said about it. Say what you will, ye wives discreet, you will never make me believe that labour, with all its terrors, can be anything very terrible, when ye incur the danger so often. I dare say I have suffered more from a fit of the toothache, the very remembrance of which would prevent my ever doing anything again that was likely to cause a return.

3 April 1813 (High Royd). *To Mrs Price,* Liverpool:

What is the matter, my dear Mrs Price, that I hear nothing from you? Sometimes I say to myself, Oh, if I had her but at my elbow, how I would twig those idle fingers of hers!

I received a letter lately from Mr Leece, to inform me of the repair of some chimnies. What sums of money have been laid out on those chimnies since the houses came into my possession! I hope, however, this is the last for some years to come. The regularity of the rent day has already, I find, been done away with.

Mrs Armitage has introduced another daughter into this troublesome world lately – six weeks ago; and although it may appear paradoxical until explained, my comfort has been considerably increased thereby. For some months after I came, Mrs A. seemed to be determined to be displeased with whatever I did; cross looks were my daily portion, and unpleasant hints were frequently thrown out. Grating as it was to my feelings to be thus treated, I continued my assiduous endeavours to discharge my duty; God and my conscience were my guides. Mrs A's manner to me determined me to keep at a distance, and threw a degree of cool reserve into my conduct that I could not divest myself of, however greatly I wished it. All at once, she has become pleasing and open (comparatively speaking), and treats me in a manner that has, as suddenly, banished my reserve. She begun to alter in this respect 3 or 4 weeks ago; and but the other day, the nurse informed me that she is always ill-tempered when pregnant, particularly at the beginning of the time. Now it so happened that I arrived here just at that unlucky period, and she has been increasing in size ever since, until about 6 weeks ago, when, being freed of her burden, she became as good humoured as she was

207

wont to be; and I now venture to meet her with that ever ready smile which I bestow on everyone, whose own countenance is too sour to return it.

Ann tells me you are likely to bring an increase of family; I wish you well over it, and comfort of the baby when it does arrive. For Heaven's sake, don't be like my mistress here, and make everybody miserable about you.

P.S. Of my brother or of my aunt, I have never heard a word – from them, at least. I think with you, that some of my relations don't wish to find me. They act most strangely! I suppose I may expect to hear by the next post from my uncle, or some one. I almost think I will write to him immediately, for he will hear reason. I am much aggrieved for the situation my aunt is in, and would long ago have visited and have nursed her, had she ever asked me.

8 April 1813 (High Royd). *To Miss Winkley,* Dublin:

Although I begin my letter at High-royd, it is with the idea that I may probably finish it elsewhere. If my aunt does send for me, what a nest of hornets am I likely to encounter! I assure you I dread going. However, I can soon satisfy them, if money is all they want; they shall have all the scrambling to themselves; I shall not stoop to do it. If I had been swayed by interested motives, I should never have resented my aunt's treatment of me because that would, to a certainty, irritate her still more.

Should I be sent for to my aunt, it is most probable I shall not return here, which will occasion a vacancy that Mrs A. must fill up with a younger person; for she will have no chance of getting a person of my years, experience, and attainments, to submit to the privations and humiliations I have done (though I could have staid contentedly, had not several considerations made it almost necessary that I should be nearer my Liverpool property). Mrs Armitage's manner has been much improved towards me lately, and has made my situation much more agreeable. I rather suspect I am indebted for this improvement to Miss A., Mr Armitage's sister, who has been a great deal here within the last two months, attending Mrs Armitage during a confinement. Miss A. and her parents (who live near us) seem to think very highly of me, and treat me with great respect. I have frequently been to tea and supper there with Mr and Mrs A. Junior, and am going today, to dine with them; yet, such is the liberality of my mistress, that I am to stay with the children until dinner is quite ready, and to return to school as soon as I have eaten it, and go again to tea. It will be the first time I have dined out since I came here; and, if such again are to be the conditions, it shall be the last. To this day's arrangement, I shall submit in silence. I was served in the same way when invited to the old gentleman's to tea last summer. I had then to return home again at 7 o'clock to hear the children's prayers. After submitting to it once or twice, I objected, preferring staying at home entirely to visiting in such a way; after which, I was permitted to stay the evening, when I did go.

As long as a governess, or any other person, is admitted into the company of her superiors, she should be treated as an equal for the time, or else it is better not to invite her at all.
April 9th.

I could smile, my dear Ann, at a part of your letter, in which you imagine your method of instruction may improve mine. After being a teacher in a school upwards of 20 years, and for more than 10 of them having made education my more peculiar study, I should not now have to learn from a girl so young as you. I am not apt to boast verbally of my knowledge, and a person must be intimately acquainted with me, before they know my acquirements.[14] I know I appear more ignorant than I am; my brother has often told me so, for he thinks me wondrous clever, considering the opportunities I have had. When very young, I was disgusted with the pedantry of some girls, who pretended upon every occasion to a great deal more than they really knew. I saw how they were ridiculed, and secretly determined never to act like them. When a person is really possessed of knowledge, it will make its appearance without any pains being taken by the possessor. But it only discovers itself to the knowing; the ignorant cannot find it.

Having expressed myself thus, I am no longer offended, my dear Ann; but having often experienced the same kind of expressions from you when we were together in Liverpool, I think it my duty to caution you, for it has given greater offence to others than to me. I could excuse it, because I well know the vanity and inexperience of 16 is apt to think more highly of itself than it ought to do; and the addition of a few years will, alone, teach it more humility; for then, the equal, nay even superior knowledge of thousands of those around us, is discovered daily.

[Journal, May 1813]:

It is well that I have so little time for reflection, or otherwise I should almost weep myself into the grave; for my present situation is a most painful one! Forgotten, as it seems, by every relative, and almost every friend at a distance, and totally secluded from all rational society here, I must sink into melancholy if my days were not so completely occupied as almost to preclude thought. The little leisure, or rather the little time I have to myself, is a good deal employed in repairing my clothes, writing letters sometimes; and sometimes I sit with my face resting on my hands, indulging in melancholy, weeping bitterly; for no one interrupts me, no voice soothes, advises, or pities.

Why am I thus treated? What have I done, Oh Father, to deserve to be thus deserted and neglected? What have I done to you, my aunt, to meet with such treatment at your hands? . . . What have I done to you, hard-hearted, selfish brother, to merit such strange cruelty of conduct?

7th. Since writing the above, I have received a letter from my aunt, in consequence of mine to Dr Hawarden; and though it is such an one as would, at any other time, have, have plunged me into sorrow and roused my indignation, it has just now affected me with the liveliest pleasure! It is a letter from my aunt, and I care not what it contains. Though I shall not even yet use the language of humility or submission (as I think I have been most unjustly, most cruelly treated), a chance, at least, of a reconciliation appears; and my heart bounds with joy at the idea. I will write to my aunt. Should my letter offend, I shall consider it as proof that nothing but the most abject language can please, and spurn at the idea of calling one to be conciliated – a relation.

19 May 1813 (High Royd). *To Miss Winkley:*

My dear, dear Ann! Do you know, that on reading your letter, I have received both a considerable degree of pleasure, and, of pain, – of pain at finding you so much grieved with a passage in my last letter. When I wrote it, I really did it with a design of rendering you a service; but, on afterwards perusing it, my heart smote me for being guilty of severity. I hesitated whether or not to dash out the cruel words. I read, in a milder tone, what appeared so angry, and I was more reconciled to them. If *I* don't reprove her, thought I, she has not another so much her friend as to do it. I will make the experiment. If she is offended, if she proudly resent, she is not the girl I could wish her to be. My heart again smites me painfully, at finding I have afflicted you so much (at the same time that I am delighted beyond measure at feeling more than ever of the goodness of your heart, and the increasing powers of your understanding). Oh! I was anxious that you should quit the dangers you were in, in Liverpool; for, as you say, so I thought, that 'your mind was poisoned by false ideas,' and that nothing would prove an effectual antidote, but the engaging in the situation which then happily offered. Mrs Edwards, though the sister of a man I highly respect, is a most dangerous woman! She, Ann, has not wanted native goodness of heart, but, in her earlier days, has wanted better instruction, and I fear is now too far gone to learn. She is unprincipled to a degree! a scoffer at religion, a despiser of all moralities , and neglectful of common propriety. Her uncommon liveliness and gaiety of temper, render her entertaining and pleasant to those who can overlook all that is Christianlike in woman. And it is this which makes her so dangerous; she vents the most profligate opinions in a manner so irresistibly laughable, as to make the poison *dreadfully* sweet! She fascinates the imagination, whilst she destroys the soul. I do not think she does it from design; her sole aim is to be admired for the brilliance of her wit; and her incorrigible vanity will, I fear, be her own destruction; (I hope, not that of others) . . . What a teacher at the head of a school! How careful should parents be, to investigate the principles of those with whom they intrust (sic) their children.

Mr Pollard is a young man of irreligious principles; *professedly* so, a Deist, if not an Atheist; and one of [Thomas] Paine's disciples. His appearance is genteel, and his manners insinuating. I pity, whilst I blame him. I would pray for him, whilst at the same time I would avoid him.

The Jackson's of Mill-Street, too . . . too depraved for description! . . . These were, all together, a *sad* society for you; and I am rejoiced that you have escaped them in your youth, before the contagion of such examples had irrevocably tainted you.

28 May 1813 (High Royd). *To Mrs Price:*

The time is fast approaching when I shall be permitted a month's cessation from my labours here, and as my affairs in Liverpool will oblige me to come there, I write to request you will take me in as a boarder, if convenient; if not, can I be with Miss Price? If neither of you can accommodate me, be kind enough to procure me lodgings as near as possible. The 18th of June is the day I intend to arrive in Liverpool; the coach goes through in a day, so it will be 9 or 10 at night before it gets there.

I have just been contemplating Wm. Hindley's Holland face, and received a Prescott letter from him, and mean to do myself the pleasure of seeing the hand that wrote it, on Monday afternoon. I prefer walking if the weather is fine, and will set out a little before 3 o'clock; should it rain, I will come by the caravan that evening.

What kind of shoulders they were on which the red cloak hung that you saw on the top of the coach, I can't say; they were not mine. I stared hard (as Miss Dannet says) from the inside of the coach, as I passed Mr Jackson's, but the windows did not serve as a frame to one single face.

How straight I write, Catherine, don't I? Hold the paper up to the light, and you will see the reason why.[15] I never met with anything so convenient before, though I know it's nothing new. When I begin to be purblind, I'll use it constantly, writing on a glass table, with a lamp underneath. What a reflection it will be to my eyes!

As planned, Miss Weeton arrived in Liverpool on 18 June and lost no time in writing to friends. Catherine Braithwaite was then staying with her married sister at Prescot, and Miss Weeton quickly acquainted them of her nearby presence. Unfortunately her visit to Liverpool was marred with difficulties, both personal and commercial. Her unquestioning loyalty towards her extended family, meant that she felt it incumbent upon her to make the difficult journey back to Up Holland, to visit her estranged dying Aunt Barton. In a letter to her good friend Ann Winkley, dated 30 June 1813, she revealed her heartbreaking experience in detail. Before returning to Yorkshire, she had planned to spend a further two or three days at Prescot, but the plan became superseded by spending time in trying to discover the whereabouts of her elusive property agent, Mr Leece.

Undated (Liverpool). *To Mrs Jos. Armitage,* High Royd:

Madam,

In compliance with your request, I called at the shop you directed me to, to make inquiries about the lamp you described. The proprietor informed me, that one with a large cut glass dish, encircled with a brass figured rim, six glass lights for candles, and a row of icicle drops, with a chain to hang it, could be furnished for £12; if additional drops were required, the price would be from £12 to £20 in proportion to the quantity of drops. The dish was very beautifully cut, but there was one valued at £15 that I admired much more; six candlesticks were placed upon a brass rim, from which was suspended glass drops, three in depth, and very thickly set; a painted glass cylinder, about 20 inches high, stood up in the middle of the candlestick. It was ornamentally painted; I think, with a landscape; and intended to contain within it, either an oil lamp or a candle. The top of the chain by which it hung, was ornamented with glass drops suspended in the manner of either icicle drops, or the weeping willow – which you please; the cylinder was in the shape of a wine-pipe, widest in the middle.

I was very nearly losing all chance of obtaining either a place for myself or my little charges in the coaches from Huddersfield. Some young ladies, returning from school, were in the coach with us, and seemed much pleased with my little, chattering companions. They asked what school they went to. I said they had a governess at home. 'Thinks I to myself, I'll pass myself off for their Mamma.' So I kept my left-hand glove on, and talked very consequentially. Shaking my head, 'thinks I to myself, these children will betray me; I fear it won't do;' and just then, Emma exclaimed, 'Oh look, Miss Weeton, see what a deal of buttercups in that field.' It was too bad, now, wasn't it?

30 July 1813 (High Royd). *To Miss Ann Winkley:*

I received your letter my dear Ann, whilst I was with your sister; but so very unsettled did I feel all the time I was with her, that I scarce knew what time I had for writing, or what to say to you; one vexatious delay or other, defeated every little plan of pleasure, and my whole vacation dwindled away without my being able to leave Liverpool except a visit for a day and two nights Prescot; and another, about the same length, to Holland.

My visit to Prescot was as agreeable as so short a stay would admit of. Mrs T. Jackson, whom I went to see, and Miss C. Braithwaite, both urged me to go to see my aunt. Anxious enough I was to see her; but, so treated as I have been, it was a hard struggle to subdue my resentful feelings. I hesitated for some days, but at last summoned resolution enough to go, writing first to my aunt to prepare her for my reception, though not waiting to know whether I should be received. With aching heart, I stepped into the canal packet; the company however soon became amusing to me, and for a time drove away all uneasy sensations. My cousin Latham's second son met me at Appley Bridge, and I walked from thence, dreading the coming hours, to which every step reluctantly hastened me.

My uncle opened the door of his house, with a faint 'how do ye.' I trembled as I walked into the parlour, not knowing whether I was welcome. I asked various questions respecting my aunt's health, which were very coolly answered. 'Are you for stopping here, or going to Mrs Braithwaite's?' he inquired. Such a question set my lips a-quivering, and a coldness spread over my face. 'If I am not welcome here,' I said, 'as I cannot go back tonight, I must try if they will take me in.' Tea coming in just then, I was going to rise, as well trembling knees would permit. 'Your aunt will not see you,' said my uncle. 'Then I had better go,' I replied, as I endeavoured to stifle some convulsive sobs. My uncle looked at me, and in a softened tone, said 'But I will make you welcome, Nelly.'

Not all my intreaties could induce him to tell me the reason of the treatment I have, for so long a period, received from my aunt; the more I urged, the more angry he was at my speaking on the subject; he said he would have nothing at all to do with the business, and insisted on my dropping the subject.

I expressed astonishment at such cruel treatment, when I was totally ignorant of what I had done to offend; I was treated, I said, as an outcast, friendless and unprotected; and not so much as the *shadow* of an error laid to my charge! I was a condemned criminal, without being informed of the crime for which I suffered!

Not all I could say, availed me; and I am to this moment ignorant of what I have done, to offend my aunt so irreconcilably! In the course of the following day, my uncle repeatedly urged my aunt to see me (she was confined to her bed-room); but in vain. I did not desire my uncle to do this; I only twice asked whether my aunt intended, or wished, to see me; and being told not, submitted in silence. The whole of this day, my uncle was very kind to me, and we spent the greatest part of it by ourselves, in friendly conversation.

I called upon Mrs Braithwaite; the altered appearance of that house, now the master of it gone, and the boys who used to fill it being dispersed for want of their teacher, gave me such a shock, that I had no sooner sat down, than I burst into a violent fit of crying, in which I was in some degree accompanied by the widow and her daughters.

My stay at my uncle's was so extremely uncomfortable, that I determined not to stay a second night with them; so I concerted with the servant to get a sight of my aunt, unknown to her; she went upstairs rather noisily, that I might not be heard. I stood peeping at the door, whilst the girl talked to her. The irritated tone of voice in which my aunt *always* speaks now, I am told, and her ghastly countenance, were almost too much for me; I retreated, undiscovered, into the kitchen, and burst into tears. 'Oh! – I *never* shall see my aunt again,' I cried. The servant wept with me, and the tears stood in my uncle's eyes; indeed I wept bitterly. My uncle shook my hand affectionately, as he bid me farewell. I gave the servant a secret, but very earnest charge, to be kind to my aunt, for which I would reward her, and then departed.

I had not gone far, when my aunt's servant came running after me, and said her mistress wished to bid me good-bye. In the first moment of resentment, I refused; it was too late now; however, I was prevailed upon to return. We shook hands, and, 'Good-bye' was all that was said. *I* could say no more, my heart was too full. I quitted her – *never more to see her!* For so I think.

I had only returned to your sister's a few days, when I was seized with a violent bowel complaint and vomiting, which reduced me to such a state of weakness that I was fit for nothing for ten days; indeed, I am not yet recovered; I am feeble and thin to a degree.

215

I was attacked again with sickness in the coach as I was coming here, and was very thankful that I was the only inside passenger from Manchester, as I had room to lie down.

Indeed, Catherine, I was glad to get back again; the greater distance I am from Holland, and the more chearful and happy I am. I was glad to have 3 days of rest here, after the fatigue of travelling, previous to commencing my labours.

Highroyd is in a great bustle just now. Mrs Armitage's mother (Mrs Henshaw) came on the 31st of July, bringing her two little grand-daughters, who had been spending the holidays with her – Miss Lacy, and little grand-daughter; and a Miss Barker, a young lady about 16, just left school, who is under Mrs H's care, and lives with her. Mrs H., if I may judge from the short acquaintance I have with her, is quite the gentlewoman. She appears so good-tempered and so considerate, that I am at present a warm admirer of her; she treats me with such polite attention, speaks to me with so much ease and chearfulness, that if I joined in by some *greater* folks here, would dissipate all the starch very soon, in which I generally feel enveloped when I am in *the presence*. I had many a laugh to myself when I first came here; for, really Catherine, I could plainly see that my *master* and my *mistress* did not know how to treat me, nor *what to do with me*; and their distant manner froze me so, that for the life of me, I could not tell what to do with myself when they were by. My arms and legs were unusual incumbrances; my hands were quite in the way; and my bottom! Lord help it! When I walked out of the room, it felt three times as big as it ever did before, and I thought it shaked most uncommonly!

Miss Barker is a good-natured lump of a girl, with a very pretty face, flaxen hair, and beautiful complexion of lilies and roses. She is peculiarly fortunate in having a home with Mrs H. Her father is living, but she, being a natural daughter, cannot so comfortably live with him, as he is married; yet he intends to provide for her. Her mother was, I think, a relation of Mrs H's. Miss Lacy is a sweet little creature, not 5 years old yet; her accent and manners, so elegant! her temper so endearing! That I feel already much attached to her. The contrast between her and her cousin Armitages, Is very great; they are the rudest, most untractable set of children I ever had to manage; and I am afraid old Daddy Time will not manage them much better, till he quietens them with his scythe. I am certain I could reduce them to order if I had them to myself; but spoiled, vulgar children, of boisterous tempers, can never be reformed *at home*, by any governess.

The roads about Highroyd are excessively rough, and in Winter, scarcely passable. Miss L. complains bitterly of them. 'We have no such roads in London,' said she one day; 'they are straight there! and so smooth! I can run upon them without falling and hurting myself.' The beauties of the country compensates, in my long-legged opinion, for the badness of the roads that lead you to survey them; though really, walking here is, even to me, almost as much of a labour as a pleasure.

4 September 1813 (High Royd). *To Mrs Price:*

Returned again to solitude, and for the present restored to health, I commence an epistle to my dear Mrs Price, that ought to have been written some weeks ago. Mrs Henshaw, Mrs Armitage's mother, has been spending above a month here, and only left Highroyd on the 30th. of Aug. During her stay, the house has been all animation and gaiety. I determined to indulge myself, and descended to supper every evening; not for the sake of what I could eat, but of what I could hear and see. Mrs Henshaw is a sensible, good-tempered, benevolent, well-bred woman; she has won my esteem and admiration entirely. She always welcomed me, when I entered the parlour, with a smile and some little observation or other; so different to Mrs A's gloomy, and I could say almost say, sulky countenance, that acts like lead upon the spirits of one so easily affected by the expression of the features as I am.

I feel more at home here now than I have done any time since I came first into Yorkshire; and could be very comfortable if it were not for the perverse and violent tempers of the children. And they really are terrible; whether I can ever subdue them, is doubtful. For a few months before the holidays, I flattered myself that I had reduced my pupils to greater order than they had ever been before; but – the holidays have undone all, and again have I all to do. Such screaming and shouting and incessant loud talking I dare say you never heard in any family before; and such everlasting quarrelling. For a month since my return, the two boys *never* attempted to say a lesson without throwing themselves into violent fits of passion; screaming dreadfully, if I persisted in making them say it. I have at last resorted to the rod, notwithstanding it is so repugnant to the present mild system of education; and if you had heard their screams, you would have thought I was really killing them, when frequently I had only struck their clothes; but for the last week, I have made them feel it, and I have found the benefit of it, though my reward from the two Mrs Armitages, is sour looks and cool treatment. A mother must indeed feel for her children, and so do I feel for them; my spirit droops under such a task; but my duty to God is to fulfil the duties of my present situation; which I cannot do by indulging the children in their perverse ways, as their mother has done. The eldest girl, for some weeks, would not study a single lesson. She sat with the book or slate before her, doing nothing. What would you have done in such a case? I requested, persuaded, insisted; but she would only smile carelessly in my face, and toss her head. I then incessantly confined her at play hours, till she had finished not only her present lessons, but all which were in arrears. Cool looks from Mrs A., were the consequence; Sarah Anne's health would suffer, she thought. So I thought; but something must be done, and as Mrs A. did not propose any better way, I persevered, notwithstanding her unjust treatment, though a frequent fit of weeping was the consequence; and I think I have conquered. Miss A. is again become not only tractable, but affectionate.

[Journal, October 1813]:

It is nearly two years since I received a letter from my brother, or wrote one to him; judge, then, you who read these pages and know what I have suffered from him, what must be my feelings this evening, on receiving a letter directed by his hand! What would it possibly contain? . . . I opened it hesitatingly, but dared not to read it; my heart beat quick; perhaps my uncle, too, was dead!

For some days I have thought – have felt almost convinced it was so; my spirits have been very low since my aunt's death, and many a gloomy idea has possessed my thoughts; so much so, that my own dissolution has appeared momentary. Two evenings ago, I sat some hours alone by the parlour fire, Mr and Mrs A. being both from home. I felt extremely faint, as indeed I had done for some time. I trembled with weakness, and fancied that if I shut my eyes, I should faint away. I suffered the servants to go to bed without exerting myself to speak to them; I had not the strength to rise from my chair . . . I felt *so* friendless – my aunt dead, in enmity with me; my brother, to all appearances the bitterest enemy of his sister, and the person who had set her against me – and from motives so mean! so base! For the sake of £100 or £150 which *perhaps* she might bequeath me . . . perhaps it might be more – it might be £200.

How weary a world this is! When such a brother as he once was, can take so much pains to bereave his only sister of every friend! I wept at the thought, and further reflected, that so unprotected as I was, where could I find a home when I wanted one? . . . I could not tell . . . God help me, protect me; and forgive my mistaken brother!

The melancholy state of my mind, and the feebleness of my body, made me alive to *any* impression of a gloomy nature; and the dismal howling of a dog, just as the clock was going to strike eleven, the sound of which seemed to be just outside of the kitchen door, terrified me so, that, finding the use of my feet, I ran precipitately up stairs, and hastened into bed. I now felt I should *die* if I shut my eyes – as if the whole of life were centred in my heart and head – as if I had no feeling, no sensation, but that of breathing and thought! At length, after some hours, I became more like a living mortal; my limbs grew warmer, and I fell asleep.

The next morning, I arose, still feeble and depressed – I felt as if I were certain my uncle was dead – though I know not why I should think of *him* . . . This evening, when my brother's letter was given to me, it was like a confirmation of my fears – for what else had induced *him* to write? Perhaps it was an explanation of his conduct . . . what a joyful idea! I read; my delight was somewhat damped on finding it a proposal to live with my uncle, in a style of the most studied indifference; but for the direction, I should scarce know for whom the letter was intended. The first words are, 'You have already been informed of the death of my aunt. I find my uncle very dull, and it has occurred to me' – &c. &c. – and concluded with, 'Yours, T. R. Weeton.'

The abrupt beginning, without *any* address, and the cool conclusion, argue no returning affection. Oh! If I do see him again, I will endeavour to warm his heart with more Christianlike sentiments. I have begun my letter with 'Dear Brother,' and ended with, 'Yours affectionately,' and I wrote what I felt, notwithstanding his cruelty towards me.

Both niece and aunt were, sadly, to remain unreconciled to the end of Margaret Barton's life. She died on Saturday morning, 25 September 1813.

Now despairing of that understanding and love for which she yearned, Miss Weeton plunged into deep and miserable self-absorption. Weeks passed before she wrote the following (undated) letter for the attention of Tom. It relates routine life at High Royd, without reference to her deep-seated emotional turmoil. Only in the final paragraph does Miss Weeton hint at what is really troubling her – the suspicion that Tom was suggesting that she should return to Up Holland and live with her Uncle Barton, without Tom having first consulted her uncle. Whether or not the letter was ever sent remains unknown:

The principal amusement I have, is in going to or from Chapel on a Sunday, which is occasioned by the friendly attentions of an old, respectable, sociable farmer, named John Schofield; as we walk together, he often regrets the death of his wife, and speaks so affectionately of her, that I cannot but admire the goodness of his heart. I tell Mrs A. that he is my beau, and she often jokes me about him. I am afraid that you wont admire my taste, when I tell you that he is upwards of 70. He one day said, that old as he was, he would marry again if he could find such a one as his wife. If he were but an *old gentleman*, instead of being *nothing* but an *old man*, I really think I would give him a hint to make an offer, for I like old John vastly; he tells me his grievances, and I try to console him.

Whilst the long days lasted, I was always *let out* with the children, morning, noon, and evening. Every morning, I was busy making them gardens, they assisting in bringing, or carrying away, manure, planks, stones, weeds, &c., and frequently going into the fields to collect wild-flower roots. At noon, I went into a little overgrown wood, where once had been a pretty walk, but Mrs A. had suffered it to be neglected. Here, with a pair of great hedge-clippers, I worked for an hour before dinner, literally cutting my way; my little companions, with forks and rakes, assisting in carrying away heaps of slain. Should I remain here, this wood would become my hobby horse. Mr A. has given me leave to have a few trees cut down, to open a view, and to plant an arbour in their place; this will occupy my leisure hours next Spring, and my little ones please themselves with thinking what a delightful place the wood will be, for playing in at hide-and-seek. In the evening, we took a walk. But now that Winter has arrived, all these amusements are put a stop to. I wish . . . I wish Winter was over!

I shall be obliged to you, when you write, to inform me whether you think my Uncle does, or does not, wish me to reside with him. I wrote to him immediately after I received your last letter, but have received no answer. What can be the reason?

27 November 1813 (High Royd). *To Miss Winkley,* at Mrs Price's:

My dear Ann will, I suppose, have been expecting to see me for some days; and I must confess I feel considerably disappointed at the result of my uncle's determination – to go into lodgings with a tenant of his, who lived on an estate of my uncle's near Holland. The proposal, coming from my brother, gave me reason to conclude that he was authorised by my uncle really writes very kindly. He says his house was in such confusion after my aunt's death, and his servants behaved so ill, that he intends to give up house-keeping, for a few months at least; he will keep the house and furniture as they now are, until he has tried how he likes his lodgings. I should have liked to have lived with him, merely because I could have enjoyed *some* society; here, I am totally shut out of it.

May I request the favour of Mr Price to call upon all my tenants without delay, to inquire into the precise state of their accounts; for I much fear Mr Leece is neglecting my affairs most sadly. Oh Ann! To have the prospect of *going home,* as it were, after not knowing what home was for near *seventeen* years, and then to be disappointed! . . . think how it must sink the spirit of a deserted, friendless female. How ardently I do long for *a home*! But I suppose there must be none for me until I arrive at the grave.

2 December 1813 (High Royd). *To Miss C. Braithwaite,* Holland Priory.

I wish my brother had not written, without knowing my uncle's sentiments, for it has placed me in a very awkward situation. For near two months I was in daily expectation of a summons, Mrs A. was inquiring for a successor, and last week received intelligence of one, to whom she has since written backword. When Mrs A. received intelligence of this young lady, I desired that if she felt the slightest disapprobation of my method of instruction, and thought this young lady (of whom she had heard a very high character) would suit her better, that she would not hesitate a moment in saying so; for the children's interest must be the first consideration. She said that she had not any wish to change, for she thought that the children had made wonderful improvement; and George, in particular, she could wish not to change his teacher until next Summer, when he must go to a public school.

My uncle says that my aunt has left a parcel for me, directed by her own hand. A few weeks ago, I had determined never to receive it, whatever it might contain; for my uncle does not seem to know; but Mrs A. advises me to send for it, and in the hope that it may contain an explanation of her unaccountable conduct towards me, I have been induced to comply, and shall be obliged to you to request my uncle to send it by any conveyance he thinks the best, and to tell him that Rd Jackson owes one year's rent, due Nov 12th last.

My health is restored again, and my spirits too. Mrs A. treats me more and more pleasingly as the time passes on; we are almost like two familiar friends, and many a piece of would-be wit passes between us.

There is going to be a ball at Huddersfield (they say). I almost wonder, for there is such a saving spirit throughout this country, that I feel a little surprised at the intelligence. Here, do nine of us sit in an evening, for near two hours, round *one* candle. To be sure, six of 'em are the children; but I really think my neck is grown longer with trying to get near enough to the light to see to thread my needles. However, by way of drawback, what I gain by length of neck, I have the consolation to suspect I lose in a stoop of the shoulders; which is very well you know, for goodness knows I am quite tall enough.

Soon after I first came here, I was telling the little Armitages that I had formed but an unfavourable opinion of their manners on my arrival, but that I began to think they had good hearts. 'And do you love us better now?' said they. 'Indeed I do.' 'Well, and I'll tell you what,' said George, 'do you know, we called you ugly-face at first.' And do you like me any better now?' 'Oh yes, we do! You are so good to us, and tell us many things.'

P.S. Since writing the above, a *most dreadful* accident has happened! 3 of Mr Armitage's houses in Huddersfield were burnt down the other night, Nov. 30th. owing, it is supposed, to the carelessness of a servant boy, when going to bed. The boy, and a servant woman, were burnt to death. The tenants of the houses were severe sufferers; two of them were able to save nothing but themselves.

Neither a letter nor a parcel arrived from Uncle Barton. Unable any longer to do justice to her work as governess, Miss Weeton obtained permission from her employer for special leave of absence, to investigate the inexplicable conduct of her relations.

[Journal, December 1813]:

I went, on the 13th of December, to Liverpool, to settle my affairs there, and wrote a Note to my uncle to beg he would send the parcel by Wm. Hindley on the following Saturday, Dec. 18th. I called on Wm., but he had brought no parcel; he gave me a letter from my uncle, in which he said several things – viz: gowns, a muff, and a bonnet – were left by my aunt, but that my cousin [Latham] had been so unwell the day before he wrote, that she could not come up to his house to take them out of the drawers. This, to me, appeared a strange kind of evasive language; there had been many days besides that one, in which my cousin might have packed up the parcel; and my stay in Liverpool being very limited, if I did not receive it *then* (on the 18th) I must return without it. I was much hurt and perplexed, and, not knowing what to do, at last I concluded on going to Holland the next morning, Sunday, Dec. 19th, in Wm. Hindley's cart, and went accordingly.

I first called at Mrs Braithwaite's, not knowing where I should find my uncle, as he had talked of taking lodgings, and had not informed me in his previous day's letter whether he had left his house or no. Mrs B. begged I would be her guest whilst I staid in Holland, and I very gladly consented. My uncle being at Church when I arrived in Holland, I waited till he got home. I then called upon him, and sat about half an hour; he requested me to take tea, and sleep at his house. I declined it, as I had promised Mrs B.

to return to tea. I have since wished I had taken tea with him, as he appeared to be in a more communicative humour than usual, and he might have treated me with some confidence, and have told me many things which I was anxious to know; but afraid to keep Mrs B. waiting, I soon left him, thinking I could make a longer visit the next morning. Whilst I staid, he said that it was indeed my aunt who had reported that I had *gone off with a gentleman!!* And that she did it, because she knew not what was become of me, and was *afraid* it was so! My brother, out of *delicacy* to my *aunt*, had not confessed to me who it really was that told *him* so; but now that my aunt was dead, he did not doubt but that Thomas (meaning my brother) would tell me all about it . . . I was astonished and filled with horror! that . . . my aunt could *so positively* tell me, in the presence of my cousin; that she had never said any such thing, nor had ever any such report been circulated, with by her or my cousin; and that *no one had ever told my brother so.* Gracious Father! And could my aunt so deliberately, so villainously, deny her own words? and be so depraved, so dreadfully wicked, as to charge my brother with inventing such a *lie*? . . . She *did* do it – and – Oh merciful Father! has died in the dreadful sin . . . Heaven have mercy on her wicked, guilty soul!

My brother's *delicacy* to my aunt! roused my utmost indignation. *Delicacy* to the wanton defamer of his sister's character! and when he knew from the first, that his sister was perfectly innocent; even from the *appearance* of evil; was she free. Where was his delicacy to his sister! to suffer his aunt, or any other person, to speak ill of her in his presence, and never to resent it? . . . Contemptible, time-serving fellow! My aunt's money, or my uncle's, was of much more value to thee, than thy sister's esteem and affection. Take their money, if thou canst get it! And mayst thou never suffer for the meanness thou hast been guilty of to obtain it.

I was so overwhelmed with grief and wonder that my aunt should have suffered her last moments to arrive without ever confessing her injustice to me, and clearing my brother as much as she might have done, that I scarcely attended to the rest of my Uncle's communications. I did just recollect hearing him say, that 2 gowns, a black and grey sarsenet [a thin silk], a muff and tippet; and marone [wine coloured] velvet bonnet, were left to me by my aunt. Until then, I had never heard what she had left me. That to my brother she gave a purse containing 40 guineas in gold, and £10 in Bank notes; and the same to my cousin Latham A purse for me she had left in his care, sealed; but, thinking of sending it by Wm. Hindley the Saturday before, he had broken the seal, and found a ring and five £1 notes.

The latter part of this information I caught but imperfectly, so absorbed was I in thought; and when it passed my ear, I thought that he must be alluding to something else. He said he would give me, in the morning, whatever was left me by my aunt; so, thinking I should then know whether I was mistaken, I took leave for the evening. As I proceeded to Mrs B's, I felt more and more convinced that my Uncle really had broken the seal; but whilst there was a shadow of doubt, I would not condemn him for a breach of trust, of which perhaps he was not guilty.

Unwilling to speak ill of my aunt now she was dead, I did not mention any part of uncle's communication respecting her to Mrs B's family, except what I thought my Uncle said of the purse, which formed the whole subject of our conversation for the evening; and the whole family seemed much hurt and astonished about it. 'If my Uncle really had been guilty of such a mean, scandalous trick,' Mrs and Miss Braithwaite both said, 'they would believe him capable of any piece of villainy; they had heard it often said, that my aunt, notwithstanding the offence she has expressed towards me, had yet made no difference in the division of her property, but had left me equal with my brother and cousin.'

I called upon my uncle next morning, at 9 o'clock; he said but little; ordered the servant to fetch down the parcel of cloathes, and went himself to fetch the purse. He gave it to me, with the seal broken!!

He gave no reason for it, that he did not choose to send it by Hindley, without knowing how much it contained, as the man might have been robbed. 'But then, you did not send it by Hindley, Sir?' To this, he gave no answer. 'And he is a man of such approved and long-tried honesty, that I could have trusted him with it.' '*He* should neither trust him, nor any one,' he replied, 'with uncounted money? Or that the parcel contained any money, if you did not tell it? As I had requested you to send it by Hindley, all responsibility was taken from you; and *I* could have trusted him.' 'It was out of care for my interest,' he said, 'that he did it.' 'If you could not trust the parcel by Hindley,' I replied,' 'why did you open it? And why did you not inform me so, in your yesterday's letter? in that, you did not so much as mention it. Indeed, Sir, you should not have opened it.'

My uncle rose from his chair in a violent rage. 'Do you mean to insinuate,' he said, 'that I took any money out, or that the purse does not contain as much as your aunt sealed up in it?' 'I know nothing about it, Sir; I only wish you had not opened it.' 'It is just the same as accusing me of stealing money out of the purse,' said my uncle, as he paced the room. I was silent. 'Your aunt left £180 to be equally divided amongst you all, at my death; she could not legally make a Will, and it shall be as I please, whether you ever have it, or no; it shall be according as you behave; so you had all of you better take care!'

I could scarcely suppress a smile at this; for the mighty sum, for which we were to be so very circumspect in our behaviour, would only be £60 a-piece; and we might wait 20 years for it, for anything we knew. 'As to that, uncle,' I replied, 'I well know you solemnly promised my aunt, some years ago, to fulfil her wishes, and gave her your permission to make a Will; and your word ought to be as good as law.' He made no reply to this, but sitting down, began to write in an Account book. I rose, and saying good bye, left the house, never more, perhaps, to see it.

I had heard from several people, some months before her death, that my aunt had made no difference in the disposal of her property, leaving me equal with my brother and cousin; and so I believed she did; it was very unlikely that she would *seal* up £5 and a ring *not worth* 7s.

It appears quite as unlikely that my uncle should be guilty of defrauding me of so small a sum as £50, when he is placed so much above want; a man, too, so constant an attendant at Church; of such apparent, and boasted, integrity; of principles so rigid, that he never forgave any deceit practised against himself; but – my aunt herself placed no confidence in him, and many little mean actions speak against him, well known by different individuals.

My cousin Latham will submit to any meanness to forward her interest in the world. To supplant me in my aunt's favour, she invented many a mischievous tale to set my aunt against me; represented me as proud and high, that I was above my relations, and that I spoke with the greatest contempt of my aunt and uncle, and ridiculed them at every opportunity. By these mean arts, she obtained her purpose – *in part*, i.e., if my aunt really left me no more than this £5 – but is, on the whole, dreadfully disappointed; she expected that my aunt would wholly exclude me, and that she had considerably more to bequeath. Finding a seven years labour in all the arts of hypocrisy and falsehood, have availed her so little, she has now cause to repent bitterly that she took so much pains to exclude me, who could now have been so great a friend to her. Had I gone to live with my aunt, my uncle would most probably have wished me to remain with him, and I should naturally have drawn him more closely to the interests of our family, merely because he would have seen more of us than of any other family; and because, having no relations of his own except a distant one, whom he has never noticed for years, he would have had no other family likely to have attached themselves to him. My absence having now totally estranged him from his late wife's family, he has adopted a little boy of that distant relation, and very likely will leave him all he has. My brother and cousin now perceive the consequence of their narrow-minded policy – and never were the guilty so deservedly punished!

My cousin, with the mean facility which she well knows how to practise, has already turned sides, and would endeavour to persuade me that she has a great respect for me! She complained much to me of my uncle's behaviour to her since my aunt's death; and, indeed, he really has acted meanly. My aunt left my cousin all her cloaths, with the exception of the few things given to me; my uncle retains the cloaths in his own possession; is highly offended if anything is said about them; and does not say when he shall give them up. He has given several garments to his servants and others, which were indeed not his to give (if my aunt's dying wishes, and his solemn promises to her, were to be at all regarded). Whilst I was at Holland last, my cousin called upon me in the afternoon, over-abundantly civil. I, in return, was not uncivil, but cool. I felt disgusted at her effrontery in expressing so much affection for me, in the presence of the Braithwaites, whom she knew had been frequent hearers of her malicious insinuations against me. She took leave with expressions of concern at the shortness of my stay (only one whole day). She came again after tea, saying she could not bear the idea of my departure, without seeing me once more! I felt so displeased at her fawning conduct, that I could scarcely forbear expressing myself with some asperity – but – she was too contemptible, and I forbore. As I had occasion to see a tenant that evening, I rose to quit the room; she followed me. As we went through the street, she thrust something into my hand. 'What is it, cousin?' said I; for the night was dark, and I could not imagine what it could be. I thought it felt like a small parcel of scrumpled paper. 'Never mind,' she said, 'at present; you'll see, when you get home.' Frank Braithwaite was escorting me, and supposing it was to be kept a secret, I put it in my pocket. On my return to Mrs B's., I found a *pound* of *gingerbread*, which had just been sent to me as a present by my cousin! I took the little parcel out of my pocket, and found it to be a yard of handsome broad lace, not much worn, and recognized it to be some which my aunt once had on a cap. I shook my head, exclaiming to myself, Oh, cousin, cousin! do you think that gingerbread and lace can make me atonement for the injuries you have done me? At the same moment, I resolved she should never be one shilling richer for anything I possessed. She seems to think she can make a mere feather of me, and blow me which way she pleases. Whilst there was anything to be had from my aunt, she took every pains to keep me at a distance; since her death, she thinks she can draw me back again; for she knows I have much more to leave than my aunt has left. She succeeded in the first, but she will find the second impracticable. In what consternation she appeared, when I told her of my uncle's determination – that it should be as he pleased, whether we ever received the money left by my aunt to us, at his death. She imagines we could claim it, perhaps, in right of my Grandfather Rawlinson's Will, as my aunt died without children. I had the Will in my possession, and promised to look at it when I got to Liverpool; and I confess I felt a malicious kind of pleasure in being enabled to inform her, by means of Miss C. Braithwaite, that she had nothing more to expect, for my Grandfather had left his daughters the full possession and disposal of their fortunes.

On her return to High Royd, Miss Weeton sent a rare letter to Mrs Green, wife of the Lakeland artist, in which she expressed that she could do nothing to further her husband's 'interest' in Yorkshire. The reason being was a marked reluctance by Yorkshire folk to spend money unnecessarily:

> I was sorry I do could nothing for his interest here; the people in this part of Yorkshire appear to be *all* a money-getting, but not a money-spending people. Taste and Science are words I never hear. Mr A. himself is in the woollen trade, and works like a slave in his warehouse, and constantly attends the Huddersfield weekly market. He keeps neither carriage nor in-door man-servant, is extremely economical, and makes all his domestics work as hard as himself. I am most excessively confined; so much so, that I think I shall not stay above 6 months longer; reading, music, or any other relaxation are almost out of the question. If I do leave Highroyd in the Summer, I should much like to spend a few months near Ambleside; do you think I could obtain lodgings, or board on moderate terms?
>
> The country here is very pretty and romantic. Highroyd house stands alone, and very high; we have an extensive, and in some points, a fine view, from the front windows; but no view here equals those near you; and the confined life I lead, makes me almost hate the country in which I am so imprisoned.

4 February 1814 (High Royd): *To Miss C. Braithwaite:*

> I have been a long time, my dear Catherine, in finding time to write to you. It is not that the frost has had any effect upon my ink; although that might serve just as well for an apology in such intensely cold weather, as most apologies made by dilatory correspondents. On second thoughts, I almost wish I had given you that as a reason; it would have been something new; for, 'want of time,' is such an old hack, everybody mounts upon the back of it when they are going to write a letter.
>
> To tell you that I have been in want of a subject, would be so humiliating to my fancied variety and elevation of ideas, that I – I – I – do not like to confess it. Besides, I have felt myself very much out of humour lately, and if I write in ill-humour, perhaps I might make you as ill-tempered as myself; for I feel it is an infectious disorder, and I should be sorry to *spread* it – I was going to say, *propagate* it – but it is such a shocking word for a *delicate female* (say an Old Maid when you read it Catherine) to use, that I forbore to insert it.

Mr Armitage is one who occasions me many a serious reflection, he appears so intent on the riches and honours of this world, and so totally forgetful of those of the next. He is a man of sense, talents, information, and industry, but every talent seems to be directed solely to the acquiring of riches and rank. He sets a great value on titles, and one day said that he thought a reigning monarch ought to confer titles on those who had, for two or three successive generations, been wealthy. Imagining that he was alluding to his own family at the time, I was silent; but often perceived the value he placed on *such* honours, I have since taken occasion to remark, that no titles conferred dignity in my opinion, except such as were obtained by merit; and that Knighthood in particular was so frequently bestowed, that it had fallen into contempt, and become a frequent theme for ridicule; that even the King himself made a laugh of it; and several times, when asked, with a smile, if he were one of Peg Nicholson's knights,[16] or if he had obtained his title by *nothing* but carrying an address? My mouth must not open again here on this subject; for, only a few weeks ago, *Mr* Walker, of Leicester (an own uncle), carried an address to the Prince Regent at Belvoir Castle, from his very loving and loyal subjects, &c., and returned – *Sir* William. I dare not laugh here again on this subject; but – thoughts are free, you know, and I did think that Mr A. himself will endeavour to obtain some such Knighthood before he dies; my pride would rise too high for such a title. I would at least be a Baronet, or remain as I am, were I similarly situated. Mr A. has several times expressed his surprise at those, who, having carried addresses, declined the consequent honour.

Mr A's parents are strictly religious and charitable; the latter virtue is as little known here as the former, and I am surprised, that with such parents, Mr A. should be so worldly-minded. He seems to possess a much greater portion of humanity than his wife; she really is not kind-hearted. Were I to treat her children as she treats her servants, I should not long be here; she is angry with them if they are ill, poor souls!

19 April 1814 (High Royd). *To Miss C. Braithwaite:*

I am answering your letter, my dear Catherine, a little sooner than perhaps you expect; but I do it in the hope of hearing from you again before I leave Highroyd, which will be about the middle of June. I wish I could conveniently leave now; my own affairs will hardly permit so great a sacrifice to Mrs A., as that of staying two months longer. I would not have left Mrs A., had she treated me like one of the family. Mr and Mrs A. are both very unpopular, I find, in this neighbourhood, from their pride and extreme illiberality; and change their servants so often, that they can scarcely get any to live with them. I have certainly been much better treated for the last twelve-months, but am still a tenfold closer prisoner than any other governess in this neighbourhood, and am staying at home this afternoon (Sunday 17) for want of a decent bonnet to go to Church in. Mrs A. knows this, but neither offers me a holiday, nor a conveyance to Huddersfield to buy one; and I'll stay at home these two months before I'll ask her.

We have lately got a new curate at our village chapel, from, [or] at least a native of Winstanley, near Holland. His name is Winstanley.[17] He has prominent eyes and wears glasses; can you tell me anything of him? I *think* I have heard of his being at Mr Banks's (sic),[18] and being a favourite there. He seems to obtain considerable respect, but as he appears to be a literary kind of character, his conversation will be above – or – quite out of the way of the Yorkshire gentry here, for *trade* is their learning. His unassuming, easy manner, gains him friends. Mr A. and all respectable of the village (Honley), have called upon, and invited him. He has dined once here; I had no opportunity of speaking to him.

What glorious, blessed news we have had week after week, my dear Catherine, from abroad![19] It will restore health to the sick, gladden the sorrowful, and make the poor rich. I wish my aunt had lived to see this day! But – perhaps she is doing better.

24 May 1814 (High Royd). *To Mrs Price:*

I have been in the daily expectation of hearing from you for a week or two, until at last my little stock of patience is exhausted; and, with scarcely time for writing, I am bustling at it as if business of the first moment depended on my present exertion and hurry. I hope to leave Highroyd in 3 weeks from this time; I don't precisely know the day. As I hear nothing from you, I feel a little uncertain as to the place I must come to in Liverpool; will it be convenient to you to take me in? I shall be much obliged, if you can. Do not tell the tenants the time of my coming, lest they should remove in the meantime without paying arrears. If Mr Leece would only see after the tenants up to the present, it would be much the best, and I shall soon release him from the trouble.

I am just now labouring under a considerable degree of vexation, from a circumstance ludicrous enough in itself, and which I have treated as such, until it has become too serious to laugh at. The country-people here have got it into their heads that I am going to be married to an old farmer of 74, with about £30 a year (on which he alone subsists); from no other foundation that I know of, than our chatting together as we go to Church on Sunday – the only time I ever see him. The old fellow may have something in his head of the kind, and may have said as much to his neighbours; but such an idea never would have occurred to me, but for one of Mr A's work-people, who mentioned it to me, and said it was reported that I was leaving Highroyd on that account. I now recollect many of the old man's speeches. I laughed at the compliments at the time, and joked again, imagining the difference of age, manners, and rank, were a sufficient licence and protection. He would sometimes wish himself 30 years younger, for my sake, and that he possessed a thousand a year, and he would bestow it all on me. I never returned this fine compliment, except by a laugh; but I have now reason to believe he is crazy enough to think seriously of it, from his conduct towards me. For several Sundays past, I have been obliged to go and return by different routs to avoid him, he waylays me so perpetually; if I am before him, I walk fast; if behind, slow, to avoid his company; and find some difficulty in doing it without publishing my reasons. Were I staying longer, I would complain to Mr A.; as I go soon, I am in hope to prevent the subject from spreading, by my apparent ignorance of it. I have thought more seriously of the affair, since last Sunday. I was stared at in a most unpleasant manner at Church, by several country-men, who then looked at old John, and laughed. If I were to make a stir about it, a greater noise would be made, which I hope to prevent by my speedy change of residence.

I used to respect the old man, because I thought him good-natured and friendly; and when he complained of and lamented the loss of his wife (who died 4 or 5 years ago), I pitied him – little thinking I was gaining his affections!

So ends the final letter despatched from High Royd. The next recorded letter is sent from Liverpool.

27 July 1814. *To Miss Sarah-anne Armitage* at High Royd House:

My dear Sarah-anne, your new governess will be with you soon, I suppose, and I dare say you are very anxiously expecting her, and wondering what kind of one she will be; she is sure to be very fond of you, and very good to you if you are obedient, respectful, and affectionate.

When I left Highroyd, I spent a fortnight in Liverpool. One evening I went to see an exhibition of Androides; I will only tell you what that means; I will only tell you what I saw. There was a very pretty, baby house and a dog sat on the front step, so little that you might have covered it with one of your baby sugar basins. The man who shewed everything to the assembly, placed a very little plate of artificial fruit, such as grapes, oranges, pears, plums, cherries, &c., before the dog, and told it to take care of it; and do you know, the little dog said 'bow wow!,' and every time the man spoke to it, it barked as if it knew what he said; and when the man stole some of the fruit, it howled and barked and whined, in a most piteous manner! How ingenious the man must be, to make such a dog; for I suppose it was nothing but wood. A little doll, not so big as yours, stood at the door, and when the man told it to fetch any fruit, it went in, shut the door, and in two minutes, came out again, bringing whatever it was sent for; one time, an orange, another a bunch of grapes, &c. The man called for a chimney-sweeper, and bid him go sweep the chimney. A little figure, about two inches high, dressed like a chimney-sweeper, came creeping through a side-door, went in at the front-door, and in five or ten minutes, popped his head out at the top of the chimney, held up his brush, and shouted 'sweep!' Then he went down again, and bye and bye, he came out again with a bag of soot, and went away. There were many other things wonderful, but I have not room to describe them.

After I had been a fortnight in Liverpool, I went to Up-Holland, and staid a week with Mrs Braithwaite; my brother called upon me to pay some money owing to me, and shook hands very affectionately. I well remember, my dear Sarah-anne, how rejoiced you said you should be when my brother and me were friends again; and the innocent, endearing warmth with which you, and George, and Emma, begged me to inform you of such an event taking place and I now tell you of it, that I may afford your good little hearts a pleasure, so nobly disinterested in yourselves, and so gratifying to me.

It would not be to a correspondent that Miss Weeton would record the details of her encounter with her brother, but to her Journal alone. The 'interview' between brother and sister took place in the parlour of Mrs Braithwaite's Abbey home at Up Holland.

[Journal, July 1814]:

My brother called upon me at Mrs Braithwaite's, and was shown into a front parlour. I was at work in a back parlour, when I was informed it was my *brother* who wished to see me. It threw me into such a state of agitation, I could with difficulty keep my seat. Miss C. B. urged me to compose myself, and go to him; I attempted, but could not rise. Catherine very kindly poured me out a glass of wine, and held it to my mouth – I could not drink it. 'Shall I shew him in here,' she inquired. 'Oh, stop a little – well – yes, do.' He was shewn in, and held out his hand in a very affectionate manner. I feebly squeezed it, and sat down, and took out of his pocket, 5£ notes, which he presented. I grew a little more composed, and faintly asked if I should not give a receipt. 'Perhaps it might be as well,' my brother answered, 'for Partington's satisfaction.'[20] I wrote one, and a miserable scrawl it was. He observed that he was very late on his way home, and must go very quickly (he had been with his wife, spending the preceding day at Bispham,[21] and had staid all night there; and coming through Holland on his way home had detained him). I answered, I knew that Saturday was a busy day with him; and then, his children recurring to my recollection, I was on the point of asking some questions respecting them, but . . . my heart filled, and I could not speak. A short silence ensued; my brother rose, and, taking my hand, affectionately squeezed it, and said 'good bye.' 'Good bye,' I faintly answered. I tried to rise, but my knees failed me, and I could not move. I was going to fall from my chair, but, resting my head on my hands, and leaning over the table, I supported myself; my brother left the room.

I burst into an agony of grief, for all hope of future intercourse seemed to be lost; why did my brother call, if he meant not to vindicate himself?

The above is the *whole* account of what passed in this interview, and yet . . . could it be imagined that my brother took advantage of these few circumstances again to traduce me!! He *has* done so. He has reported that I refused to shake hands with him, or to salute him. I can only imagine that he has told this *lie* to irritate my uncle still more against me, with the view of keeping us separate as long as my uncle shall live; it certainly being more to my brother's interest to be without a rival in my uncle's favour. Should my uncle die before me, I have no doubt but my brother would immediately seek a reconciliation with me; for, having obtained all he could from my uncle, his next object of attack would be myself; if he defer vindicating himself until my uncle's death, *he shall never* have the opportunity after.

Miss Weeton was right to be suspicious of her brother's motive, his avaricious nature would eventually bring about disaster for his sister and the destruction of his professional reputation.

NOTES:

1. Sarah Ann, born 29 July 1805.
2. George, born September 1806.
3. Joseph Armitage's wife eventually became the mother of 15 children.
4. By Miss Weeton commenting: 'I feel little what becomes of me,' and being 'tried at the great day,' far from revealing a depressed spirit, indicates her complete trust in God. Christian teaching emphasises that the length of a person's life is unimportant. Its emphasis is on its quality, i.e. a life lived by way of obedience and faith.
5. Miss Weeton's matter-of-fact comment that a 'governess is more a prisoner than any servant in the house', is supported by Charlotte Bronte. She commented that even in a 'kindly and friendly household, full-measure was extracted'.
6. Miss Marianne Armitage was nine years younger than Miss Weeton.
7. Miss Weeton's brief references to individuals connected with Luddite activities can be referred to in more detail in Frank Peel's book: The Risings of the Luddites (1880). It can be accessed via the on-line version at 'The Luddite Link.'
8. Emma, born 22 November 1807.
9. Joseph, born 24 April 1809.
10. It would seem that Mr Armitage was not in the habit of spending money on printed matter. Not only was he averse to spending on educational books for

his children, but neither did he take in newspapers. For the duration of her stay at High Royd, Miss Weeton had to arrange for a supply of newspapers to be sent regularly from Liverpool.

11. It is clear from Miss Weeton's letters, that whilst the Armitages lived in constant fear for very good reason, she did not.

12. From the moment Miss Weeton purchased the cottage in May 1808, Dick Jackson proved to be a 'slippery' tenant. She finally transferred the cottage, with its tenant, to her brother in part settlement of a sum due to him under the terms of their mother's Will.

13. Miss Weeton's hard-headed Yorkshire employer loaned her No 1 of Vol. II of the Edinburgh Encyclopaedia, by D. Brewster. She read it 'at various intervals.'

14. Miss Weeton's correspondence reveals herself as someone who was always tactful in the company of her employers. When corresponding with friends, however, she did not always cease to be 'the governess.'

15. Laid paper was made in a mould with wires across it in parallel lines to form a watermark.

16. Peg Nicholson's Knights were the recipients of easy knighthoods conferred upon them for their loyal addresses of congratulation to George III. This followed an attack upon the King's person in 1786, by Margaret Nicholson, a poor demented woman. Under the guise of presenting a paper to him for his examination, she struck him with a knife, which penetrated the cloth of his coat only. After being confined for 42 years, she died in her 99th year.

17. The Rev T. R. Winstanley was one of a succession of curates who officiated during the suspension (for reason/s unknown) of Rev Robert Smith, M.A., the holder of the living at Honley from 1802 to 1845.

18. 'Mr Banks's' refers to Meyrick Bankes (I), who succeeded his father in ownership of Winstanley Hall, near Wigan, in 1803. The Winstanley estates comprised much coal-bearing land, and had been owned by the Bankes' family since being purchased from Thomas Winstanley in 1595.

19. Miss Weeton is almost certainly referring to the successful battles against France towards the end of the Napoleonic Wars. During April 1814, Marshal Nicolas Jean de Dieu Soult, Commander of the French forces, agreed to an armistice and Napoleon Bonaparte abdicated.

20. The £5 was interest paid on a loan to a Mr Partington, of Leigh.

21. It is believed that Thomas and his wife had stayed at Bispham Hall, located at Billinge, two miles south west of Up Holland.

SEVEN

Betrayal and persecution

Wigan

September 1814 – February 1822

ON THE FIRST day of September 1814, Miss Nelly Weeton became Mrs Nelly Stock. She was married at Holy Trinity Parish Church, St Anne's Street, Liverpool, to Mr Aaron Stock, a Wigan man and a widower. Born 24th January, 1776, Stock was 11 months older than Miss Weeton. The choice of church[1] was possibly one she knew whilst living in Liverpool between 1808 and 1809. Like all women who married at that time, in the eyes of the law, once married, Miss Weeton no longer existed as an individual. At a stroke, her personality became incorporated into that of her husband. With marriage came the legal obligation of giving up all her shrewd investments and savings to her husband.

The first time we learn of Aaron Stock is a fortnight before the marriage. He was a cotton-spinner by trade, and owned a cotton-spinning business in Wigan; operating in a factory located off Chapel Lane. The building was leased from the Scott family, the in-laws of Thomas Weeton.

Through the family of his wife, Thomas Weeton would have known of recently widowed Aaron Stock. He may also have known that Stock was struggling to keep his business solvent. The result of such knowledge by someone who was financially opportunistic, as Thomas was, would have led him to realise that the Scott family would not want the insecurity of knowing that their property was leased to a tenant with financial problems.

Where and how Miss Weeton met Aaron Stock is not known; she does reveal an 'attack of the vapours' on two occasions, in the company of a certain 'man of the cloth.' He was believed to be a Rev Thomas Saul, who twice stayed at Dove's Nest, Ambleside, during 1810. In letters to Miss Winkley (11 May and 21 November 1810) she stated:

> 'I cannot say I ever met with a man so agreeable . . .' and 'I wish he were either less agreeable, or would take himself away; his presence is too much for me.'

Beyond becoming personally-overwhelmed in that encounter by presumably sexual attraction, there are no further clues in her correspondence and journal entries (extant), which would indicate a passionate interest in any particular individual. Having said that, there are clues as to why she made the seemingly uncharacteristic impulsive life changing decision to marry. It is understood that she was empathetically drawn towards Calvinist non-conformity. It is also known that she longed for a home of her own:

> 'How ardently I do long for *a home*! But I suppose there must be none for me until I arrive at the grave.' [Letter to Miss Winkley, 27 November 1813].

During her ceaseless activities at High Royd, Miss Weeton had experienced moods of intense gloom, triggered largely by the irritable nature of Mrs Armitage during the latter's pregnancies. There had also been times when she felt intensely isolated from friends in Lancashire. Perhaps at a time of deep melancholy, in that bleak and isolated house, she suddenly forcibly realised that at 38 years of age, she would soon be past child-bearing age.

Despite Miss Weeton's difficult relationship with her brother during the previous two years, she decided to write to him, asking him to obtain a 'character' reference concerning Aaron Stock. This is evidence, yet again, of her unshakable loyalty to family blood, rather than employing her normally excellent intuitive qualities. Time and time again, by his actions, Thomas had revealed to his sister that loyalty to his wife and the Scott family was a far greater priority than concern for his sister. Naturally, Thomas gave her a satisfactory report of Stock's character, and with that she was duped into marrying an unfeeling and violent brute. For his part, Stock got exactly what he wanted: the answer to his severe financial difficulties and a way out of impending bankruptcy.

Stock was a regular worshipper at St Paul's Independent (Congregational) Chapel, Standishgate, Wigan, and was a very good friend and associate of its Minister, Rev Alexander Steill. In the eyes of Thomas Weeton, Stock's regular Chapel attendances, when offset against his financial difficulties, would seem to have been sufficient to recommend him as a suitable husband for his sister.

To be fair to Thomas Weeton, knowing-of a person is far removed from knowing a person. It may well be that Thomas knew that Stock was a committed Calvinist and regular member of the congregation at St Paul's Independent Chapel, that does not mean he also knew that Stock was, in outward appearance only, a sincere Christian[2] and upright pillar of the community. It is also uncertain as to whether or not Thomas knew before his sister's marriage, that if she either married or died, according to the terms of their mother's Will, he stood to gain £100. In addition, Stock gave liberally, but indiscreetly, to Missions and Schools. (Miss Weeton later opined that his sole motive for charitable giving 'lay in those causes that issued lists of subscribers for public edification and emulation').

Immediately after the marriage, the groom brought his bride to his home at the rear of his factory. It was a home that bristled with potential for wicked intent. Chief mischief-maker was his step-daughter, Hannah Gilbert, also a younger daughter, Jane Stock.[3] In addition, there appears to have been a succession of easily influenced servants, one of whom would never miss an opportunity to prejudice her master against her increasingly-isolated would-be mistress.

Aaron Stock's financial difficulties and threat of bankruptcy had been far from short-lived. In later correspondence to her husband, Miss Weeton reminded him of just how difficult her life had been in the years following their marriage:

> You required me to repair all your cloathing, excepting shoes, and I dare say you remember how readily and good-naturedly I submitted to your wishes. I disliked exceedingly patching breeches, coats, waistcoats, and even neck-kerchiefs, besides darning stockings up to the very knees; but to please you, I did it chearfully.

The impression you made upon my mind, was that such extreme shabbiness must proceed from the continual danger you felt yourself in, of becoming bankrupt, and for 6 or 7 years, I was in the constant expectation that we must all end our days in a workhouse.

Just nine months and nine days after the marriage, a daughter named Mary was born (9 June 1815). Sadly the birth of a daughter did not bring-about unalloyed joy for the mother. Severe depression of spirits, exacerbated by the resentful members of that unhappy household overwhelmed Mrs Stock. In order to recuperate, she travelled to take the 'salubrious air' of Southport, considered then to be the place where 'invalids every year derive essential benefit.'

In a letter to Mrs Stock's cousin Smith, then comfortably living in the Wade household in the Isle-of-Man, she wrote:

I recovered from my confinement very rapidly indeed, to the surprise of everyone who knew me, and quite unexpectedly to myself. My little one was healthy, and for above a month, we went on very well; we were then both taken very ill – the child appeared too weak to be weaned, and I was no longer able to nurse it. A wet-nurse was procured, and then I went to Southport for a few weeks [to recuperate]; the child recovered rapidly. I laboured under so great a depression of spirits, that my recovery was very slow.

Since my convalescence, I have been much engaged with sewing, making short-clothes for Mary; my friends all flatter me in saying she is a beautiful child; she is very fat and lively, and I hope will prove a source of peculiar comfort. I think of having her weaned in a few weeks; and as we are to remove to a much larger house[4] in a month or two, we shall of course be very busy, particularly myself. I am sorry to wean the child so soon, but the nurse's conduct has been so very reprehensible, that I must part with her. She has behaved well to the child, and had she been commonly civil to me, and in any degree trusty, I would have kept her some months longer. If Mr Stock would consent, I would go over to Liverpool soon, for two or three days; but he will not let me stir anywhere; no powers of rhetoric work on him, so I must be contented at home. I should much like to see some of my friends there.

Joyful loving affection that would normally greet the arrival of a new-born child, remained absent. Mrs Stock experienced nothing other than firm enmity from her husband. Additionally, a cavilling coterie of family and servants united in their calculated and continued spite towards their besieged mistress, whom they continued to consider to be an interloper.

Despite violence and increasing threats of more violence, concern for the safety and care of her child became her overriding preoccupation. Whilst Mary remained unharmed, bruises to her mother became commonplace. Daily she felt her life to be in danger, 'attended with constant terror for many months, supposing each hour might be my last.' Constantly she was on her guard against blows, sometimes at the back of her ear; all unprovoked and when least expected. She even became afraid of being poisoned, afraid to eat or drink anything that her husband may have 'meddled with,' even though though her response to her husband's authority was never questioned.

When considered alongside the overriding law of the land regarding the absence of married women's rights, not surprisingly she acquiesced at all times to her husband's authority. Unchallenged subservience then applied to the vast majority of women.[5] Additionally, as a Christian, Mrs Stock would have been influenced by Biblical teaching.[6]

By the summer of 1816, there appears to have come about a sort of 'truce' between husband and wife. Taking advantage of the situation, Mrs Stock, daringly defied the Liverpool ban, to visit old friends there. Later she wrote to Mrs Price with a detailed description of a walk, with her infant Mary, through the streets of Wigan. She also tells of the preparations for Wigan Fair, to be held on 23 May, 1816:

22 May 1816 (Wigan). *To Mrs Price:*

I have been very comfortable since I left you; Mr S. never said a word on his return that could lead to the subject of his displeasure when we parted in Liverpool; and I was equally cautious.

I have been much diverted with Mary today. I took her by the hand, and she walked all the way from hence as far as our late

241

house in Chapel-lane. She has so many things to look at, that I
thought we should scarcely ever arrive. She stopped at every open
door, to look into the houses. There were many groups of little
children in the street, and she would walk up to them, and shout
at them; she set her foot upon the step of a door where there
happened to be a cake-shop, so I bought her a cake; and then
she wanted to stand still in the street whilst she ate it. I thought
her first walk should be to her who first nursed her, as she lives
in Chapel-Lane. I knocked at the door; I had to wait a little, and
Mary, too, would knock. After our visit was over, we walked
to see a neighbour who lived opposite to our old house; many
people were at their doors, and Mary stopped to look at them
all, and if they had infants in their arms, she stood some time.
Many laughed, and said she was a sharp little thing. She went
up steps at one house to a child of 3 or 4 years old (with a little
help), who gave her what he was playing with. The noise of looms
in a cellar next attracted her attention; she struggled hard to go
to the windows; but she is so fond of kicking, that I expected
nothing less than the breaking them, so I enticed her to go after
some poultry, and there was a little race. It is the first walk she has
had from home, but I mean often now to take her short distances.

The 'truce' between husband and wife also seemed to have
brought about the amelioration of at least one servant: 'Our
servant Alice has behaved extremely well since I came home, that
I have great hopes of her becoming valuable.' A happy spirit of
carnival was also in the air:

The town is going to be in a great bustle this week; for the
fair commences tomorrow [23 May], on which occasion, it is
usual for everybody to clean their houses thoroughly, to whitewash, paint, &c.; the confectioners begin of baking for the fair
a week beforehand; and the shop-keepers to polish, and set their
wares, in the neatest order; large caravans enter the town with
wild beasts, monsters, and Jugglers; likewise wooden horses,
whirligigs, gambling tables, barrel organs, fiddlers, and hordes of
beggars; to add to the *usual novelties*, a handsome new Cloth Hall
will be opened, built by Mr Tennant, and *everybody*, I suppose,
will go to see it.

The now more confident Mrs Stock indicates that she was
gradually becoming her old self, especially-so in connection with

her excellent organisational ability over her newly-developed system of household management. In triumph she wrote:

23 June 1816 (Wigan). *To Mrs Bessy Price:*

I could smile at your thinking that I had been so long my own mistress, because I had remained so long unmarried. I never was uncontrolled more than 2 years of my life. No-one, used to live in another person's house, can be said to have much of their own way. You don't know what it is, nor how great a trial and breaking of the temper it is, to keep a school, or to be a private teacher; married to one of so peculiar a temper as I am, it is scarcely worse.

I know how little success you would have, could you take my place for one year. Much as you think you could effect, you have not the most distant idea of such a situation, nor can words express it; yet I am indeed much happier of late than I was, entirely owing to being determined not to submit to a continuation of ill-treatment. Had I not acted with greater spirit, had I continued to take every means to please (which was taken for a principle of fear), I must have lost my senses or my life. The man who rules by tyranny, can never be obeyed in affection; he is submitted to from fear, and delights in abject submission; it gratifies the pride of his heart to see everyone trembling around him. But mark! The tyrant in power, is ever the abject slave when humbled; he knows no medium, and the only way of living peaceably with him, is . . . not to be afraid of him; for . . . tyrants are always cowards. By way of experiment, I have acted on this principle for the last 10 months; and with so much success, that we have all much more peace than we had. But don't suppose that I cease trying to please; it is my daily and hourly study; and you would think so, were you to live here. It is only where my own comfort is materially concerned, that I assume a resolute conduct. I love too much, to grieve my husband when I can make him comfortable.

I again repeat, that I am much happier than I was last Summer; I am better treated; and my little Mary is so sweet a tempered creature, that she is the delight of my heart. How blest I am in every way; my heart glows with gratitude to the Mighty Father, for he is drawing me nearer and nearer to him. I have been tried as it were in the fire, and I am delivered.

Having recently moved to a more commodious and rather impressive Georgian town house of three storeys, Mrs Stock was now beginning to see herself as a Wiganer – up to a point.

In her regular walks around the town and meeting more and more ordinary townsfolk, she would have been forcibly reminded that her educational attainment was far in excess of her contemporaries. This would be noticeable in her syntax, her extensive vocabulary and non-vernacular speech; although her flat vowels would have indicated having resided North West of the Pennines with an a south of the River Ribble intonation.

In an age of deference, Mrs Stock's 'difference' would have been respected, rather than resented. Society's norm was to respect ones betters, or perceived betters. It would be a mistake to refer to Mrs Stock as a 'snob;' she never pretended to be anything other than herself. She would, of course, have felt intellectually superior to many, for she was a voracious reader who had loved words and the use of words since childhood. She had been a child who 'burned,' without success, 'to learn Latin, French, the Arts, the Sciences.'

She did not question her place as a woman in the male dominated society of early 19th century England. Even in the darkest days of her marriage she never failed to refer to her husband, in all correspondence, as 'Mr Stock.' She did, however, question the historical injustice of men's contempt for women as being inferior in intelligence and wisdom. Furthermore she believed that men who considered women as inferior because of their lesser physical strength, 'debased themselves' as being 'unenlightened.' Irrespective of status, quite naturally she preferred to socialise with those who were not only intellectually able, but also morally upright. Moral rectitude, instilled by her mother remained ever-present. As a result, it is perfectly understandable why Mrs Stock would scorn those who aspired to a higher status, by confidently copying the manners of the upper classes, yet who remained woefully ignorant:

23 October 1816 (Wigan). *To Mrs Price:*

At present, my dear friend, I have plenty of time, and abundance of inclination for writing to you; and, besides these,

244

some degree of matter more than can at any time be collected in a town like this. I wish you would come and see me; the coach-fares are so very low, that now is the time for travelling. We are very comfortably fixed here, and I think you might spend a few weeks without being unhappy.

We Wiganers have begun to raise our heads and commence a literary career, that perhaps may exalt us to the top of Parnassus.[7] What think you of a Wiganer being able to compose, to write, to print, or publish!!! Is it not most extraordinary! *We* have got no farther than a penny, and three halfpenny pamphlets; *we* are only in our noviciate; but even these are most astonishing . . . for Wigan! And as I feel some pride at being an inhabitant of a place that is at length beginning to shew some slight signs of intellect, I feel some additional consequence in being able to join myself to this bright community, and, in speaking, to say *We*!

For some time, perhaps 3 or 4 years or more, there has been a debating society in Wigan, supported and conducted by some low fellows, principally journey-men;[8] and they have gone on unnoticed, except now and then affording a good joke to their masters. One of them once got into the room; a servant of his got into the chair, but when he saw his master there, he was so confused, the debate could not go on, and the exclusion of strangers was gravely voted.

Lately a shoemaker's son, of the name of Burdekin, a warehouseman, feeling some strong impulses, and mistaking them for the effects of Genius and Patriotism, has opened his mouth in this society; and being looked upon as a great man among them, he begins to think himself very great indeed; and, from leading a few poor illiterate fellows, would all at once take upon him to conduct the house of Lords and Commons, the King, Queen, Prince-Regent, all the Royal Dukes, the Princes, the Princesses, and Nobility and Gentry of all descriptions; it is only the poor people whom he thinks capable of conducting themselves.

To assist him in this arduous undertaking, some experienced-headed Reformers from Liverpool, such as Rushton and J Smith, have of late frequently attended here, and have been honoured with the presence of hundreds of vagabonds. The richer inhabitants of Wigan begin to be seriously alarmed; and the Mayor, a short time ago, remonstrated with the Reformers respecting their meetings;

they were deaf, and ridiculed his interference. Then came out a little letter advising peace and patience, and perseverance in well-doing; a simple, well-meant thing, supposed to be written by Mr Pigot, late curate here. A very hot answer was instantly returned by a Reformer, in which were a great deal of hard words, and no *little* vulgarity and scurrility, interspersed with a *little* Latin, and of course, a *little* Dr Holme, a young apothecary of *little* repute. Soon after, a third pamphlet was born, said to be produced by Dr Cowley, a man of some talents; the bantling was very witty, and had more sense and argument than either of the other two; but should it not become any larger, will, like the other two, be soon forgotten. The Reformers treated this with great contempt; it was not worth answering; and indeed there were some questions which it may not be convenient to answer; however, they do not mean to stop here, and these new-fledged authors mean to have more feathers yet in their wings.

The bravadoes of the Reformers, and the fears of the Loyalists, are amusing to an indifferent Observer. The former imagine that they have quite frightened the latter, and laugh exultingly; the latter are not quite easy, but laugh contemptuously, and at the same time, prophesy riots the ensuing Winter by the meddling of these would-be Reformers. Should riots really ensue, perhaps I may laugh with neither side. Many people are seriously uneasy.[9]

Mrs Bird, Mrs Weeton's sister, has got to such a pitch of drunkenness, that she is the talk of the country. The other day, she was carried home almost senseless; and in her way up Holland streets, was followed by a mob, hooting and hissing. Mr Bird has at last determined on separating, and my brother is to meet him in Wigan next Tuesday, with deeds to that effect.

My little Mary improves, and is the delight of all; she is just 16 months old. She does not say a word yet, notwithstanding which, she has a thousand little engaging actions. Her hair is very light, and curls all over her head like a little mop; and she is all over so fat and so soft. I have many a kiss in the course of the day, and many a laugh at her little droll ways; her father would be quite lost without her, and I am sure, so should I. I wish I had another . . . but hush! Don't tell.

Where is Mrs Edwards; have you ever heard? How are Mr and Mrs Langdon, and Master – but come and tell me with your own mouth, and I will not now ask you any more questions. I often call at your uncle Hawarden's, for I am almost lost for want of society. I cannot ask them here, so I call there once a week; they always receive me in a friendly manner. They have been painting and beautifying the outside of their house and that adjoining, which is let to a straw bonnet-maker, and fitted up stylishly.

You would hear of a coach being overset here lately, opposite to the Eagle Inn.[10] Many were severely hurt; but their heads were proof, being *Wiganers*. One man's head was fractured, but he came from Bolton.

My servant Margaret, notwithstanding what Hannah thinks of her temper, is the best by much that I have had since I came to Wigan; and I am really very comfortable with her. She is very steady indeed, and cleanly, and pays more respectful attention to me than any other person in the house. I found it necessary, soon after she came, to tell her how I was situated with regard to Jane; that she would take every means of setting her against me; and Margaret told me that she had already attempted it with her, but assured me she would always strive to conduct herself so as to deserve my approbation, and I have had no reason to repent the confidence I have placed in her. Her temper breaks out sometimes, but it is nothing compared with what I have suffered from all the rest; I can easily put up with it.

Sadly all was far from sweetness and light within the marriage. An undercurrent of resentment and hate was welling-up in the heart of Aaron Stock. A letter to Mrs Price proves to be a harbinger of impending personal tragedy:

4 November 1816 (Wigan). *To Mrs Price:*

Dear Friend,

Perhaps when I exclaim how enviable is your lot in possessing a husband so kind, that where he is, your heart is treasured; his home, your paradise; I ought much rather to say, how much above you am I blessed! My heart is driven and buffeted about, seeking where it may find rest; and, having none on earth, will, almost of necessity, be driven to heaven. Mighty Father, may this indeed be the result of my afflictions! Then shall I be blessed to the utmost of my wishes, and the misery I now endure will be an eternal cause of gratitude. My husband is my terror, my misery! And I have little doubt, will be my death. I earnestly wish I could obtain a situation at Mr Wade's or elsewhere; I would not hesitate a moment. I shall never live to educate Mary, unless I quit this place.

Early in 1818, behind the locked door of her room (and her prison), Mrs Stock decided to obey her natural impulse and attempt to write something very different than anything previously. It was to be a diary, entitled: *Occasional Reflections, A.D. 1818*. Its purpose was to pour out her innermost thoughts to God, at a time when her faith was wavering, because of marital stress:

A.D. 1818. An intention of marking a few domestic events, but more particularly the religious state of my mind, induced me to attempt a kind of Diary. But so painful and heart-rending have been the occurrences of the few days which have yet passed in the New Year, that agitation, anguish, and despair, have driven all thoughts of religion away. Have mercy! Have pity upon me, Oh my father! And enable me to sustain Thy chastening hand with more submission and humility. Forsake me not at this trying time, and help me to see which way I should act, so as to please Thee and save my soul.

Is it Thy Will that I submit to the tyranny of him who so cruelly uses me, and abuses the power which he has over me? Oh, that I could say that it were any other than my own husband. He that should nourish, cherish, and protect me; he that should protect me, so that even the winds should not blow too roughly on me – he is the man who makes it his sport to afflict me, to expose me to every hard-ship, to every insult. Or am I right in struggling to free myself from his griping hand?

Bitter have been the years of my marriage, and sorrowful my days. Surely the measure of them is full! My life, my strength, cannot sustain many more such.

Jan. 5th. Turned out of doors into the street! In the anguish of my mind, I broke out into complaints; this only was my fault. I took a chaise to Leigh; my brother not being at home, I dismissed it and stopped two nights. He brought me home with an intention to effect either a reconciliation or a separation. He could do neither. Mr Stock wants me either to remain at home pennyless, as an underling to his own daughter, or to be kept by anyone that will take me. I cannot agree to such a reconciliation, or such a separation, whilst he has plenty of money. I am obliged totally to withdraw myself from any domestic affairs, in obedience to my husband's orders; to live in an apartment alone; not to sit at a table with the family, but to have my meat sent to me; and amuse myself as I can.

When, and how will this end?

Jan. 10th. Still in my solitary confinement. Had a new cloak brought home, and the first thought on seeing it, was, Well! I have made sure of this, however (having long wished for a Winter garment of this description, and not had it in my power to obtain it). Alas! . . . how presumptious! That very night might my soul have been required of me, disease have seized me, or fire have destroyed both it and me, and all else I possessed. But Thou, O Father, hast been very merciful. Yes! Although my husband makes me, as it were, a prisoner in my house, I have a Peace which he knows nothing of, a Joy which he cannot take away. Oh! That his heart would soften, and that he might repent.

Even though, for good reason, Mrs Stock had at last become suspicious of her brother's motives, in sheer desperation she felt there was no choice but to try to solicit his help. She interrupted her *Occasional Reflections*, to despatch a letter to her practising lawyer brother, Thomas, who was now also Clerk to the Leigh magistrates. It candidly reveals the pitiful details of her circumstances and it brought about a prompt response – for reasons additional to his sister's desperate plight:

14th January 1818 (Wigan). *To Mr Weeton:*

Dear Brother,

I feel a strong reluctance to saying any more on a subject which now appears to me altogether hopeless; and after this week, be assured I will never more distress you or Mrs Weeton by the sight of me, or of anything that can remind you of me. My late exertions have only been like the weak struggles of a drowning insect, and if I cannot now be rescued, I must inevitably sink! I would not, at this time, have applied to you, had it not been frequently said to me – 'Why do you not apply to your brother? As your brother lives so near, it is his duty to protect an only sister from the ill-usage of an unkind, unfeeling husband.' I have often replied, 'What can my brother do? If he can do nothing effectual, it is cruel to distress him.'

It was not from mere momentary resentment that I came to your house. I have suffered bitterly by much the greater part of the time since I came to Wigan; and the time when I suffered most, was *when I endured most patiently*. I am at length most firmly convinced, that had I but strength and resolution to act with greater spirit, we should both live more peaceably. I am generally treated in such a browbeating, sulky, contemptuous manner, that I become abject and spiritless; if, like a worm, I shew a little impotent resentment, I am kicked and trampled on. Could I but assume more spirit, I should be treated with more respect; or, if a few individuals would interest themselves for me, the fear of what the world may say, would induce Mr S. to treat me with more appearance of kindness. But he overawes all who come near to him; even *you* feel it. Although many despise him, none dare shew him so much outward attention, it is a tacit encouragement to his tyranny at home. I have long found that he grows worse by submission (I do not mean, to his reasonable wishes), and that resistance to his cruelty, although attended with terrible effects for a time, *ensures more peace afterwards*.

On every trifling occasion, he is ordering me out of doors, until I am quite weary of hearing of it. Did you ever know what it was to be unwelcome? And did you feel happy in that place? If you had daily proofs that your wife wished to be quit of you, would your domestic lot be enviable?

Mr Stock is a man of that kind that would like a fresh wife every three or four months; his behaviour has been so unkind to me, that I wish it were in his power to change. It was supposed by many of his acquaintances that he was tired of his first wife long before she died, and that his unkindness hastened her end. Now it is my lot, and he will teaze me to death; I see no escape. Were he generally as kind as I this [last] Summer knew him to be for a few weeks, to live with him all my days would be most desirable, and to leave him, my greatest grief.

His saying I never was the first to be friendly, is false; I have numberless times made the attempt. I acknowledge that his repulsive manner intimidates me so, that my attempts are feeble; generally, by striving to enter into some conversation with him, or by some little delicate attention, which *would win a heart like yours* directly. When I have attempted to put my arm around him, he has often pushed it away from him so rudely, that his hard gripe has hurt me exceedingly; the few times that I tried that way, I never recollect that it succeeded.

In his quarrelsome humours, which occur often, I can do nothing right; and when perfectly placid, and he has nothing else to find fault with, my looks are ridiculed, my thin face, my haggard countenance, and skeleton figure. I seldom reply; I make ill-natured reflections on him or his relations, let him say what he will of mine.

My principle ground of complaint is the being kept so totally without money, at times when he is angry with me; his frequently refusing it to me, and, at the *same time*, and for the *same purpose*, giving it to his daughter, to Hannah, or to the servant. With what patience I have generally borne this insulting usage, they can, any of them, testify, although continued for many weeks at once; and since I came to this house, at one time for a period of from 10 to 12 months; now lately, for 2 months or more. Frequently, when sitting with him, I have recollected something that was wanted, and have gone into the kitchen to send the servant to him to ask for it; this is a *very common* occurrence; and as common to me to requesting dinner, &c. they know that he will tell them sooner than me; this is not just for a day or two, but a daily conduct for weeks or months at once. Any alteration or improvement about the house or garden, I hear of first from servants.

This invariable kind of treatment, naturally is the cause of my losing all authority and respect in the house; and at such times, it is a regular thing for Hannah or Jane to conduct the house, just as they please, without thinking it at all necessary to consult me. Further, the family know, that to please Mr Stock, they must set themselves against me; and as I have neither money nor power, they can insult me as they please. I can neither punish, nor dismiss. If I complain, I am threatened to be turned out of doors, for there is no living with me. 'Why do you, then?' I reply. 'Let Jane and Hannah be mistresses, and let me go.'

In his ill humours, which I have told you continue for so long, it would be a crime of the first magnitude to sit down with him at supper; like a cat, I sit by and watch, but dare not touch. If it be shell-fish, sausages, &c., he eats all up, and however I may long, I can get none. I must either fare as the servant does, or go without. He frequently buys fruit, which he always locks up from me; if I am in favour, I get a little; but that is so seldom, that it chiefly falls to Mary's lot, and he will sit eating, by the fire, without offering me a taste. But I have discovered that he treats himself, chiefly when out of the house, with fruit or anything very nice, eating it out of doors, or elsewhere. When he had quarrelled with me, he used to refuse helping me at dinner. I took it up warmly, and he has not done it lately; he only revenges himself, by not helping me to cheese.

I do not recollect that I ever was the first to begin a quarrel, until the last time, because he would give me no money.

As an argument, which I strongly insist upon in my own defence – if I were so bad to live with, do you think me cheaply bought off, for £70 a year?[11]

He well knows that I am such a check upon Hannah, Jane, and the servant, that much more of his property would be wasted, or spent extravagantly, than it now takes to keep me. If I were so bad to live with, Hannah and servant would be glad to leave. I can easily prove that every servant I have parted with (through Jane's and Hannah's mischief-making), have been desirous to remain, or come again, except one; and I have had 6 or 7. Many of my acquaintance can tell you, that they do not like, or dare not visit me, owing to Mr Stock; none of his acquaintances can say the same of me.

Some of his intimate friends can tell you of his stingy fits; and I can tell you, that in those fits, he is terrible at home.

If I remain here, my proposition is:

1st. That on no occasion of quarrel, I am ever again deprived of Money for house-keeping, and for my own and Mary's cloaths. I would prefer a regular weekly sum for one, and an annual one for the other, half a year paid in advance.

2ndly. Wholly to give up house-keeping to Jane or Hannah, and have only an allowance for cloaths, and pocket-money; and to live like a boarder in the house; I shall very willingly accede to this.

I will then give up my time to Mary's education, to reading, music, the cultivation of plants, or anything else that may make for peace, and prevent my interference in the family.

Peace I must insist upon; either in the house, or to be permitted to depart in Peace.

Leigh is a little over seven miles from Wigan and Thomas realised that as Clerk to Leigh magistrates, the two towns were too close for comfort. Thomas could ill-afford the gossip and adverse publicity that a marriage break-up within his extended family, might cause. As a result, his earnest desire was to preserve the peace at all costs. Thomas did his best by visiting the Stock's home to intercede on his sister's behalf. Whilst it may have helped to calm the situation, unfortunately there would be no quick resolution; Thomas Weeton was as impotent before the law of the land as all others. It would be six more years before Mrs Stock would be free from persecution, intimidation and penury. Throughout 1818, the stress and turmoil of her marital circumstances dramatically reduced her letter writing, in favour of entries in *Occasional Reflections*:

Jan. 16th. My brother came with a view to assist, if in his power, to put an end to the unhappy state in which Mr Stock and me were. It was done. My hopes are not very sanguine; but should this peace be of short continuance, or should it be more lasting than before, may I bear meekly. Shouldest Thou again afflict me, let not despair, let not anguish of soul, drive me again to such a degree of madness as lately possessed me! I shewed little of it, but Oh, how did I feel it!

Jan. 18th. Having gone to Holland on the 17th, to stay 2 days at Mrs Braithwaite's, I received a message from my uncle, requesting to see me. I called upon him, and he offered me an asylum at his house, should I ever want one. He had heard how I had been situated lately, and was then ready, he said, to take me in. I told him that a kind of reconciliation had taken place [with her husband]; that his offer, notwithstanding, had released my mind from an anxious burthen; for I did not know where to go when turned out before. At the same time, I would do all that was in my power to avoid being placed in such a situation again. I had ever striven to act as a wife ought to do; in the same way, I would endeavour to continue. I could not promise more.[12]

Tuesday morning, Jany 27th. Went with Mrs Scott to the Catholic Chapel,[13] to see high Mass performed, and the consecration of the stone for the new Chapel. It was the first time that I had ever been in a Catholic place of worship. I have often heard their forms and ceremonies much ridiculed and highly censured, and have felt much pained at the want of charity in my Protestant friends. I have thought their bitterness equalled Roman Catholic bigotry, and felt much inclined to think they were not quite so ridiculous as they were represented. What I witnessed this day, filled me with the utmost astonishment, that so many millions of people, possessing as much natural sense and discernment as myself, could be so led by such boyish pageantry, or imagine for a moment that Christ, whose 'kingdom was not of this world,' whose life in it was utterly void of grandeur or finery, should be pleased with that now, which he sensured whilst he was amongst us in his human nature.

Jan 31ˢᵗ. Hard of faith as I know I am, and much as it grieves me that I remain so, I should be completely an Infidel of the Roman Catholic profession were it the only Christian profession on earth.

The pomp observed in many of our Protestant Churches, and the frequent profligacy of the clergy, first shook my faith to the foundations; first discovered to me, that I was no Christian. Had I not been forced to reflection by these means, I should have gone on heedlessly to my last hour, imagining myself to be a very dutiful child of God all the time, trusting in my own works. Turning disgusted from the pompous folly of our Churches and Clergy, and knowing nothing of the Dissenters,[14] the apparent simplicity of the Quakers had strong attractions for me. For years I went on thus settled, never being fortunate enough to become acquainted with one religious Protestant family or individual, yet seeking them wherever I went.

During 1818 she spent three months in Liverpool before acute financial pressure became an embarrassment to her. To take prolonged advantage of the charitable nature of friends would have been repugnant to Miss Weeton's sensibilities. She took her quill once again to make an entry during November:

November 29ᵗʰ. It is long since I recorded aught in these pages, which were intended to have been devoted to the spiritual state of my mind; to mark from time to time the progress I made in holiness; and to be a warning to me lest I, like Lot's wife, should look back again.

Although I have not, I hope, turned back, my progress is scarcely perceptible. I have been under the influence of such

254

gracious words from the pulpit ever since I came to Liverpool (Sept. 16), that surely I am not hard-hearted and rebellious to the last degree, surely I shall grow in grace, for now I have no excuse. I have many hours each day full of leisure for devotion. I cannot grieve now, as formerly, that I have not time for reading the word of God; but, let me ask as each hour passes, as each day closes, have I improved those hours? And what is the sum at night?

Oh never, never let me rest, my God, when my heart wanders from Thee. Draw me perpetually as hitherto. Warn me, counsel me, afflict me, so Thou but secure me! And if I am again the mistress of a family, let nothing hinder my taking many opportunities each day to pray with them, to read them in the Bible, and to teach them of Heaven as God shall give me utterance. Let not the dread of being scoffed at by my husband for pretending to sanctity, any more have influence with me.

Dec. 16th. I am now on the eve of doing something which will materially affect my future situation. In the morning, I set off to Leigh, for I must either bestir myself, or starve. I have waited 3 full weeks for a remittance; my brother has kindly lent me £5, but I must not live on credit. If great exertions are necessary, I have great exertions in contemplation.

Oh, my Father, let me go forth in Thy strength. Work for me by what means soever Thou seest best. Desert me not in this hour of great trial. Be my Guide and my Counsellor. Give me the wisdom of the dove; and oh, have pity on me, and more particularly for the 3 ensuing days, in which I have much to do. Deal gently with Thy servant; let not the anguish of mind I must expect to endure, Oh! Let it not quite overwhelm me. Give me much strength.

And with those heart-rending words, Miss Weeton's *Occasional Reflections* ends.

The year 1818 is also significant in increasingly bringing to the fore the vital importance of the only child of the marriage; in particular her importance to her mother as a delightful companion during periodic exclusions from the Stock home. Mary also proved to be a vital substitute for Mrs Stock's now dwindling list of correspondents. Now aged three, Mary was becoming the

255

subject of dispute, either through hateful obstruction, or because of her mother's genuine desire to give the child an educational advantage in life.

At this time Aaron Stock began to indicate a desire to separate Mary from her mother and give her the benefit of an education himself. In addition it would also deprive Mary of her mother's influence for long periods. Sole consolation for Mrs Stock in this arrangement would be that Mary would no longer be exposed to the evil influences that surrounded her in her father's home. Mrs Stock submitted to the arrangement that Mary should be placed in the 'care' of Mr and Mrs Grundy, joint principals of Boarding Academy for Young Ladies, at Parr Hall, St Helens.[15] Parr Hall was an ancient building (now demolished), in the Blackbrook area of St Helens, and had been associated with Queen Catherine Parr's ancestors. In 1778 it was described as 'a capital mansion house.'

It is doubtful that Stock would have been aware that all was not well at the Academy. Mr Grundy was said to be inclined to amorous dalliances with his staff of single young women, while at the same time Mrs Grundy was in the process of drinking herself to death. Thankfully during her time at the Academy, Mary did not appear to have suffered any violent ill-treatment, but she rapidly became very thin whilst under the Grundys' care. It also became noticeable that Mary soon lost 'some of her engaging little ways' that had so endeared her to her mother's heart.

In order to ensure the continued patronage of Stock, the proprietors of the Academy were under strict instructions from him concerning visiting arrangements. These were designed to adversely affect Mrs Stock's relationship with her daughter. Also, through her husband's connivance with the Wigan Postmaster, Miss Weeton's letters to her daughter were deliberately intercepted. With Mary safely out of the way at the Boarding Academy, Stock had thus cleared the way to destroy his wife's determination to assist in her daughter's educational development.

A single letter by her mother has survived, addressed to Mary but never despatched. It is written in a larger than normal clear and legible script, with unusually generous line spacing, in a style didactically suitable for a young mind:

256

31 December 1819 (Wigan):

My dear Mary,

According to my promise, I have sent you a little servant [doll] to wait upon the young ladies that Mrs Grundy was to bring with her from Liverpool. Her name is Ellen. I am afraid you will have a great deal to do to teach her, for she has never been in service before; but she is perfectly honest, no rambler nor a tell-tale; and as to her indolence, if you set her a good example, it may perhaps have a wonderful effect.

I have made her a few cloaths, and furnished your cradle, and it has amused me very much; for indeed it is a pleasure to me to do anything for my little darling girl. Now you must be very contented, and not wish anything more for a long time; for there are thousands of little children who cannot get any of those comforts which you enjoy every hour of the day. Think often of this, my dear little Mary, and as often as you do think of it, thank that Heavenly Father who is continually taking so much care of you. You are no better than those poor little girls that go about selling cold potatoes. God makes some poor, and some rich, to try which serve him best: but let no one, my dear, love and serve God better than you. How you must do this, I have often told you; but if you forget, ask Mr or Mrs Grundy; they will tell you at any time, for they are very good, and very clean; and indeed they are very kind to you. Tell them your mother wishes to be very respectfully remembered to them.

I have written my letter in a large hand, in hopes you will try to learn to read it yourself. When Miss Knight comes to school again, I think I will write to you by her.

Give my love to your little companion, Miss Watt.

Your affectionate Mother,
N. Stock.

From the winter of 1819, until after Mrs Stock's legal separation in January or February 1822, persecution became relentless; exacerbated by the autocratic Revd Alexander Steill, minister of St Paul's Chapel, Wigan.

The degradation and humility that Mrs Stock was forced to endure during that period is revealed in a 12,000 word letter sent to her brother after her separation. Extracts from the letter are as follows:

Repeatedly turned out destitute; twice imprisoned – the first time for a first offence of the kind; the 2nd, *perfectly innocent*, having myself been beaten almost to death; several times obliged to flee for my life; the time when I broke the windows, if I had not by that means forced my way in, I must have been out all night, on the cold and wet pavement of a dark November night. I had then been turned out only for complaining, whilst enduring exceedingly unkind treatment. I was threatened with being sent to a Lunatic Asylum, only for asking for food. Cloaths I could not procure until I got them credit; and that I did not attempt, only for the last year that I was with him. The second time I was in prison, was on a false oath; yet you said I acknowledged that I struck the man. I did not strike the man, and how you could construe the passage so, I know not. I should like to see that letter again, for I took no copy; for, owing to anguish of body from that dreadful beating, and distraction of mind at being at the point of being a 2nd, time sent to prison by my husband out of revenge for my procuring a warrant for him, I could not copy it.

With my bruises thick upon me – bruises such as the Doctor said would have mortified had I not been so extremely thin – was I imprisoned for two days, and you would not bail me out! Oh, oh, you unnatural being. I had no money, and no provisions were sent to Kirkdale house of Correction for the want of bail (since you would not do it), when J. Latham and G. Oakes [for whom she had performed a kindly office as far back as the year 1809] of Holland, came over and bailed me out. Oh! this was a climax of misery! 'Tis strange I did not lose my senses, to think that I should have such a husband and such a brother!

At 8 o'clock that night, my bruises still undressed, and pitiably emaciated, I had to walk with these men to Holland, 4 miles. The night was dark, wet, and winterly; but now among friends, and I was nursed, and soothed, and comforted. Mrs Braithwaite's door was open to me, if my brother's was not – and her door is often open to the friendless.

I soon returned to my miserable home, for I dared not stay long away, now expecting nightly or daily to be murdered – or worse, sent to a Lunatic Asylum in my right mind; for so I was threatened; and I had no help to expect from you (for so you had assured Mr Stock)! I had no earthly help, no help but of heaven, and I endeavoured to resign myself. I expected to be again turned

258

out, although Mr Stock lived in another house, and to be driven out destitute as I had often been, so that I kept myself locked up day and night in my bedroom, going out only by stealth in the evening, to fetch provisions, and let Dr Hawarden's see that I was in Wigan, and alive. On returning one night, I found my room on fire, and my bed burnt! I almost solemnly declare that I was not in the house when the fire commenced. In my opinion, it was done to procure my transportation, or perhaps even hanging; for I had no help to expect from you. I wish it had been investigated. I could easily have proved my innocence, and have brought home the charge guilty.

I had now no bed! As I was reduced lower and lower in affliction, I often exclaimed – what next? After lying some nights on a Sofa, rolled in blankets, I found shelter at the kind Mrs Braithwaite's of Holland.

All was not lost on brother Thomas, despite the inconvenience, he soon came over to Wigan from Leigh, bringing with him his respected friend, Mr Marsh of Westleigh, a Magistrate on the Leigh Bench, under who Thomas officiated as Clerk. In such august company, there can be no doubt that Thomas would have behaved impeccably:

> You did indeed strive to serve me, and paid all the expenses at the Inn that day. Mr Marsh was unsuccessful (to prevail with Mr Stock to allow me a separate maintenance); but I was not the less obliged; and I repeat my thanks to you, as I shall to him if I have the opportunity. But it had long been too late for anything but the strong arm of the law, and that you would not assist me in (keeping true to your promise to Mr Stock). Your cruel neglect was the astonishment of great numbers in Wigan, who said you would be quiet if I were in murdering.

If Stock had proved adamant with regard to separate maintenance, he was by no means averse to a Deed of Separation. Having already appointed his solicitor (Mr Henry Gaskell), before whom both parties had entered into recognizances to appear at the Sessions, it remained only for Mrs Stock to name her solicitor. Brother Thomas, however, displayed an unsolicitor-like reticence in representing his sister, and refused to answer any further enquiries from his bereft sister. Speculation about

Thomas's lack of action is far from difficult to understand, he had previously made it plain to his sister that because Stock was renting a factory in Wigan, belonging to his wife's mother, he had threatened to give notice to leave the premises if Thomas gave him any offence. Two other reasons put forward by Thomas were that he 'dreaded the expence (sic) it might involve,' and most pathetically, that his wife 'would not let him.'

Despite Thomas Weeton's vacillations, hope finally came from another source, but not before further humiliation of his now abandoned sister. Mrs Stock had become very much dependant for her bodily sustenance on the charity of increasingly hesitant and apprehensive friends. Alternatively she could sign the Deed of Separation, which had already been drawn up by another legal representative, and signed by Stock. That other legal representative was revealed as none other than Thomas Weeton himself, acting on behalf of his new client, Aaron Stock. The choice for Mrs Stock and its implication was clear: Sign or starve. The choice was hers. Furthermore, beyond hearing the content of the Deed read out to her once only, she was not allowed to read it for herself. 'Game, set and match.' Mrs Nelly Stock was a beaten woman.

The alternative to signing in ignorance was possible starvation, lunatic asylum (she had previously been threatened with the lunatic asylum), or prison. Nor would her brother act as a bondsman for her. She signed the Deed[16] at the end of January (or early February) 1822, with the comment: 'I find I have forever signed my child away!'

Events leading to the signing of the Deed of Separation, were recalled later by Miss Weeton, in a letter to a sympathetic friend:

> He [brother Thomas] came to me at Mrs T. Marsden's, to persuade me to agree to the terms which Mr Stock insisted on. His unbrotherly-like conduct roused my greatest contempt, and I would not listen to him. I never saw him afterwards, or heard from him; and I hope never more to do so! . . . When, in two or three weeks after, the Deed itself was presented to me by Mr Ackerly (Mr Gaskell's clerk) to sign, I was obliged to sign it in great ignorance of its contents (not being allowed to read

it, but only to hear it read by the clerk), for the sake of getting immediate subsistence, as people were unwilling to trust me on Mr Stock's credit.

Under the Deed's provisions Miss Weeton was limited to three annual visits to her child. The visits were to take place only in the presence of a proprietor of the Boarding Academy for Young Ladies, at Parr Hall, St Helens, (Mrs Grundy or her partner). The most outrageous condition was not only to forbid her residence within a two-and-a-half-mile radius of Wigan, but also to prohibit her visits to the town upon any pretext whatsoever!

Eventually she openly defied that prohibition, yet the quarterly allowance continued to be paid to her (through an agent). The reality is that not even in the anti-feminine times of George IV it is extremely doubtful that the validity of such an agreement would have been upheld in an open court.

Seven-and-a-half years after marrying, Miss Weeton now found herself childless, a wreck of her former self and in receipt of an income in the form of a dole. The property she had once owned, plus her investments gained by business acumen, rarely found in one of her sex, remained in the hands of her former husband. Furthermore, Aaron Stock took the opportunity to damage his former wife's creditworthiness, by paying her the agreed £70 per annum allowance, quarterly in arrears.

Once more a wanderer, Miss Weeton, then retired from that place of 'mental barrenness' – Wigan – to the scene of her often difficult childhood and early womanhood, also the place of 'scandalous licentiousness' – the village of Up Holland.

NOTES:

1. Miss Weeton would have freely chosen Holy Trinity Parish Church for her marriage, but by law she had to be married by a Church of England parson. It was not until the Marriage Act of 1836, that Protestant Dissenters and Roman Catholics were allowed to marry in their own places of worship.
2. There is evidence (almost one year after their marriage) that Aaron Stock could offer free-use of his fists. The local Sessions Rolls of the period record: 'On the 17th July, 1815, Aaron Stock, cotton spinner, entered into recognizances (his sureties being Richard Eccles, surgeon, and Thomas Astcroft, a stone-mason) for an assault on Robert Balshaw, a cotton rover.' (S.R. 60/25).
3. Aaron Stock's first wife was Elizabeth Gilbert, widowed wife of John Gilbert, a grocer. John and Elizabeth Gilbert had five children, Samuel, Jane, Edward, Hannah and Thomas. Samuel and Jane Gilbert had died prior to Aaron Stock's marriage to Elizabeth. Aaron and Elizabeth had two children, William and Jane. William had died prior to Aaron's marriage to Miss Weeton. (See also Appendix III).
4. The Stocks moved to a larger home in Standishgate, Wigan, very close to the centre of the town. (See image No. 16).
5. Not until the Divorce Act of 1857, did the many former marital injustices begin to be addressed.
6. St Paul instructed: 'Wives, submit yourselves unto your own husbands, as unto the Lord. For the husband is the head of the wife, even as Christ is the head of the Church, so let the wives be to their own husbands in every thing.' (Ephesians 5:22-23).
7. Parnassus. The name of a mountain in Greece, overlooking the Gulf of Corinth. It was sacred in antiquity as the home of the Muses.
8. Historically, a journeyman was one who tended to live and work for a master. It was normal that they too would aspire to becoming masters. Collectively, journeymen were brother labourers of one class, who shared meals together. A proud fraternity of skilled men of the trade.
9. Not surprisingly, people were uneasy because of the recent Napoleonic Wars. The wars had resulted in exorbitant increases in the price of food. Reform was in the air throughout the country; commerce was interrupted and supplies of foreign corn were extremely small. Wheat had reached an enormous price. After the war Parliament resolved to keep out foreign corn as long as English wheat was at, or under, 80 shillings a quarter. The advantage and benefit was to farmers only. Workers already reduced in circumstances through the lowness of wages, suffered even more. Justice was sought through agitations and riots in 1817 and 1819.
10. The 'Eagle Inn' was the Eagle and Child public house. Later it became the Royal Eagle and Child and latterly the Royal Hotel. It was located on the corner of Station Road (now The Grand Arcade) with Standishgate, where once was Woolworths (now W. H. Smith).
11. Before her marriage, Miss Weeton had enjoyed an income of £70 per year. She was eventually to make that same sum a year, a 'conditional' for leaving her husband.

12. There is no evidence that Miss Weeton ever saw her uncle again. Thomas Barton died 21 October 1820, aged 78. He is buried with his wife, Margaret, in Up Holland churchyard. His legacy of £60 (less £6 Legacy Duty), was forfeited, in its entirety, to Aaron Stock.
13. Believed to be St John's R.C. Church, Standishgate, Wigan. 'Mrs Scott' is possibly the mother-in-law of Thomas Weeton, who appears to have some sympathy for Mrs Stock.
14. Refers to the 'New Dissent' known as 'Methodism.'
15. 'St. Helens: William Grundy. Boarding Academy. Parr Hall.' *Baines's Lancs. Directory, 1825.* As an educational establishment for young ladies, Parr Hall was advertised in successive directories, up to the year 1855. It is not known when the Academy ceased to be run by the Grundys.
16. Attempts to trace a copy of the Deed have failed.

EIGHT

Rejected

Up Holland

April 1822 – May 1824

EARLY IN 1822, Miss Weeton's access to her daughter Mary became more difficult than before she signed the Deed of Separation. During the Christmas holidays of 1821, she had not been allowed any contact and was now restricted to infrequent and conditional interviews with her at Parr Hall, near St. Helens, some seven miles distant from Up Holland where, in April, Miss Weeton took up residence. She was now an exile from Wigan living in cramped lodgings at Ball's farm[1] near the summit of a hillside overlooking the town. Sadly, a further 18 months were to elapse before she would meet her daughter again.

In common with the surrounding countryside, the Balls were experiencing considerable hardships, so Miss Weeton was to witness close at hand the after effects of the Peninsular Wars. These had never before concerned her; neither had she ever before observed its deleterious effects. She would now eat her comfortless meals alone, for Mr and Mrs Ball, together with their servants and labourers, worked unremittingly in order to survive.

Mr Ball and his wife were grateful for the meagre amount that Miss Weeton could afford in rent that would help them to stave off either enclosure or foreclosure. She was there as a stranger among those who could not spare the time to care for her if she ever became ill. The only place of comfort for her might have been the nearby church of St. Thomas The Martyr, but its impassive repetitive liturgy, seemed only to mock her pain-filled heart and spiritual needs. She was, however, able to find acceptance and to it, rather than contend with him; but the guard took up my cause, and a long scuffle ensued; once or twice I thought between them they would have overturned the coach. I then begged the guard to say no more, and I rode the rest of the night on a very dangerous outside seat behind, backwards: we were four upon it, and it was too short by much, for the number; but every seat was equally crowded: it was very necessary to keep my eyes open, for the least drowsiness, and I should have dropped headlong: the man on my left kept a constant motion with his head upon my shoulder, up and down, the night through, being heavy to sleep; the brim of his hat endangering my eyes: the guard and he quarrelled again, but neither good words, nor bad, had any effect. I expressed my obligations to the guard, and begged him to trouble himself no more with the man, and so made peace; for the Irishman seemed determined to have the last word, and the last blow, had they quarrelled for a week: the iron rail bruised me sadly, I was so jammed against it. About 6 in the morning, one of the Irishmen in front, left the coach; when I saw that, down I dropped, and up into his seat like a cat, and was much more comfortable, although I had one on my left, as filthy as possible, and his head likewise jolting against me perpetually: it was intolerable! I very quietly requested he would let his head nod on the other (the out-) side; I thought the man would have beaten me; the coachman then interfered, and they had a long quarrel, and at last a scuffle, as the driver was determined to hurl him off the coach unless he behaved better; I was really frightened, and could not but weep: the women in Ireland must have a dreadful time with such fellows. A young woman on my right, the only female companion I had had, and she had passed a dreadful night; an Irish pig driver on each side of her, and another in front, snoring, and resting their heads against her, to present themselves falling. I extracted sweets from bitters, and still enjoyed the ride, and the prospects, arriving in Liverpool at 11 o'clock the morning of the 30th July (Friday)

12. A sample page of Miss Weeton's handwriting. Over 400 words were normally written on a page size of $7^{1}/_{2}$ x $6^{1}/_{4}$ inches (190 x 160 mm) and each letter averaged some 1400 words. The above page refers to her return stagecoach journey 'outside' from London to Liverpool, on July 29th, 1824. At Birmingham the passengers changed coaches and "took up 6 Irishmen of the lowest description." *Courtesy of Wigan Archives and Local Studies.*

Drawn by T.C.Dibdin. from a Sketch by Mr Hughes.

Engraved by J.H.Kernot.

13. 'Dove's Nest, Ambleside, Westmoreland, c.1835. Drawn by T. C. Dibdin from a sketch by Mrs Hughes, engraved by J. H. Kernot. That 'charming seat' (now 'The Samling'), was the place where Miss Weeton lived and worked as a governess, from December 1809 to February 1811. It is located about one mile south of the town centre. *Courtesy of Jean and Martin Norgate.*

14. Regatta and Boat Race, near Ferry House, Windermere, c.1810. Drawn by T. Unwins, engraved by J. Lewis. "On the 25th of July there was a Regatta held at the Ferry Inn, opposite the large island, five or six miles below Dove's Nest," wrote Miss Weeton to her brother on 15th August 1810. *Courtesy of Armitt Museum, Ambleside, Cumbria.*

15. 'Bridge House, Ambleside,' c.1820. William Green (1760-1823). Mr and Mrs Green and Miss Weeton became very good friends, and she accepted an invitation to become Godparent to one of their 'numerous' children. *Courtesy of Abbot Hall Gallery, Kendal, Cumbria.*

Standishgate. Circa. 1836.

16. Standishgate, Wigan, 1836. The property on the extreme right was the residence of Mr and Mrs Aaron Stock from 1816 until early 1822. It became the home of their daughter, Miss Mary Stock and her mother, from 1828 until 1844. The site is now occupied by Marks and Spencer. _Courtesy of Wigan Archives and Local Studies._

17. St Paul's Congregational Chapel, Standishgate, Wigan, c.1900. It was built in 1785, on behalf of the Countess of Huntingdon's Connexion. In the early years of the 19th century the church moved towards Congregationalism. Its minister from 1809-1832 was Revd Alexander Steill (1768-1832). Steill was a good friend of Aaron Stock, the vindictive and violent husband of Nelly Stock. The original building (pictured), was demolished in 1902. _Courtesy of Wigan Archives and Local Studies._

18. Market Place, Wigan, 1831, drawn by Thomas Whitehouse. From an original drawing by John Harwood, 1824, and engraved by Henry Winkles. *Courtesy of Wigan Archives and Local Studies.*

19. Handloom weavers' cottages, Wigan Lane, Wigan, 1904. The type of cottages Miss Weeton referred to as she and her daughter, Mary, walked the streets of Wigan on May 22nd, 1816. "Many people were at their doors, and Mary stopped to look at them all . . . the noise of looms in a cellar attracted her attention." *Courtesy of Wigan Archives and Local Studies.*

Fashionable Spring Walking Dresses.

20. Ladies in fashionable spring walking dresses, 1808. One is wearing a 'gypsy' hat, secured with a ribbon over the crown and brim, held with a bow beneath the chin. The other is in wearing a 'chip' bonnet, made of thinly cut pieces of popular or willow wood chip, plaited or woven like straw but sturdier and less flexible. *Editor's collection.*

21. Jane Weeton, nee Scott, (1780-1831), wife of Thomas Richard Weeton. British (English) School, c.1803. *Courtesy of Wigan Archive and Local Studies.*

22. Thomas Richard Weeton (1781-1845). Solicitor of Leigh, Lancashire. Husband of Jane and brother of Miss Weeton. British (English) School, c.1803. *Courtesy of Wigan Archives and Local Studies.*

23. A stagecoach leaving London, c.1820. Miss Weeton would have travelled on this type of coach 'outside' to and from London, in the summer of 1824. Note the low iron support rail which stopped passengers from falling onto a wheel. Miss Weeton remarked 'the iron rail bruised me sadly.' *Editor's collection.*

24. Greenwich Park, London, 1835, by George Cruikshank. To Miss Dalrymple, in Liverpool, from Miss Weeton, staying in London, dated June 8th, 1824, she wrote: "On Whit Monday (7th), I went to Greenwich Fair, a highly wrought scene of fun, frolic, and folly . . . Here were innumerable groups walking about and innumerable groups amusing themselves by getting to the tops of various hills in the Park, and, taking hold of hands, 2, 3, or 4 together, they run down with the utmost speed; often some unlucky wight [person] places himself just before them as they are at full speed; down they tumble over him, and over one another, men and *women*, boys and *girls*." *Editor's collection.*

some comfort in the home of the Braithwaites. But circumstances there had changed dramatically from the happy days she remembered. The master of the house was no longer there; gone too was the income from Mr Braithwaite's academy. Mrs Braithwaite's health was in decline and her daughter Elisabeth was consumptive. Both mother and daughter were increasingly unable to participate in the work of the household and garden. Elisabeth's eldest sister, Margaret, was now happily married to Mr T. Jackson, Master of the Assembly Rooms at Prescot near Liverpool. Mr Jackson had also provided a home for another sister, Mary, the youngest daughter of Rev Braithwaite. It now fell solely upon the shoulders of Catherine to sustain the bodily comforts of the Braithwaite family.

A number of Miss Weeton's correspondents were now no longer alive. Gone were Mr and Mrs Chorley of Liverpool; also Mrs Edmondson. Mrs Dodson, Mrs Green and Ann Winkley, seemingly were all now consigned to be mere episodes of the past. Contact with the young Armitages was perfunctory and would soon cease.

Despite regrets, Miss Weeton's latent desire to write never completely abandoned her. Soon the compulsion to write began to overwhelm her. First to her beloved daughter Mary, then to Miss Hawarden, to Mrs Marsden, and to Mrs Grundy of Parr Hall. In addition her ever-expanding Journal entries increasingly consumed more and more time.

The following two letters (to her daughter and to Miss Hawarden), reveal that Miss Weeton began to suspect that her letters to Mary were not reaching her, and came to the conclusion that her letters were being intercepted:

3 September 1822. (Up Holland). *To her daughter Mary* (at Parr Hall, near St Helens):

> I have expected to hear from you for some weeks past, and wonder why you have never written to me. Write soon, my love, if Mrs Grundy will permit you, or I shall think you want to forget your mother. I have never received one letter from you, yet you wrote to your father almost a year ago, and I hope now you will write often to me. The sight of a letter by your dear little hand,

would be a great comfort to me, and I hope I shall see one in a few days after you receive this.

It is now many months since I heard anything of you. I earnestly hope you are well; but I never hear whether you are well, or ill.

I am still living at Up Holland with Mr and Mrs Ball, and spend my time very agreeably, often going out to tea. Mrs Braithwaite is exceedingly kind to me, and so are Miss Braithwaite's. I sometimes go to dinner, and remain with them until bedtime; and if I am 3 or 4 days without calling, they express themselves quite concerned; and they are such intelligent people, that their conversation is always pleasing.

I was at Southport a few weeks ago. Mrs Ball and I went together; we remained there 3 weeks. A very agreeable and genteel party were lodging in the house with me, and Miss Louisa Barge, a little girl of 7 years old, was quite a play-fellow for me. We got each a poney and rode on the sand hill, and made a sand oven, and sand pies in large cockle shells. I was the bakehouse woman, and Louisa, a servant, and made the pies.

I talked to Louisa about you, and we wished you were with us. I often laughed at her, for she scolded me for burning the pies and spilling the syrup, and sometimes I quite upset them, and then she had more to make; and just when we were tired of that play, and going to play at hide and seek, she said, 'Let us jump our oven in.' So we got on the top of it and jumped. It gave way rather suddenly, and down we both fell, laughing, and half buried. We soon got away, and played at hide and seek until we were tired.

I bathed frequently, and sailed several times, and now find my health much improved.

In the hope of hearing from you in a few days, I will conclude now with desiring you to present my respects to Mr & Mrs Grundy.

18 October 1822 (Up Holland). *To Miss Hawarden*, Wigan:

About 7 weeks ago, I wrote to Mary, and sent the letter, by Ed Melling, to the Wigan Post Office, knowing him trusty, and not daring to send it by M Forster. I requested an early answer from my little darling, hoping Mrs Grundy would have the goodness to set her to the grateful employ. More than a month passed, and I heard nothing. About a fortnight ago, I wrote to Mrs Grundy to enquire if that letter had ever been received. To this I have yet had no answer. To make quite sure, I will try another plan. I will write again and beg of you to give it to Will Kelly, the Coachman, that he may deliver it himself; for perhaps Mr Stock may have intercepted the other at the Wigan P.O. Don't tell Kellys from whom it comes, although he and his wife always interested themselves very kindly for me.

Perhaps you could get him to find out whether Mary is now at Parr Hall, for I have strong suspicions that she is not there, and that Mr Grundys' are commanded by Mr Stock not to publish at present that she is removed.

If Mary is at Parr Hall, I must consider some method of proceeding different to this which I have pursued for so many months, of being patient, and submissive. My spirits are exceedingly depressed. I think I shall quite sink unless I can see my child.

Inclosed is a letter to Mrs Marsden (which I shall be obliged to you to deliver) on a very different subject, but which I shall request her to communicate to you.

Oct. 21st. Since writing the foregoing, I received a letter from Mrs Grundy. I will send it to you on account of one passage in it, a statement of Mary's, quite mysterious to me. She has not been at Holland, neither have I ever seen her since last March at Parr Hall. Shew it to Mrs Marsden, and return it when convenient. Discover, if you can, whether some trick was played on the poor child whilst last in Wigan.

19 October 1822. (Up Holland). *To Mrs Grundy*, Parr Hall:

Having written to Mary nearly 7 weeks ago, and after waiting some weeks for an answer and receiving none, I next addressed a letter to you. I have still received none. If these letters never reached you, be kind enough to inform me by return of post. If they have been received by you, I intreat you to tell me why they were not answered, inclosing your letter in a cover directed to Dr J. Hawarden, Wigan, who will safely forward it to me. My letters have been intercepted, and possibly may be again.

If my letters safely reached you, oh, how could you act so unchristian a part by me as not to notice them. Is it respecting the mother as the father? Is it doing as you would like to be done to? That my husband has ever treated me with the utmost contempt, is no excuse for such treatment from any other. Even if he has given you any such directions, it is not your duty to obey them. The fear of losing a pupil cannot surely be of such moment as that you should treat a mother unjustly to please the father. You did treat me with great kindness, and I was very grateful for it.

The calumnies which my husband has so industriously spread, should have no weight with you until you had heard both sides. I declare most solemnly that they are all false; and I should not be condemned unheard, not considered guilty, because I am accused. As I understand that you have listened to Mr Stock, and as I find that you have acted in consequence, it is but an act of justice to hear me. Do not use me contemptuously before you know whether I am deserving.

Mr Stock is afraid of anyone seeing me, or hearing me, in my own vindication. He knows he cannot stand that test, and for that reason he has ever endeavoured to shut me out of all society. Yet I never told anything but Truth, nor will I ever depart from it.

I would now be silent, if he would but let me; but my continued sufferings justify me in speaking and acting in my defence, for even here has persecuting spirit follows me, and he is endeavouring to get me shut out from the comforts of Religion! Oh! That his heart might be changed before it is too late, for it is dreadfully hard and cruel.

So long as my child is with you, I shall consider it my duty to take every pains to clear myself from the falsehoods which have been heaped upon me. I do not want to accuse my husband, but I must defend myself. I can do it with Truth; and if I could but have the opportunity afforded, I could prove myself entirely innocent from even a thought of ill, and still more so of the deeds he talks of.

You will not refuse to give my love to my little Mary? Surely you are not forbidden to do that?

Oct. 21st. I had just written the foregoing, when I received your letter. I cannot comprehend what Mary means in saying she was lately at Holland, and saw her mother. I did not see her, nor ever heard of her being here. Has some trick been played upon the child, to deceive and bewilder her; was she taken to some other place and told it was Holland – which might be easily done, as she can know but little of the place – and shewn some other woman instead of her mother? Yet I think she cannot so far have forgotten me.

Surely, in resembling her father's family in features, she does not at the same time resemble them in falsehood.

You should not have told Mr Stock of Mary's preparing to write to me. This is the first time I have ever requested any thing I did, respecting Mary, to be kept secret from Mr Stock, but now I think I am justified in it. If you will not let her write, let me beg that *you* will instead, about twice in each half year, that I may know the progress she makes in learning, and the state of her health; and say whether my letter to Mary can be received or not. Do not ask Mr Stock respecting it.

In the light of largely negative responses to Miss Weeton's desire for active participation in a faith community, it may be helpful to assess the importance of her proclivity towards regular worship and her faith.

Worship at the church of St. Thomas The Martyr at Up Holland proved unacceptable, the result being that she decided to travel one mile south to Salem Independent (Congregational) Chapel in the village of Far Moor (Orrell). There she soon became a committed and popular Sunday school teacher.

Unfortunately her new-found role was not to last. Murmurings began to circulate that that she was not a fit and proper person to be involved in the life of the chapel. She firmly believed, not without good reason, that the culprit was Rev Alexander Steill, of whom she opined had 'been calumniating me in the bitterest manner' to Rev Holgate.

Miss Weeton's husband, Aaron Stock, had long been a regular worshipper at St Paul's Independent Chapel, Standishgate, Wigan, he was also a good friend of the chapel's minister, Rev Steill. That friendship had, in turn, effectively barred Miss Weeton from worshipping at St Paul's.

Despite the best efforts of Rev John Holgate, in giving Miss Weeton a fair hearing by visiting her at her home, a later formal meeting at the chapel, was not unanimous in wanting Miss Weeton to continue teaching.

19 October 1822 (Up Holland). *To Mrs Marsden:*

I have been in hopes to have seen you here long ago; and all Summer I have thought you would be coming some day or other to see me, when the means of getting here were so easy by the Coaches from Wigan daily. They yet continue several days a week, I understand, but perhaps will not continue long. Let me have the pleasure of seeing you very soon, for a few days, if you will put up with half of my bed.

The congregation at Farr [sic] Moor [Independent] Chapel, are about to form a regulated body for the first time since Mr Holgate came amongst them; but, keeping it secret from me, innocently and unsuspectingly, a few weeks ago I expressed my desire to join with them, whenever that happened; but so reserved were Mr Holgate and one or two others, of their intentions, and so cool to me, that I thought something was wrong. Last week I became more urgent, for I began to find that they meant to get the formation of a Church completed without informing me. In consequence of my repeated inquiries, Mr Holgate said he would call upon me, which he had never before done, and, on the 16th he came.

Judge my feelings when I found that Mr Steill had been calumniating me in the bitterest manner to him, so as to make him believe that I should only bring disgrace on the Society; and that my name, if appearing in the list to be presented to Mr Roby[2] (who is expected on the occasion), would make him judge unfavourably of the whole, if such as I were admitted!

Mr Holgate is a most worthy man, I do believe, but in this instance he has acted in a most unchristian-like manner. *First, he has condemned me unheard; secondly, because I was accused, he treated me as guilty;* and thirdly, treating me in this manner yet *keeping secret from me of what I was accused,* by which means *I was excluded all opportunity of speaking in my defence,* or *procuring any testimonials in my favour.*

I vindicated myself to Mr Holgate as well as I could, but my spirit was so excessively cast down, I was almost unable to speak. I told him that he had heard but one side, and that, my bitterest enemy; that to prevent my representing the excessive cruelty with which Mr Stock and his whole family had used me, I was nearly excluded all society. I earnestly desired he would find whether Mr Stock or Mr Steill were to be believed, and how dreadfully I was treated.

He seemed impressed with what I said, but still deferred receiving me into the Church, as it could be done at some other time, still expressing apprehensions of Mr Roby.

The humblest Christian would almost spurn at thus being introduced into a Christian Church, as it were by stealth. Whether I shall consent to this or no, I shall consider.

You will see that my former doubts must have been much as propose myself to join any Church . . . and to be thus rejected, is trying indeed!

You did not condemn me unheard. No! In the midst of the deepest affliction, you came to comfort, and not to condemn. Your almost first introduction to me, was in tenderness and pity to my sorrows; and these brought you, when prosperity had never done it; you visited me at times when others fled far from me, in sorrow and in prison, and your own door was ever open to me for comfort.

Oct. 22. As I have kept this letter a few days, I will tell you what passed on Sunday, the 20th.

Ever since I came to reside in Up Holland, I have attended as a teacher in the Sunday School at Farr Moor. I have gone regularly; no weather hindered me. Punctuality, perseverance, and patience, gentleness, and industry, were my undeviating rules of conduct (as they always were at home in my husband's house). On Sunday morning I went as usual, but feeling an intention to resign if I were still considered as unfit to be a member. This I would first ascertain.

I had a good deal of conversation with Joshua Tunstal, a young man very active in the school (Mr Holgate was gone to Rainford [Independent Chapel] for the day, and Mr Toothill[3] supplied his place). I found from Joshua that my character had been a subject in several meetings. I inquired what were the charges against me. I could not get to know. I then requested to meet my accusers, that they might give me an opportunity of defending myself; strenuously asserting that I was confident I could clear myself.

Accordingly, after evening service, they assembled in Mr Holgate's parlour, who was then returned. Imagine what I felt on going in and seeing ten or twelve illiterate, coarse-looking, poor men and women, before I had voluntary brought myself, and who appeared to receive me as a poor criminal, come only that they might pronounce sentence; for I found that I had previously been tried and condemned, not in a Christian kind of way, but like the inquisition in Spain, where the criminals were never confronted with their accusers, nor told what they were accused of. So it literally was here. I trembled as I sat down; but you know my ideas of strict Christian conduct, and these supported me.

For a long time, no one spoke. At length, the silence was broken by Mr Holgate, (for my feelings overpowered me, so I could not begin first), who gave out a Hymn and Prayer. Next, Mr Toothill. Then again a total silence. At last, I spoke to Mr Holgate, requesting to know of what I was accused, that had been thought sufficient to prevent my being taken in amongst them at this time, and complaining of the great injustice done me in keeping the whole of their proceedings so totally secret from me in regard to their intentions of forming a church at this time, which I had only known a few days, and of what had been going on respecting me for several months; that they had heard only what my husband and Mr Steill had reported – my bitterest enemies; and had, on the other side, never inquired from my friends; and this was not doing by me as they would any of them like to be done by.

Mr Holgate spoke of the very favourable character he had heard of me by all the neighbouring people, but there were one or two present whose minds could not be easy to receive me, and he asked me if I could be content to be elected by a majority only, and not unanimously. I asked what these had to say. Not one person spoke. I rose, and bid them all good night.

My heavenly friend was with me, and I left them without any feelings of resentment. As a Christian society, they have made a poor beginning. May they become wiser.

If I hear no more of them, I go no more near them. There is only the Church [of England], and the Methodist Chapel at Lamberhead Green. To one of these I must go.

On the 21st. (Monday night) Mr Roby come to form them into a Church. Of course, I did not go.

There is no evidence that Miss Weeton went back to the Church (of England), or even attended the Methodist Chapel at Lamberhead Green.[4] It is almost certain that attendance at either would have been referred to in her correspondence or in her Journal at a later date. Instead it would seem that she decided to defy the ban on entering Wigan to join the congregation of the newly-built Hope Independent (Congregational) Church, Wigan.

We might observe that despite the discouragement from those expected to aspire to higher values, there is no indication that Miss Weeton questioned Christian truth at that time.

12 December 1822 (Up Holland). *To Miss Dalrymple,* 44 Seymour Street, Liverpool:

I have been in hopes of hearing of you for some time, and fear your health is little better yet, as you have never written. A few weeks ago I almost determined on coming to Liverpool for a week or fortnight, but as I have since concluded on deferring the journey, I cannot be comfortable any longer to delay writing to you, to inquire after your health; be kind enough to let me know by the bearer of this, who regularly goes from Holland every Friday to Liverpool, arrives that evening at Fairclough's (bottom of Dale Street), and returns next day, leaving Liverpool about noon.[5]

Since my temporal affairs have been more settled (my mind in consequence having gained more composure), I have come to the point which you have with so much zeal laboured to bring me: but what will you think when I inform you of the great discouragement I have met with at Farr Moor Chapel?

From the first of my coming to Up Holland, I attended the Sunday School at Farr Moor, with the utmost punctuality; it is a mile hence, yet no weather hindered. The girls I taught were exceedingly attentive and attached to me; they increased in numbers, and I pleased myself with thinking that I was as a Missionary in a little obscure corner, where no one else scarcely would give themselves the trouble to labour. Here the talent which the Mighty One had given me, would not be hid in a napkin; and yet, if He blessed my labour, I might be of great and lasting use amongst a race of beings almost lost in barbarism, in a way so quiet that my name would never appear in Annual Reports, or Missionary Chronicles.

Having a mile to walk, and my own apartments to attend to before leaving home (the people of the house I live in, do nothing for me), I rose early on Sabbath mornings, setting out soon after eight, and dining in the Chapel on a currant bun, as I had to teach all afternoon; and often staying evening service, so that I did not return home till at night.[6]

All went on very peaceably. I attended to my own class, and interfered with no one else. I grew more and more attached to the place, and thought, now have I 'found rest for sole of my foot'. [At this point Miss Weeton once again related the events leading up to her rejection of Rev. Holgate's conditional offer for membership of the Chapel at Far Moor].

Do they, in the Churches at Liverpool, condemn any unheard? Oh Miss Dalrymple, I have suffered so much from this unmerited treatment, my spirit is sadly cast down; it has deprived me of many a night's sleep. I once thought I would come over to Dr Raffles[7] about it, but . . . I begin to feel almost reckless.

Mr Holgate has not altogether rejected me. My past conduct was the ground of his rejection, therefore I will not come until that is cleared; for I cannot bear to come to be looked upon with a suspicious eye by those members he has received, few of whose past conduct will bear looking into; thus to come before a set of people consisting entirely of colliers, weavers, and labourers! Here the business rests.

Many of the congregation are much hurt at the treatment I have met with; the parents of the children I taught, particularly. They say it is owing to Mr Holgate's borrowing books of Mr Stock, who has an excellent Calvinistic library, and that if he admitted me, Mr Stock would lend him no more. Mr Holgate I still believe to be a worthy man, but he has had improper advisers, and has been too ready to follow their counsels. Mr Steill is a very worldly-minded kind of man, haughty, and over-bearing, and of a most bitter temper, and not a fit companion for any inexperienced minister.

1 January 1823 (Up Holland). *To Mr Stock,* Wigan:
My dear Husband,

I have heard that my Mary is with you for the holidays: consider a mother's feelings, a mother's affection, and grant me the favour of seeing her at Holland, if it be only for a week, I earnestly entreat you.

It is very long since I saw her, and if you have any compassion for me, and any desire to afford Mary a real pleasure, you will at once liberally and generously afford us a gratification that will warm our hearts towards you with gratitude.

If you will but comply with this wish of mine, I will send for her in any way you may appoint, and return her punctually to the time you fix: only let me beg you will grant me as long a time as possible, considering that I never saw her last Summer, nor the Winter holidays previous.

Let me be favoured with as early an answer as possible, and it will still further oblige,

Your affectionate wife

E. Stock.

Despite the most courteous tone of the letter, it did not bring about a response. Meanwhile, in her pitiful state, Miss Weeton, had interested the wealthy Mr Stopford (through whom she received her quarterly allowance). In his response, Mr Stopford made repeated efforts to achieve the setting-aside of the unjust Deed of Separation and its outrageous restrictions, especially so with regard to the infrequent contact between mother and child; all to no avail beyond an insulting diatribe by Thomas Weeton, to Mr Stopford, against his sister.

In the spring of 1823, Miss Weeton broke her silence to write to her daughter, at Parr Hall.

16 April 1823 (Up Holland). *To Miss Stock,* Parr Hall:

Will you not rejoice to see another letter from me, when I have been silent so long? I know you will, whilst at the same time you will wonder why I have been so long in writing. Indeed, my love, I had hoped to see you long ago, and for that reason I waited until I was certain whether I should be allowed to see you soon or not. I begin to think I must see you no more; but surely I may write and tell you how much I love you, and how glad I should be to see you. More than a year has passed since I saw my only darling child.

I continue to lodge at Mr Ball's, in Up-Holland. I have a Bed-room, and a parlour to myself, and, being very much alone, I sometimes feel it very dull. Mr and Mrs Ball are strict-principled, and tender-hearted people indeed. I respect them highly. They treat me with great respect, and so do all their servants; for, being farmers, they have many. They are so busy every day with their cows, their farm, that they have little time to sit in their parlour, so that I have very little of their company. They wish much to see you.

Mrs Braithwaite is in a declining state of health. I fear she will never be well again. Mr Stopford's have left Holland about 3 weeks ago, and have gone to live near Roby Mill, about 2 miles hence. I am sorry they are gone so far, they were so kind to me. During Summer I shall often take a walk to see them.

You see, Mary, I introduce you as it were to all my friends.

Miss Dalrymple is, I dare say, almost as old as I am, and not at all pretty; but she is such a worthy, religious woman, that I esteem her highly. She has been unable to walk for more than a year, owing to exerting herself too much, when she was well, in going about to collect money for the Bible Society, the Missionary Society, to distribute Tracts, and to visit the sick poor as a Member of the Benevolent Society, by whom they were assisted and relieved. She is recovering, but very slowly, and is so chearful, it is quite pleasing to see her. Oh, Mary, if when you grow up, you know where to look for comfort, and to find it as we have done.

22 April 1823 (Up Holland). *To Master J. Armitage,* Free Grammar School, Manchester:

I felt most exceedingly pleased on receiving your last letter of April 12th., in addition to the usual well filled one at Christmas last; for I scarcely expected, that so young as you were when you last saw me at Highroyd, that you would recollect or care much about me. I was much attached to all of you, and esteem, and it gratifies me much to reflect that I gained what I wished.

You will be 14 on the 24th. inst., an age, Joseph, when many boys are very thoughtless, and often very unfeeling to those unfortunate animals that fall into their power; let no example lead you to be so, and I feel a hope that you possess a mind of some compassion and refinement – a hope founded on the desire you express to learn to play the flute.

Music has a powerful tendency to humanize the disposition, and a fondness for it, I always think, speaks highly for the temper of any one. I am glad your friends encourage your desire, and with a good instructor, I dare say you will improve quickly; and when you are at home, you may help to form a complete band of Musicians, with your brothers and sisters. If Sarah-Anne wont take any other instrument, she may assist with a marrow bone and cleaver. Does George play any? As to Emma, she is, I suppose, quite an M.D.

You will be seeing all your brothers and sisters, I suppose, at the expiration of two months. Give my love to all who remember me. Probably, were they to see me now, they would scarcely remember my features again; they were all so young when last saw me, and it is nearly 9 years ago when I left.

I shall be glad to hear from you at any time, and I hope you will write me a longer letter, for I dare say you are never at a loss for a subject; any thing interesting to you, would be so to me, and you may write as familiary as to any other *old* acquaintance.

8 May 1823 (Up Holland). *To Mrs Price,* 35 Seymour Street, Liverpool:

The time has, I think, arrived when I may begin to hope for the fulfilment of the promise you half made of coming to Holland when the weather should be warmer and the days of such a length as to make such an excursion agreeable. After you have received this remembrance, I shall begin to expect you every week until you actually arrive; so let me beg you will not be long, and come with an intention to stay as long as possible.

I went to Wigan last week last Sunday (May 4) to Hope [Congregational] Chapel, where Mr Ralph preached; since his death, Mr Marshall [see Appendix VII] from Macclesfield has succeeded to the school. I was most gratifyingly received (for I have not been at the place, since I ceased to reside in Wigan, until the 4th. inst.). Mr Marshall and several others told me that when I left, the school diminished lamentably, and continued to do so until lately. It now revives again. My old pupils are all gone, except two or three who are become teachers. They received me most affectionately. I think I shall go often when the weather permits, taking my dinner in my pocket, as I did last Sunday, and eating it in the School, or at Mr Marsden's, father-in-law to the minister.

When afternoon service was over, I called to see Dr and Mrs Hawarden, and took tea with them. The Dr is no worse; his intellectual faculties appear as clear as ever. I found him standing by the window, reading the small print of some Magazine without glasses. He spoke with his usual chearfulness, and with that degree of wit and humour which you know is so strikingly peculiar to him – but his tongue falters – his deafness increases – and his limbs tremble under him!

Two very fashionable-looking young men have become boarders with them; they conduct a shop lately opened in the Millgate by a Mr Lee.

[Journal, May 1823]

May 4th Sunday. Went to Wigan to Hope Chapel for the first time since I ceased to reside in Wigan.

May 11th. Went again to Hope Chapel, returning that morning to Holland. Was invited to dine at Mr Alston's and accepted the invitation.

18 Spent this day again at Hope Chapel, having stayed all night previously at Mr Marsden's. On Monday the 19th. (having likewise stayed at Mr M's on Sunday night) I attempted to go to St Helen's by Coach at 6 o'clock that morning, and got into the coach for that purpose; but not having taken a place, I was obliged to get out again, as all the places were engaged previously, so set off home, arriving there by half past 7 o'clock.

22d Thursday. After dinner walked to St Helen's from Holland; saw Mr Taylor, the solicitor; stayed all night at an Inn; saw Mr T. again next morning,

23d Mrs Braithwaite died in the evening, just after I had called to inquire how she was, on my way to Wigan, where I again went to be ready for Chapel.

June 2nd. Mrs Braithwaite was interred in the morning; in the afternoon, saw my brother, his wife, and son, at my cousin Latham's.

18 Wednesday evening. Mary came home to her father for the holidays.

22 Having left Holland the evening before, spent this day at Mr Marsden's, and the Chapel. Heard of Mary, but made no attempt to see her.

25 Went in the evening to Wigan; found Mrs Hawarden a little recovered, giving me hopes that I was not yet going to lose another mother; for one went when Mrs Braithwaite died.

29 Went to Chapel; wrote a short note to Mr Stock in the afternoon, requesting to see Mary, but he only insulted the boy who took it, threatening to kick him out of the house. This day I heard that Mr Stock was thought by many to be almost insane; indeed, I had been hearing for some months before of many corroborative circumstances. A few days ago, he was seen going up Millgate without his hat. About a month ago, he was carrying a bundle of papers through Chapel-lane, flourishing them about like a ballad singer.[8]

27 June 1823 (Up Holland). *To Miss Dalrymple*, 44 Seymour Street, Liverpool:

I ought to take blame to myself for not writing to you long ago. I was not expecting to hear first from you, and I have had no sufficient reason for deferring it so long. I was really anxious to hear of you, and hoped to have heard some tidings by Mrs Price many weeks ago, and had desired that she would inform me. As she never answered my letter, I had concluded she had not received it; but yours of the 12 inst. informs me she has. I was rejoiced to hear from you, although concerned to find that you were still so weak; it appears that your recovery is not so rapid as could be wished, but yet you have hope.

I have been going on since I was at Liverpool, in a sort of every-day jog trot way. 6 or 7 weeks ago I began to go to Hope Chapel in Wigan, on a Sunday morning, taking my dinner in my pocket, and returning at night; since when, I have gone on a Saturday evening, taking a bed at Mr Marsden's. Whether I can continue it long, I cannot say, for Mr Stock will probably raise some obstacle. I have for some time past concluded on going into some kind of situation, the first that offers that may be eligible, or into some way of business, for I cannot get forward with the law suit I told you of, my brother preventing me. He is, on all occasions, my enemy. With a sincere, steady friend, and an able attorney, I firmly believe I could have gained it.

My stipend would keep me with moderate care, but I cannot have those domestic comforts here which a home of one's own affords. I seldom know what it is to have a comfortable dinner, and all my meals are solitary. If I am sick I have no one to nurse or comfort me; if I am well, there is none to converse with, for which reason I often go out to Miss Braithwaite's, and to Miss Dannett's; but as it not convenient to do this at times, I am left much alone. I have lost a kind and long tried friend by the death of Mrs Braithwaite, about a month ago; she had been gradually declining all winter, and I regret her loss much.

As I find Mary is come from school to her father for the holidays, I do not mean to be far from home until she returns to school, in hopes I may obtain his leave to see her. I then think of going to Southport for a time.

Should I get some situation in another neighbourhood, it may possibly be where there are more opportunities of enjoying religious society for I often sigh to find, that when I have been for a time estranged from the society of pious people, and a place of Christian worship, I feel sadly weaned from them, and am almost inclined to look upon them, and it, as a piece of error and fanaticism, and wonder not at the many who speak or write under such impressions. But when again I mingle amongst them, the sky of Heaven opens upon me – but, placed where I am, what can I do? I must either seek lodgings elsewhere or draw a little circle around me here of untaught souls, and commence leader, for which I am not fit or able. I wish some one would plant, and then I would work as under gardener.

To Miss C. Armitage, Milnes Bridge, near Huddersfield: [Dated 12 October 1823; but a note states that 'the above had been prepared in July last, but was not sent until the present date'].

The letter which I received from you all at Christmas last, was very welcome, and found me at Holland, in better health and spirits, and greater comfort and tranquillity, than any preceding one since I left you. I am much restored indeed in health my situation is, as may be supposed, very comfortable in many respects, yet very comfortless in others. The enjoyment of rising and retiring to rest in peace, free from any fear, and spending the day free from any distressing anxiety, with no other employment than that of attending upon, and amusing, myself, is surely valuable; but then, on the other hand, the solitude necessarily attendant on residing in lodgings, eating every meal alone, no one to converse with me to enliven me in health, or sooth in sickness, is exceedingly sinking to the spirits; so much so, that I intend to engage in some situation or way of business as soon as I can meet with anything eligible. My income is too small to admit of my keeping house, and the support of a servant; and unless I can make a home of my own, I prefer employment.

Since I came to Holland, Mrs Braithwaite's kindness has been unremitting; one or two days every week I spent there; but . . . this friend is gone! She died about 5 months ago; she had known me from a child, and was like a mother to me. Her daughters make up the loss to me as much as they can; but whenever I go to the house, there is one wanting.

Mr Stock wants to insist upon my being bound not to see Mary more than 3 days a year, the days to be exactly specified, and a heavy penalty attached, if I were to see her at any time. I reject such a proposal with indignation; but the consequence is, that he does all in his power to prevent my seeing her at all, and I have seen her only once for the last 19 months.

In May last I walked over to Parr-Hall, only 7 miles hence, for I am not rich enough to hire a conveyance. I saw Mary, and staid 3 hours with her. When I arrived at her residence, I expected to have been refused admittance, for such were the orders I understand Mr Stock to have given; however, I was politely received. You may imagine how my heart ached at going thus to see my child; and when she was introduced to me, a 14 month's estrangement had caused us both to forget each other! Mary knew not her mother! And her mother hardly recognised her child, her only one!

Mary looked timidly and cooly at me; she was exceedingly pale and thin. By degrees, we became more and more affectionate, and she chatted with me quite familiary. My heart ached to discover a very wrong system of education pursued for my child; but I must submit to it in silence. *No father is fit to educate a daughter*, and Mary, thy lot and mine is very sad!

1 July 1823 (Up Holland). *To Mr Stock*, Wigan:
Mr Stock.

I again write to intreat that I may see my child. Why is it that I am thus debarred the natural right of a Mother? If no Christian feeling influences you, if no principle of duty to your God has any weight; nay, if only moral decency is disregarded by you – reflect a little – and consider that the very brutes act not thus inhumanly, except a few of those most horrible of all animal creation! But even these know not that they are fathers. Oh, if you have any thing manly about you, shew that you have, by acting like one. Oh, if you have any soul-like feeling that there is a Mighty God, incur not His everlasting displeasure, by acting so contrary to His example and to His laws; for the power and the wealth which He bestows upon you are but lent to you to do good with, to make even the widow's heart to sing for joy. But I am as it were – a widow – yet is my husband living. I am childless – yet my child is not dead. I am likewise comparatively poor, yet is my husband rich.

Who has made me a widow? – You.

Who has deprived me of my child? – You.

Who has made me poor? Oh, that I could say 'twere any other but – You.

As regards my child, why deprive me of the comfort of her society, when you would in no way suffer yourself? You could see her just as much as you now do. It is in your power to make us all happier, for you would surely feel a pleasure in acting kindly towards me. There is a pleasure in doing good, and do you not know it? There must be a misery in inflicting evil, and have you not felt it?

Do you not love Mary? Why then deprive her of the comfort of a mother? If you sincerely loved her, you would study *her* comfort and satisfaction. When in your house, what female society has she, capable of giving her proper instruction? – none. Too ignorant are they, and of language and manners not for her to copy; and when she leaves school, she must come home to be the companion of servants.

Do not educate her thus, I earnestly urge, but let her have the advantages of a mother's solicitude, which she may have, although we reside in separate houses, for I do not urge to live with you myself; but it might be managed so, if you had the desire to act with liberality of feeling towards me, that we might both have the enjoyment of the society of a child that is dear to, and which I surely deserve, if it be only for the exemplary patience I have shewn you since I left you.

[Journal, July 1823]

July 1st. Packed up Mary's doll, to send it to her with all its cloathes, and took it to Edward Melling, to take to her at her father's in Wigan the following morning, along with the preceding letter.

2d Wednesday. When Edward returned, he brought the doll back with him, informing me that he called at a shop near Mr Stock's (as I had directed him) to inquire first if Mary was still at home, and was there informed that Mary was, on Monday morning, 30th. inst. Sent off by Coach in a hasty and rather mysterious manner. For the remainder of the day, I was almost inconsolable, so bitter and inveterate a spirit is so perpetually manifested against me by my husband. However, I began to take comfort that my child was from under the care of such a father, for she is better anywhere than with him.

3ᵈ H. Latham told me he was going to St Helens, and I instructed him to discover whether Mary was at Parr Hall or no; at night, he called on his return and told me she was there. I was now quite easy about her.

9ᵗʰ My brother-in-law, Wm Stock, came with his wife and youngest daughter, who is dying of consumption. I requested them to let her come for a few days try change of air and scene. They dined and drank tea with me, and then took leave, their little Margaret remained with me.

12 Packed up Mary's doll again, and sent it her to Parr Hall by a Wigan Coach.

13 Sunday Mornᵍ. Took Margaret Stock to my cousin Latham's to spend the day, whilst I went to Wigan, where I arrived at half past ten in the morning, thoroughly drenched by a tremendous thunder shower. Remained drying myself by Mrs Marsden's kitchen fire until noon. Went to Chapel in the afternoon.

16 Margaret Stock returned home by Coach.

19 Spent the Sabbath at Wigan, paying Mrs Marsden for my board for seven Sundays, reckoned as one week.

22 Set off in Mr Ball's cart to Appley Bridge, at 12 o'clock, accompanied by Miss Dennett; sailed from thence in the packet to Scarisbrick Bridge. From thence we had a pleasant ride in a Landau to Southport,[9] Where Miss Dennett's niece Catherine joined us in a day or two. Mrs Walmsley, where Miss D's lodged, had not room for me; I therefore engaged lodgings at Mr Lowe's for a week. Found two very agreeable female lodgers of the name of Heatley, from Manchester (sisters-in-law).

23ᵈ Bathing, and walking, visiting Miss Dennett and conversation with the Mrs H's agreeably occupied the whole of this day (Wednesday).

24ᵗʰ Sailing and bathing, walking and visiting Miss D's, and riding with Miss C. D. And party, occupied the time most amusingly until the [end of sentence omitted by Miss Weeton].

26ᵗʰ when Mrs Heatley and I went with a party in a boat to Lytham; the day was beautiful, and although we were both very sick as we went, I yet greatly enjoyed the sail. We soon recovered on the landing at Lytham, and, purchasing something to eat at a confectioner's, we went into the Church-yard and sitting on a tomb-stone, ate a most hearty dinner, after which we rambled for a mile or so until it was time to return; we were not at all sick on our way home.

31ˢᵗ As the Mrs H's had left Southport, I paid Mrs Lowe for my lodgings, not liking solitude, the expence, and my little stove of a bedroom; neither the continual drunkenness of Mrs Lowe, nor the want of principle in the servants; and removed to Miss Lowe's, sisters of Mr Lowe, where I could be at half the expence with honest sober people.

[Journal, August 1823]

August Passed the time as before, very agreeably, until yᵉ 8ᵗʰ, when I hired Mr Lowe's horse, and rode alone to Crossens by the shore, and returned through Church Town. When near Southport, I felt for my watch to see how long I had been away, as I paid by the hour, and to my astonishment, my watch was gone! The shock was such that I was not able to return to look for it, although I knew I had it after I had mounted. I proceeded home, and making known my loss, Mr Lowe very good naturedly directly took his horse and rode precisely by the rout I had taken; in the meanwhile, I sent the Bellman, who had not finished his round ere Mr Lowe returned with the watch. At Crossens, it was found lying on the road by a boy, who took it to his mother; from which, it seems it must have been thrown out of my pocket by the high trotting of the horse. The first person Mr Lowe met with to make any inquiry of, was this very boy, who immediately said he had found it, and on restoring it, Mr Lowe gave him 5s. [shillings]. I was much pleased on seeing my watch again; it was a valuable, very old-fashioned gold one, given by my father to my mother immediately after they were married. The boy's honesty merited a better reward, and if ever I should be in the neighbourhood again, I will try to find him out.

14ᵗʰ Set off to Liverpool, outside the coach from Southport,[10] on a tremendously wet morning. Had I not taken my place the day before, I would not have gone. I shall take care how I secure a place again, when there is no absolute necessity to go to a certain day, unless I could at the same time secure the weather. The wind blew so furiously, no umbrella could be opened or carried. The coachman was very attentive and kind to me; he gave me a stout rug to cover my shoulders, and another to cover my knees; and in this elegant costume, I rode through Ormskirk and Liverpool to the Inn there, as heedless and contented as possible, the rain soaking through all the way, driving in at a little crevice between my hood and my neck, and trickling in little streams down my back, so that I was literally wet to the skin; and when I descended from my elevated situation, my cloaths were so entirely wet, that I found I was a woman of much greater weight in Liverpool than I had been at Southport. However, my rugs had kept me warm, so that when I took them off, I went smoking all the way to the coach stand, and procured one to convey myself and luggage from Red cross Street to Russel Street, to lodge a short time with Mrs Roxburgh, where I got well dried after my smoking, and received no injury to my health.

18 Took Miss Roxburgh with me in a steam packet over to Birkenhead. For some time previous, I had had some thoughts of engaging in some business or other on Mrs and Miss Hawarden's account, whom I desired if possible to assist, as they are likely to be destitute, I fear, before long; and their kindness to me at a time of extreme distress, when turned out by my lunatic husband, and not knowing where to shelter, was such as I hope I shall never forget. With this view, I went this day to Birkenhead, thinking that taking in lodgers or boarders, and accommodating tea parties, might answer. I reconnoitred accordingly, looked at several new-built and unlet houses, and thought it probably would succeed, if they would like to come so far. On many succeeding days, I traversed many parts of Liverpool and neighbourhood with this view, intending on my return home to inform them of the result. Had an exceedingly pleasant sail and walk back.

30 Sailed at 8 o'clock this morning with Mrs Moneypenny and Miss Hawarden in the Steam Packet, to Bagilt in Wales.[11] Mrs Moneypenny and Miss Hawarden rode in a Car to Holywell; I preferred walking there alone. The day was serene and lovely. I joined them at Holywell where we dined and went to see the well and a little of the surrounding country, and then proceeded all together in a Car. The same afternoon to St Asaph, where we stopped at the Red Lion. Miss Hawarden and I took a short walk before bed time.

31ˢᵗ Sunday Morng. Miss Hawarden and I, rising early; took a walk towards Rhyddlan, and returned to Mrs Monepenny to breakfast. As these ladies were Catholics, I left them and went to the Cathedral. I was rather amused to see them enter soon after, thinking it would never be known by their friends in Wigan. Thinks I to myself, now if I should tell!

It appeared here as if 'praising and singing to the Lord' was a vast of trouble, very hard work, a great deal of pain, and much expence, there were so many people – men and boys – regularly employed and paid to do it; so hot, too, did it make them, and some of them pulled weary faces – so unaffected simplicity of primitive Christian worship. After service, as we walked round the Cathedral yard, the Bishop's housekeeper invited us to walk in the palace garden. We were pleased with the civility and entered; it was neat and retired. On coming out again into the Cathedral yard, we found the gates all locked! We were in a dilemma now, for there was no way out. We traversed round and round, and last sat down in patient despair for half an hour or more, when luckily a boy passed by one of the gates. We sent him to the proper authorities, who came and let us out. After dinner, we all walked to Rhyddlan, viewed the ruined Castle, and returned to tea. Miss Hawarden took a great fright in the night on hearing a noise she could not account for; she made such a fuss getting up, and walking about and screaming out most shrilly and valiantly – Who's there? enough to have scared a whole host of thieves or hobgoblins; and because there was no answer, she was more terrified than before. She walked to the window, and catching sight of a man going to the necessary (being moved thereto in the dead of the night), she begged of him to call the landlady; he promised, but forgot – unfeeling man! She then dressed herself, determined to sit up the remainder of the night, to protect Mrs Moneypenny and me. I wished her fast asleep many a time, and begged, if she could not sleep herself, to suffer me to rest, for I feared neither robbers nor spirits. She became more quiet, but sat up a long time. It was only a dog lying outside the room door.

[Journal, early September 1823]

Sept 1st Rose early, and set off from St Asaph with Miss Hawarden, to walk to Bagilt, leaving Mrs Moneypenny to follow in the Car. Miss Hawarden and I breakfasted at the Druid, a little public house by the road-side, where we had a hearty breakfast and a good deal of hearty laughing at the shriekart of the previous night. Walked forward with renewed spirit to Holywell;

took another peep at the well, and then continued to Bagilt, so little fatigued with a 13 miles walk, that for my part, I could have proceeded to Flint and back on foot; however, we joined Mrs Moneypenny at a Car to Flint; returning to Bagilt to dinner. At 4 o'clock, we set off in a Steam Packet for Liverpool, and arrived there at 8 that evening.

4 & 5th Spent these days in visiting Miss Dalrymple, Mrs Price, and in walking. Saw a pretty, small house, in Toxteth Park, I should like much to reside in if I had but furniture; the situation is so beautiful, and the rent 18£.

7th Sabbath Spent this morn⁸ at home in solitude; went to dinner at Miss Braithwaite's where I had slept the last night, they very kindly meeting me at the late hour of my arrival, to invite me lest my own bed should be damp. Sat all afternoon and evening with Miss B's; returned home to sleep, my bed having been well aired by a good fire for some hours.

12 Took a walk to Wigan; found my little niece, Margaret Stock, declining fast.

14 Went to Hope Chapel in the morning; carried buns in my pocket, for dinner, which I ate in the vestry at noon. Took tea at Dr Hawarden's, and after attending evening service, walked home.

19 September 1823 (Up Holland). *To Miss Dalrymple*, Liverpool:

According to my promise of writing to you soon. I begin the performance. On the morning that I left Liverpool, as it was very fine, I preferred walking a part of the way, to riding the whole of 20 miles or more in a cart. So footed it very agreeably all the way to Prescot, carrying my dinner in my basket until noon, and then eating it by the way, about 2 miles from Prescot. I was downright hungry, and ate a large part of a twopenny loaf. I would rather have a repast in such a way, than sit down to a stately, luxuriant dinner table. At Prescot, I called on Mrs T Jackson,[12] and I sat 3 hours with her; at 4 o'clock, the cart arrived, and I was jolted in it for the next 5 hours, over as rough a road as any in the country, at the rate of $2^1/_2$ miles an hour. We Holland people out-do you in Liverpool in travelling, for I seldom hear of your travelling at this rate, except to the Church yard, where few are in a hurry to go.

I have felt very unsettled since I returned here, for I have been such a rambler for the last 2 months, that I cannot all at once relish sitting still.

I made some inquiry at Prescot respecting lodgings, but Mrs J. could not inform me of any at present. I dare not attempt to think of Liverpool; rents are so high for such small incomes as mine. The place Miss Eden so kindly mentioned, I set out to inquire about, but my heart failed me before I got there, for I was certain, accommodations such as I wish will be 20£ a year or upwards; and if I pay so much for rent, I must be abridged of many other comforts and enjoyments.

I have inclosed a Copy of the Deed of Separation between me and Mr Stock.

The Deed alone should be the guide, or what was a Deed made for? The very idea that Mr Stock *can* get it altered if he will, because he now finds it as does not like, is shocking, and, I should think ridiculous. *I* may then do the same, for there is not one Article in it that I would not alter, if I could. I was forced to sign it as it is, or starve; the alternative was dreadful, so that I did not voluntary consent to it in its present form; yet, having signed it, I am obliged to abide by it; and so should Mr Stock.

I find that Mr Wallace is Mr Gaskell's Counsel, as well as Mr Taylor's, so that after giving his first opinion, he had probably been consulted by Mr Gaskell, Mr Stock's attorney, and thus has applied to on both sides.

In consequence of many falsehoods which my Brother has uttered, and other unbrotherly kind of treatment, I found it necessary about 6 months ago, to write in my own vindication, and if possible, to put a stop to his doing me more mischief. I send a Copy – it is rather long, but I leave you at liberty to peruse it or not.

[Journal, late September 1823]

21st Set off from my home about 10 o'clock, to walk to Parr Hall, to see my little darling Mary, whom I had not seen since May 23d. I told no one where I was going. Not being well acquainted with the road beyond Billinge,[13] I walked near a mile in tracing and retracing. About half past 12, I arrived there. When Mr Grundy entered the room he looked so grave and solemn, not the least smile embellished his features, that I thought it was a prognostication of a refusal to see my child. However, I brought a chearful countenance, and kept it, which seemed to impart some of its influence to Mr Grundy, for, by degrees the cloud on his brow disappeared, and he brightened his eyes and relaxed his mouth, and became very chatty and agreeable. He touched upon no topic relating to me or my child; a mother's anxiety touched my heart, for I began to fear they were conveying Mary away somewhere, she was so long in coming. In about a quarter of an hour, my little sweet one came into the parlour, looking very pale and very thin. She looked so glad to see me. In a short time, dinner came in to me on a single plate. Mary was called away to dine with her schoolfellows. This was unusual; she had always before dined with me, in the little parlour in which I now was, except twice when I had gone with her to the large dining-room. I suppose it was some order of Mr Stock's, to degrade me in the eyes of my child. However, I ate my dinner, asking no reasons, nor making any observations. I had come to enjoy for a short time, the company of my child, and strove to the utmost to drive away the approaches of dejection on being treated in so unmerited a manner. Mary came to me as soon as she had dined, but was soon called away again, to prepare for a walk. Mr Grundy evidently wanted me to depart – unfeeling being! Knowing that I had walked 7 or 8 miles, and had to walk as many more, I surely wanted resting time. I appeared not to observe his manner, or take his hints, for I determined to stay as long as I thought was proper. Mary coming in again with her bonnet, I desired she might remain with me, as my stay could not be so long, and she was suffered to do so, Mr Grundy scarcely leaving us for five minutes; in obedience, I dare say, to Mr Stock's instructions. It is a matter of indifference to me whether we are alone or all the world is present. I neither mean to run away with the child, nor to say anything to her that I fear to have known; the greatest openness, and the strictest integrity, have ever marked my conduct, and ever shall. At half past three, I too leave, Mr Grundy and Mary accompanying me a little way. Heaven bless her! a time may come when this distressing mode of seeing her may be done away with. If not – Thy will, Oh my Father, be done. With thy help, I can resign myself chearfully, for, in a few years, death will silence us all, and then what matters it?

On leaving Mr Grundy and Mary, I went with alacrity and speed, and arrived at home about half past 5. Very little fatigued. Thanks be to Him who gives me spirit and strength.

22^d Went with Mrs Ball to dine with Mr and Mrs Stopford. Miss Bird was there, and Mrs Mylchrist from Southport unexpectedly arrived. She told me Mr Stock was going to purchase a house at Southport, intending to reside there.

26 Sunday Spent the day at Wigan [Hope Chapel] as usual. My little niece, Margaret Stock, died, after a long illness, and on Wednesday the

29 was interred.

[Journal, early November 1823]

November 3rd, 5th, and 6th Spent greater part of these days at Miss Braithwaites, as well as many previous ones not noticed here. Catherine was at Dalton, at her cousin Prescott's, Miss P. being in very low spirits, a malady unhappily inherent in the family. Elisabeth, a constant invalid, wishes for society, for which her youngest sister, Mary, is unfit, being very subject to fits. As I am much at liberty, I can go at almost any time, and be, as they kindly tell me, a consolation to them; and it is a very agreeable change to me, from the solitude of my lodgings, to society at once intelligent, enlightened, and, what is best of all, strictly conscientious.

7th Walked to Wigan, to inform Mrs Marsden that I would, for the Winter, cease spending the Sabbath at Wigan, as the days are too short to go in the morning and return after afternoon service; and my bed being only slept in by myself, would, I feared, be damp.

9th This day, about 4 o'clock in the afternoon, Mr Stock's father died. He was an old man [age left blank in her Journal] years of age, and had lain in a helpless state for 5 or 6 years, from rheumatism which he contracted by being a brewer's journeyman. His only unmarried daughter, Margaret, attended on him, and supported him to the last, he having little or no property of his own, and receiving little, very little, assistance from his other five children. His eldest son, my husband, was best able to support him, but he suffered him to want the comforts, and almost the necessities of life.

11th The passing bell for the old man's death was this day tolled here (at Up Holland).

13th My father in law was buried here this day, about one o'clock, in rather a pompous manner, his previous circumstances considered. I expected this would be the case, Mr Stock thinking probably he could blind the world to his undutiful neglect by a hearse, 3 chaises, and a dinner for 40 people at the interment of his father. The cost of two thirds of this would have made the old man very comfortable during some months of his life, and have been better spent. It is rather singular that my husband's father, and my mother, are interred within one grave's breadth of each other, without any previous intention of any party.

As Mr Stock did not cause any one to inform me of his father's death, or send me any mourning, I have therefore thought it advisable not to wear any. I can feel the same respect for the old man, without any ostentatious shew, and I can ill bear the expence.

I was in hopes this event might soften his heart a little, and that something like humanity would touch it; but – he could not finish the funeral dinner before he began to pick a quarrel with his brother William at the table, before all the company, by insulting his wife! 'William,' he said, in an abrupt, peevish, and sleering manner, 'whether are you or your wife president?' Mr Stock has made many attempts to prejudice Wm against his wife, and on this occasion, she was not invited; but as many other female relatives were even more distantly related than she, Wm was hurt that she should be neglected, and brought her with him, and seated her by him at the dinner table; for she has ever conducted herself in a most respectable manner. This public insult wounded Wm deeply; he was so confused, he scarcely knew what he replied, but said, 'My wife is president, because I choose to make her so; and I shall always take my wife's part as long as I live.' Saying this, he rose, greatly agitated, from the table before he had quite finished dinner, and taking his wife, quitted the room. She burst into a flood of tears; Mrs Perkins, too, one of Mr S's sisters, could not restrain herself, but left the room to give vent to her grief, but soon after returned, Wm and his wife came to me at my lodgings, and returned no more to the funeral party; their minds were so deeply hurt, that they were some time before they could become composed. I could not help but weep with them, having myself so acutely suffered from the same malignant spirit. Wm, with all a Christian's meekness, prayed for his brother; his wife, in the true spirit of charity, joined him; and so most sincerely and earnestly did I, that the Almighty would turn him from the evil of his ways, ere his days were ended.

21 November 1823 (Up Holland). *To Miss Stock*, Parr Hall, near St Helens:

How often I wish to see you and hear you talk; your childish prattle would be very entertaining to me. But it is a pleasure that is denied me, and I most probably must never have the comfort of your society so long as I live. May the Almighty supply to you a mother's loss!

Although I have not the society of my little darling, yet my spirits are wonderfully chearful. I work, and read, and sing, and walk, and write all day long; and in the evenings, go and converse at Miss Braithwaites, or Miss Dannett's; and on Sundays I go to Wigan, to the Chapel there.

Indeed, I never was so happy in all my life as I have been since I came to Holland; every body is so kind to me. The poor people, as I pass them, bid me good-morrow, or good-night, so cordially; and the little children call after me, quite pleased if I call them by name, or smile – every one has a pleasant word for me or a chearful look – God blesses me, Mary.

I spent a great deal of time at Miss Braithwaite's, the second sister, has very ill health indeed; she has an asthmatic complaint, which confines her to the house for at least 8 months every year, and since Mrs Braithwaite's death, she has been more alone than ever she was in her life before; for her oldest sister, Catherine, is so busy, looking after the farm and attending to housekeeping, that she has little time to sit with her, and Elisabeth wishes me to be with her a great deal – poor Elisabeth! I fear we shall lose her before another year is over; she declines, evidently, and is worse this Winter than the previous one.

She is fond of rug work, and has done a great deal in a superior and beautiful manner, but she seems to be less able to amuse herself with it now, than she was wont to be. She has a memory wonderfully strong and correct, and can converse upon most subjects with great ability; her manners are very ladylike, yet she has a diffidence and humility that render her very amiable. Catherine, the eldest, is kind-heartedness personified; her manner is not elegant, but she is full of animation, wit, and drollery; she makes herself a slave to the whole family. You will suppose, my dear Mary, that they are very agreeable companions to me; and as I have known them from infancy, they are like sisters to me.[14] Thus you will perceive, my love, that I am very comfortable. I could fancy that I often hear that heart-piercing, anxious little question of yours, whenever I see you – 'Mother, are you comfortable?' Yes, my dear, I am indeed. I should be more so with you; but if I must not live with you, I make myself as contented as I can. God gives me so many blessings, that I should be a very disobedient child of his, if I were to grieve because I had not every thing I wished.

I should be very glad if I could receive a letter from you, if it were ever so short.

[Journal, late November 1823]

Novbr 23 Sabbath This day, Matthew Stock's (my brother-in-law) wife died at her mother's house; thus there has been a death in the family every 2d Sabbath for 3 times successively.

Went to Church to-day, and sat for the first time in Mr Morris's pew, having engaged with him for a sitting during the Winter months.

Dec 1st Went early in the afternoon to Miss Braithwaite's, to tea. Elisabeth has been declining, I think, for some months, much more rapidly than usual. She has suffered many years from an asthmatic complaint. 3 or 4 days a violent bilious attack has confined her to her room, and she looks most wretchedly reduced and deathly. In the evening, received a Bill, drawn out to my brother, by Mr Battersby, for Legal advice &c. in the year 1821. My brother sent it by Peter Latham.

2d Went down in the evening to see Miss E. Braithwaite, and found her but little better; she had never left her bed the whole day.

Dec 3d Went early in the afternoon to Mrs Heyes's, of Holland-Moor, to tea. It was then fair; whilst I staid, rain commenced and the wind rose, and on my return it was very rough; however, I got snugly home at 8 o'clock. The wind increased, and blew a perfect hurricane through the night. No damage was done at Holland worth mentioning.

This day Mrs Grundy died at Parr Hall.

9 December 1823 (Up Holland). *To Mr Stock*, Wigan:
Sir,

The time draws near when our little daughter, Mary, will leave school for a while, to enjoy the recreations so necessary to her age, and the comforts of a home where those nearest and dearest to her should assemble with her at the dame fireside. Let her have two homes, and deprive her no longer of the affectionate caresses of a mother – that parent which is ever most necessary to a daughter's welfare, and who alone can pay that minute attention to her moral and religious principles, and her daily and hourly conduct, which is absolutely necessary. Let her time at the approaching vacation be equally divided between us. Your business will frequently call you away, and she must then be left to the care of a servant, an evil that has been the ruin of numbers, has been the ruin of poor Jane, and will be the ruin of Mary if it be suffered. Yet it will be exceedingly hard upon Mary, if to avoid this evil, she must be kept perpetually at school, and thus have *no recreation, no change of scene.*

It is the duty of both of us to do considerable violence to our own inclinations and feeling when the welfare and comfort of our child is at stake; and this might be without any inconvenience to you.

I hear you are about to give up housekeeping in Wigan, and intend to reside principally at Southport. If this be true, you will then, I dare say, have no particular objection to my residing altogether in Wigan, if I wish to do so? I should be glad if you would consent to this – but then, where is Mary to be at the holidays? What respectable, well educated female will take charge of her at these times, and supply a mother's place? None but a mother's can, or will, act a mother's part. To spend the holidays at school, will be a comfortless, unhappy way for the poor child, and be in danger of depressing her spirits to such a degree, as eventually to undermine her health – indeed, *she is suffering now* from the great confinement she endures, and has endured, from 4-and-a-half years old; it must be a stronger constitution than hers that can bear it. Growing girls up to twice her present age, require much more air and exercise than it is possible they can have at a boarding school.

If you still refuse me the comfort of my child's company, and her the advantages of a mother's care, let me intreat that you will make it up to me by allowing me those comforts which you can well afford me, and of which I stand in need, by increasing my income and giving me a little furniture, that I may have a home of my own, and the attendance of a servant. Should I be attacked with a long sickness, as numbers around me are, what must become of me? My present income will neither allow me a nurse or a doctor; but even in health, I should have the comfort of a home of my own and a servant's assistance. My wishes are so reasonable, that you surely cannot deny me; for if you comply with all I have asked, it would, I should think, add a pleasure to your own heart to reflect that you were doing a husband's duty, by treating your wife as yourself. There should not be a single enjoyment on your part that is not equally allowed to me; yet I do not ask a tenth part, much less an equal share.

I have heard that you have reported that I have many things of which you do not know how I obtained possession, that belonged to you. *I assert in the most solemn manner*, that it is not so. You saw me pack up *every thing*. I left many things behind me in the hurry of packing up, which belonged to me; but I by no means conveyed anything away unknown to you. The strictest integrity ever marked my conduct, but a melancholy reward I met with!

The fire which took place in my bed-room, Mr Bird and Mrs Alston told me you laid to my charge. From this horrid accusation, I could easily have cleared myself, had you but told me that I was suspected; why say it behind my back, and not say it to me? I could at the time have easily proved my innocence. *I was not in the house when the fire begun.* How it happened, I know not. I gave the alarm instantly on discovering it. I had been above an hour and a half absent from the house. I gave the alarm in less than one minute after I entered, and which I could then have proved; and John Johnson himself said it had not been on fire above a quarter of an hour, so that it certainly took place whilst I was out. Besides, why should I do it? Everything I possessed in the world was in that room; it was but little, but it was all to me, and had it been destroyed, no Insurance Office would have remunerated me; neither would you, nor any one else.

My perfect innocence on this occasion prevented my having an idea that any one could suspect me; but knowing that you had been accused unjustly on one occasion, my anxiety that night (unkind and cruel as you had been to me), was to clear to you. What a contrast between your conduct and mine! For this reason, I got several people in after the fire was extinguished, to shew them that all that belonged to the house, was still there. I unlocked every drawer, cupboard, and box of which I had any key, and shewed them the contents. I shewed them your bookcases, on which I knew you set so much value – and all *to vindicate you.*

Consider this, and let you heart soften towards me, and be a little more liberal. Let me have free access to my child, that I may do a mother's duty to her, and which she really stands in need of.

For all Mrs Stock's restrained pleadings, her husband remained unmoved.

[Journal, December 1823]

Dec 9 From this period, I have been so greatly occupied in attending the wants of my dying Elisabeth, that I have neither had the time nor inclination to write here until now (21st). Poor Elisabeth! how she has suffered, and how gratefully she ever acknowledged the attentions she received. When shall I see her like again.

Her sister Catherine's assiduity in attending the dying beds of her Father; then her eldest sister Anne; a few years afterwards, her mother (24th May last); and now, her dearest, and most loved sister Elisabeth, is beyond all praise. May she have her deserts!

Catherine and Elisabeth were nearest of an age, which naturally caused them to be more together. Their dispositions differed materially, but their excellencies were equal. They grew from infancy sweetly united together, like two roses on one stalk. Although Elisabeth was the younger, her judgement was more cool, and corrected Catherine's warm-hearted impetuosity. Elisabeth possessed a superior talent in delineating flowers on canvass; Catherine was content to assist the progress of her work, by filling up the subordinate and laborious parts. Elisabeth from her youth was sickly; and asthmatic complaint prevented her taking much exercise; Catherine was ever ready to supply her every want. What one planned, the other could execute. In laying out their flower garden, or in any other amusement, their tastes were very similar. Catherine, with peculiar activity, would finish almost by the time Elisabeth suggested. Catherine's drollery, wit, and humour, enlivened Elisabeth's fine taste and peculiar delicacy of manner, were the delight of Catherine's heart. Together, they budded, bloomed, and expanded – but now! – one sweet rose has faded – withered – dropped – and how sad the other looks without its wonted companion. I fear it will wither soon. Poor Elisabeth! when I forgot thee, my memory must have entirely lost its faculty. Elisabeth had the greatest rectitude of principle; her manners were very lady-like; delicacy of sentiment, with decision of judgment, were finely contrasted. Her memory was most extraordinary. In History, she would frequently allude to minute circumstances with a wonderful precision, as well as to events of greater importance. In Genealogy, she was quite a Court Calendar; she amused herself much with reading, and long remembered whatever she read at any time, she did it so unostentatiously and with so much simplicity, that it slipped by, as it were, at the time; after-recollection would bring it again in full force of surprise at a memory so unusual. In Geography, too, she was very clever, and in many other things which I cannot just now commemorate. She excelled in whatever she attempted. When but a girl, and in better health, her superior cookery and domestic management were her mother's boast.

Poor Elisabeth! when shall I see thy like again.

For some years she had been confined to the house; for 7 or 8 months each year; but seldom missed joining the family at any period, before dinner, in the usual sitting room. Reading and rug-work were her principal amusements. She was fond of the society of a few, but could never bear many; the one, she did not like to be without – the other, distressed her; and gratified am I to think that I was frequently one of those few (not that I am vain enough to suppose I should have been so often selected, had the circle of Elisabeth's neighbours been more numerous; in a village like this, there are few to choose, have that liberty – and then, she pitied me; and pity induced her mother, her sisters, and herself, to invite me often).

Since her mother's death, I had observed her decline very rapidly; yet, if any feeling of affliction on that account had injured her health, she concealed it. Still her rug-work and her books had charms to amuse – until lately; for, ill and spiritless indeed she was, when these failed. At last, she could no longer – she could no more – and about 3 weeks ago, she took to her bed, from whence death only could remove her.

Yet, under all these accumulated sufferings, she was so grateful to the Almighty for the many comforts she enjoyed! How delightful it was to hear her speak her gratitude, and thankfulness. She had a sweet spirit! She had no want, she said, but it was supplied; food, medicine, attendance, lofty and airy apartments; the best of sisters, and many kind friends.

On Thursday, Dec. 18th, she was seized with a kind of stupor; death had finished his work, and left her to expire in peace, after a few hours of something like ease. It was about half past 12 at noon, when she seemed more inclined to sleep than usual; about 4 o'clock, she roused a little, and conversed with intellects as clear as ever. Mrs Gaskell, a favourite friend, had come to see her that afternoon; about 7 o'clock, Mrs Jackson and Miss Mary arrived (her two sisters from Prescot), and although still sadly overcome with a deathlike drowsiness, she exerted herself to talk to them with great chearfulness all night, until 2 o'clock on Friday morning, when they retired. Catherine soon after adjusted her pillows, and then laid down on a bed, close by; poor Catherine was heavy with her previous watchfulness for many nights, and great bodily fatigue, and fell asleep; at half past 5 o'clock, she started up, finding she had laid too long; she wondered at Elisabeth's stillness, put her curtain aside, and found her – dead!

Just in the attitude of sleep in which she had 3 hours before left her, with her head resting on her hand, she found her, as if she had never moved – so peaceably she departed,

Friday, Dec. 19th 1823, at the age of 32 years and 7 months.

Dec 24th Went down to the Abbey to see Catherine and Mary, and was shewn by Miss E. Leatham into the chamber of death, to take a last look at those features once so blooming and animated, but now pale, still, and lifeless. Death! Thou art awful – but thou and I have long been acquainted; seldom an hour passes that I forget thee, or a day which brings not reflections of thy power. When the night comes, I resign my spirit to the Father whom I love most dearly, not certain that these mortal eyes may ever again see the light; and in the morning, I rise as one who has but another day lent to them; so loosely, as it were, does the garment of life hang upon me.

25 Christmas Day On this, my Birthday anniversary, I have completed my 47th year, and have enjoyed more earthly comfort for the last 12 months than I ever remember to have done for the same length of time.

Dec 26 The interment of Miss E. Braithwaite took place this day, at 12 o'clock. My anxiety to hear something of my child, induced me to set off to Wigan. I called at various places, but could hear little – only that she was fetched from school on Monday, the 15th, in a gig.

27th Saturday Heard that Mary was seen the day previously, in the street, with her father.

(I have forgotten to say in the right place, that on my birthday, I finished a Will, on which I had for some time before been employed, having a right to make one, by a clause in the Deed of Separation between me and Mr Stock. Mr James Ball, and his nephew, Henry Ball, witnessed it).

29 Packed up a few toys for my little Mary, and wrote a note to Mrs Alston, requesting her to give them to her; and to intreat Mr Stock to let me see my child during this vacation.

30 As the Year is so near a close, I have this day made up all my money accounts, and having only received from Mr Stock, 3 quarter's annuity within the year - £52. 10s. – and my expenditure £64. 7s., I was £11. 17s. involved. This year, having received the full income of £70, and my expenditure £64. 18s. 7d., I have recovered a little - £5. 1. 5d. – which repays part of the last year's debt, and leaves yet behind £6. 15. 7d.

Drank tea with Miss Dannet in the evening, and passed it very agreeably with her and her intelligent, unassuming friend, Mr . Holcroft.

[Journal, January 1824)]

6th Having heard nothing respecting my child, walked over to Wigan this morning, and heard that Mr Stock was still inflexible, and was exceedingly angry with Mrs Alston for sending the toys to Mary at his house; at which, she is so offended, that she considers me as extremely ill used.

12th Went to Miss Dannett's to tea: the heat of the room was such, that I received a violent cold, and was for several days in a burning fever; and at the same time an inflammation in my mouth, and gathered gums. By Saturday following, I was recovered.

22^d Took tea with Mrs Ball, and met Mrs Morris and Mrs Walker. Mrs Morris is a woman of peculiarly amiable disposition, and fascinating simplicity of manner, combined with good sense. How unfortunately she has married; the only child of her parents, and having a handsome fortune, it is all squandered away most unaccountably by a hog of a husband, and she now toils amidst a numerous flock of fine-looking boys and girls, like a galley slave. Mrs Walker, a shop-keeper in Holland, is a woman of such strange manners, that I should never be surprised to hear she was become deranged. She is greatly to be pitied. The anxiety of business, and a family of 5 or 6 children to support, will be too much for her. I admired most her sentiments, they appeared so correct; but the nervous twitching manner she had, almost forced a smile even from pity's self.

February 2ᵈ I have long contemplated writing a History of my life, and yet have deferred it from month to month, from what must appear a very strange reason by any one who sees the quantity of my writings – the reluctance I feel to attempt writing. Whether it proceeds from indolence, or some other undefinable motive, I cannot say; but whether I have a letter to write, a journal, or an account, it seems a task to me; and yet the activity of my mind perpetually urges me to it. It is a strange contradiction! But are we not all strange contradictory beings.

This day I arranged my books and writing materials on my table, determined to begin, when such a depression of spirits seized me at the melancholy retrospect, that I could not commence. I wept, I trembled, and my soul utterly refused comfort; like Rachel, I wept for my child. I tried to pray, to sing a hymn, but could do neither. I passed the whole day in melancholy inaction; the next day the same. I attempted to sew, I put it away again; I took my flageolet, but it pleased me not, my mind was not in tune; and, living by myself, I had not a human being to speak to. If I had, it would often make me more chearful, and would help greatly to restore my composure when my spirit is cast down.

4ᵗʰ (Wednesday) This morning I was enabled to overcome my unwillingness to commence my history, and made a beginning, since when, I have proceeded by little and little; but if I get on no quicker hereafter, I shall be a long time finishing it. It is for my daughter's sake I am desirous to do it, and on her account I feel it absolutely necessary.

12ᵗʰ I think of my Mary from day to day, and mean immediately to make another attempt to see her, let Mr Grundy treat me as he may. I think he means well upon the whole, but Mr Stock has taken so much pains to prejudice his mind against me, that he is influenced to obey Mr S's tyrannical directions much more decidedly than he ought to be if he were really a Christian; which I hope he is almost.

18 (Wednesday) Left home a quarter before 10 o'clock this morning, to go to Parr Hall. I walked by the way of Winstanley, the Bear in the Ring, Senela Green and Black brook. I had just sat down in the parlour, when Mr Grundy came in, looking exceedingly solemn. Whether he really grieves for the loss of his wife, or no, I cannot say. I am not inclined to give him credit for it. I fancy the jewel of joy is within, enclosed in a case of *black shagreen*. We had a good deal of conversation respecting my seeing Mary. Mr Grundy informed me that he was awkwardly situated in regard to her, but he would endeavour to procure some precise instructions, and for the present, Mary should be introduced to me. She came, little darling, as soon as she was summoned, and embraced me most affectionately. She is extremely tall for her age, and very thin and pale, but says she is well. I staid with her more; for her father, in his mad passions, declared if I do not cease attempting to see her, he will place her where no one but himself shall ever know. Poor Mary, what is to become of her?

I got home at half-past-five, very little fatigued.

As I told Mr Grundy that if I had not much more liberty of seeing my child, I should certainly return to Mr Stock and run whatever risk I may of having my life sacrificed by his brutality, and requested him to inform Mr Stock of my determination, perhaps ere another year has elapsed, I may have breathed my last. Oh, my Father! look with pity on thy oppressed servant; extend thy protecting arm over me, and put into my heart what Thou wouldest have me do. If I go to my husband, go with me; if I should not go, put such obstacles in the way as shall entirely prevent my attempting it; be with me at all times, for if Thou forsakes me, I am lost. Oh, be with me, and protect me.

22ⁿᵈ Past the Sabbath at home, and in going twice to [Up Holland] Church. From this time, I intend going again to Wigan on Sabbath day; the weather and length of the days will now permit me to go in time for the morning service, and return home after afternoon service. Sometimes, in an evening, I read a sermon.

26ᵗʰ Took a walk to Wigan after dinner, and accidentally met with my nephew, William Stock, in Moyle's, the tea-dealers, shop. Some months ago I had had some conversation with him about purchasing an organ; the subject was again resumed, and he now

301

walked down with me to Atherton's, in Queen Street, who is an organ-builder. I was pleased with what I saw and heard there, and I am strongly tempted to order one; but although he says he can make a good one for 15 to 20£, yet it is a serious sum to me, and I must deliberate a little.

29 Sabbath day, and the 5ᵗʰ in the month, February. Went to Hope Chapel; met Mr Stock in Hope Street. It is the first time I have passed him since we were separated. We both passed without seeming to notice each other. He was coming from Standish,[15] near which he last Wednesday went to reside, at the house that Mr Ainslie, Mr Standish's steward, lately lived in. Mr Stock, I am informed, gave 100£ for fixtures, has ordered 20 new chairs at 2 guineas each, a set of dining tables, an elegant new bed, and a new gig!!! and is to give 80£ a year for the house and ground.

[Journal, April 1824]

April 10ᵗʰ (Saturday). Set out this morning at half-past-one o'clock in Wm Hindley's cart from Tower Hill to Liverpool. About 3 o'clock the wind rose and continued for some hours to blow off the road, showers of snow and hail were very frequent. We were four passengers in the cart (a covered one), and notwithstanding the storm and the loneliness of the hour and the road, I was very warm, comfortable , and contented. The storm abated before 6, and at 7 [the following morning] we arrived at Liverpool.[16] I went to Mr Roxburgh's in Russell St, to breakfast, having brought the materials with me in my basket. The principal object of this journey was to ascertain the expences of a journey to London, and to obtain the necessary Maps and Tours, that I might become acquainted with the country I had for some time contemplated passing through. I dined at Mr Price's, and afterwards called upon Miss Dalrymple, and at 5 o'clock, again entered Hindley's covered cart, and arrived home between twelve and one at midnight, very little fatigued.

14ᵗʰ Walked to Wigan to make further inquiries respecting the London roads and coaches from Manchester, as Mrs Stopford wishes her daughter and Master Barlow to go that way, and to go with me under my protection.

30 Friday Having waited for 2 or 3 days for fair weather, that I might walk over to Parr Hall to see my little daughter once more before I went to London, I set out this day at 10 o'clock. The morning was fair and bright, but the wind blew quite a hard gale, and I had great difficulty in forcing my way through it, for it blew right in my face. I had for some weeks been rather weak and indisposed, and, on setting out to-day, almost despaired of accomplishing so long a journey on foot; but a mother's heart can do great things. The farther I proceeded, the more light and active I felt, and I arrived at Parr Hall at half-past 12. Miss Hammond, the teacher who was engaged on Mrs Grundy's death, opened the door, and as I followed her through the writing room, my little Mary, who was there, advanced to me immediately, and we retired together to the little back-parlour where I always sit when at Parr Hall. Feeling apprehensive that Mr Stock may remove my child some time when he thinks I am quite unprepared for such a blow, and she may be placed where I could not discover her, I had prepared a card with a direction for Miss Dannett of Up Holland, and gave it to her now, telling her, that if ever she were removed to any other school, she must take an opportunity, in private, of writing to inform me where she was, and with whom, and to direct for Miss Dannett (for if my name was on the direction, it might be intercepted at the Post Office); and be very careful with whom she intrusted it, to put it there.

The child is so young that I fear she will hardly be able to manage such a business, should there be occasion. This is the beginning of my instruction to her to do any thing in secret; but after much hesitation and mature deliberation, I have come to the decision that if I had taken no such precaution, I should have been sadly wanting in duty as a mother. That it should be necessary, must lie at Mr Stock's door; and on his head be the guilt. If he would act as a husband and a father ought to do, there would be no occasion to keep anything secret from him; it would be a crime to attempt it. I told Mary to put the card at the bottom of her box, and shew it to no one; and if any one should see it, I think they would not know what it meant. I staid with her until 4 o'clock, and then returned home, less fatigued with a 12 or 14 miles walk than might have been expected.

May 4 Took tea with Miss Braithwaite; was seized whilst there with vomiting, and was very ill all the evening.

6 May 1824 (Up Holland). *To Miss Stock,* Parr Hall, near St Helens:

When I left you, my dear Mary, last Friday, I forgot to turn up the road through the wood, which Mr Grundy once shewed me when he and you took me a part of the way, but walked down the road for almost a quarter of a mile, and found a way through some fields, near a good brick house on the left. Perhaps this way was as near, and I was in no danger of losing my way whilst I had Billinge beacon in view; for I had to pass near it, and through the village of Billinge, which appears to me to be about half-way between Holland and Parr Hall.

I met with few people on the way, and those passed me quietly and civilly; indeed, my dear love, wherever I go, no harm happens to me, nobody injures me, or puts me in fear. You asked me if I was not afraid of robbers. No, my dear, because I never was robbed – by strangers. It seems to me as if, because I had no earthly protector, that God was with me wherever I went, and took care of me himself.

I had a pleasant walk, although rather tired. I took shelter from a shower of rain at Mr Gaskell's, of Ox-House,[17] where they very hospitably gave me some refreshment, and I then went home quite rejoiced that I had had the pleasure, I am sure, when you reflect that I am passing my time as agreeably as I can, and that all the addition I could wish for, would be the society of my dear Mary to chatter to.

I expect to set off for London on Wednesday next, May 12th. I shall meet the Liverpool coach at Prescot, along with Miss Stopford and Master Barlow (a youth from the neighbourhood of London, who is an apprentice to Mr Stopford). Miss Stopford is going on a visit to Master B's friends, and I anticipate a very agreeable journey with them. As the journey is a long one, and I never travelled so far before, I feel somewhat anxious for you, my love; but if I should die, and you never see me more, may the God who has supported and protected me, take equal care of you, and – you will never be forsaken.

I hope your throat is better, and that you are now quite well again. When you are at liberty, go out into the garden as often as the weather permits; and always be out of doors when you can, that you may grow stronger, for you look very pale and delicate, and there is nothing better for your health than being much out in the open air. I believe I should be stronger if I were to go more out of doors, and I intend to be very little in-doors until winter returns.

I must remind you of the approach of your birthday. You will be 9 years old on the 9th of June, which is about 5 weeks hence. You may be assured that I shall think of you when the day comes, and wish you every kind and good wish; but I suppose I shall be far distant at the time.

I have written to you now, because it may perhaps be several months before I could conveniently write again.

[Journal, May 1824]:

From the 4th to the 12th of May, nothing occurred but the usual routine of rising, eating, and going to sleep again. I made little other preparation for my journey to London than procuring my cloaths to be all washed, and taking care not to leave a single halfpenny owing. If I can but give in as clear account at the day of judgement, as I keep with my fellow-creatures from day to day, with what confidence I shall appear before Thee, O my Father. But the debts Thy children owe Thee must be cancelled; they can never be paid.

I am now 48 years of age, and since I left my husband, have increased in bodily health and strength, so much as to be better than I ever recollect being, for so long a time, at any period of my life; and have an apparent prospect of a constitution to last me perhaps 15 years longer – yet, ere another sun sets, these eyes may have been closed for ever; ere another day dawns, these limbs may have become stiff and cold; but Oh, if I am but with Thee, Thou Great and Mighty Un-nameable, what need I care.

In this state of mind, I set off for London; considering it to be very probable I should never reach it; when such numbers are killed by the overturning of stagecoaches, what right have I to expect to escape? I prepared no finery, for I did not mean to wear it. The cloaths I had, were good enough to wear where I was wholly unknown.

Miss Weeton's methodical plans were now put into action. She caught the London stagecoach at Prescot, on Wednesday, 12 May 1824, 'setting off exactly at 2 o'clock outside all the way to London.'

NOTES:

1. Extensive research has failed to find any reference to, or map reference to the location of Ball's Farm, Up Holland.
2. Rev William Roby (1766-1830), born Haigh, near Wigan. Considered instrumental to the revival and rapid growth of Independency in Lancashire. Founder of the Lancashire Congregational Union (1806). For a brief period Roby preached on behalf of the Countess of Huntingdon's Connexion, at St Paul's Chapel, Standishgate, Wigan. In 1795 he was called to become minister of Cannon Street Congregational Church, Manchester, before becoming minister of Grosvenor Street Congregational Chapel in 1807. Grosvenor Street Chapel became known as Roby's Chapel. A new church was built at Longsight, Manchester, in 1972 and named Roby United Reformed Church.
3. Rev John Toothill (1760-1839), born Wilsden, near Bradford, Minister of Rainford Congregational Church, near St Helens, for over 50 years. Buried at Rainford together with his wife, Sarah, who died in 1852, aged 89. (See also chapter 4, note 20).
4. In 1790 a 'Wesleyan' Methodist Chapel, or a 'preaching house' was first built a little over a mile distance from Up Holland, at Lamberhead Green, Pemberton, near Wigan. The site is now a small park/memorial garden in Chapel Street.
5. Anthony Billington, carrier. 'Roe Buck, Old Haymarket, A. Billington, Up Holland and Wigan on Friday, and returns on Saturday.' *(Gore's Liverpool Directory, 1825).*
6. Sunday school hours were necessarily long, as a regular course on instruction in reading and writing had to run parallel with Bible instruction. For the majority of children, the only chance of acquiring an education was on Sunday.
7. Rev Dr Thomas Raffles (1788-1863), born Spitalfields, London. Secretary of the Lancashire Congregational Union (1826-1863). Known as a 'dominant minister' at Great George Street Congregational Chapel, Liverpool.
8. In Miss Weeton referring to Stock's idiosyncratic behaviour as a sign of insanity, may appear to be exaggeration born of understandable resentment. She had already been threatened with incarceration in a lunatic asylum by Stock. Unknowingly, her comment proved to be an omen for what was to come. (See Aaron Stock, Appendix III).
9. 'To such as are more disposed to economize money than time, the canal packets offer a cheap conveyance from Liverpool and Manchester as well as on the whole line of the intermediate country to Scarisbrick Bridge, where a number of handsome carriages are stationed to convey passengers to this place of fashionable resort [Southport], being a distance of about five miles.' *Baines Lancashire Directory, 1825.*
10. 'Coaches: During the bathing season. ECLIPSE to Liverpool every morning at 8, rets. at 7 in the evg.' *Baines Lancashire Directory, 1825.*
11. 'Bagilt: CAMBRIA, sails with goods and passengers to Bagilt, near Holywell, Wales, every day, at eight morning.' *Baines Lancashire Directory, 1825.*
12. Mrs T. Jackson was the younger Braithwaite sister (Margaret), having married Thomas Tellaw Jackson in the year 1808
13. Billinge is situated 5 miles south west of Wigan and two miles from Up Holland.

14. Catherine and Elisabeth Braithwaite were, at that time, aged 41 and 32 respectively.
15. Standish is located three miles north of Wigan. 'Standish: Stock, Aaron: Mfr. Prospect Hill'. *Baines Lancashire Directory.*
16. The cart travelled at approximately $2^1/_2$ miles per hour.
17. Ox House Heyes is located on the boundary between Up Holland and Billinge. It had been the home of the Gaskell family from the 17th century. The last Gaskell to live there was James Gaskell, a well-known musician, who was organist at St John's C of E, Church, Pemberton, near Wigan. After being unoccupied for some time Ox House became the new home of Up Holland Grammar School from 1878 to 1952.

NINE

Adventure by stagecoach

London

13 May – 30 July 1824

THE 30 YEARS or so of the 'golden age of the stagecoach' ran
from about the beginning of the 19th century to the mid-1830s.
Following the opening of the Liverpool and Manchester railway
in 1830, travel by stagecoach began to decline. In 1824 Miss
Weeton was in her 48th year; in that year she took full advantage
of the stagecoach at its most advanced to experience an exciting
journey to London.

Her usual mode of travel was to walk, often for distances
up to about 15 miles (including the return journey). This had
the advantage of costing her nothing other than time and shoe
leather. For longer distances that could not be undertaken by
the more comfortable canal packet, she would take the more
expensive stagecoach and suffer the discomfort caused by deeply
rutted roads.

Such journeys were at best uncomfortable and at worst
dangerous; the result of an overturned coach would be either
serious injury or death. Miss Weeton was content to suffer such
discomfort and despite the added danger of sitting outside,
preferred this to sitting inside next to an uncouth or unwashed
stranger.

During the 1750s a stagecoach journey from North West
England to London took $4^1/_2$ days. By the 1820s road
improvements effected by John Macadam had reduced a
journey from Liverpool to London to 'only one night on the
road,' but that excluded bed and breakfast at an inn in favour

of continuing to travel throughout the night, stopping only to change the horses.

An advertisement in the *Liverpool Mercury*, in 1815, for the *Umpire*, which may have been the stagecoach on which Miss Weeton travelled, detailed its route from the 'Saracen's Head Inn,' Dale Street, Liverpool, at 1 o'clock, every Monday, Wednesday and Friday afternoons. Stops for refreshments were extremely hurried: 'Supper allowed 30 minutes, Breakfast allowed 30 minutes, Dinner allowed 30 minutes.' The *Umpire* would eventually arrive at the 'Saracen's Head Inn,' Snow Hill, London, during the evening of the following day.

Miss Weeton approached her proposed London journey in her usual methodical manner, by acquiring maps and a copy of a well-known guide book entitled: *The Picture of London*. Her recorded itinerary to and from London, gives us a fascinating glimpse of early 19th century life throughout the land; also of how sparsely populated was England before the 1830s. Passing through various towns and villages, she describes her experiences at the various inns and the shortness of time allowed for meals, before travelling onwards.

Miss Weeton's ambitious sightseeing plans reveal her to be a lady of resolute spirit with a thirst for adventure. Her enthusiasm for visiting all the recommended tourist places, described in *The Picture of London*, seems to have had no limits. It would appear that she had set off with the idea of trying to achieve a record in terms of miles walked in London and the number of attractions visited. She was far too imaginative to engage in repetition, but many of Miss Weeton's days in London do become rather tedious reading. For that reason, whilst her journeys to and from London, as recorded by Edward Hall in *Miss Weeton's Journal of a Governess*, are repeated here in full, only the sightseeing highlights of her visit to the capital are included in this edition.

On arrival in the metropolis, she realised that her copy of *The Picture of London* guide kindly loaned to her by a Mr T. Jackson, was 20 years old, and quickly replaced her out-of-date copy with an up-to-date 1823 (23rd edition).[1] The title page states that it is: 'A correct guide to all the Curiosities, Amusements, Exhibitions,

Public Establishments, and Remarkable Objects in and near London; with a collection of appropriate tables, made for the use of Strangers, Foreigners, and all Persons who are not intimately acquainted with the Metropolis.'

22 May 1824 (London). To *Miss Dannett*, Up Holland:

On leaving Holland, May 12th, Miss Braithwaite very kindly accompanied me a long way over the fields, and when we parted, I proceeded very comfortably, and arrived in Prescot at about 20 minutes past 4 o'clock. The following morning, we went to Mrs Jackson's garden, and made several calls. After dinner, Mrs T. Jackson, Miss R., and 2 or 3 more accompanied me to the coach, on which I set off exactly at 2 o'clock, outside all the way to London. Miss Stopford and Master Barlow were snugly fixed with 2 middle-aged ladies, who travelled the whole way. At Rainhill, as the ostlers were fixing fresh horses, one of these got dreadfully frightened, and fell twice in the shafts; the 2nd time, they had some difficulty to raise it, and then it backed and twisted so among the other horses, that although there were plenty of men, they had some difficulty to manage it. I expected an overturn. At last, we set off, at as great a speed as the coachman could drive; the poor horse got well whipped the whole of the stage. The inside passengers knew nothing of their danger until it was nearly over; outside, we were never more than half full, which was very agreeable to me.

At Warrington, I found my luggage at the Inn where the coach stops, quite ready at the instant. The air was so piercingly cold, that I immediately availed myself of some of my wrappings, and my wool-lined beaver gloves were a treasure to me. The air was so cold, and the sky so nearly without sunshine, as entirely to divest the surrounding country of any picturesque beauty; and the whole road beyond Warrington seemed a continued flat, few passers-by to enliven the way; and not a gentleman's carriage, scarce a chaise, only three or four gigs, and as many horsemen, until within 40 or 50 miles of London. We passed through Lichfield at midnight, only stopping ten minutes. We had previously had our tea at 9 o'clock, but I was then detained with Miss Stopford upstairs, that I did not get half enough. At Lichfield, therefore, I was so starved with hunger as well as cold, that a 10 minutes warming was most gratifying at a roasting kitchen fire.

Mrs Jackson had furnished me with a small bottle of brandy, and I here applied the hot kettle to some of it. I had not ventured to touch any before, for fear of being sleepy. I now found the cold air had power enough to keep me staring wide awake. I gave Miss Stopford some, and then set off again, famished but refreshed. Mrs Jackson had given me some potted shrimps, and a good lump of cold tongue; but these, hungry as I was, I could not eat. Some bread which I had provided, vanished long before, and if I had some more, some biscuits, or some of Peggy Hodson's[2] buns, I could have feasted; for I am a graminovorous (sic) animal and not a carnivorous one, and in this, you and I perfectly agree. As I had no food on my stomach to warm me, I applied to my bottle *many was the time and oft*, although I was cautious to take no more at once than a table spoonful and a half, one third brandy! By this means, I got on through the night very well. My head and face were covered with a thick cotton handkerchief, tied under my bonnet.

A lunar rainbow was observable near 2 hours, but very faint, which showed there was heavy rain southward. We had none. This was the first lunar bow I ever saw. At 6 o'clock [a.m.], we stopped at Lutterworth, to breakfast, to my great comfort. I took care this time to accommodate nobody, but let everyone look after themselves; for I have not found, in this business, that spirit of accommodation from others which I had a right to expect, but a very great deal of selfishness. I took a hearty breakfast of coffee, and mounted the coach much better for it.

This day was colder than the preceding one, and more cheerless as we came along the greater part of the day. The country might have been depopulated, we saw so few living beings; I think I did not see above half-a-dozen in Buckinghamshire. We stopped to lunch at Northampton. Miss Stopford and Mr Barlow would have nothing, and when I saw the table covered with cold meat, ham, etc., and not a potatoe or a tart, I set off to buy a loaf, but before I could find a bread shop, the coach was going, and I was obliged to go away empty, and without knowing how blessed are the hungry – when they are filled.[3] In a very ill humour, I rode on; for, although keeping it to myself and troubling no one with my vexation, I inwardly grumbled bitterly at my own easiness of temper, which constantly makes me a sufferer to other people's humours; and, what is worse, I receive no thanks for it. Had I

311

pleased myself, I would certainly not have travelled in such weather.

When 40 miles of London, it began to rain, and continued the remainder of the way. It was now *quite delightful!* My frequent application to the bottle, whilst it prevented cold, at the same time added to my drowsiness. I had no difficulty to keep awake in the night, but now I was in continual danger of literally *falling* asleep. I have great reason to thank Mrs Jackson for the brandy, for I believe it preserved me from taking cold. As greatly as I have puffed about my *frequent application* to the *bottle*, I have at least half of it left yet. Mr John Barlow met us at Islington, and put me into a coach. Miss Stopford and Mr James were quite well, and very little fatigued. We had many a bit of chatter through the coach window. I drove to Mr O'Donoghue's; it was about half-past-5 when I got there. He very kindly requested me to take tea, which I gladly did, and then walked to my lodgings with my landlady's daughter.

I got to bed as soon as I could, and never woke until near noon the next day, quite well, and ready for breakfast, which I took in Mrs Benson's room, while she ate her dinner. I did nothing that day but buy in some provisions and coals, and went to bed again about 7.

Next morning, Saturday the 15th, I arose, completely refreshed. It rained incessantly this day and the day before, and I only went out with a rice pudding to the bakehouse.

On Monday morning, the 17th, after examining my map, I set out at half-past-10, to deliver Mrs Ducker's letter to Mrs Johnson in Queen Street, Clerkenwell. In passing Whitechapel Church, about a quarter of a mile hence, I saw a great crowd, and mingling amongst them, I was told the Bishop of London was going to hold a confirmation there; so I played truant, and went in, and witnessed the whole ceremony. When it was over, I was glad to go home and dine, for Dr Littler's[4] medicine and my subsequent journey, have given me a keen appetite. Off I set again after dinner, and got to Mrs Johnson's without further let or hindrance, easily finding my way. I staid tea with her, and we had a deal of chatter. Mrs Johnson took me over the way to the lodgings. I have not yet agreed for them, for though I like the situation and vicinity to Mrs J, I don't like the room, it is so small. I shall stay here one month, for I like my present lodgings with Mrs Benson. It is a very light, airy situation, and I can see fifty times as much sky as I can in my parlour at Holland. It is a fine wide road, and very lively.

Tuesday, the 18th, I spent at Mr Barlow's. I had received an invitation the day before to go, guided by two little gentlemen, old playfellows of Mr James's. As it was so far distant, we were requested to leave home at 9 o'clock. We did so, and arrived at Hamstead a little after 11. I had been told, when at Mr O'Donohue's, that Mr Barlow had had a severe attack of palsy, and I found that James and Miss Stopford had never seen him; nor had the family dared to tell him of their arrival. He is very nervous and ill, and faint hopes of his recovery. It is very probable that I shall see Miss Stopford no more here. It is such a terrible distance, near 6 miles. The family were so stately and reserved (a mother, 3 daughters, and 2 sons), that I did not like my visit, and don't desire to repeat it. You will take care, I hope, to show this letter to no one but Mrs Dannett, and Miss C Braithwaite, for you will see there is much in confidence.

I have *accidentally* heard that it is quite a settled thing with the Barlows that James is to marry Miss Stopford. Whether this is as well understood at Roby Mill, I cannot say, but I think it will not be for Miss S's happiness. She is an artless, unambitious girl, and this family, I fear, are exceeding proud, over-bearing, and anything in temper but sweet.

Wednesday, 19th. I was confined at home all morning, cleaning, going errands, and cooking. After dinner, I took a long walk through the city by way of spying out the land, and walked round St Paul's, but did not go in. I came home well tired.

20th. I set out in the morning to Mrs Johnson's, to conclude about lodgings, and found them engaged. It is of little consequence, for I did not like the room; it was so close and small. I rested all the afternoon, and after tea I walked along Shadwell and Ratcliffe Highway to see the Tower (only the outside), and London Bridge. It was the 1st time I had seen the river, and I was much pleased with the walk. My morning's walk to Mrs Johnson's, which is a very long distance, and this, fatigued me so, that to-day (the 21st) I must stay at home to recruit. My time has hitherto been so taken up with cooking, cleaning, and going errands, that I am half tired before I set out. The going up and down 2 or 3 pair of stairs so continually, adds to the labour as well as to the consumption of time. Next week, I intend to begin serious operations, and view the interior of some buildings of which at present I have only seen the outside.

I have now given you a long Journal of my Week in London. I am quite pleased with my visit, and enjoy myself much; but having everything to do wholly for myself, I can see but few objects in a week, and must therefore take a longer time to see all, than one who has everything provided for them.

Mr T. Jackson lent me a Picture of London, but when I here begun to examine it, I found it of so old a date, 1803, it would not do; so I went to Lackington's, and bought one for the present year,[5] for there is no possibility of doing without one. I only got it yesterday I can now go out with confidence, as I shall know constantly how to proceed.

From 70 or 80 caravans, each as large as those which usually convey wild beasts, are passing daily to the East India docks, and return filled with tea to the India House. What an amazing consumption there must be in England.

It will probably be next week but one before I can send a letter to Miss Braithwaite, for I must not spend much time in writing, I find.

31 May to 2 June 1824 (Mrs Benson's, No 5 George Terrace, Commercial Road). To *Miss Braithwaite*, Up Holland:

You will before now have seen my letter to Miss Dennett, I dare say, so I will not repeat what I have said there. You will neither expect nor desire that I shall give you an accurate description of what I see, for any printed book on the subject will, of course, be far better. In a correspondence like mine, where I feel as if writing to friends who are interested in what pleases, amuses, employs, or befalls *me*, and who I suppose wish to know how *I* proceed, I think it better to relate such things concerning myself as may entertain those far away, who desire to be acquainted with them; and in this case, I think egotism (if it literally mean writing about my own affairs) necessary, and a compliance with your wishes, and not a reproach. On this plan, then, I will proceed until you request me to alter it.

I certainly was greatly pleased with my journey hither, although the weather was not the brightest and most pleasant. Many an object as I passed along, amused and interested me, and no consideration could have induced me to travel inside the coach; the guard offered me an inside seat in the night, but I declined it, for the night was light, though not clear, and it was not near so cold as the following day; many a drunkard's candle did I see, lighting him to bed past midnight, and a waiting family for the absent. Litchfield Cathedral looked solemn and grand, though passed hastily. I peeped in at many an opened bedroom window, unclosed by early risers to purify their rooms as the morning dawned and the day advanced; and many a sickly invalid, I fear, would be startled from their slumbers by the guard's noisy horn; which was of no use that I know of, for the coach made noise enough. Riding on a coach is very easy; I never felt tired or benumbed with it.

About noon the second day, the scene grew more and more animated; towns were more frequent, and villages thickened; they increased in beauty too, the nearer we approached to London. Mr McAdam's[6] name was on many a board as we approached; thanks, ten thousand thanks to him, I say, for the easy ride I had had the whole of the way. I should have been more shook if I had journeyed from Wigan to Southport; but on these roads, the traveller has all the pleasure without any of the fatigue.

Whilst at Mr O'Donohue's, before I proceeded to my lodgings the evening of my arrival, a Miss Steel and I were for a short time alone. She told me that Mr Barlow's intended their son James for Miss Stopford. I thought it was singular I should *come to London* to hear Holland news. I think it is only conjecture at this end of the tail by the end. (Don't tell how I came by this, or I may get my own tail pinched for it; and Miss Steel's too) – for when, on the following Tuesday (the 18th), I was spending the day at Mr B's, the *most marked attention to Miss Stopford* was constantly paid, to the utter neglect of poor I. I had been requested to leave home at 9 o'clock, that I might have more time to rest there. I thought this kind, and did so. The two boys, Master B's late school fellows, and myself, arrived at 11. We found Miss Stopford and James preparing for a long walk to Regent Street, etc., and had we been half-an-hour later, they would have been out. I thought it very odd, as I knew no one else. I, out of over politeness, requested that our early arrival might not prevent their walk, as we were too much fatigued to go with them. They went, and I and the little boys, sat by ourselves almost 2 hours before any of the family came near us. At last, Miss Barlow came in, and her eldest brother. Some time had elapsed before any refreshment was offered. Ann and James returned, and they *all* sat down to a game of teetotum,[7] Miss Barlow and all, leaving me quite in a deserted seat.

There are 3 sons and 3 daughters in this [Barlow] family. James is the youngest. The house is handsomely furnished, the rooms a good size for a single house. I saw 3 women servants. They are a very plain-featured family. James is the handsomest. I really think, prejudice apart, that they are not a good tempered family. James is very rude, slovenly, and overbearing and shewed no feeling for his father, but was most troublesomely noisy, although he knew his father was not to know that he had come home.

Poor Ann [Stopford], I fear, will be made a sacrifice for her money, and will not know nor derive any advantage from it; and James Barlow has not the delicacy or feeling to appreciate the value of a girl like her. She is at present a sweet, innocent, affectionate girl, and I wish she might meet with a mind like her own; but an unfeeling son cannot make a good husband.

I am much pleased with my visit to London. The first view I had on coming was in passing under the arch at Highgate; and really, it was grand. The city appeared so immense, and St Paul's, that emperor of buildings, towering amidst the whole. For some days, the confusion I naturally felt, prevented my distinguishing objects individually. I now begin to feel almost naturalized.

I wished to see the General Post Office, so on the morning of the 22[d] (Saturday), I took that letter all the way there, instead, of putting it into one of the receiving Houses nearer at hand. It is a gloomy, dark place. A new Office is commenced building on another site, and much need there is of it. I find it necessary when going to some places in the city, to keep my attention quite awake, or I should pass by many a grand place, and not know it. So it was now; I was close by the P.O., and could not tell which was it.[8] I expected to have seen a crowd about the place of entrance, all bustle and business, but it was perhaps to inquire, and went up a gate way. When I had deposited my letter (and it requires some sagacity for a stranger find the right hole), I turned inattentively to come out, and issued forth at a place totally different to the one where I entered. 'If I could but mind what I am about,' thought I, 'I shall be finding all the fellows p - - - - - g against the wall in this narrow place.' I opened my eyes and minded my way, and going cautiously round, got again into Lombard Street, to the spot where I had entered, for otherwise, I should not have known where I was.

I get off my Lesson from my Map at home, and drawing a rough sketch of the precise places I mean to walk to, if I deviate, I am bewildered – like a child saying of his task who, if he be interrupted, must begin again. Having my little sketch in my hand, I knew now which way to turn. My plan was to spend the day in reconnoitering, which I find quite necessary, as I have no companions to go with me. I went to St Paul's, intending to be there during morning service, and no more, at this time; but on entering, the doorkeeper informed me that there would be no service until the 10th of June, as the workmen were now putting up scaffolding and benches for the annual assemblage of children at that time. I paid the usual 2d and never did I see so grand a sight for so little money. I rambled an hour or more over the whole ground floor of the building. I wished for you to view what I saw. It far surpassed anything I had imagined amongst beasts; in comparative size as an elephant; but in real beauty – to what shall I compare it? It is rich in ornament, but not loaded. Between 30 and 40 fine marble monuments adorn it. Such works were new to me, and my feelings were highly wrought upon. First impressions are often most exquisitely vivid. The shutting of a door now and then, the occasional knockings of a workman's hammer, resounding like thunder, had a fine effect as the sound wound up and reverberated within the dome, dying away by degrees as I ascended to the top. I left, with a determination to revisit it soon, and see the whole. I shall not be able to obtain admittance on the 10th for want of a ticket, as they are not sold.

I next proceeded up Ludgate Hill, and part of the way along Fleet Street. The market here is the dirtiest heap of lumber I ever saw.[9] There had been several heavy showers of rain that morning, and the streets in some places were near ancle deep in mud. At the crossing places, there were such long strings of vehicles of every sort, that foot passengers had to wait a considerable time to catch an opening, and then it was run that run could. It was fine fun for me, for I like a good excuse for a run. There were famous long rows of us, and the longer we stood, the worse it was, for the line lengthened. It was market day too, and the carriages could only pass on at a foot's pace, like a funeral train. I could see neither beginning nor end of them. At last, I skipped across like a Columbine – only I plunged one foot in a mud hole.

On the 26th, I went to St Paul's, and saw the whole, from the vaults below, to the Ball above. I purchased on my way there, a quire of large paper, the benefit of which you are now receiving.

June 2nd. I have never seen nor heard a word from Miss Stopford since the day I was there [at the Barlow family home, Tuesday, 18th May]. She might have written, at least, as I do not know her address precisely, (and she does mine), nor Mr Platt's. I shall be obliged if you will request Mr Stopford to remit my Quarter's Annuity on the 21st of June, as he proposed, through Mr Platt (all except what was paid for my Coach fare by Mr Platt's address, and I will call upon him. It will save postage.

I shall be glad to hear from you as soon as convenient.

8 June 1824 (London: No. 5, George Terrace. Commercial Road). To *Miss Dalrymple,* Liverpool:

Since I arrived here, I have often thought of my promise to write to you, but other and prior promises at Up Holland have prevented my fulfilling it before this, and my time has hitherto been so fully occupied, that I find I must let little writing serve. I have no attendance at my lodgings, and having all my own cleaning, cooking, errands-going, and waiting to do my self, much of my time each day is taken up with it.

In a few days after my arrival, the weather brightened, and I have enjoyed the novelty of the scene much, and think of remaining here until the middle or the end of July. I am about half-a-mile from Stepney, in a pleasant, healthy situation; but it is too remote from the west end of the town, to admit of my having seen anything as yet of the gay scenery there. For that reason, I have taken lodgings in Lambeth, at No. 16, Carlisle Place, and go there on the 10th. inst.

On Whit Monday afternoon (7th.), I went to Greenwich fair, a highly wrought scene of frun frolic, and folly. I was highly diverted with the nonsense and mirth of which I was a spectator, and could laugh now when I think of it. A grand fair is held there in Whitsuntide, for three days. I had to walk a mile and half, and then, taking boat, was ferried another mile. the boats here are of a much narrower and lighter construction than I ever remembered at Liverpool. We were 10 passengers – 6 of them lads, to my joy – though in other boats no larger, I saw 14 grown-up people. The weather was so hot, that the waterman stripped his jacket soon; by and bye he swelled so with heat and exertion, that – first modestly apologizing – he unbuttoned the waistband of his breeches – We all sat as still and grave as judges.

Hundreds of boats and thousands of passengers, all for the same destination, together with the extreme beauty of the day, made the scene most animated. As soon as I landed, I saw people as old as myself, mingled amongst the young, swinging away merrily in the large boat Swings, shouting, laughing, and screaming, as they mounted aloft in the air, like hey-go-mad. 'This is the finest fun we have had to-day,' shouted some – Need I tell you that I did not get in? I walked on to the Park, which is always open to the public; it is a most lovely place. Here were innumerable groups walking about, and innumerable groups amused themselves by getting to the tops of various hills in the Park, and, taking hold of hands, 2, 3, or 4 together, they run down with the utmost speed; often some unlucky wight [person] places himself just before them as they are in full speed; down they tumble over him, and over one another, men and women, boys and girls. I sat on the grass, watching this sport until I was tired of laughing at it. I was surprised to see such a number of genteel people there, spectators like myself; but still more, so many well dressed ones actually joining in it. As to servant girls, apprentices, and others of a worse description, the wonder is not so great. The shows too, were in great numbers – and the grotesque figures!!

Many of these fellows make clever speeches for their purpose, as Mr Canning or Mr Brougham;[10] and Mr B. and Mr C. might just as soon have been show men. How can any boast of the superior understanding of the human race, when they see so many, naturally as wise as themselves, making themselves more ridiculous than any other creature living? If they would but reflect justly, they would see how full of folly the wisest of them are, and what a slight shade of difference between them and an idiot.

6 July 1824 (London). To *Miss Catherine Braithwaite,* Up Holland:

I wish I could do by this letter as you have done by yours, and save you the expence of postage. I was beginning to be anxious to hear from you, when your letter arrived. The bearer had paid immediate attention to it. I got it by the twopenny Post.[11]

Balloons are going up here almost weekly. On the day I last dated my Journal to you, the 2nd of June, one went up from some where not far from Pentonville (one of the villages adjoining London on the North). I knew nothing of it until I got into the Aldgate, on my way to put my letter to you into the P.O. It was then 3 o'clock, the very hour advertised for the ascent, so I hastened to Blackfriars Bridge, as I knew the wind would bring it that way, and I could not possibly have got to the place of its ascension had it risen punctually to the time. After waiting an hour and a half, I saw it come, and rise out of sight over my head, in fine style. It descended very safely, I afterwards heard. Not so the one which had gone up a few days before. You will have heard of poor Harris's awful fate. His balloon I did not see, not having heard of its intended ascent until after the Catastrophe had taken place. When I heard of it, I was glad I had not seen it.[12]

Whilst I was at Mrs Benson's, I was sadly out of the way of hearing of anything going forward in or near the metropolis; and if I had heard, I was too far off to benefit by the news. Harris's funeral was going along the road, as Graham's Balloon was ascending – how unfeeling!

Thursday, June 3rd. I went after dinner to the Tower, to see the Jewel Office. I was rather disappointed here, for all the grand baubles (worth, I suppose near a million of money; perhaps two of three) are contained in a place no bigger than a recess for a sideboard. The place is perfectly divested of daylight, and shewn by lamplight. It is well enough to see for once, but had I the choice, I would prefer seeing the emerald isles of Winandermere (sic), the ruby coloured setting sun, its golden rising, the silvery clouds, the azure sky, or even the simple yellow butter cup. The admission for one person is 3s; the armoury 3s. I thought both sights too costly, so declined the latter. A Warder conducted me from the Tower Gate to the office and back, a very kindly, good natured old fellow. The costume of a Warder is very antiquated – scarlet coats, with skits full all round like petticoats, flat crowned broad-rimmed hats, etc.

4th. Set off after breakfast to see a few streets with comical names to them – *Cloth* fair, *Petticoat* Lane, *Curtain* Road, *Threadneedle* Street, and passed through the Court of Bartholomew Hospital, Charter House Sq., but could not get the least glimpse of the school and gardens, they were so enclosed by high walls. I next walked all round West Smithfield, quite full of cattle. I could fancy I heard their roarings and bleatings now; it is a very large square – it smelled woefully. I then went to Paternoster Row, near St Paul's – a narrow dark, dirty street – and called at Longman, Hurst, Rees, Brown, and Orme's, to ask on what scale my map was drawn, as they are the publishers of the Edition of The Picture of London which I have; and lo and behold! L.H.R.B. and O. Could not tell! Pretty fellows! – No thanks to them, however, I have since found it out by my own self, after *persevering* efforts and *intense* study. A pack of Lazy, Hoggish, Rascally, Blockish, ganderlike Oafs!!!

5th. The next day, I was so weary with the many miles walk I had had the day before, that I could not go out till after tea, when, going past Shoreditch Church, I went a long way up the Kingsland Road. I found I could not get into the country; truly, if once you get into London, you can get none out; my feet are not able to take me out, however.

6th. Sunday. I rested myself by going 3 times to Chapel.

7th. I rested at home, all morning, that I might be able to go to Greenwich Fair in the afternoon, it being Whit Monday. After I landed, I saw 4 shows and gave a gratuity for $3^1/_2$d; bought a penny worth of gingerbread and got cheated; laughed at myself, and walked on. (It is unnecessary to repeat here what is sufficiently detailed to Miss Dannett in the preceding copy).

10th. Packed up in the morning and *flitted* in the afternoon to my new lodgings, 4 miles Westward.

13th Sunday. Went to Rowland Hill's Chapel in the morning;[13] and to St Margaret's Church, close by the Abbey, in the afternoon.

15th. I went to the opening of a new Independent Chapel (Brunswick) in Mile end Road, in the morning and evening, which, as it is 5 miles off, caused me a walk of 20 miles. I was much gratified indeed, but so weary when I got home, that the next day I never stirred till after tea, and then went by Carlton Palace;[14] found as it were by accident St James' Palace, Burlington Arcade[15] and the Haymarket Theatre. Passing a Jew's shop window, I saw abundance of labels pinned to various articles, very humorously, e.g. 'Guineas taken with delight,' 'Sovereigns received with joy,' 'Double sovereigns with transport,' 'Half sovereigns taken with avidity,' 'Crowns hailed with pleasure,' 'Half crowns received gladly,' 'Shillings quite welcome,' 'Sixpences, as many as you please,' 'Pence will be looked on with smiles,' 'Halfpence will not be refused,' 'Farthings rather than nothing,' I have never been able to find this shop again, not noticing at the time what street it was in. I see many a droll sight as I go along the streets, and many a hearty laugh I enjoy by myself at home. I would prefer having some one with me to enjoy and join in the laugh, but that cannot be. Whilst I was at Mrs Benson's, I bought my coals and potatoes of Mr J. Thurtell, own coz [cousin] to the noted J. Thurtell.[16]

The London fellows provide for themselves one convenience, which is no where to be seen for the women, who many a time want it as ill – p - - - - - g places are provided in many a snug corner, and on all the Bridges, just like little sink stones; my nose many a time tells me they are stinking stones. "Commit No Nuisance" is brazenly posted on every wall and good building, even on the Churches, a shame that it should be so necessary.

We are not half sharp at Holland; why, one person here makes his bull to draw a cart; and dogs are quite commonly put to that use here. Catherine, do *you* keep a bull, and make Mary drive. Oh! As I pass the shop windows, and see many a tempting thing billeted – 'Only this,' and Only that –,' I find to my cost, they are sad money traps, and I Only have my money melted out of my pocket, I hardly know how.

Well might my feet become so swelled and painful, when the heat of the weather is considered (for the Summer was a peculiarly hot one), and the little previous exercise I had been in the habit of taking. I am astonished at my own strength, but – I have a kind Friend above, who permits me to have some enjoyments, in pity to me for those He thinks proper to bereave me of for a time.

18th. I was busied at home all morning, cleaning; after dinner, I set out, determined to find where Mrs Burne resided, or persevere daily until I did. I recollected, that on my way the day before, I had passed a Register Office, and as one thief is said to be the likeliest to catch another, so it occurred to me it would be in this case – and I was right, for the mistress of it directly informed me where to find Mrs Burne, viz, 24 Howland Street, Fitzroy Sq. I went home quite pleased, and spent the evening in writing to her [Miss Weeton kept no record of this letter].

On the 25th, I set out to try to find Mr Platt, as you had not procured me his address, which after some trouble, I managed.

Do you know, Miss Stopford had never made the least inquiry after me. I was above 3 weeks at Mrs Benson's after I had given myself the trouble of a 12 miles walk to go to see her; and during that time, she never wrote, came, nor sent. When I changed my lodgings, she of course could not know where to find me. I was completely thunderstruck when Mr Platt informed me that Mr Stopford had not made the slightest mention of my money to him – it's all of a piece! With little enough of money left, I have to wait 10 or 11 days till Mr Platt hears of a remittance. I was made to appear like some swindler, asking for money not belonging to me. Mr Platt told me Miss Stopford was now at his house. I neither offered to call, nor left my address, as it was not asked for, but said I would call again at the warehouse on the 5th of July. I next went forward to Mrs Benson's; she said J. Barlow had called 3 days after I left, and when he heard I had changed my lodgings, he walked off before Mrs Benson could tell him where I was gone to; for I had told her.

27th Sunday. After dinner, Mrs Hudson, with whom I lodge, proposed that her husband and son John, should take me through the Parks and Kensington Gardens; she is so lame, she goes little anywhere. I was desirous to see the Parks, with their Sunday company, and really it was amusing. It is just like what I have read Ranelagh was, only this is out of doors.[17] I saw one person there from Wigan – Mr Swift, who was an apprentice with D Cowley, but I never had any acquaintance with him, I did not speak to him now. I suppose we traversed this day not less than 15 miles; my feet, in consequence, suffer from these many and long walks. In other respects, I never was in better health.

The 30th. I went for the first time to the British Museum, and staid near 7 hours. My poor feet were sadly swelled, and yet I could have no mercy on them, nor on my dinnerless stomach. Got home at half-past-four, and never sat down the whole time. The distance, going and returning, 5 miles.

July 4th. I went in the morning to Surrey Chapel and heard Mr Elliot, of Devizes, preach. In the evening, I went to the Magdalen.[18] The place was full, but I was not particularly pleased; it was very formal and insipid. I shan't go again.

5th. This morning, I went to Mr Platt's Warehouse, No 38 Cateaton Street – apparently a very fatherly, tender hearted kind of man. I sat chatting with him about half-an-hour, while my money concern was going on. He said he was going with Miss Stopford into Lancashire in about 3 weeks, and asked me what time I should be returning. I said, in about 3 weeks or perhaps a month (we got nearer the point). He did not say that Miss Stopford ever mentioned me or wished to see me, and I was equally silent. I should be glad to know whether she has thus instructed from her parents. I shall certainly inquire into it when I return. I have not fixed exactly when I shall return; but present my respects to Mr and Mrs Ball, and tell them I shall be preparing in about 3 weeks, and then they may expect me by Anthony Billington some Saturday night from Liverpool (I'll come none with Miss S.).

I never heard of the King's going in state to prorogue Parliament until all was over; was it not mortifying? I have never seen any of their Royal faces yet; I have likewise missed two reviews in the Parks, and have not seen any.

Write to me as soon as you can. Perhaps you will hear more from me until you see my phiz.

Would you take an early opportunity of requesting Miss Hawarden to do me the favour to desire Miss Bullocks (Mr Henry's daughters) to call on Mary? Or, if they can get to see her at Chapel, to ask her if she has any doll but the one I dressed for her? If not, I will bring her a tall, jointed one. If her father or any one else has given her one, I will bring her something else. I would rather her father knew nothing of it until I return, and then I will manage the rest. Your early attention to this would oblige me greatly. Miss Bullocks had better not tell Mary *I* want to know, for the poor child cannot keep a secret; but inquire as a mere matter of curiosity of their own.

6 and 7th. Heavy and incessant rain prevented me from walking for these two days. It rendered me a service, as I had plenty of employment in writing letters and memorandums, and repairing stockings, &c., as well as setting my apartment in order; besides, I obtained a necessary rest and a recruit of strength for further long walks. I always considered a rainy day as a very kind friend with a homely face and a dark garb. Had the weather been altogether fair, I should probably have exerted myself in walking until I had brought on a fever, for the heat was intense.

10 (Saturday). Went immediately after breakfast to a Review in Hyde Park; saw the Duke of York[19] for the first and last time; likewise the Duke of Wellington and Lord Hill; I could not learn

the names of the rest of the officers. The heat was such as to
endanger the lives of both men and horses. The fat Duke of York
looked, as we say in Lancashire, 'as if he wur aw of a swat, and
welly meltit, and smoort,' with his high fur cap and wrappings
round the neck. The spectators had plenty of scampering to keep
out of the way, and yet get a good view. It was a high treat to
me; for, amongst so great a crowd, I passed unnoticed, although
wholly unaccompanied by any one I knew, as old as I am.
Sometimes a few of us chose to stand our ground, close to the
muzzles of the muskets as they were firing, but hanging down
our heads, and setting up our shoulders to protect them; the noise
was completely stunning, and the clouds of smoke blackened our
faces and half smothered us; when it was over, we were bold
enough to laugh.

12. Went over Westmr. Bridge to George St., to see Lord
Byron's funeral.[20] Waited amongst the crowd opposite his house
for more than 2 hours. At length, the procession set forward; I
followed it to the top of the Haymarket, and then returned home.
Afternoon, walked with Mrs Spearmen to Doctors' Commons.[21]
Mrs Spearman was a neighbour of Mrs Hudson's, where I was
going to consult a Proctor, wishing to be separated from her
husband, and I had a desire to see the place. The heat was at this
period so intense, I could go very little out.

July 14th. The heat was still excessive, and about noon, distant,
yet loud and aweful thundering began. I would not have ventured
out this day, but in the hope of rendering a service to Mrs
Jackson of Prescot, I had for several weeks attentively noticed
the advertisements in the newspapers, which I saw almost daily;
last evening I saw one in the Morning Herald, for a Housekeeper
and companion to an elderly gentleman. This I thought would
exactly suit Mrs J. I set out amidst increasing thunder, to Mr
Rennie's, 59 Charlotte St., Rathbone Place. I was shown upstairs to a small, but elegantly furnished drawing room, in which
was an elderly gentleman of very pleasing appearance. He told
me he had already engaged one; he said not less than near 30 had
applied the day before. I felt very sorry I had not seen the paper
sooner, and made an earlier application. Got home to tea. The
thunder now increased, and the lightening the *most aweful and
incessant I ever saw*! Long as I live, I shall recollect it; it continued
till 9 or 10 o'clock. The rain was very refreshing.

Number of Miles I walked from the morning of June 17 to the evening of July 16, 133$^1/_2$.

20. Remained at home all morning, cleaning; walked out after dinner and espying some of Gaskell's Eye Snuff[22] in a Druggist's shop window, went in and purchased a box, 1s. 1$^1/_2$d, purposely that I might have an opportunity of inquiring where Mr Irving[23] preached, of whom so much has been said, and such immense crowds of the Gentry, Nobility, and even Royalty. I obtained the requisite information, and lost no time in going to reconnoitre the place. I had wished to hear him from the first of my coming to London, but could not tell where in all the wide Metropolis he was to be heard of, since Mrs Benson, Mr Hudson's, my Picture of London, nor my Evangelical Magazine could give me no information. I examined, many a time and oft, the numerous Portraits of him in the Print shop windows, but they never told me where he preached, or where he lived; and I was too shame-faced and too poor to enter and purchase, by way of paying for the information. Now, hearing from the Druggist's shopman that he preached at the Caledonian Church, Cross St., Hatton garden, and that tickets were requisite, I proceeded direct, and passing the Church, went to an open door of a Milk house, where I saw a woman cleaning a cream mug. She very readily told me how I was to manage to procure a ticket; I was to write a letter, stating my request, and giving my name and address. I returned down Fetter lane home.

24. Mr Hudson, with whom I had lodged ever since I left Mrs Benson's, had been a master carrier, but was reduced in the world, and now worked as a journeyman. By his first wife, he had 4 children living; the 2 eldest were boys of 14 and 16, remarkably fine looking youths, who worked at their father's business; the two younger were girls, Ann and Keziah, of 10 and 8 years. The youngest was a most diseased child, yet fat and rosy; one eye had run quite away, and the other seemed to be wasting fast, and gave her great pain; one elbow, too, was diseased, and the arm gradually wasting; added to this, her temper was very bad, and all together, she gave her father great uneasiness. To add to the calamities of this afflicted child, she had now been near a fortnight ill of the small pox, and was completely loathsome. Poor, poor Keziah! How thou didst suffer; yet we thought she appeared very likely to recover; and it she did, she would be one

326

of the most deplorable objects ever seen; but her constitution seemed naturally strong.

Mr Hudson's second wife was sister to his first, and consequently, aunt to her first step children. I felt greatly concerned when I heard of this, but made no observations to them about it. Mr Hudson was an uncommonly fine-looking man in every respect, his figure tall, athletic, and portly; his countenance, voice, and manner, most benignant and impressive. He laboured hard for his family, working over hours on his own account at home when his other work was done. I felt high respect for him, and had become quite attached to the family; and in all appearance, so had they to me. The present Mrs Hudson was a little weakly woman, with one leg shorter than the other. Mr Hudson had married her for the sake of his children. I spent many an agreeable hour with her, for she never left the house, and no acquaintance called but Mrs Spearman.

July 25th. Went to the Caledonian Ch., Cross St., Hatton Garden, in the morning, to hear Mr Irving. My letter box the previous Wednesday, had not been noticed; but this, I was informed by the mistress of the milk-house, was scarcely to be expected, as applications were so exceedingly numerous, that the Elders, who could only give as many tickets a there would be seats in the Church, were obliged, in justice, to send them in rotation according to the earliness of the application, and numbers had to wait 2 or 3 Sabbaths. I however could not wait, for, ere another Sabbath had passed, I expected to be far away at Liverpool. I ventured without a ticket. When I arrived at the door, the carriages of gentry and nobility continued in a line the whole of Cross St. and Kirby St., and a crowd at the door of the elegantly dressed people. I had taken care as regarded my own dress this day for, however contrary to Scripture, there is scarcely any obtaining decent treatment in plain cloathing. I often attribute the civilities I receive, to my dress. On speaking to one of the Elders at the door, who was receiving tickets, to ask if I might be allowed to enter without one, he with very great civility replied, that it was against their rules, but however, we will say nothing of it – giving me a nod to pass on. I got very agreeably situated in the gallery.

Mr Irving's appearance struck me as peculiar; he appeared to me in physiognomy, dress, and manner, like the wild genius of the mountains. I was exceedingly impressed; his eccentric gestures frequently excited the smile of the congregation; yet it was the smile of approbation, for his manner and language appeared quite natural, and peculiarly his own. I should much like to know the opinions of others respecting this preacher, for I have not yet heard a single one.

July 26th. On setting out this afternoon, I inquired at Charing Cross respecting the rout of their Coaches, for the fares everywhere were the same. As these did not travel the way I wanted to go, I went into Piccadilly, and from the Spread Eagle Office, corner of Regent St., a coach was driven through Oxford to Liverpool. I particularly wished to see Oxford, so resolved on going by this coach. I returned down to Charing Cross, along the Strand, Cheapside, to the end of Aldgate, as before stated, and on arriving home, found poor Keziah had died whilst I was out! I was thunderstruck, for I had all along thought she would eventually recover – It was a providential release, for, had she recovered, she would have been a heap of disease. Poor, suffering child, thou knewest no comfort in life.

27th. Ann Hudson was now taken ill of the small pox, although she had been vaccinated a few years ago; she had them very mildly during my stay.

28 July. Took a place outside the Coach to Liverpool, to go on the following morning at half-past 5 o'clock. In the evening I packed up.

Number of miles I walked since July 16th. 104 miles.

The whole distance, then, will be as follows for the 11 weeks which I resided in London.

From May 17th to June 16th. 213$^3/_4$ miles.

From June 17th to July 16th. 221 miles, which added, will be 538$^3/_4$ miles.

29 July. Set off outside the Coach from the Spread Eagle Office, Piccadilly, at quarter before 6 o'clock. Very agreeably to me, the passengers throughout this day were few and well behaved, the morning as lovely as it could be, and the whole day's ride most delightful. Windsor Castle was a grand object, adorned as it was with the early morning's sun. Oxford was a grander object than I had expected; but previously to this, Henley-upon-Thames delighted me most; it appeared to be in a lovely, romantic country. I was quite gratified with the sight of Oxford, although upon a Coach and never descending; yet I made good use of my eyes the short time we stopped. I had provided basket store sufficient in buns and biscuits, and for a drink, a bottle of cold tea; for I had learned to be wiser now than to touch any strong drink during my journey. My life was in imminent danger on my journey to London on account of the drowsiness occasioned by the brandy and water I took. It was but little, at the most a half pint bottle, more than half filled with water, but not in general being accustomed to any strong liquid, it took deeper effect, and the more so as I was exposed to the air so many hours. Even as it was, I should not have taken any with me, while ignorant of injurious effects, had not Mr T. Jackson in a manner forced it upon me, from the kindest of motives, thinking it quite necessary for me. My own experience teaches me quite the contrary; and I believe, that if there were no strong drink in the world, and little other than vegetable diet, there would be less disease, and greater length of life and greater rectitude of conduct; for stimulating food and inflaming liquors cause most of the vices and wretchedness of society.

So little have I heard of what is going on in the world for the great part of my life, or even in England, that I was quite astonished when we arrived at Leamington, never having heard any thing of the place but its name; it appeared to be a very beautifully built and fashionable watering place. It was about 6 o'clock in the evening when we got there. The coach stopped near half an hour, during which time I got a good warming at the kitchen fire; for, hot as the weather still was for walking, I found it rather cold riding, towards evening. I think we had passed Warwick just before; having no maps or any other means of reference, I cannot just now recollect on which side of Leamington Warwick was situated. The sun was setting low as we passed through, and its fine rays upon the Cathedral and Castle added much to the grandeur of their appearance. I cannot here forbear breaking out into exclamations of rapture, awe, gratitude and praise to the God of beauty and of wonder!

Within thy circling pow'r I stand
On ev'ry side I find thy hand;
Awake, asleep, at home, abroad,
I am surrounded still with God.

Amazing knowledge, vast and great
What large extent, what lofty height!
My soul, with all the pow'rs I boast
Is in the boundless prospect lost.

When I think of the beauties my Heavenly Friend has this Summer permitted me to witness, my souls swells with feelings indescribable, and is ready to burst the bands of the body, and fly upwards instantly to worship at his throne.

When we got to Birmingham, it was just dark, and I could see little else than a vast number of fires and lighted windows. At the Inn, we changed coaches, and took up 6 Irishmen of the lowest description, which wholly destroyed the comfort of the remaining part of the way, by their selfish rudeness. One of them had usurped my seat. I was quietly submitting to it, rather than contend with him, but the guard took up my cause, and a long scuffle ensued, in which I thought, between them, would have overturned the coach. I then begged the guard to say no more, and I rode the rest of the night on a very dangerous outside seat behind, backwards.[24] We were four upon it, and it was too short by much for the number; but every seat was equally crowded. It was very necessary to keep my eyes open for the least drowsiness, and I should have dropped headlong. The man on my left kept a constant motion with his head upon my shoulder, up and down, the night through, being heavy to sleep, the brim of his hat endangering my eyes. The guard and he quarrelled again, but neither good words nor bad had any effect. I expressed my obligations to the guard, and begged him to trouble himself no more with the man, and so made peace, for the Irishmen seemed determined to have the last word and the last blow, had they quarrelled for a week. The iron rail bruised me sadly, I was so jammed against it. About 6 in the morning, one of the Irishmen in front left the coach; when I saw that, down I dropped, and up into his seat like a cat, and was much more comfortable, although I had one on my left as filthy as possible, and his head likewise jolting me perpetually. It was intolerable! I very quietly requested he would let his head nod on the other (the out-) side. I thought the man would have beaten me; the coachman then interfered, and they had a long quarrel, and at last a scuffle, as the driver was determined to hurl him off the coach unless he behaved better. I was really frightened, and could not but weep; the women in

Ireland must have a dreadful time with such fellows. A young woman on my right, the only female companion I had had, said she had passed a dreadful night, an Irish pig driver on each side of her, and another in front, snoring and resting their heads against her, to prevent themselves falling.

I extracted sweets from bitters, and enjoyed the ride and the prospects, arriving in Liverpool at 11 o'clock, the morning of the 30th July. (Friday).

I am so far from indulging in that general prejudice which the majority of the English have against the Irish, that I ever feel a great deal of pity for them, as an oppressed and neglected people; and the viciousness and violence of their tempers and conduct is a great deal owing to want of education, and the residence and example of their land-owners. If it were possible to hold the seat of Government 4 months in the year in some central part of Ireland, it would effect a wonderful change in that country for the better, and be no injury to our own.[25]

On leaving the coach at the Blue Bell, in London road, I proceeded directly to Mrs Roxburgh's, 4 Russel St. Her lodgings were all let. She recommended me to a Mrs Cash, 4 Bridport St., where, as soon as I had dined, I went to bed at two o'clock in the afternoon, and slept soundly till 8 the following morning, Saturday, July 31st.

NOTES:

1. The 1803 edition was printed by Lewis and Co. for John Feltham. The 1823 (23rd edition) was printed in London for Longman, Rees, Orme, and Brown, at Paternoster Row, who continued to publish *The Picture of London* until the mid-1830s. Various editions are available via a 'print on demand' service.
2. A noted baker at Up Holland.
3. '. . . everywhere and in all things I am instructed both to be full and to be hungry, both to abound and to suffer need.' (Philippians 4:12).
4. The Up Holland apothecary.
5. The 23rd edition.
6. John Loudon McAdam (not Macadam), (1756-1836), shares with Thomas Telford the distinction of having made possible efficient coach routes.
7. The Teetotum was a kind of top, hexagon or octagon shape, with all sides numbered.
8. The old Post Office was situated in Lombard Street.
9. Fleet Market, which stood in the middle of the street, was opened for the sale of meat, fish, and vegetables in 1737. In 1829 Farringdon Market was

built to house this offence to sight and smell, but the project long proved unremunerative.

10. George Canning (1770-1827), Tory statesman. In horror of the French revolution Canning attached himself, in 1793, to liberal Tory, William Pitt ('The Younger'). Lord Brougham (1770-1868), inventor of the Brougham carriage. came to prominence as a result of defending Princess Caroline, later Queen Caroline, against George IV, who wanted to divorce her.

11. The twopenny post operated only within the London area, country postage continued to be based upon mileage until 1835.

12. 'May 25, 1824, Lieut. Harris, R.N., ascended from the Eagle Tavern, City Road, with Miss Stocks; the former killed by the too rapid descent of the balloon.' Timb's *Curiosities of London*, 1855. Harris had apparently allowed too much gas to escape through the valve. His female companion was only slightly injured.

13. The Surrey Chapel, in Blackfriars Road, was an ugly, octagonal building, of the Calvinist Methodist denomination, built by the famous preacher, Rowland Hill, in 1783. It was closed in 1881.

14. Carlton Palace, the town residence of His Gracious Majesty, George IV.

15. Burlington Arcade was a great novelty, built in 1819.

16. J. Thurtell was the principal in a notorious murder case. He was tried and executed for the murder of Wm Weare in the early part of 1824. His accomplice, John Hunt, was sentenced to be transported.

17. *The Picture of London* refers to a prohibition concerning Kensington Gardens: 'With regard to Kensington Gardens, no servant in livery, nor women with pattens, nor persons carrying bundles, are admitted into the gardens. Dogs are also excluded.'

18. Magdalen Hospital, St George's Fields, was opened in 1758, 'for the relief and reformation of wretched young women . . . The hours of divine service are a quarter after eleven in the forenoon, and a quarter after six in the evening; and on account of the fascinating pathos of the singing, which is performed by the females (screened by a curtain from the general eye), no place of worship in the metropolis is more worthy the attendance of a stranger.' *The Picture of London.*

19. Prince Frederick (1765-1827), Duke of York, was the second son of George III.

20. Lord Byron died 19th April, 1824, at Missolonghi, Greece. His body was brought back to London, where for seven days the putrefying remains lay in state in the front parlour of Sir Ed. Knatchbull's house in Great George Street.

21. Doctors' Commons, was the ancient seat of Doctors of Law.

22. Miss Weeton had perfectly good eyesight in daylight, but found writing by candlelight very trying to her eyes.

23. Edward Irving (1792-1834), was the son of an Annan tanner. He became a Scottish minister and founder or the Catholic Apostolic Church. Came to London in 1822, as Minister at Hatton Garden Chapel, where his preaching soon made him famous. In 1833 he was expelled from the ministry of the Church of Scotland for his heretical views. The title of 'Holy Catholic Apostolic Church' was assumed by his followers.

24. Miss Weeton's description of: 'a very dangerous outside seat,' was because the only thing to stop a person falling from the coach was a low iron support rail.

25. At this time, Irish immigrants and cattle drovers were a vexation, particularly in Lancashire.

TEN

Hope awakened

Prescot, near St Helens

August 1824 – May 1825

MISS WEETON HAD long been dissatisfied with her isolated situation at Ball's Farmhouse, Up Holland. More than ever, she was determined to leave at the earliest opportunity to an area of 'busyness.' Added incentive was the desire to be nearer to her daughter, Mary, residing at Parr Hall Boarding School for Girls, St Helens. As a lone female, walking 7 miles between Up Holland and Parr Hall, Miss Weeton was beginning to feel increasingly vulnerable in the sparsely-populated countryside. She wrote: 'The loneliness of the road was my greatest fear, and no stated conveyance to go by; and to hire one expressly was too expensive, so that I was forced to walk . . .' Another consideration was that in her opinion, Rev John Holgate, minister of Salem Congregational Chapel, Far Moor, had treated her in an 'unchristianlike' way, necessitating her having to walk four miles to worship at Wigan.

Prescot, near St Helens, was to be Miss Weeton's preferred location for a new home. This had the advantage of friends already living there, and therefore contacts to advise on the possibility of obtaining lodgings on favourable terms. Margaret Braithwaite, a friend since childhood, and daughter of the late Rev John Braithwaite of Up Holland, had married a Thomas Tellaw Jackson. Mr Jackson was Master of the Prescot Assembly Rooms; he also owned another house nearby, occupied by Mary Braithwaite, another sister to Margaret.

On the morning of 3 August 1824, Miss Weeton set off to walk the 11 miles to Prescot from Up Holland, to call on Mrs

Jackson, with a view to discussing suitable accommodation in Prescot. A fortnight later an entry in her journal explained her planned removal from Up Holland:

[Journal, August 1824]:

16. I had little to do now but prepare for removing to Prescot, by informing my acquaintances, and taking leave of them. Mrs Ball was in Liverpool; I had seen and left her there, and now intended informing her of my plan as soon as she came home; for I had not the heart to do it when I met her in Liverpool. I knew she would be hurt, and Mr Ball too. In a few days she returned, and with some difficulty to my own feelings, I told her of my intentions. She was so aggrieved that I almost repented of having thought of leaving them; yet it was for my own comfort. I value the two old people greatly, for they are very deserving of esteem.

27th. Walked to Wigan to take leave of the Hawarden's – of the poor old Doctor for ever! unless we are permitted to meet and know one another in a future state – and of Mrs Marsden.

28th. Walked to Parr Hall to see Mary, my dear, dear, child Mary, and spent some hours with her most delightfully, walking in the garden together a long time. Whether I must ever see her again, is doubtful, for Mr Grundy told me that Mr Stock had again enjoined him not to let me see her without his previous permission. I fear I shall be forced back again to my husband's home, or that her mother should be there. I walked back with great ease, and little or no fatigue, and perfectly safe. 14 miles.

Sept 1st. Saw my furniture loaded in the morning, and then, taking an affectionate leave of Mr Ball's family, walked to Prescot, 10 miles. The heat of the weather still continued intense; I several times sat down by the wayside to cool and rest. In the course of a few days after my arrival at Prescot, I got very snugly fixed, and Mrs T. Jackson's kindness renders my abode here very agreeable; for I often call.

9 September 1824 (Prescot). *To Miss Stock*, Parr Hall:

On opening the parcel, you will find I have recollected your requests. As I found, when I saw you, that although you might know how many inches or feet were in a yard, you had not a distinct idea of the real length of an inch, foot, or yard, I have sent you a small ivory case with a ribbon marked for a yard, with 36 inches. I bought it in London, and ask a shilling for such a one. I expect you will keep it very neat, and not spoil it by childishly amusing yourself with repeated unrolling and rolling it. I have inclosed 4 different kinds of Gimp,[1] of 4 and 2 yds length, as you may perceive when you measure it, (my mother once had Gowns trimmed with it – perhaps 60 years ago); a little narrow green ribbon, which is of little value; it may serve you to draw your doll's work-bags. Of these I have still many yards left, and I shall think them well used, if they afford you, my love, any gratification. The green ribbon is part of a large box-full my mother (your grand-mother Weeton) once had; they were taken in a prize which my father captured during the American war, between the years 1775 and 1782. The vessel was Spanish. The surgeon in my father's ship had the box of ribbons, amongst other things, to his share, and made a present of them to my mother.

Print for patchwork is sold by weight, in small bits such as I have sent you. I purchased it in Prescot market, 4th inst. The man asked 2s. 8d. p. pound. I thought it would be sufficient for you for the present. The piece of patchwork is out of a Quilt I made above 20 years ago; it may serve as a pattern. The Hexagon in the middle was a shred of our best hangings; they were Chintz, from the East Indies, which my father brought home with him from one of his voyages. He was never in the East Indies himself, but probably purchased the Chintz in some foreign market. My mother bequeathed the bed to my brother, and I suppose it is now worn out. I suppose your patchwork is only for the amusement of leisure hours, and that you will manage it entirely yourself; your ribbon measure may be useful to help you to cut your paper pattern exactly.

I have no white muslin, but may perhaps buy you some in the Spring. The old cambric muslin I know will be useful to you to cut into patterns for sleeves, bodies, caps, tippets,[2] &c., preparatory to cutting out real ones. It is so old, you need not be afraid of wasting it. I have thus, I think, provided you with materials for amusing leisure hours for a few months, in rainy or cold weather; for I particularly wish you never in fine weather to stay in doors, or spend your play hours in, or out, in sedentary amusements. Your health, strength, and spirits, absolutely require that you should have enough of sitting still during your unavoidable studies.

I hope you learn the Theory of Music, alone with the Practice; and that you understand the composition of many of the pieces you have learned to play; at least, in a great measure. I have understood that any modern teachers begin with uniting theory with practice, in teaching little children, so I hope you will be as clever as others; don't be afraid to ask your teachers frequent questions respecting the meaning of any thing in your lessons you do not understand.

You told me you did not much practice speaking French; do not let diffidence prevent you, for if you do not learn to speak it now, you never will speak it well, and all your time and your father's money will be quite thrown away, as is the case with a young lady I know, who has been learning the language 7 or 8 years, who would be as unfit to travel in France as any person who never attempted to learn.

[Journal, September 1824]

Sept 15. Had an exceedingly pleasant walk to Liverpool and back. 16 miles. The practice I have had in London this summer, makes me think little of such a walk.

Sept 29 (Wednesday). The death of Dr Hawarden [17 September 1824], made me feel anxious to see his widow and daughter, and I set off this evening by the coach, to see them. I found them, as I expected, grieved but resigned. I staid all night, and walked over to Holland the next day.

Oct 20th. Wrote a letter to Mary, and took it myself, along with a little print for patchwork, to the cottage at Parr Hall gate; had I been an hour earlier, I should have seen Mary, walking amongst the rest of the ladies – so the old woman at the cottage told me. I can take care to go sometimes at this hour on a Thursday, when Spring returns, if not before; but now, the rain, and storms of wind are almost incessant. I will be tolerably quiet for the Winter.

20 October 1824 (Prescot). *To Miss Stock*, Parr Hall:

You would feel a little surprised perhaps, on receiving a pound of raisins with so short a note enclosed. I will tell you how it was. My old and very great friend, Dr Hawarden, died Sept. 17; when I heard of the event, I determined to go by way of Holland; and to procure some cake or fruit for you at Wigan, and leave it by the coach. When I changed my plan, it was at too late a time to allow me to write you a longer letter. The raisins were not the best, but I really thought they were the wholesomest; for the best raisins have so thick a skin as to be almost as indigestible as leather; it should never be swallowed, nor indeed should the skins of any fruit. Do not think you are guilty of any extravagance in not eating the skins of fruit; it is a sin to eat them, because they injure the stomach; and eventually destroy the health.

I walked from Holland on the Saturday morning, and got home, not at all tired, about 11 o'clock; and it is 10 miles. I am very snugly fixed here for the present. I intend to take a small house if I can obtain furniture; a year ago nearly, I did petition for some, but was not successful. I will try again; I should much wish to have a home of my own.

Last week I took a walk to Liverpool, which is 8 miles. I dined at Mr Price's, and called to see Miss Dalrymple, who continues to recover; she was seized near 3 years ago with a spinal complaint, which is of tedious cure; 2 issues in her back, and frequent sea-bathing are her best remedies. She is such a pious, religious woman, that I respect her highly. She invited me to stay all night, but I declined it, for I was so little fatigued, that I could walk back again very well; and if not, I could ride by a coach for 1s. or 1s. 6d.; however, I managed to walk.

The weather is now becoming very stormy and winterly, and I shall be obliged to be much in doors; but I am seldom at a loss for amusement; my Flageolet, and Harmonicon,[3] my books and my needle, are an ever-varying source of pleasure; and thinking of you, my dear, dear little girl, and praying for you and your father, occupies many a portion of each day.

I was much pleased with your very correct sentiments on several subjects, the last time I conversed with you, as regards your companions and your daring to set your face against actions that were certainly wrong. When you prove another, so it in an affectionate manner, not angrily, and then you will deserve to be treated yourself.

Good bye, my dear girl.

[Journal, November 1824]

From the above date (October 20th) up to the present time, Thursday November 18, I have scarcely gone out, owing to the heavy rains, and almost perpetual hurricanes. My time has passed most agreeably in sewing, music, copying music, reading, and bringing up the arrears of this journal.

About a fortnight ago, I received a Letter from my cousin Latham of Holland, with a Bolton newspaper, in which Mr Guest of Leigh has exposed my brother's inconsistency of conduct and bitterness of spirit, at great length; it corroborates what I have said of him, for I have suffered greatly from him; he has done me irremediable mischief by his calumnies.[4]

14 December 1824 (Prescot). *To Miss Stock*, Parr Hall, St Helens:

The basket, my dear Mary, which accompanies this, is stored with the Doll's Dinner Service I mentioned to you when I wrote about 3 weeks ago – 2 small Dutch dolls, that may serve as little daughters to your larger one; they wont require much dressing, for they are born, as you may see, with stockings, shoes, and gloves on, and their hair ready curled; a frock, and one petticoat, are quite enough to wear at once; they need no further underclothing. You will have some old cloaths of your own which you may cut up for the use of all your dolls; perhaps a coloured tabinet frock, and a few other things that are too little for you. If you have not sufficient, I am sure your Father will let you buy, at Wigan, any thing you want. One of the little ladies cost 10d. and the other 6d.

A Cocoa Nut, and a hundred Walnuts (that is, 120, or 6 score to the hundred) I have likewise inclosed; offer your father a part, my love; I know he is fond of them; but do not on my account eat more yourself than 6 or 8 in a day of the Walnuts; a larger number would make you ill, and take away your appetite. The Cocoa Nut was 6d., the Walnuts 1s. the hundred. I tell you the prices of such things, and to give you as much knowledge as I am able of the prices of many of the common articles of sale; for you will never be fit in daily use. Do not open the basket until you get home.

I have written this letter by candle light, which is rather distressing to me, for I cannot do with less; yet I can see almost anything with bright day-light; but I think you will read it easily.

Your holidays are very near; I hope they will be spent very agreeably.

Christmas-day, Dec. 25th is my birthday; don't forget me on that day.

3 February 1825 (Prescot). *To Miss Hawarden*, Wigan:

I have been expecting to hear from you, my dear Miss Hawarden, for this fortnight past, as Mrs Bent said she would inquire if Mary was returning again to Parr Hall, and inform you that you might let me know. May I ask the favour of you to write immediately, to inform me where she is?

I have been passing my time in almost total solitude since I was with you; but it was much the same at Holland – and much the same at Wigan, and – all my life time; still, I can never be so used as to be reconciled to it. So it is with all females of small incomes who have no families and few or no relations; if forced to live in lodgings, they are shut out from domestic comforts and a social fireside – the very kind of life that the most valuable part of either sex would prefer. A single woman so situated, is a poor lost creature, and those who ought to be the protectors of such, are often the insulters! the ruiners! and the persecutors! Oh, what a heavy judgement will those fathers, those brothers, and those husbands have to undergo, who are the cause of so much female suffering.

I have certainly passed this Winter more comfortably and chearfully than the 3 preceding ones, for my present *cage* is light, which the other was not.

I have not been in Liverpool since I was with you in Wigan, until Monday last, when I left home a little before 9 and had a very agreeable walk, the road was so dry. On my way, hearing a gig following me where there was no footpath, and the middle of the road overspread with logs of wood, I turned round to see on which side the gig was overtaking me, that I might give way. I was on the right side, and I found the gig was coming on the same side. Immediately I crossed through the mud to the left side, and had scarcely done so, when the gig was driven across likewise, and I was in danger of being run over. I looked at the driver, and was surprised to find the gentleman who had so little politeness to an unprotected and accommodating woman, was Mr Kearsley of Wigan, who was driving, and Thomas Sutton with him. The sight of Thomas was like a dagger through me; he is a perjured wretch, and for the present, he is suffered to triumph in his perjury. The natural buoyancy of my temper enabled me to soon surmount the effects of this little mean insult, and, finding a decent young woman on the road, we continued the remainder of the way together, for mutual protection. How very common it is for men to insult unprotected woman, for whom there should be a universal feeling of pity; their very helplessness should be their safe-guard, and it should be a common principle of honour and feeling in all men, ever to afford protection to, and at the least, to avoid insulting an unprotected woman.

I walked half way back again, and then got into the caravan[5] just before dusk, for I dared not walk alone by moonlight; one of the male passengers observed that all four on our side (for we were 7 in all) were none of us very heavy. I replied, that whenever I travelled, I always found it very convenient to myself and my companions, to be thin; for I required little more than sky room, and of that there was always plenty. When about a mile from Prescot, the same man said, he thought we should get home by moonlight. 'We surely shall,' said I dryly, 'or else we must ride all night,' for the moon was then shining finely, and likely to do so till 5 o'clock in the morning – at which speed, had we not arrived by moonlight, we must have been 11 hours in going a mile, as it was then 6 o'clock in the evening. I set the whole company a-laughing; for I durst have wagered all England, to travel in a one horse carriage at that rate, and have been the winner.

Give my kind respects to your mother.

8 March 1825 (Prescot). *To Miss Stock*, Parr Hall, St Helens:

It is near 3 months, my dear, dear Mary, since I last wrote to you. Have you been thinking, my love, that I had quite forgotten you? If you have thoughts so, I do not wonder; yet indeed, my dear child, I never do forget you. I do not certainly know where you are, and that uncertainty has prevented my writing before now; but in the supposition that you are at Parr Hall, I last make the attempt. Do you often think of me? Do you often talk of me? I hope you do, for you have not a better, or a more sincere friend in the world. I cannot give you money, nor that which money has bought; but, Mary, I can bestow that which millions of pounds can never purchase – mother's love.

I dare say that it will give you pleasure to know that I am well. I am blessed indeed with excellent health; and have been for 3 years, growing stronger as I grow older; but that can only be for a time. I expect the usual approaches of infirmity which age brings, but I am at present as lively, chearful, and healthy, as I was at 25 years old; and yet I am 48 – very near 50, Mary, is it not? Your father is 49; he is just 11 months older than I am; your father's birth-day is on the 24th of January, and so is my brother's, your uncle Weeton of Leigh; which is rather remarkable, only he his 5 years younger, I suppose you never see him – he is no friend of yours.

I have been very comfortable at Prescot since I came to live in it; the people I live with, treat me kindly and respectfully, and wait upon me in almost every thing I want; but I always, wherever I am, take care to give as little trouble as possible.

11 March 1825 (Prescot). *To Miss Hawarden*, Wigan:

Your information, my dear Miss Hawarden, that Mr Stock had purchased an estate in West Derby, was quite new to me; neither have I been able to hear any thing further;[6] whether he is going to live at it, who lived there last, what he has given for it, or the exact situation. I should like to know some additional particulars.

I am writing to you upon paper which I bought in London at 5d. per Quire, so don't be saucy and call it shabby. I shall inclose yours in one to Miss Braithwaite on a sister-sheet; and sure it was bought in Lunnon [London] too, for did I not buy it there my own self; and if I could but have known how long I should live, I would have bought as much as would have lasted my life; and, alack a day, I did not buy one Quire, and sorrow to me, I may happen outlive it, and then what will I do.

Have the Literati of Wigan commenced a Newspaper yet? I apprehend they have not, as I have seen no announcement. Perhaps if they knew – the learned ones of Wigan – that so able a pen as mine might be engaged in their service, they would proceed; tell 'em, will you?

Why did you not remind me, when I was at Wigan at Christmas, to mend or make you some pens? I am sure I was as willing, as able; don't neglect the next feathery opportunity. Bring some Quills with you, or old Pens to renovate,[7] as soon as Lent is over, and stay a while with me at Prescot, and we can see Liverpool some day; for next month, I have no doubt but we shall have some fine weather.

Give my kind respects to your Mother.

11 March 1825 (Prescot). *To Miss Braithwaite*, Up Holland:

How are you all going on in Holland? as like vegetables as ever? or do you approximate to locomotive steam engines?[8] are you torpid in the Winter at your *foreign* country? Or do you burrow in holes in some seasons; or are you like piss-i'th-mires,[9] minding nobody's business but your own, and always swarming on your own hillock? I am fond of natural history, and should be glad to know, having heard little of your *distant* land lately, or of what kind of creatures grow there.

Give my respects to Mary, and tell her I am looking forward to the period when the light of her countenance will shine upon Prescot, as I am led to expect it will be next month.

Remember me to Mrs Ducker and Miss Dannett; and say to Mrs Dannett, that I have never called upon Mrs Green about the lodgings, as the situation is not open enough. I think I shall not move until I can find apartments in Fall Lane or the Market-place, at a rent not exceeding what I give here. The worst of it here, is, my bed it too small for more than one person, so that I cannot offer half a bed to a friend for a night or two, neither could I cook in the day, so that I must look out for better accommodation before very long.

[Journal, March 1825]

Sunday, March 20 I had, from the first of my coming to Prescot, intended that as soon as the Winter was over, and the weather fine enough, I would make a practice of going to St Helen's on a Sunday, or any other day that was likely for Mary to be met with: this day, therefore, I set out immediately after dinner, and walked through St Helen's, and about a mile beyond I saw Mr Grundy's young ladies approaching over the bridge, a little on this side of Parr Hall; and for fear they should see me and perhaps take Mary back again into the house, and so prevent my meeting with her, I slipped into a cottage close by, until they all arrived opposite to it. I then issued forth and joined my little darling, who, with two others, was walking close after two of the teachers. I fell into the rank and walked to St Helen's. Miss Hammond seemed agitated, but what cared I? She appeared inclined to be insolent when I apologized for coming in such a manner; but I avoided altercation – what an unfeeling world this is! None but married women seem to have tenderness.

I chatted to my dear girl as well as I could, but our peculiar situation threw a great deal of restraint upon us. Mr Grundy and Miss Jackson were no where to be seen – courting perhaps. I left Mary near Tontine Street, thinking it was as prudent for the present not to go to Chapel with her. I can meet her there, perhaps, some day if Mr Grumblety does not make a fuss and write to Mr Stock about it – which I hope he will be simple enough to do, for I wish Mary to be taken away from the school; so that I shall effect the latter purpose by going on Sundays, if I miss the other; and either is better than as it has been. Poor Mary may be kept up for a while, but that cannot last for ever.

22ⁿᵈ. Set off to Liverpool on foot at half-past-8 o'clock and prevailed with Mrs Price to accompany me from Seymour St. to Mr Perkins, 14 Roscoe Lane, brother-in-law to Mr Stock, to request his mediation, and that of Mrs Perkins to prevail with Mr Stock to let me have some more liberty in seeing Mary, and to increase my income. Mrs Perkins was not at home. Mr Perkins was so kind and friendly, that I was quite rejoiced and grateful; he promised me to make the attempt.[10] I returned home, feeling as if God had prospered my going out this day, as well as on Sunday.

25 March 1825 (Prescot). *To Mr Stock*, Standish, near Wigan:
Mr Stock

Let me request your considerate and calm attention to what in this letter I am about to urge. A strong sense of duty alone is my motive, and a friendship for you as sincere as ever was in the bosom of any human being, notwithstanding all the afflictions you have caused me.

It would be very consoling, could I be permitted to use a term warmer than that of friendship; let me at least ask for yours in return; be my friend, and be no longer my enemy; and in the present instance, let me beg that a candid and benevolent construction may be put upon what I say, and upon my intentions; and indeed, upon all occasions, for I never had any sinister motives, I never was selfish, I never was malicious. Your benefit, and that of your family, was my sole study from the hour I married you, of which I give you daily proofs.

Allow me those comforts you can so well afford me. If you gave me 200£ a year, it will only be what you ought to do, when your own circumstances are considered; and you would never miss it. It would be far from half your income; yet you swore to endow me with *all your* worldly goods, which surely means one half of every thing. I swore the same oath, and *gave you all*; and never, whilst I lived with you, asked for any thing in return but your affection and tenderness, friendship and protection, your confidence, and as much money from week to week as would merely keep the family in comfort. Was I unreasonable? Oh no, and if you had not been made the dupe of mischief makers, we might still be as happy a couple as most in our own rank. Those evil counsellors, who were constantly endeavouring to poison your mind against me, were your enemies; under the insidious cloak of friendship, they were only studying to obtain money from you, or some advancement by your means, unfeelingly working your misery as well as mine. I saw plainly into their views; then, what was the intense anguish of my mind, when I saw you fall into their snares, entrapped by their fine, fawning, flowery speeches.

Be assured that my enemies are yours; and they are only mine, hoping to get something out of you; for were you poor, and I rich tomorrow, they would the same day turn from you, and endeavour to keep up your prejudices against me, by ridiculing and speaking contemptuously of me – they are but bloodsuckers! If they were Christians, they would strive daily to make peace between us. But let your own sense of a Christian husband's conduct, induce you to treat me more liberally.

I only wish for what you can spare, without depriving yourself of a single comfort – a better income, and the same liberty of seeing my child that you have. My income is much too small, considering your circumstances; you would raise yourself much in the estimation of all respectable people if you would not act so penuriously towards me. I can but just procure myself the common comforts of life, but my narrow income shuts me out of either genteel lodgings or society. There are many families of great respectability, who have known me from a child, and with whom I could now be on terms of intimacy, could I afford it.

It is certainly a hardship that I must be obliged to live in other people's houses, or in a little mean house by myself. A comfortable, small house, respectably furnished, and one servant, with the means of dressing respectably, and of enjoying intelligent society at a moderate expence, is not an unreasonable desire. I ask no more than 200£ a year *for life only*, and your means are so ample that you would not even feel the poorer for it. And reflect how meek and patient I have been ever since I left you, although you have made me suffer daily; yet my conduct in every respect has been most exemplary

I have heard a report that you have settled 600£ a year upon Jane. If this be true, let me intreat that you will alter it. Is not Jane equally a child with Mary? And why make a difference. Had you left Mary only 200£ a year, I would not have said a word.

You and I are verging upon 50; when Mary is grown up, we may be both dead, and if Mary has not Jane for an affectionate sister, she will be but a lost creature, with all her money; for, as to my brother's family, his unnatural conduct in never calling to see her, is proof enough what she has to expect in that quarter. I earnestly hope that you will consider this, and be not offended with me in touching on a subject that I have long had at heart.

Oh, that you would, with the feelings of a Christian husband, as well as a father, yet listen to my wishes, in allowing me to see my child without restraint. She would be better under my care than that of any other person; she has not been placed under the care of any one equally able to instil firmer principles into her mind, or more decided piety. You are not aware, perhaps, that when you took her from me, you placed her with a drunken woman; and that she is permitted to visit occasionally at a house where the mistress of it is a drunkard. She has never looked so well since she was taken from under my care, as she did before; and if she must have a chance for health and strength, a mother's care is necessary.

I have written at great length; excuse me, for I have but seldom troubled you. Look with an eye of candour on what I have said, and attribute none but the kindliest motives to me.

Yours respectfully
N. Stock

[Journal, March 1825]

March 29th Tuesday. As Mary had requested me last Sunday but one to buy a few Prunes and some Spanish Juice for her, I had no way of conveying them to her but by taking them myself to the old woman at the cottage, near Parr Hall gate; so this morning I purchased, and took them. It was a lovely morning, and I had a very pleasant walk. I sat about quarter-of-an-hour with the old woman, who promised to take up the parcel to the Hall, and give it to the cook, which she said was the only way, for otherwise

Mary would not get it. When I had arrived within a quarter of a mile of St Helen's on my return, I heard a horse following; the rider was on the trot, but slackened pace when he came up with me. I had my parasol up, and never turned my head to look at him, but kept my face covered with my parasol whilst he was approaching. I was imagining it might be Mr Grundy following me, to give me some information or other, and when for a minute he walked by my side, I peeped a little under my parasol, and saw the legs of a fine horse, and the accoutrements of a well saddled one, but raised my eyes or uncovered my face no further – how fortunate that I did not! For, when he had got a few yards before me, I ventured to look out, and – beheld Mr Stock! dressed in a beautiful dark puce-coloured coat, and every thing else corresponding. He was either tipsy, or one of his nervous agitations had come upon him; he wriggled and twitched upon the horse most comically, pulling the horse to stop, and whipping to make it go. At length, the harassed animal tried what a trot would do, and away they went, jogglety, jogglety, and were soon out of my sight. Mr Stock never saw my face, and whether he knew me, I cannot say; I suspect he did.

It was very unlucky I should be overtaken so short a way from Parr Hall; had I been nearer Prescot, I should not have cared; he will suspect my errand, and the old woman at the cottage will be prevented admitting me again – it cannot be helped now!

It was Mary herself who told me, that her aunt Perkins last Christmas, when she was at Mr Stock's house for a part of Mary's holidays, urged him every day to alter his present system as regarded his wife and child. I had not an opportunity of asking Mary more particularly what it was precisely that her aunt said to her father, but it raised my hopes so much, that 2 days after, I walked to Liverpool and called on them.

9 April 1825 (Prescot). *To Mrs Stopford*, Roby Mill, near Up Holland:

In acknowledging the receipt of the Quarter's annuity, due 25th of March last, I address myself to you, my dear Mrs Stopford, and through your medium, to express my thanks to Mr Stopford for the attention he has ever paid to the transmitting the money so regularly.

I am glad to find, from Miss M. Braithwaite, that she believes you are all in good health. I was inquiring particularly after

Mrs Smith, and she informs me that she is very active and well, considering her years, which I was much pleased to hear; for I have always felt a great respect for her. When Mrs Braithwaite was taken, I felt as if I had lost a mother; but there are three left, that have at one period or another, been as mothers to me – Mrs Smith, Mrs Hawarden, and Mrs Marsden; they shewed kindness to me when I was in affliction, and may Heaven be their reward.

I cannot but express my approbation at your kindness in giving an asylum to poor Mrs Littler.[11] I feel deeply concerned for her. I had long suspected that she was a sufferer like myself; hers is a situation most miserable! none can have even a distant idea of it, but they who have suffered likewise. I hope she will have friends more willing to exert themselves for her than I ever had, that she may not fall a sacrifice, as I have done, to brutality, depravity, hypocrisy, falsehood, and an unfeeling world.

Had I one real friend *even now*, I should not be deprived of my child as I am, and pining, friendless, and in solitude, a wanderer on the face of the earth, without a home, and no prospect of any thing better so long as I live. And what is painful to the last degree in situations like Mrs Littler's and mine, when our husbands use us cruelly, the whole world are open-mouthed against us too, instead of pitying, soothing, and comforting us. A wife, though her conduct be as correct as mortal's can be, yet if her husband unnaturally drives her from his roof, from the ferocity of his own disposition, she is avoided as if she were infamous. This is cruelty to cruelty; yet so have I found it, and so I fear will Poor Mrs Littler. My heart bleeds for her; but if she have any determined friends, they may do much. Your family are tender-hearted, we can both say, and much comfort have you bestowed upon us.

A few months ago, I heard of an affair as regards Miss Stopford, which pleased me greatly – I mean, that she made her father and mother her confidents, as regarded Mr Battersby; yet the company I heard it in, were all against Miss Stopford for having done so, and called her silly and foolish, and said she would know better another time than tell her papa and mamma. Tell her from me, as one of the sincerest friends she has, that she never can know better, and that I hope she will invariably act in the same way. Whoever advises her to keep any thing secret from her parents, are her decided enemies, and theirs too; they are only seeking their own interest, and if she had no prospect of any fortune, they would not give themselves the trouble so much as to speak to her.

[Journal, April 1825]

Sunday, April 10. At one o'clock in the afternoon, I took a walk to St Helen's to meet my little darling again; an unusual trepidation and anxiety seized me as I went, but exerting as much fortitude as possible, I endeavoured to divert my thoughts by the beauties of the scenery; for indeed, my indulgent Father had gilded the prospect by a glorious sun and a clear atmosphere. I proceeded to the farther part of St Helen's, but had not met my child. My knees trembled so, that I went into one of a row of cottages where a fruit shop was kept, and requested leave to sit down. A very neat-looking young married woman was in, and was very civil indeed. As I sat waiting, I told her my situation as regarded my child, and she seemed to pity me much. I said I was afraid that when Mr Grundy and Mr Stock found that I made a practice of meeting her on the way to Chapel, they would prevent her going; but I had no other method left, and I considered it to be my duty to see her in any way I could. I was afraid that this might be the last time; and I added, 'Judge then what must be my feelings at this moment,' – for I was very faint.

Bye and bye Miss Jackson, the head teacher, came past, and whole train of boarders; my anxiety confused my sight, and I could not recognize my Mary. I sat in a corner by the window, so that they could not see me; for I was afraid the young woman might suffer some unpleasant treatment on my account if they saw who afforded me shelter; for such is Mr Stock's unceasing bitter and dreadful persecution against me, and I should be sorry that a single human being should lose so much as a penny on my account, or have one uneasy moment.

When the whole of the Parr Hall family had passed, I issued forth and hastened to overtake them, that I might be quite sure whether Mary was there. I asked Miss Hammond, one of the teachers who walked last, whether Mary was there; she replied she was at the front, with a very haughty, forbidding nod, which I cannot soon forget. Oh, my Father, have pity, have pity on thy suffering servant! Thou knowest that from my fellow creatures I deserve not this cruel treatment.

I hastened forward and saw my Mary next after Miss Jackson; the change from Winter habiliments to Summer ones, had been one means of preventing my knowing her. Miss Jackson spoke and looked kindly. Heaven bless her for it! but it is in her very nature. We were soon at Chapel, and I determined on entering, that I might enjoy the sight of my child another hour. Miss Jackson directed me to the Pew next Mary's. During service, Mary became very faint; poor child! I know thy feelings are harassed. One of the young ladies, apparently about 14, looked at me with a peculiar degree of compassion. On coming out, Mr Grundy and Wm. Woodward might tell Mr Stock that he had seen me at Chapel in Mr Grundy's pew, as if Mr G. encouraged me, and so perhaps he was explaining.

I took leave of Mary at the Chapel door, timid and spiritless, afraid of going to too great lengths; yet Mary's indisposition would well have justified me in going part of the way homeward with her. I have repented ever since that I had not; but I have not the spirit of a mouse. I was just arrived at the outskirts of St Helen's when two young women speaking to me by name, requested I would go with them home to tea. I hesitated a moment, not knowing them, but their looks were kindly, and I, expressing myself pleased with the friendliness of their manner, accompanied them. They led me near a mile, and I began to wonder where they were taking me to. At length, they made up to a gentleman's house and grounds. Will they lead me to the front door, thought I; but I inquired not. At last they entered a cottage in an out-building, where was an elderly, sickly-looking woman, laid on a sopha, and there I sat down.

They had heard of my situation, and offered me the calling there at any time when I wished to meet with Mary at Chapel, as it lay between St Helens and Prescot, and in Summer is a very pleasant way through fields. The Almighty raises me Comforters among the poor, if I want friends among the rich. They appeared to be a pious family, and told me they rented the garden belonging to the late Col Fraser, whose house it had been which I had just passed. I felt much pleased with the mother and daughters; there was a good deal of fine expression in their countenances.

15 April 1825 (Prescot). *To Miss Dennett*,[12] Up Holland:

The very great kindness, my dear Miss Dennett, of your conduct towards me, and your long continued friendliness, and likewise that of Mrs Ducker, induces me at this time to make a request, which if you comply with, may possibly be of essential service to me, and will, I hope, be no great trouble to you, although it must be some.

I will state what it is. A few months ago, it was suggested to me by one who well knew Mr Stock's temper, that if I could get a petition to him, drawn up as a testimonial of the natural goodness of my temper, my patience, mildness, disinterestedness, integrity, piety, generosity, humanity, &c., and signed by those who have known me well, that it would be the most probable means to induce him to permit me the frequent and *unrestricted* liberty of seeing my child. My talents, my prudence, or my abstemiousness, he never called in question, I am told. These, therefore, are not so necessary to insert; yet it may be as well to include them.

When this was first mentioned to me, I knew not how to set about it; for I could not write it myself in my own praise; neither could I tell who to apply to; but my distress about my poor, delicate child, urges me to lay aside all nicety and diffidence, and ask you – if you can conscientiously, and with that regard to truth so evident in all I have ever known of you, and which I desire you to adhere to now, assist me in forwarding such a business. I think Henry Latham, with your instructions, would be well able to draw it up, so as to be taken for signatures to all those in Holland and its neighbourhood who have long known me, and are willing to do so; for I would desire none to sign who cannot do so heartily.

For a little while I would have kept very secret, until it is drawn up and I have seen it, lest any thing should require altering; for that reason, as my Cousin Latham is not very good at secret keeping, if you would be kind enough to send for Henry to your house, I should be obliged.

The children I had at school, can testify how far from severe, or violent, I was with them, and how fond they were of me at all times, so that even in play hours they were not happy without me; it was quite an affectionate contest amongst them, which should be the nearest to me, who should go to walk with me, or spend a Winter's evening at my house. My cousin Latham knows that I never charged her a farthing school wages for her two boys, yet at that time I was very poor. I had generally one of Mr Billington's for nothing, and sometimes two; and many other children I taught gratis.

Miss Heyes, of Holland Moor, would I think, obtain some signatures. The Hootons of Orrel Post, and others.

When completed, if Mr Stopford could be induced to present it to Mr Stock, and could call in the aid of one or two respectable gentlemen besides, they might render me an essential service. As an act of benevolence, Mr Stopford might be induced to prevail with Mr Gaskell of Holland, and of Wigan too, to assist him. And, if, after all, there is no good done, it can do no harm; and you shall all have my lasting and sincere gratitude.

I should be glad if Miss Braithwaite and Mr Bird[13] would assist in promoting it. I have not mentioned it to Mrs T. Jackson, but mean to do so.

Every one I have lived with, I am sure, would sign it (out of Mr Stock's family), and many of my servants.

If several gentlemen together, of wealth and influence would call on Mr Stock with it, I sincerely believe he would comply, particularly if Mr Gaskell of Wigan would be one.[14]

16 April 1825 (Prescot). To *Miss Hawarden*, Wigan:

As you promised to write again, I thought I would write no more till I had first heard from you; but having seen my Mary's account with the Robys, It has occurred to me that Mrs Roby, whom I know to be a feeling woman, might be prevailed on to exert herself with Mr Stock to induce him to allow me to see Mary without *any restrictions*. Could you be prevailed upon to try your powers of persuasion with Mrs Roby? and to induce her likewise to use her utmost influence with Mr and Mrs Alston; for I do think something might be done; if they would frequently speak to Mr Stock upon the subject; saying a little at a time, and representing it to be his duty to shew kindness to me (for hitherto, I fear, they have encouraged him in his bitterness).

Mary's health requires a mother's care; there is not a girl in the whole school who looks so ill. Mr Grundy always represents her as enjoying good health – with no better motive, I fear than the emolument of her board; for I hear a very poor character of him, both in Prescot and St Helen's, for meanness, avarice, and bad temper. Mrs Grundy, it is said, never knew a moment's happiness after she married him. It is very necessary that Mary should, for a year or two, be unconfined in any school, or she will be thrown into a consumption; besides, it is astonishing to many, that Mr G.'s school should flourish as it does, with a widower like him at the head of it, and a set of young unmarried women only, to manage it. I have a high opinion of Miss Jackson, but she cannot act against Mr G's will in any thing; her situation depends upon pleasing him.[15]

I do not wonder that Mr Grundy should have taken the pains he has, to prevent my coming to Parr Hall to see Mary, after what I hear; he is afraid I should discover deficiencies which cannot be observed in general by any visitors at the house, owing to his retired situation. He has stood in his own light, I think; for I heard a few days ago that Mary was to leave the school, which, I hope is true. Had Mr Grundy been quiet, I could have gone to Parr Hall, and no one scarcely could have known it, it is so secluded; but now that I have been forced to resort to the method of seeing her on the way to Chapel, she will not remain long, I dare say. If she be taken away soon, she will probably be sent elsewhere; but if Mrs Roby would lose no time, but to get her husband likewise to second her, Mr Alston's, or any others who have any influence with Mr Stock, something may be done.

I went to Liverpool purposely about 3 weeks ago to see Mr and Mrs Perkins (Mr Stock's sister) on the subject. Mr Perkins only was at home; he promised his influence, but I fear Mrs Perkins is against me as I never have heard more. I have since written to them very earnestly, but have received no answer.

[Journal, May 1825]

May 7th Saturday. I went to Liverpool this morning, in the caravan, to make the necessary inquiries as to the facility of procuring lodgings in Bangor, lest if I set out and could not easily procure them after my arrival, I should be obliged to return again the following day by the Packet I went in. Mr Dalrymple says I need not hesitate; for, so early in the season, I am sure to obtain lodgings any time after I get there.

8th Sunday. Set out at 1 o'clock to meet my Mary again at Chapel; this is the third time that I have done so. Just arrived in time to see her and her schoolfellows enter the Chapel, and I followed in, seating myself in an opposite Pew. When service was over, I joined her and walked part of the way towards Parr Hall with her, and but for the rain, would have gone farther. We had a good deal of chatter. I thought she looked rather better. eight-and-a-half-miles.

9th. I left home at 12 at noon, and walked to Holland (11 m.), for I found, from Miss Dannett's answer to my letter, that she was become quite a different woman to what I had ever known her before; for indeed, her letter was so cool and unkind, that it required all my fortitude to bear it with composure, and I never saw any unkindness when I was with her, and I have always heard that she expressed the greatest esteem for me to others. She decidedly refused my request in her letter; but I found when I saw her, that she was still what I had ever seen her before, and complied without hesitation, and even with apparent pleasure, to serve me. How unaccountable are these things! I took no notice of the unkindness of her letter, to her; some other time, I may.

On Tuesday, I sent a boy to fetch Henry Latham, who came that evening and put the business in such a train, that I can do without being obliged to the unwilling; for I have reason to think that a great number will cordially sign the testimonial to my disposition and character. There is nothing like bestirring one's self in one's own affairs. Miss Dannett thought that I wanted her to go about the country to get signatures. No such thing! but I knew she could easily *send* to various places, she knows so many people, many of whom, passing her door, would readily have done it and have forwarded it themselves without giving her the trouble of going beyond her own gate. Miss Braithwaite and Miss Heyes promised to sign.

13. Walked to Liverpool after dinner, to inquire the hour the Bangor Packet would sail on Thursday, the 19th., and to request Mrs Roxburgh would permit me to sleep there the previous night. I intended to ride home in Southern's caravan, but had walked 2 miles towards Prescot before he overtook me. I then got in. (10 miles).

15 Sunday. Immediately after dinner, I set off to St Helen's to see my Mary once more; as I was a little too soon for Chapel, I walked down the road from St Helen's to meet her, about half-a-mile, and returned with her to Chapel, sitting in an opposite Pew. As soon as service was over, Miss Jackson, the head teacher, crossed over to me, and told me Mr Grundy desired her to ask me if I knew the consequence of my repeated visits to St Helen's. I knew well enough the purport of the question, but thought there might be something further. 'What consequences?' I inquired with a smile. 'Mary would certainly be removed,' she replied. 'If

I don't see her at all, it matters not to me,' I said, 'where she is.' (I had like to have said, nobody will be the loser but Mr Grundy, but caution prevented me). 'If I can see her here,' I continued, 'I shall wish her to stay; if not, I care not where she is.' 'But,' said Miss J., 'it will be such a loss to the child.' (Thinks I to myself, I can't see that; well done, Mr Grundy's vanity, to think there is not such another school in England). 'The loss of a mother,' I replied, 'is the greatest loss she can sustain, and it shall not be my fault if she is without one.'

We then left the Chapel, and continued talking as we walked down the street; my little darling held my hand and we gave each other many an affectionate squeeze. Tears were in Mary's eyes; bless the tender-hearted child. Whilst Miss Jackson continued to represent to me the *dreadful* and *tremendous*, the *deplorable* and *terrible* consequences of my coming to see Mary, I vindicated myself most strenuously. All of a sudden, Miss Jackson popped into Dr Gaskell's shop without saying and left Mary and me quite alone; this was an expected delight, so we walked on above a mile, and got a great deal said. She asked me for a coloured miniature portrait of myself, and I requested some of her copy books and drawings, and a little of her needle work.

At last Mr Grundy overtook us. I took not the least notice of him; at length he opened his mouth, and he spoke, but only on indifferent subjects, to which I replied civilly. Not a word did he say upon the subject of his instructions to Miss Jackson – a mean fellow, to load a blunderbuss for her to fire, and dare not produce a pop-gun himself.

At last, Miss Jackson came up, just as I arrived at the wooden bridge near Parr Hall gate, and I then took leave, and affectionate leave, of my Mary, possibly for the last time! When she found that I stood in the road looking after her, she continued turning her dear face to the last moment, as she walked on to the house. When the hedge intervened, she continued jumping up to look again at me, and again. At last, she quite disappeared. Oh, what hearts of stone those are that can separate mother and child. I got home, weary and depressed. 12 miles.

16 & 17ᵗʰ. Were passed in preparing for my journey.

Since early spring Miss Weeton's thoughts had again been turning to adventure. This time it would be a tour of North Wales.

NOTES:

1. A kind of silk or lace.
2. Tippet – a neck covering.
3. Mouth organ.
4. For notes on the career and ultimate ruin of Thomas Richard Weeton – see Appendix II.
5. The 'caravan' would be that of Sothern's, which plied daily (with the exception of Tuesdays) between Liverpool and Prescot. The term 'caravan' was usually applied to Pickford's vans, for the transport only of goods.
6. West Derby is a suburb of Liverpool. Mr Stock did not take up residence there.
7. Steel pens had been introduced as far back as the year 1803, but Miss Weeton was true to her quill. Her writing is firm and bold over this period and her office as quill-mender must have been greatly appreciated by her friends. Owing to the rapid wear of quills, they were usually purchased by the score, among those unskilled in the art of 'fining.'
8. 1825 was the year of the opening of the Stockton and Darlington line for passenger traffic. The Bill for the Liverpool and Manchester Railway was presented to Parliament in that year but was rejected. However it was passed in May 1826 and opened in 1830. All of Lancashire was, in turn, gripped with excitement.
9. Ants.
10. Subsequent to her visit to Mr Perkins and his promise to attempt mediation on her behalf, she subsequently made an impassioned plea by letter to Mr Perkins, along the lines contained in the letter to her husband, dated 25th March 1825.
11. Wife of Dr Thomas Caldwell Littler. There is a tablet to Dr Littler in Up Holland Church, recording his services as a surgeon in the district for 27 years. Judging from Miss Weeton's letter to Mrs Stopford (9 April 1825), it would appear that Dr Littler's marriage had been as disastrous as was her own.
12. Miss Margery Dannett, of Holland Grove, died in April 1846, aged 75, though she was not at that time residing at Holland Grove. Miss Weeton varies the spelling of her name – sometimes Dannett, alternatively Dennett and also Dennet.
13. The Rev John Bird, B.A., assistant curate of Up Holland Church, 1812-1821; perpetual curate 1821-1844. He succeeded the Rev Thomas Meyrick, who died 'unmourned' in 1821. John Bird was also the wise choice as headmaster of a private school, not only had he married, secondly, Miss Catherine Braithwaite, one of the former headmaster's five daughters, but his family had sufficient influential social connections on Merseyside, which ensured a steady stream of boarders to Up Holland. 'The Parsonage' (now Upholland Conservative Club), was rebuilt in 1822 and became the place of residence for boarders. Bird died 30th March 1844, aged 59, and buried 'amidst a great gathering of parishioners.' His wife, Catherine, died 9th February 1848, aged 59.
14. Nicholas Heyes, the three local Gaskells, and Mr Stopford are all listed in a contemporary Roll Book, as Surveyors of the Roads.
15. Historian, Dr Theo. C. Barker, wrote a series of articles for a St Helens newspaper in the 1960s. His thoroughly researched account reveals a very different William Grundy from that described by Miss Weeton. Dr Barker

describes Mr Grundy as 'a very capable man and pillar of the community of St Helens.' In 1819 when Mary Stock was sent to Mr Grundy's Parr Hall boarding school, he was considered 'a pillar of the Independent Chapel in town [St Helens].' And 'for the next 20 years, church records are full of his bustling activities.'

It is clear from Miss Weeton's correspondence that she was suffering great stress at this time. The physical strain of many miles of exhausting walking to visit her daughter would have been enough to weaken even the most ardent spirit. Added to which was an ever present anxiety that she might even then not catch a glimpse of Mary, let alone be allowed to join with her in conversation. On the occasions when she was permitted to speak to Mary, she witnessed a gradual deterioration in her daughter's physical health. In such circumstances, it is hardly surprising that Miss Weeton was inclined to believe the local gossip, concerning the character of Mr Grundy, rather than employing her usually excellent ability to make accurate character assessments.

ELEVEN

The call of the hills and valleys

North Wales

May – July (?) 1825

ON THE 18TH of May 1825, Miss Weeton travelled in a caravan from Prescot to Liverpool. There she dined and drank tea with Mrs Roxburgh, before visiting Mrs Dalrymple and her brother, where she then slept and breakfasted. Armed with the Rev William Bingley's North Wales Guide,[1] she set off the following morning at 9 o'clock to catch the Llewellyn Steam Packet.[2] It was a fine summer morning. Being first on board for a place in the low cost 'steerage,' Miss Weeton took full advantage of the time, to simply contemplate the stillness of everything before her, musing that her necessarily frugal plan 'ill suited her inclinations' because it 'throws me amongst the lowest classes, I am obliged to be constantly on my guard, and at the same time to keep up a certain degree of reserve to prevent familiarity.' One hour later they set sail.

As the boat proceeded along, the stillness of the morning soon became superseded by a cacophony of 'steam, steam engine paddles, a double drum, clarionet (sic), fiddle, and a French-horn.' Miss Weeton's thoughts began to turn to whether or not she should continue with writing her Journal, but then almost immediately the thought of her beloved daughter, Mary, came into her mind and she decided to continue with it 'for her sake.'

On landing at Garth Ferry (for Bangor) her immediate priority was to find suitable lodgings; a task much harder than she had expected. The problems were a combination of language and price. Many of the residents spoke no English and many asked extravagant prices. At last she discovered a 'respectable-looking' man by the name of Mr Wm. Pritchard, and his house-keeper. She agreed a price of six shillings for a week's bed and board.

After tea she strolled towards the Menai Suspension Bridge,[3] about two miles away, before returning to sleep very comfortably in her bed, convinced that it was free from 'dampness, bugs or fleas.'

[Journal, May 1825]:

20. I went down to the waterside and over the Ferry to visit Beaumaris: the road was very pleasant, although the day was hot. I rambled a good deal round about the town, and got home to a 3 o'clock dinner; took tea like-wise at 5, that I might have time to mount the hill just above the town of Bangor. I was entertained to discover that every body's *back premises* were exposed to my view as I stood first upon one pinnacle, and then upon another.

When I returned, Mr Pritchard sent for his daughter (who is in a respectable service near), to talk with me; she speaks English well. She is such a pretty, genteel, innocent-looking young woman, that I greatly admire her; intelligent and modest.

22ᵈ Sunday morning. I arose quite refreshed. I wonder how it is, that at 48 years of age, I should have so much of the elasticity of youth, both in body and mind; for I am as playful as a child. I went to a congregational Chapel at half-past-10. I was too soon; the place was filled with men and boys. I felt quite confused at being the only female, for they were employed in teaching and learning in Welsh. At 11, they every one went out, and for a few minutes I was left totally alone, expecting to be locked in if I had not my wits about me. Soon, an entirely different class entered, and a preacher, and the service was conducted in English.

May 23ʳᵈ· Monday morning, after breakfast, I went to see the pillar erected in honour of the Marquis of Anglesea, beyond the new Bridge at Bangor Ferry. I crossed the ferry in company with 3 or 4 horses, and 2 as wild Welsh cows as ever were ferried over, besides a number of men and women. I had a very extensive prospect from the top of the rock on which the Pillar is erected. After dinner, I walked down to the shore at Garth Ferry, strolled over the Hill above it, and amused myself with my spying glass, remaining some hours.

24. Wrote to Miss Dalrymple this morning. She is the only person who has asked me to write during this journey, and I shall therefore, I think, write to no other.[4] Not a person in England knows at this moment where I am, or appears to care. How we are neglected when we are in adversity! What anxiety there would be about me, were I affluent! Oh, my Mary, if ever you read this, feel for your mother, and be grateful for those who shewed her kindness.

There had been heavy rain in the night; a hard gale of wind succeeded; notwithstanding, I ventured over at Garth Ferry after dinner, to take a stroll round about Beaumaris. Few people ventured upon the water this day; but I am so fond of water, that a trifle does not prevent my sailing. I have the opportunity but seldom; only when I leave home. I am a sailor's daughter, and perhaps inherit a portion of his taste and spirit.

The sun shone clearly upon the mountains, except when a cloud glided between, and the water was blue as the sky; every place looked beautifully. I rambled round Baron Hill, and up many a road where I could go without asking leave; for I dislike to do that. I want to go no where, where man, putting up his sign board, says proudly – 'thus far shalt thou go, and no farther!' Strolling towards the shore, I perceived a bathing house, where, finding two women, one of whom could speak English, lingering idly about like myself, I was glad to have a bit of chatter. The wind blew roughly, but setting our backs to a high wall that sheltered us from it, we conversed a long time; then, taking leave, I turned homeward. The ferry man at Garth is a singular looking mortal, very corpulent, and very short; he rolls about the boat like a hogshead; coarse features, and a rough voice, with plenty to say; but I find he can argue on two sides of the question – so a fig for that man's sincerity whose ingenuity rises above it.

26 Thursday. An annual meeting was held this day at the Market Place in Bangor, by the Ministers of the Independent denomination. I attended morning and afternoon. There was something primitive in thus standing out of doors to hear preaching; it reminded me of many parts of the Acts of the Apostles. As well as of the preaching of Jesus. It is not at all uncommon with the Dissenters of the present day,[5] but it was unusual to me. I felt concerned to see none of the wealthier part of the community attending; are they ashamed of it? Two ministers lodge here for the time, but they appear somewhat shy; they should follow the example of the great Apostle Paul, and be 'instant in season, and out of season;[6] but there are many who can preach better than converse, yet conversation is the most powerful means of conversion; preaching is but secondary to it; as was the first and only means by which an impression was made upon my mind, of the truths of religion and its comforts.

27. As thin as I am, and as skinny and bony, yet my bones cannot be dry bones, but must be 'full of marrow and fatness,' or I could never be able to endure such long walks, and be so little fatigued; my feet swell sometimes, but I can skip like a lamb amongst the rocks, and enjoy the sport, after a 10 or 12 miles walk. This day I rambled about 16 miles.

28. I examined Menai Bridge today very minutely, yet cannot discover how the passengers are to get on, or off, at the Anglesey end; the other end will have a fine entrance, but this is as yet not discoverable. The sun shone brilliantly upon the mountains, all except Snowdon. I saw it with great distinctness in every part fronting towards Anglesey, but the sun seldom touched it, and blackness was its distinguishing vesture all afternoon. All the week it has been veiled with the blackest clouds, and 'thick darkness has covered it.' And why? it is very little higher than several mountains near to it, which have only had mists and rain upon them, but not near so aweful looking, nor often invisible.

This day's walk was about 11 miles.

29 Sunday. I did not go out, except to Chapel in the morning, and took only a short walk in the evening. The sun shone very clearly, but the air was piercing cold, that there was no comfort without a fire, and I sat chiefly by it.

30. I crossed at Garth Ferry immediately after dinner, and walked to Bangor Ferry; a rout I had not before taken. The view from this side is the most beautiful of any I have seen in the vicinity of Bangor, and if I wished to reside in its neighbourhood, it would be here. Snowdon, as well as all the other mountains, was peculiarly clear and bright.

31st. At 9 o'clock this morning, I left home to walk to Conway (15 miles). I would have gone by a stagecoach, had there been any; but a Mail only travels there at 7 o'clock every evening through Bangor. I felt a little timid at the idea of accomplishing so long a walk, and to return on foot next day. I had never attempted such a task for near 15 years, when, at the Isle of Man near 15 years ago, I one day walked 36 m. This morning was extremely fine, and I enjoyed the beauty of the scenery greatly. Beaumaris bay was in full tide The road under Penmaen Mawr is certainly awful, and today it was, all the way, very lonely. I felt somewhat afraid, and as it proved, unnecessary.

Before I reached Penmaen Mawr, I passed 2 men lying at one side of the road, basking in the sun. One had a bundle of printed papers, which I suppose he was going to cry through the streets of some town, detailing some wonderment for a half-penny each; the other, apparently an Irishman, had nothing with him which bore a semblance of any intended employment. These two were presently joined by a man coming from a gentleman's house, with a barrel organ at his back. They arose, and walked at his pace, which could not be very quick considering his burthen. I perceived this, and proceeded very nimbly, that I might get out of sight of them; but the road ascending as I approached the mountain, I could not outwalk them. I turned, and found the organist had left them, and they were close behind; I preferred having them before me, so I stood to look over the wall to the sea, and they passed quietly. It would have been easy in this part to have robbed, and thrown me into the sea, without discovery; but I perceived 2 or 3 passengers approaching at a distance, which determined me to stop a little here. I sat down, and ate the bread and butter which I had brought with me, and they went out of sight. 4 or 5 miles farther, I again came unexpectedly upon them, lying, as before to rest. I passed as speedily as possible, and got safe into Conway. I dare say the men had no unlawful thoughts.

As I had loitered much upon the road, it was 3 o'clock when I got to Conway. I soon found the ferry and crossed it. The chain Bridge building here, is not nearly in so forward a state as that at Bangor Ferry.[7] It will be a beautiful object to some of the gentlemen's seats on the opposite shore. I rambled a good deal about, before I set out to look for a bed for the night; then, calling at a little shop, I inquired where I could have a private lodging, and was directed over the way, where I was soon engaged.

The vicinity of Conway is peculiarly romantic. I was glad I had walked so far to see it. I retired early to rest, much tired with an 18 miles walk.

[Journal, June 1825]

June 1st Wednesday. In the night, I heard the roaring of a storm – and the previous evening was so lovely! I arose at 8; the storm continued, but it was yet fair. I hastened to eat breakfast, that I might return. I dared not stay to see more of the place, which I had intended, for I saw the storm would increase, and I must return to-day, as I leave Bangor to-morrow entirely. I had a prospect of walking a few miles before much rain fell; so, giving the landlady a shilling, which was 3 times what she asked (I found my own provisions), I took leave at 9. The wind blew furiously, and when I had gained about 7 miles, the rain fell heavily; the remaining 8 was winterly indeed! I was drenched thoroughly. I looked for each succeeding mile stone anxiously. When at last I got home, between 1 and 2, every part of my dress was wet; the rain had run off my bonnet, down my neck, wetting me inside as much as out; for I had no umbrella or cloak. The wind had blown in my face all the way, furiously, and yet when I got dry cloaths on, I was very little fatigued with a 15 miles walk. Let me raise a thought of gratitude to Thee, Oh my Father, for this!

3^d. As Thursday was so wet and stormy, I was obliged to defer my removal to Carnarvon to to-day (Friday), and had a very agreeable walk, the roads not dusty, and no more wind than was necessary to keep the air from being too hot.

6 June 1825 (Carnarvon). *To Miss Dalrymple,* Liverpool:

I have just got myself comfortably settled at Carnarvon, after a fortnight's sojourning at Bangor, so now I hope I shall hear from you soon.

When I had been near a week at Bangor, I took a walk to Carnarvon, to take lodgings there, previous to removing thither; it is so very uncomfortable to go any place, and have a place of abode to seek afterwards.

Mr Price's reference was of great service to me. I soon found out Mrs Evans's daughter, who assisted me, and took me to a Capt Hughes's, where I have engaged a bed-room for a month at 4s. per week, and the accommodation far superior to those I had at Bangor at 6s. I was imposed upon there, but I shan't fret about that; it was no ruinous concern; they took advantage of my immediate want of lodgings at a lower price than 10s. 6d. I could have had plenty, at that rent, for a sitting and bed-room. Mrs Evans knew how to manage; she would have taken me herself, but I did not like the closeness of the situation. Here, I am opposite to the river and shipping, and have a fine view of the Castle, and a pretty green hill over the river, surrounded with wood. I have a side view into Castle Square; for you must know, Ma'am, I am in Love Lane, and really love the Lane very well. An animated view from my window is really necessary, where I am so much alone.

For 5 or 6 days after I got to Bangor, the weather was hot; it then became severely cold, but the air was peculiarly clear, and the sun shone with great brightness. Last Tuesday, May 31, I walked to Conway. It was as if I had the whole world to myself; nothing living was visible but a couple of sea gulls. The first thing on my arrival was to visit the new chain Bridge. It is quite a miniature piece of work compared with Menai Bridge; it will be not be long before it is finished. Had the succeeding morning been as fine as the previous one, I would have seen more of the neighbourhood. I arrived in Bangor at 2 o'clock P.M., like some poor wretch just saved from drowning. However, when I had put dry cloaths on, I was not a jot the worse, and I am very glad I assumed resolution to go the journey. I should have been very sorry to have missed seeing so singular and romantic looking a place.

The storm continued with unabating fury till next day at evening; the people reeling in the streets as if they were tipsy, the wind drove them about so rudely.

The family I have left, and the one I am come to, can neither of them speak English, except a *very* little, which causes some droll mistakes often, besides being mortifying to me; for I am *rather* fond of talking, which is somewhat *surprising* in a *woman.* The market women try me first in Welsh, but when they find they can make nothing of me, they speak in English rather than lose a bargain.

Since the English have visited them so much, they have most of them, in towns, been obliged to learn that language for interest sake; and probably in another century, the Welsh will have become almost extinct; for national schools are universal in the principality, and I think the children are taught in English.

I have as great a loss in religious services as any thing; for they are comparatively few, and very short, to what we have them in England. I consider myself happy, however, in finding both families I have lodged with, professedly pious people.

If you have an opportunity, please to let me be remembered to Mr Price's. Mr P. is one who will leave no stone unturned to serve a friend; he fears no trouble.

[Journal, June 1825]:

June 8th. The storminess of the weather is still such as wholly to prevent my going out, except a few errands; the wind, as well as rain, is violent. I find from the papers, that there was a tremendous thunderstorm at Manchester the night that I was at Conway. It seems to have let loose an amazing quantity of wind. For amusement, I have been obliged to resort to a circulating library (Pool and Harding's). 'Brighton on the Steyne,' a satirical work, was the first I got hold of. I would not have wasted my time with it, had I known what kind of a composition it was; a deal of profligate sentiment is elicited, and the vilest conduct towards women, particularly wives, treated with the utmost levity, as a very trivial kind of offence; nay, even as affording much amusement; and characters ranking high as to title and warlike achievements, are little, if at all, censured for the most diabolical conduct towards women, when, if there be one crime of greatest magnitude, it is that!

If man injures man, the injured has a great portion of power to defend himself, either from natural strength of body, of resolution, of the countenance of many of his fellows, or from the laws; but when man injures woman, how can she defend herself? Her frame is weaker, her spirit timid; and if she be a wife, there is scarce a man anywhere to be found who will use the slightest exertion in her defence; and her own sex cannot, having no powers. She has no hope from law; for man, woman's enemy, exercises, as well as makes those laws. She cannot have a jury of her peers or equals, for men, every where prejudiced against the sex, are her jurors; man is her judge. Thus situated, thus oppressed, she lives miserably, and by inches sinks into the grave. This is the lot not merely of a few, but of one half, if not two thirds of the sex! That a man who will use a woman with cruelty, is a coward, a despicable villain, may be asserted by one of his own sex who has perhaps some share of probity. He is so. But then, according to that assertion, there is a prodigious number of cowards and of villains; I may justly say, seven eighths. I scarcely go into a house in which there is not a fornicator, a seducer, an adulterer, a tyrant. Even here – see a poor suffering creature in the person of Mrs Hughes. She is consuming with a vile disorder, given to her by her wretch of a husband. She is in continual pain, and must die; she cannot be cured. To see such a sweet, innocent, mild-tempered woman, in such constant agony, rouses the utmost indignation against the fellow who could prove himself so like a fiend, yet this is not an uncommon case. My own experience of the world shews me many such. What numbers of men murder their wives; and that, by the most cruel of all means – slow torture.

11. Intending to go to market this morning, I deferred going to market, the embarrassment pursues me as regards the language. I applied to two or three butchers before I could make a purchase, and then was indebted to a young woman passing by, to become my interpreter. I am so easily repulsed, so soon disheartened, that I am ill fitted for this rude world; my mind is too delicate for a mingled multitude. I often think of the poet Cowper, for I think I am much like him in disposition and sentiment; I do not mean in talent.

I do certainly observe myself to be looked at here more than I ever recollect before; for why, I cannot discover. Perhaps because I am a stranger, and alone; then, I am taller and thinner than most women, and very plain-featured – yet, I think, not so ugly as to attract passers-by – perhaps I am; few of us know how we appear in the eyes of others. Many of the country people I meet on the road, bow or courtesy to me, as I were of some rank or respectability of appearance; but the market people turn almost one and all to look after me, and when I inquire the price of any thing, ask exorbitantly. My dress is very plain, that I may pass unnoticed; a dark print, no way remarkable in the make of it, and a bonnet likewise plain. Strangers, I should think, are so common here, that they would excite little attention.

12. There was no English service at the Chapel to day until half past 3 o'clock, so I sate at home writing my journal (which was a week in arrears), all morning and evening.

13. The 2^d set of books from the library please me much more than the first; the first had certainly much wit, perhaps talent, but I can make no allowances talent misapplied. These – 'The Paris Spectator,' translated by W. Jerdan, are worth reading. There is a great deal of good sense; and the manner, style, and variety, render the work highly interesting.

I left home this morning to cross the Tal y Foel ferry at 9 o'clock. The conductor told me, when I arrived on the pier, that it would be quarter of an hour before a boat would go. I thought this would allow me time to fetch some thing I had forgot. I hastened home, and returned within time – and the boat was gone! and I had to wait $1^1/_2$ hour for another. I remained on the terrace all the time, lest I should be again disappointed. When at last I got into a ferry boat, it was 11 o'clock. The weather this week has become intensely hot. Only 5 or 6 days ago, the air was so cold as to render a fire in my room quite desirable, and for 2 days I had one. Setting sail so late, I had to endure the whole heat of the day; whilst I was on the water, it was refreshingly cool, but when I landed, it was scorching. I trudged over a dusty, uninteresting road, through Newborough, and seeing a Church a little beyond, I went and seated myself on a low grave stone, on the most shaded side of the Church, and ate some bread and butter, the only dinner I had provided.

Newborough is a city of hovels; and the Church, like almost all I have yet seen in Wales, as comfortless and shabby within as an old barn. I often see Churches or Chapels marked on my map, which I use, is to discover if possible some building without a chimney.

When I had rested and refreshed myself, I proceeded; I soon got amongst sand-hills, for my object was to get to the sea shore, to look at the shells, and then to go to Llanddwyn rocks, light-house, and perch. The view of the Carnarvonshire mountains was very grand to-day, and all that coast; for I could see from Penmaen Mawr, all the way to Braich y Pwll most distinctly. The view under my feet, and for a couple of miles or more before me, was dreary, blinding, and cheerless; sand, marsh, star, and bare rocks, composed the barren prospect. As I mounted sand-hill after sand-hill, I began to ask myself why I wearied myself so? What induced me voluntarily to undertake these profitless labours? What pleasure was there? For indeed, these succession of sands, for a much greater way than I had anticipated, the heat, the pain to my eyes, had almost been too much for me; yet the natural perseverance of my mind urged me on, and when at last I arrived at the water's edge, on the Malldraeth sands, about 2 miles above Llanddywyn, I felt as if my labour was repaid. I am passionately fond of water, and now it was the more delightful as the tide was just beginning to flow; the breeze was cooling, the sands firm, and covered with shells, the water a beautiful purple; it was now 3 o'clock, and the sun would soon abate of its fury, and the view southward over the bay was fine indeed. I stood admiring, or rambled about in a luxury of delight. I rejoiced I had come.

I arrived at home about half-past 7 o'clock, after a walk of 15 miles, besides being on my feet $1^1/_2$ hour at the terrace before I left in the morning. Tea, and a warm bath, and a good night's rest, enabled me to rise quite refreshed and well next morning. Should I not thank Thee, my Protector, and my Supporter, for all these mercies?

Tuesday, June 14. To-day I enjoyed the luxury of resting, yet not wholly still. I wished to see the baths that the Marquis of Anglesea has lately constructed; I was told they were quite elegant. I went this morning, and took a cold bath, which I liked so much, that were it not for the expence, I would go every day whilst I staid. When the place is considered, the retirement, convenience, and comfort, one shilling is cheap for a single bath; very cheap, and can never, I should think, pay interest for the money expended. It would be dear to me, merely on account of my circumscribed income.

I like to be alone when I dress and undress; many people have no scruples of delicacy in this respect. My excellent mother was strict in this part of our education; for my brother was taught to have as great a regard for personal modesty as I was, and never were we exposed to each other in washing and dressing, as I see most families of children are. From a child, I could never bear to suffer any one to be witness to my preparing for bed at night, or to quit my room in a morning, nor any exposure of a person at any other time. I introduce this subject here, with the impression that my darling Mary may happen to peruse what I write. You have no mother to teach you, my love, as I had; and no other person will ever supply my place. You will not, most probably I fear, learn true modesty at a public school; and you are unhappily deprived of the precepts and of the example which your mother could have set you.

The afternoon I sat at home, repairing stockings, &c. To this, Mary, my mother ever required me to pay the strictest attention; and I have never since disobeyed her. I am not afraid to take off my shoe at any time, for I have no holes, or soil, to hide.

In the evening, I had a short, but pleasant walk to Llanbeblic Church, and turning to the right over some fields, rambled along the Seiont. All the children in Carnarvon, apparently, were here assembled together, sporting on its banks, or in its stream; here a group of boys, thereof girls, for nearly half a mile.

I began to meditate an ascent of Snowdon; of course, alone, for I knew nobody.

June 15. Set off at 8 this morning on the Mail to P. Aberglaslyn, with another passenger, a poor young woman, with a little girl of 2 years old. She was going to her parish![8] Her husband was a sailor, and for 2 years had deserted her; for the last 15 months she had heard nothing of him. How frequent are these instances of cruelty to wives! What hard hearts men have, and how little punishment they meet with for this description of profligacy. If they steal a sheep or a horse, they are pursued and hung; to desert a wife is a thousand times greater crime; yet no police pursues him for this – is a wife no better than a sheep or a horse? Is her misery to be nothing accounted of? The very parish officers take no cognisance of a husband's desertion, whilst she asks for no money from them.

At Pont A. I left the Mail; it was between 11 and 12 o'clock, for we had stopped above half an hour at Beddgelert, to rest the horse, who, poor thing, had to accomplish the whole journey. During this pausing time, I sat under the shade of a tree in the Inn yard, quite at my ease. At P.A. I sat on the battlement of the Bridge, eating part of the bread and butter which I had brought from home, and then walked slowly to a spot I had noticed in passing, near Llyn Cawellyn, where I had to begin my ascent; and, feeling able and eager, I ventured.

I had got up about one third of the way, when, being thirsty, and a tempting rill just by, I took off my bonnet and bent my head to the water, drinking very comfortably. I had provision in a small bag, but a drinking vessel I had forgotten; the drink – the best of all liquids, I knew the Provider would furnish. It was now near 2 o'clock, as I judged by my shadow; for my watch I had left at home for fear of accidents. Just as I raised my head from the water, I saw a gentleman descending with his guide, at a short distance. They espied me. I had already left the regular path a little, merely to quench my thirst; and now deviated a little more, purposely that they might not distinguish my dress or features, lest, seeing me at any other time, they should know where they had seen me; and I should dread the being pointed at in the road or the street as – 'That is the lady I saw ascending Snowdon, alone!'

The guide, seeing I was out of the path (only because he was in it, if he had but known), calling out to me, but I was *quite* deaf. He continued shouting, and I was *forced* to hear; he was telling me to keep in the copper path, &c. I knew the way perfectly well, for my Map and Guide had been well studied at home. I could find from what the gentleman said, that he imagined I had called for the guide at his dwelling, and finding him engaged upon the mountain, had gone so far to meet him; for he intreated the man to leave him. 'I can do perfectly well now,' he repeatedly said. I never turned my face towards them, but walked as fast as I could, hanging down my head; the Guide again giving me some directions – with the best intentions, I am sure, and partly, I think, as a little stratagem to draw me nearer; but I had no fancy to be the heroine of a tale for him to amuse future employers with, and to describe me as young or old, handsome or plain, ladylike or otherwise; and if he could have drawn me near enough so as to have known me again, next thing, perhaps, I should have figured in some newspaper; or some tourists, glad to fill a page of their journal, would have crammed me there, as 'A singular female!' – I am not thus ambitious. No! No!

To the Guide's civility, I twice called out, 'Thank you!' But now my deafness had left me, I had got a stiff neck. When I had mounted a considerable height above them, I turned, and saw the gentleman standing looking up after me, with his hands on his sides as if in astonishment, and the Guide trudging downwards, vexed perhaps that it should be seen that any body could ascend without him, – and a woman, too! and alone! for the lift in his shoulders seemed to indicate as much.

It was my wish to ascend on the Betttws side, to cross over the summit if practicable, and descend at Llanberris. I knew it would lengthen the journey greatly not to descend where I had commenced, but I did not like to do it. I wished to have an entire range and view down every side. I persevered, and reached the first height; I was now higher than ever I had been in the world before. I had often turned and sat down to rest and look at the prospect, but here I remained some time. I could count at one time, from 10 to 14 lakes, some of them mere pools certainly, and a sea of mountains rising in every direction, like wave beyond wave; not a cloud was to be seen, but a slight haze partly obscured the distance; nearer objects were quite distinct. Had I ascended either 1 or 2 days sooner, I should have had a brilliantly clear atmosphere, but timidity had prevented my bringing my resolution to the sticking place sooner. Even this morning, on rising, I felt irresolute. I had passed most of the night disturbed by distressing dreams (and dreams of any kind are very unusual to me), occasioned, I dare say, by the feeling of anxiety with which I had retired to rest; yet I knew that as I was not obliged to go, I could any moment return if I saw a prospect of danger. Here I stood, perched on a ridge like a crow on the point of a pinnacle; not a human creature could I see anywhere; for aught I knew, I had the whole mountain to myself. It was a grand elevation; an eastward precipice exceeding deep, I dared not look down, standing. I laid myself flat, and examined it; fatigued and a refreshing coolness, made me drowsy, and I had nearly sunk to sleep. I jumped up to shake it off, and proceeded.

Not far before me, the path wound along a most aweful precipice. Now I *was* startled! for the first time. This was wholly unexpected. I could not recollect that I had read of such a road, either in Bingley or Williams. I thought when once I was at the top, the summit would be, and that I should not be obliged to encounter any rocky ridges like these before me. I hesitated some time; there was no crossing lower down. I must either return home as I had come, or climb the only way there was. I reflected, numbers of gentlemen and many ladies must have crossed before me; certainly then, I may. I had taken the precaution, on coming to Carnarvon, to write my address on a card, both to my lodgings there and my dwelling at Prescot, and wore it in my pocket, so that if any accident should befall me, whoever found me would discover where to apply. I could not be amused at thus wearing my direction *inside.*

Thus – I was directed *inside*, but I hoped to be brought safe back again. Strange feelings and ideas mingle! the next moment I raised a thought aloft to Him who is the Highest. Be my Protector still, I said. He heard – and on my way I sped.

Whilst crossing the ridge,[9] perhaps 100 yds., perhaps 22, or even more, for I was too terrified to ascertain – the precipice on my right and left both, was too much for my head to bear; on my right, if I slipped ever so little, nothing could save me, and Oh! It looked like an eternity of falling; it seemed to my giddy head, half a mile down. I drew my bonnet close over my right cheek, to hoodwink me on that side. On the other side there was a low ridge of rocks to hold by, and I soon crossed. I breathed now, and again surveyed the dangerous road. Often have I read of such paths, but truly I suspected the authors of exaggeration. I beg their pardons now. I will be less incredulous in future.

When I attained the second summit, a boisterous wind blew upwards from the bottom; this was a phenomenon to me; it was so rough as once to blow me down; but it was safe falling on this side. Had the wind blown the contrary way, it would have been madness to brave it on the edge of the precipice; for the whole circumference of the summit, East and North, appears to me for some miles to be perpendicular for almost half a mile down; it looked aweful and grand. I could see the various post roads, winding among the valleys like a white thread; but houses or cottages I could not see one. I could have wished to remained some hours longer, but observing my shadow to have lengthened considerably (for, amongst other precautions, I had left my watch at home in my box, lest I should break it by some fall or other, or be robbed), I prepared to descend.

I found descending more disagreeable than ascending; my shoes became so slippery that I often fell, but never got hurt. The heath was dry, and the rocks flinty and polished like slate, so that it was difficult to stand or walk. I had a very long walk before me, if I descended on the Llanberris side; it would have saved 2 or 3 miles or more had I gone down on the Bettws side; but then, I must have repassed that dreadful ridge. And I dared not without a real necessity. Snowdon, on the Llanberris side, has many subordinate summits, yet very lofty ones; sons and daughters, as it were. I peeped down between each of these, and as I looked down from several of the loftier openings, the bottom was so low, I could not distinguish either houses or any other buildings, distance so levelled them with the ground. It was now about 6 o'clock, and I had at least 12 miles to walk.

At last, Dolbadern Castle appeared; a rivulet, a bridge, cottages – some upon brows, some on their sides, and others at the bottom – plantations, and gardens. What a romantic landscape! Looking upwards, how grand, how majestic; downwards, how lovely and heart cheering! for here, I, who had been for many hours, soaring Queen of the Mountains, had now arrived amongst my own species again, and on a level with my fellow creatures. I had but met with 2 men in my descent, any more than my ascent. They were cutting turf; they spoke not, looked quietly at me, but not rudely.

At 8 o'clock, I passed the Inn at Llanberris; I was then 8 miles from home. I now urged my utmost speed; for the last 5 hours I had eaten nothing, nor drank anything. Snowdon has few streams, and of these few, I could not drink for want of a cup. I tried to reach them laid down, but could not without wetting my cloaths; and I was too thirsty to eat. When I got into the open road, I passed many a tempting stream, in some of which I dipped a little bread, and it sufficed until I arrived at home at half past 10 o'clock, tired certainly, but highly gratified and delighted.

The servant girl was waiting for me, and made me tea; whilst it was preparing, which was scarcely more than 5 minutes, I drank plentifully of cold water, for I was not hot. The night was so serene and calm! And Oh! – that I may sincerely add, I was so grateful to Him who had conducted me safely home again, to a comfortable, a very comfortable habitation, after a walk of more than 25 miles.

June 16th. I arose at 8, refreshed and rested, and not the least footsore or stiff. After breakfast, I went down to the shore and bathed, and the remainder of the day I sat at home, writing my journal, until after tea, when I went to the top of a lofty rock behind the Uxbridge Arms, from whence there is a fine and extensive view.

Sunday, June 19th. I feel a reluctance at going to a Church here. I cannot make Mrs Hughes understand my questions as to where English service is performed, and when; and my natural diffidence has taken such strong hold on me, that I stay at home, rather than go to find it out myself. I find I manage best in crowds, for in London, I was as much at home as if I had always lived there. It is the language that is such a teaze. Most of the people in Carnarvon who take in lodgers, can speak English. I am rather unfortunate.

At half past 3, I went to the service in English at a neighbouring Methodist Chapel; it only lasts an hour. I feel the loss greatly of the frequent opportunities we have in Lancashire. I lose ground sadly. I condemn myself, and say, religion is not an innate principle with me, but the force of continual examples and the perpetual repetition of precepts; or why am I not as constant and as fervent by myself in my own chamber, as when influenced by mingling among frequent crowds of worshippers? Every situation has its advantages and disadvantages; I admire Carnarvon greatly, but I shall be glad to get near to my old acquaintances again in England.

This morning I received a letter from Miss Dalrymple, which was very welcome.

20th. The weather has again taken a complete change; the wind is bitterly cold, dust rises in whirls, and heavy black clouds all portend a continued storm of at least some days.

After dinner, I took a walk along the Pwllheli road, as the rain seemed to put off, for about three-and-a-half miles, but the atmosphere thickened so in many places, I dared proceed no farther; reading and sewing filled up the other intervals of the day. I have, for some years, entirely given up all kinds of needlework which has no real utility to recommend it. I do not say anything in condemnation of ornamental needlework, although I could say much, and I think, justly. If it amuses others, I let them employ their time as pleases them, expecting the same privilege. It does not amuse me. When I sew, it is to make necessary clothing, and to keep it in repair; and as my Mary may read what I write, for her information I shall be more minute in many of my observations than I should be had I no daughter; and Mary, I keep my apparel in the exactest repair; and when I lived at Wigan and had a house and family to attend to, I kept the whole quite neat. It is so little of an amusement to me, that were I rich enough, I should employ others to do it, for I think it a duty in the affluent female to let others live. I do not look upon it as a merit for any young person to make her own dresses, bonnets, shoes, or lace, if she be rich; I do consider it a merit that she should be *able* to make them; for no one so affluent but may suffer a reverse, and every female should know how to earn a living.

I consider it as so disgraceful to wear rags, or any part of my apparel with ever so small a hole in it, that I daily find at least a *little* employment for my needle; for I am too poor to buy new, frequently. My cloaths, if examined, would be found to have fewer holes and more patches and darnings, than those of almost any other person; yet, I think I am as respectably dressed, and as

373

neat in my *every day apparel*, as any of my acquaintances; though many of them exceed me in visiting dresses.

Books are my amusement, books my employment; but not novels or light reading. I have always been sadly lost for want of the means. Music has high wrought charms for me – but – my poverty has ever been in the way. I could never purchase an instrument, except a flageolet, nor afford the price of instruction even on that; yet it sweetens many a solitary hour! With care and saving, I could now procure an organ; for that should be my instrument; but I am too old. Yet, old as I am, I am strongly tempted to purchase one, as I know a person who would sell me a small finger organ for less than 20£ – a very good one. I can, self taught, amuse myself with my Flageolet; I could do so with an Organ. I have an Harmonicon, on which I could soon play tolerably, but it is too trifling an instrument to afford me any amusement.

The solitary life I lead, is not from choice; I see no way of avoiding it. In lodgings, I have hitherto found it unavoidable; and I have found no family to board with, who would take me on such terms as I can afford – such a family, I mean, as I could wish to reside with; for I could not be comfortable to mingle continually with people of coarse manners, vulgar, and illiterate. I appear to be condemned to solitude for life. I am naturally of a lively, social turn, and to be often in the company of such as possess highly gifted and highly cultivated minds, would be a gratification to me, superior even to books . . . But! God has said 'Set your affections on things above, and not on things on the earth.'[10] – and therefore appears to have specially deprived me of all those things on which I could have set my affections. Thy will be done! I see Thy mercies and Thy Graciousness in this, and am thankful.

On that beautiful but melancholic note, the manuscript by Miss Weeton's own hand, abruptly comes to an end.

Despite every effort by those closest to her from childhood, that she should abandon her 'ardour for literature,' no-one was ever able to overpower her urge to write. The fruit of Miss Weeton's ceaseless industry through quill and paper, has allowed all of us the privilege of witnessing everyday life in Georgian England through the eyes of an observant and determined woman. That she retained a steadfast faith in her God, together with a willingness to find excuses for, and even forgive those who caused her sufferings, is a testament to her strength of character Nelly Weeton would have been a remarkable woman in any age.

NOTES:

1. 'North Wales, delineated from two excursions [1798 and 1801] through all the interesting parts of that highly beautiful and romantic country and intended as a guide to future tourists.' The Rev. W. Bingley, M.A. London: printed for Longman, Hurst, Rees, Orme, and Brown (1814).
2. 'Steam Packets. Beaumaris and Bangor – *Prince Llewellyn* and *St David,* (of 75 horse-power each) sail regularly from St George's Dock, pier head, for Beaumaris and Bangor, North Wales, average passage six hours.' *Baines's Lancs. Directory, 1825.*
3. The Menai Suspension Bridge was then in the process of being erected by Thomas Telford (1757-1834). Its construction had begun in 1819. It was opened in 1826.
4. This letter was apparently written on 6th June and sent off then. Miss Weeton adhered to her resolve not to write to any other.
5. Miss Weeton was more than likely alluding to 'the new dissent' of Methodism.
6. Refers to: 'Preach the word; be instant in season, out of season; reprove, rebuke, exhort with all longsuffering and doctrine.' (2 Timothy 4: 2).
7. Commenced by Telford in 1822 and competed in 1826.
8. As soon as deserted wives became a charge upon the parish of their adoption, they were sent back to the place of their birth.
9. 'The ridge' to which Miss Weeton refers is almost certainly the knife edge ridge of Crib Goch. From there she would have to negotiate a very steep descent to reach the Lanberis road.
10. Refers to: 'Set your affection on things above, not on things on the earth.' (Colossians 3: 2).

Epilogue

That nothing walks with aimless feet;
That not one life shall be destroyed,
Or cast as rubbish to the void,
When God hath made the pile complete.

Alfred, Lord Tennyson ('In Memoriam')

FROM THE CONTENT and tone of Miss Weeton's correspondence from the summer of 1823, favourable signs of her old self were starting to become apparent. Prolonged absence from Wigan, the place of her former distress, had produced beneficial results. Old friendships and associations had been rekindled. Once more her letters and her journal testify to a renewed vigour and interest in the life and concerns of those around her. At the age of 47 her wander-lust would find temporary satisfaction in daring trips into the forbidden town, including an association with the congregation of Hope Congregational Chapel. She also took a risky stagecoach journey to London and latterly a walking tour round North Wales.

Despite the lukewarm attitude of Wigan citizens and its church folk towards Miss Weeton, during the period of her greatest distress between 1818 and 1822, they would eventually benefit from Miss Weeton's association among them. As the years advanced, her position in Wigan became reversed from that of social outcast, to that of (relatively) wealthy resident. The iniquitous Deed of Separation, which in effect barred her from contact with her child, eventually became the catalyst which gained Miss Weeton sympathy and support. This was achieved through material assistance from members of Hope Chapel and its new minister, Rev William Marshall (1792-1861).

At the time of Miss Weeton's tour of North Wales, she was contentedly living in Prescot, from where she was better able to visit her daughter, still residing at Parr Hall, St Helens. That in turn begs the question as to why Miss Weeton made the unlikely decision to remove from Prescot and return to Wigan? The answer was discovered during researches for this book: Aaron Stock, who had once threatened his wife with incarceration into a lunatic asylum, was himself admitted into Lancaster Lunatic Asylum, on 26 May 1828. He died there on 27 December 1830.

Rate books and local directories of the time confirm that Mary had become the owner of her father's property in Standishgate (Wigan Lane) and both Mary and her mother occupied the property until 1844, when the property was sold. The 1841 Census describes Mrs Stock as a 'pawn broker' and Mary as a 'teacher of music.'

No Wigan newspaper or other printed Wigan source has revealed any further information concerning Mrs Stock and her daughter after 1844. Mrs Stock died in 1849 at a time when few local newspapers were circulating. The *Wigan Times* was established in January of that year and ceased publication October 1853; both the *Wigan Observer* and *Wigan Examiner* were established in 1853. At the time of publishing *Miss Weeton's Journal of a Governess* during the 1930s, Edward Hall had given up all hope of finding any further reference to her with the words: 'It is assumed that obscurely as she lived, so obscurely she died.'

This remained the case until 1994 when a resident of Liverpool found her burial records in the registers for the Necropolis Cemetery, Liverpool. Listed as follows: Grave number 7611, Nelly Stock, aged 72; cause of death decay; date of death 12 June, buried 14 June 1849; address Bedford Street. Her death certificate confirms her age and her death due to typhoid fever. The informant is named as William Newell, 71 Bedford Street, Toxteth Park. Mr Newell was Nelly's son-in-law.

In the cemetery registers Mrs Stock is referred to as 'Nelly,' which confirms her own statement that she had been christened Nelly as recorded in the registers of St John's parish church, Lancaster. There has been some confusion concerning her Christian name because she occasionally signed her letters as 'Ellen.' The Liverpool registers also confirm that Miss Weeton, as Mrs Stock, spent at least some of her final years living with her daughter Mary and son-in-law William Newell.

Her will was proved on 15 August 1849. Most of her possessions were left to her daughter, including her books, furniture and clothes etc. The residue of her estate was left in trust for the benefit of her daughter and grandchildren. Legacies of £10 each were to be paid to the executors of the will. These were Rev William Marshall of Hope Chapel, Wigan; Richard Walmsley, attorney's clerk of Wallgate, Wigan; and Thomas Dawson, house agent of Liverpool.

But what of her precious copy-letter memorandum books? It is perhaps worth remembering that as far back as 1810, Miss Weeton had expressed concern for the future of her writings: *I have spoken freely of most of them, or their near connexions, and to whom I can bequeath them at death, I know not.* However, from the time of his arrival in 1822 at Hope Congregational Chapel, Wigan, Rev William Marshall had been her intimate and highly respected friend and confidante. To him she left her letters, memoranda and other autobiographical writings, together with her copy of 'Clarke's Commentary on the Old and New Testaments.' These were retained by him until time regrettably brought about their dispersal.

By any standards, Miss Weeton was a remarkable woman, not only because she was an exceptional letter writer, but also because of her determination to make a successful life despite all the obstacles that beset her and the discouragement of those closest to her. Her strength of character is best exemplified by her perseverance in the face of great hardship, her expansive natural abilities and her commitment to the Christian faith. Despite revealing a lack of discretion at times, she was unwavering in her loyalty to her friends. On one occasion only was her loyalty to her Christian faith in doubt, due to a deep depression during the darkest days of marital stress. Even then she was able to purge her creeping doubt in God by writing a kind of diary entitled 'Occasional Reflections, A.D. 1818.'

Her personality was such that, had fate allowed her a more fortunate start in life, she would have been capable of achieving much more than she did. A rather later contemporary of hers, the Hon Mrs Norton (Caroline Elizabeth Sarah Norton 1808-1877), following a disastrous marriage, instigated an intense pamphleteering campaign that in 1853 changed the law concerning legal protection from her husband, the custody of offspring and female earnings. By then Miss Weeton was four years in her grave but would undoubtedly have approved and, given the means, the opportunity and the support, she would have acted similarly. But without financial means or titled friends in Wigan, she was forced by Deed of Separation to leave her husband's home. That same deed banned her from residing within two-and-a-half miles of Wigan, resulting in her reluctantly relocating to Up Holland, to live in cramped farmhouse isolation.

How was she able, both physically and mentally, to withstand regular onslaughts to her dignity and to her sense of well-being? As I studied her writings, the answer became clear in two very different ways. Firstly, despite the lack of protein in her diet, she was naturally blessed with a strong constitution; all the more remarkable because she apparently lived largely on bread, buns, biscuits, eggs and potatoes, referring to herself as *a graminovorous animal and not a carnivorous one*. In addition she was tall, thin and exercised daily, through many miles of walking.

Secondly her Christian faith was a major source of inner strength, despite her personal circumstances. That in turn led me to question why did the editor of the 1936 edition, Edward Hall, state in his Introduction to the first volume: *Religion was not an innate principle in her; the irresistible attraction was a sound preacher, free from the petty prejudices of his sect, with the broad sympathies of a human outlook and expansive creed?*

That comment does not reflect the whole truth, as I discovered when I came across the actual words recorded by Miss Weeton. The first eight words of Hall's comment accurately quote Miss Weeton's own words whilst touring in North Wales on Sunday, June 19th, 1823: *At half-past-three; I went to the service in English at a neighbouring Methodist Chapel; it only lasts an hour. I feel the loss greatly of the frequent opportunities we have in Lancashire. I lose ground sadly. I condemn myself, and say, religion is not an innate principle with me, but the force of continual examples and the perpetual repetition of precepts; or why am I not as constant and as fervent by myself in my own chamber, as when influenced by mingling among frequent crowds of worshippers?*

Many who read this book will find it difficult to understand why Miss Weeton would suggest 'religion is not an innate

MISS WEETON, GOVERNESS AND TRAVELLER

principle,' within her, when the very opposite appears to be the case. Both Edward Hall's and Miss Weeton's comments require clarification: Theological illiteracy has escalated during the 20th century and continues apace today. An unfortunate casualty of ignorance is that individuals increasingly reach erroneous conclusions about Christianity. Prevailing opinion appears to confuse the word 'religion' with the content of belief. 'Religion' and (for example) 'Christianity' are not synonymous. The word 'religion' refers to the outward expression of belief, it does not indicate the content of a particular belief. Miss Weeton fully understood the difference.

Throughout her life she was a person with a deep faith in Christian truth. She was instinctively a Protestant dissenter by way of the 'old dissent' of Congregationalism (formerly referred to as Independency), a denomination which also embraced the dogma of Calvinism, although she was not inflexible when considering the 'forms and ceremonies' of others. I believe her non-bigoted attitude assisted her intellectually to separate the content of her belief from that of strict religious formality, in particular that which over-emphasised the importance of ostentatious liturgical vestments. Whilst she was attracted to Congregationalism, I do not believe she considered Calvin's doctrine of predestination vital to securing salvation (eternal life). If that had been the case Miss Weeton would never have contemplated attending a Wesleyan Methodist Chapel, which she did on a number of occasions, nor would she have attended the Church (of England) from time-to-time. John Wesley, founder of the Methodist movement from within his own Church of England, was vehemently opposed to the determinist logic of John Calvin, who rejected the saving will of God. Wesley subscribed to Arminian theology which acknowledges that Divine sovereignty is compatible with real free will in man, arguing that God bestows forgiveness on all who repent and believe in Jesus Christ; that He died for all, not just for the elect.

Miss Weeton eschewed ostentation of any kind at all times. One need only refer to her experience at the foundation stone-laying ceremony of St John's R.C. Church, Standishgate, Wigan, on Tuesday morning, 27 January 1818: *It was the first time I had ever been in a Catholic place of worship. I have often heard their forms and ceremonies much ridiculed and highly censured, and have felt pained at the want of charity in Protestant friends. I have thought their bigotry equalled Roman Catholic bigotry, and felt much inclined to think they were not quite so ridiculous as they were represented.* Then came the bombshell: *'What I witnessed this day, filled me with the utmost astonishment, that so many people, possessing as much natural sense and discernment as myself, could be led by such boyish pageantry .*

Like so many respectable folk of her generation, Miss Weeton was in the habit of attending church on the 'Sabbath' (The Lord's Day), although it was not vital for her personally to do so every single week if it was physically difficult because of bad weather, or because of the short hours of winter daylight. Whilst naturally attracted to Congregationalism, she was not obsessed by denominationalism, an unusual characteristic in her generation. She depended solely on her deep love for God and the knowledge that she was loved by God. In that sense, as Hall correctly stated, she was 'a freethinker.' Hall was also right in his comment 'the irresistible attraction was a sound preacher.' Miss Weeton was largely impressed or otherwise by the characteristics of individual clergymen, rather than the various forms of worship. She strongly censured any weakness in a clergyman that she perceived to be un-Christian behaviour. This would be observed by her as a clear lack of piety, noticeable through pride-driven haughtiness, pomposity, or by an unreasonable autocratic attitude. At all times she placed humility and love of the sacrificial kind at the highest point of human virtue. The clear importance to her of a person's personal characteristics, speaks volumes. In the final analysis, Miss Weeton considered that the proof of Christian character is best revealed in a person's attitude towards others. Respect and concern for others, far more than denominational differences and man-made doctrines, reveal the true condition of a person's heart.

In all that she was and achieved as a governess, and as a loyal friend to many, she candidly explains in exquisite detail, through an endless flow of appropriate adjectives. And in the process dispels any doubts of her having a capricious nature. Not only was Miss Weeton a consummate and passionate writer, she was also courageous. Walking and travelling alone as a female was to risk physical harm. Any fear was dispelled by the overwhelming desire to visit her daughter, Mary, when at Parr Hall Boarding School for Girls, St Helens. From Up Holland to Parr Hall, was a distance of 7 miles each way.

The excitement of adventure gave her a great sense of achievement and fulfilment. She planned and completed a walking tour alone around the Isle-of-Man, including the ascent of Snaefell where she placed a stone on the cairn on her second attempt. She also toured North Wales alone including the ascent of Snowdon at the age of 49. Her greatest adventure was to undertake a high risk return stagecoach journey to London, riding all the way on top. At that time it was well-known that serious accident and even death could often result if a stagecoach toppled over on deeply-rutted roads.

I end this book in the way, I believe, Miss Weeton would heartily approve. Throughout her writings references to God, often in verse, abound. Two such verses were written and entered together in her Journal in 1824, when she was 48 years old. The first verse is attributed to 'Watts.' Dr Isaac Watts (1674-1748), was a dissenting Independent minister and prolific hymn writer. The second verse signed 'N.S.' (Nelly Stock), is a fitting end by her own hand:

> Then dearest Lord in Thy embrace,
>   Let me resign my fleeting breath;
> And with a smile upon my face,
>   Pass the important hour of death.
>
> *Watts*

> And when to judgement though shalt come,
>   O may I in Thy likeness rise!
> And guardian angels bear me home
>   To holier mansions in the skies.
>
> *N.S.*

Nelly Stock's remains lie undisturbed, alongside those of 25 others, beneath the sod in a burial pit that was once Necropolis Cemetery, Low Hill, Everton, Liverpool. The cemetery was closed in 1898 and made into a public garden. In 1914 it was renamed as Grant Gardens.

Bibliography

Books:

Acland, Alice, *Caroline Norton*. (Constable, 1948).

Anderson, D., *The Orrell Coalfield, Lancashire 1740-1850*. (Moorland Publishing Company, 1975).

Aughton, Peter, *Liverpool – A People's History*. (Carnegie Publishing Ltd., 1990, revised 2003).

Bagley, J. J., *Upholland Grammar School*. (University Press of Liverpool – Hodder and Stoughton Ltd., 1944).

Baines, Edward, *History, Directory and Gazetteer, of the County Palatine of Lancaster*. (Wm. Wales and Co., Liverpool, Vol. 1, 1825 and Vol. 2, 1826).

Bebbington, David, *Victorian Nonconformity*. (Headstart History, 1992).

Burkett, M. E. and Sloss, J. D. G., *William Green of Ambleside – A Lake District Artist, 1760-1823*. (Abbot Hall Gallery, Kendal, 1984).

Clarke, Mike, *The Leeds and Liverpool Canal*. (Carnegie Publishing Ltd., 1990).

Constantine, Stephen and White, Andrew (Editor). *A History of Lancaster*. (Edinburgh University Press, 2001).

Jagger, Mrs Mary A., *The History of Honley*. (Alfred Jubb and Son, 1914).

Miller, Allan, *George Lyon, Up Holland Highwayman?* (European Library, The Netherlands, 2001).

Miller, Allan, *Up Holland Church, 1307-2007*. (European Library, The Netherlands, 2006).

Nightingale, B., *Centenary of The Lancashire Congregational Union, 1806-1906*. (John Heywood Ltd., Manchester, 1906).

Robinson, W. Gordon, *William Roby, 1776-1830, and the Revival of Independency in the North*. (Independent Press Ltd., 1954).

Schlenther, Boyd Stanley, *Queen of the Methodists – The Countess of Huntingdon and Eighteeenth-Century Crisis of Faith and Society*. (Durham Academic Press, 1997).

Booklets/Papers:

Log for the brig *Lively*, 1781. (Preston Record Office, DDX2743/5546).

A History of Rainford Congregational Church, 1577-1967. Compiled by Arthur Huyton, Pastor. (Printed by South Lancashire Newspapers, St Helens).

A Ramble Around The Wigan Parish Church. Compiled by W. J True, verger. (Printed by Thos. Wall and Sons Ltd., 1901).

Up Holland in the Hungry Forties. A series of 14 instalments published in the 'Wigan Examiner' between 1st April and 1st July 1933 (based on diaries written by Mrs. Mary Bird Stopford (c.1793-1848), of Bank House, Roby Mill, Up Holland. Compiled by Rev. John Bird Stopford, M.A. (1859-1934), grandson of Mrs. Stopford).

Wesley Methodist Church, Lamberhead Green – Brief History of the last 170 years, 1776-1946. (Printed by J. Starr and Son, Wigan, 1946).

The Funeral of Meyrick Bankes of Winstanley, 1827, by Joyce H. M. Bankes. (Transactions of the Historic Society of Lancashire and Cheshire, Vol. 112, 1960).

Miss Weeton's letters to correspondents and her autobiographical writings. (Wigan Archives).

Appendix I

Rev. John Braithwaite (1754-1812)

JOHN Braithwaite was born at Crosthwaite, Cumberland , in 1754 and was educated at St Bees School before moving to Rainford, near St Helens. One year later, he accepted the post of assistant curate to Rev Richard Prescott, curate-in-charge at St Thomas's, Up Holland. The assistant curate's salary of £30 a year did not prevent most of the parish work falling on his shoulders. His great energy combined with his 'itchy palm' compelled him to make money while at the same time ensuring his devotion to his career. In November 1782, four years after arriving in Up Holland, he was appointed to the headship of Up Holland Grammar School and on becoming licensed on 12 July 1783, he accepted the living of St George's, Wigan. A position he held until his death.

Braithwaite took full advantage of the snobbery of the age by changing the name of the school from 'Grammar School' to 'Academy'. At that time Grammar Schools were associated with charitable foundations, whereas an Academy possessed the more dignified status of an educational establishment. In particular, the term was used for the dissenting centres of learning that offered a university type of education to young men who were barred from Oxford and Cambridge because of their religious leanings. Of more importance to Braithwaite was the fact that an academy would attract wealthy patrons whose sons would board at his home. Girls, including Miss Nelly Weeton, were excluded from such schools.

Thanks to the detailed and vivid letters of Miss Weeton, it is possible to peep through the windows of 'The Priory', home of the Braithwaite family, located off Church Street, Up Holland. John and Anne Braithwaite had six children – five daughters and a son. All their daughters were friends, in varying degrees, of Miss Weeton; as also were the daughters of Rev. Richard Prescott.

Anne Braithwaite was the eldest daughter. The first copy-letter extant, dated 25 October 1807, was sent by Miss Weeton to Miss Anne Braithwaite, who was staying with friends in London. At the time of the letter Anne would be aged about 28. She died of a 'decline' shortly after the death of her father. Catherine was a rather condescending and supercilious friend of Miss Weeton. Margaret was much more 'genteel' and 'more accommodating' and with 'greater consideration for the feelings of others'. She also had a 'religious turn of mind' which was natural to her. She married Thomas Tellaw Jackson, of Prescot, near Liverpool, in 1808, and died there in 1851. Margaret was greatly admired by Miss Weeton. Elisabeth was rather refined with a quiet disposition in an otherwise somewhat boisterous family. Her last illness and death caused by an asthmatic complaint is touchingly recorded by her admiring friend, Miss Weeton, some 15 years her senior. Of Mary, the youngest daughter (who suffered from fits), and son Frederick, nothing is known.

Rev. John Braithwaite tried hard to play the part of a country parson, yet towards the end of his life he succumbed to drinking heavily; though it would be a mistake to look on him as degenerate. At that time drunkenness was common and even fashionable amongst the upper classes. Many gentlemen were proud to be considered 'three bottle men'. Despite his failings, the very human and somewhat charismatic Braithwaite was greatly admired and loved by his family and by his pupils, amongst whom he found great respect and affection. Thirty years after his death, at the age of 58, a group of his old pupils erected a tablet to his memory. It remains where it was placed, on the south wall of Up Holland church, above the pews once reserved for the scholars. His wife, Anne, life-long friend and 'protector' of Miss Weeton, continued to live at 'The Priory' until her death at the age of 65 in May 1823.

A.R.

References:

Chetham Society – vol. 18. *History of the Church and Manor of Wigan – Part IV.*
Bagley, J. J. *Upholland Grammar School (1944).*
Miss Weeton's writings.

Appendix II

Thomas Richard Weeton (1781-1845)

THOMAS Richard Weeton (the name 'Richard' had at some point been wrongly substituted by Miss Weeton in favour of the name 'Rawlinson'), was the youngest of four children and only son of Thomas and Mary Weeton of Lancaster. He was born at Lancaster, on 24 January 1781, four years after his sister, Nelly. As the only two surviving siblings, in childhood they were inseparable and formed an attachment that would last into maturity.

At the age of 14, Thomas was articled to a Preston solicitor, at which time Nelly plunged into a deep melancholy. For weeks afterwards she visited each place in and around Up Holland , where they had regularly been together, and wrote: 'I never should see him again as I had seen him before: his seat in church; his usual corner at home; his old clothes and books. Everything that had reminded me of the happy days that were fled'.

Within a year of Thomas ending his seven year clerkship, he married Miss Jane Scott, the youngest of the four daughters of Thomas Scott of Wigan. Scott was the owner of industrial premises in the town. Jane herself might be considered to have been a heiress by, in due course, acquiring through her deceased mother, the Greenhalgh-Willoughby estate, known as Rigby House, located at Adlington, near Standish.

On the day of the wedding the happy couple went to live with Miss Weeton in her cottage home at Up Holland. Unfortunately the accommodation arrangements were most unsatisfactory to Thomas's sister, and exacerbated by the apparently indolent nature of his new wife. Within a month of their arrival, much to Nelly's relief, Jane's mother sent a note requesting that the couple should return to live in Wigan.

By the age of 26 and bolstered by Scott money, Thomas Weeton gradually became established as an Attorney in the little township of Leigh, Lancashire, where the population of some 5,200 were mostly poor weavers. At that time the town boasted 22 licensed houses, a bull-baiting ring and a cock-pit. Thomas found it difficult to establish himself, but through perseverance and with no little encouragement from his sister, he eventually secured the bulk of the practice to be had in the town.

As his prosperity increased, Thomas became increasingly ashamed of his humble upbringing, a constant reminder being the lowly status of his sister. His socially aspiring wife continually goaded him so that any esteem that he had for his sister rapidly eroded. As Miss Weeton's letters reveal, Thomas's attitude would eventually culminate in despicable behaviour towards his hapless sister, especially during her disastrous and tragedy-filled final years of marriage to Aaron Stock.

Thomas Weeton was a man who loved open debate and its attendant publicity. He had been well educated as a boy at Mr Braithwaite's 'most excellent' Up Holland Academy and for seven years he had been trained as a solicitor. As a result he was confident and articulate; perhaps it was this very confidence that eventually led to his undoing by underestimating his 'less well educated and intelligent' contemporaries. He became involved in the cut and thrust of pamphlet warfare and scathing letters from him are revealed in lengthy column inches in newspapers. He lashed out against riotous weavers, he objected to the singing of sacred music by an opera star, and his loyalty was called into question at the accession of George IV in respect of a local celebration to celebrate the Coronation in 1820. Consequently he made many enemies who gave him little peace. Even his personal friendship with Mr Marsh, the magistrate, offered no protection in the matter of a certain Mrs Bevan's Will, during 1833.

Mrs Elizabeth Bevan lived at Laurel House, Lowton, near Leigh, and, through her extensive Lowton Estates, was a lady of considerable wealth. Then 81 years of age and with rapidly failing health, she instructed Mr Weeton in the disposal of her estate. According to Mrs Bevan, Mr Weeton fraudulently named his very good friend, Mr Philip Newton, as the main beneficiary of her will. In return for a valuable legacy for Mr Newton, an alleged sum of £500 would be given to Mr Weeton. Unfortunately for Mr Weeton, Mrs Bevan recovered sufficiently to expose the forgery. Mr Weeton tried to exonerate himself via a 25-page pamphlet, entitled 'Mr Weeton's Statement of Facts' that was comprehensively written and executed by a Leigh printer. Mrs Bevan responded with a 15-page pamphlet, entitled 'Mr Weeton, Reply to his Pamphlet Sent To Her', executed by a Wigan printer. Weeton was a beaten man. He had already lost his coveted position of Clerk to the Magistrates and his professional fees had suffered severely. He was finished in Leigh.

Thomas Weeton was constantly and grudgingly reminded of his lowly ancestry, when compared with that of his wife. As a result he tirelessly tried to distance himself from his early years and vainly attempted to tamper with reality by requesting a Liverpool book dealer to engrave seals and book plates for him.

The marriage resulted in one son, Thomas, born in 1804. Two surviving daughters followed, Catherine, born 1806, and Jane, born 1807. Four others died in infancy.

Thomas appears to have retired in 1837, either to his own home, or to the home of his son-in-law, John Darlington, and his wife, Jane, in the village of Adlington. He died there in March 1845, age 64. His wife, Jane, had predeceased him, dying in January 1831, age 50. Both are buried in the churchyard of Horwich Chapel, now Holy Trinity Church, Horwich, near Bolton.

A.R.

References:

Hall, Edward. *Miss Weeton's Journal of a Governess, Volume 1 (1807-1811), extended footnote p.48-9, also Volume 2 (1811-1825), revised epilogue 1968, p.399ff.* David and Charles (Holdings) Limited, Newton Abbot (1969).

Appendix III

Aaron Stock (1776-1830)

AARON Stock was born on 24 January 1776 in Windle, St Helens, the son of Matthew Stock, a locksmith[1]. On 9 January 1793, he witnessed the marriage of his sister Ann Stock to William Critchley at the church of St Thomas the Martyr, Up Holland[2]. Miss Weeton and her mother moved to Up Holland in May 1784. In September 1796, the Revd John Braithwaite arranged a loan of £220 to Alexander Winstanley, a clockmaker, as a mortgage against a property in Wigan. Aaron Stock was a witness[3]. Miss Weeton and her mother were friends of Revd Braithwaite and his family. Furthermore, Miss Weeton knew Mr Winstanley; she let her house to him in 1808. It is therefore possible that Aaron Stock was acquainted with Miss Weeton for many years before she first mentions him in her diaries two weeks before their wedding on 1 September 1814.

On 30 October 1796 Aaron Stock became a Freemason at the Sincerity lodge, Wigan[4]. His profession was listed in the Freemason membership register as an accomptant[5]. On 22 November 1798, Aaron Stock married his first wife, Elizabeth Gilbert[6], widow of the late John Gilbert. Elizabeth and John had issue of at least five children, two of whom died in infancy. Consequently, upon marrying Elizabeth, Aaron Stock became step-father to Edward (aged between 6 and 10 years[7]), Hannah (aged about 2 years[8]) and Thomas Gilbert (aged 1 year). About 1801, two children, William and Jane were born to Aaron and Elizabeth[9].

It is unclear when Aaron Stock ceased to be an accomptant and became a cotton manufacturer and spinner based at Chapel Lane, Wigan. On 19 March 1808 the London Gazette published a list of dissolved partnerships including that of Ralph Tindsley, John Daglish and Aaron Stock, of Wigan, Lancaster, cotton spinners. In 1809, Aaron Stock and Samuel Singleton, Wigan cotton spinners, and James Stock, a Liverpool cotton broker, agreed to become partners. The broker contributed bills amounting to £3,002 5s 7d, and allowed the spinners to draw on his own London agent 'to the amount of £8,000 each year'[10].

In 1811 Samuel Crompton undertook a survey of cotton spinning spindles, comparing the quantity of spindles in use within a thirty mile radius of Bolton. Within the survey he noted that Aaron Stock of Wigan had ten Throstle Machines of 144 spindles per machine (a total of 1440 spindles) and sixteen Jenny Machines of 130 spindles per machine (a total of 2080 spindles)[11].

Elizabeth Stock died on 12th December 1812 and on 1 September 1814, Aaron Stock married Nelly Weeton at Holy Trinity Church, Liverpool[10].

Commercial Directories of 1816 and 1818 list as cotton spinners, Aaron Stock of Chapel Lane, Wigan and Singleton Stock (the partnership of Samuel Singleton and Aaron Stock) of Princess Street, Wigan[12].

Nelly describes Aaron's brutality towards her and she suggests that his behaviour hastened the death of his first wife. In October 1821 Aaron Stock appeared in court for an assault on Nelly and was required to enter into recognizances[13] and in December of that year Nelly appeared in court for an assault on Thomas Sutton, although in April 1822 the assault was discharged. No court appearances relating to Aaron Stock and his first wife, Elizabeth have been found. In 1822 Nelly signed a deed of separation from her husband and returned to Up Holland.

On 31st December 1823 Aaron Stock's partnership with Samuel Singleton was dissolved[14] and in 1825 he is three times referred to in the trade directory as a cotton manufacturer, in Standishgate and Chapel Lane, Wigan and at Prospect Hill, Standish[15]. On 15 April 1826 he was the victim of a highway robbery for which Patrick Blake was tried at Lancaster Castle and sentenced to death for his part in the robbery. The sentence was commuted to a life sentence and Blake was transported to Australia.

On 8 May 1826, Aaron Stock was declared bankrupt. He was then living in Wigan and West Derby[16].

In a Journal entry dated 29 May 1823 Nelly said that a number of people "thought that Mr Stock was thought to be almost insane" and that she had been hearing that kind of comment for nine months[17].

Aaron Stock was admitted to Lancaster Asylum on 26 May 1828. He is described simply as a married cotton spinner, although the initial reason for his admission was not recorded. He died there on 27 December 1830, the entry simply noting that he was discharged dead. He was buried at St Mary's Lancaster.

Andrew Heyes MA(Ed)

References/Notes:

1   Parish Registers Prescot, St Helens. 1713-1812.
2   Parish Registers, Marriages, Up Holland, St Thomas. 1754-1812.
3   Lancashire Archives, Preston (Ref: DP/443/2/28/1/9)
4   Library and Museum of Freemasonry, London. Freemasonry Membership
    Registers: *Register of Admissions: Country and Foreign, vol II, Fols 1-649*
5   A now obsolete word meaning Accountant.
6   Parish Registers, Marriages, Wigan, All Saints. 1754-1926
7   Currently no records can be traced to provide Edward's date of birth.
    However, based on records relating to his siblings, as the second son, his age
    would be between 6 and 10 years at the time of Aaron Stock's marriage to
    Elizabeth Gilbert.
8   The 1841 census records Hannah's age as 45yrs, suggesting a year of birth of
    about 1796 and giving an approximate age of 2yrs at the time of Aaron and
    Elizabeth's marriage (HO107; Piece: 604; Book: 3; Civil Parish: St Margaret
    With Bishops Fee; County: Leicestershire; Enumeration District: 5; Folio: 7;
    Page: 7; Line: 10; GSU roll: 438750)
9   In the 1861 census Jane is recorded as aged 60 years. If this is correct she
    was born about 1801 the same year William Stock was born. However the
    accuracy of census returns cannot be guaranteed. There appears to be no
    record of their births and Miss Weeton's letters do not provide any assistance
    in clarifying their years of birth.
10 Edwards, M.M., 1967, *The Growth of the British Cotton Trade 1780 – 1815*,
    Manchester University Press
11 Townend, M., 1985, *Wigan's Textile Industry* (Wigan Local Studies) pp146.
12 *The Commercial Directory, For 1816-17. Manchester, England*: Wardle and Pratt,
    1816. pp342.
    The Commercial directory, for 1818-19-20: J. Pigot, 1818.
13 In Criminal Law, a person who has been found guilty of an offence can be
    required to enter into a recognizance whereby he agrees to keep the peace in
    the future.
14 Paget, J.W., 1824, *The Law Advertiser Volume 2*. London: J.W. Paget 5 Quality
    Court, Chancery Lane.
15 Baines, E., 1825, *History, Directory, and Gazetteer, of the County Palatine of
    Lancaster: With a Variety of Commercial & Statistical Information ... Illustrated by
    Maps and Plans, Volume 2*. Liverpool: Wm. Wales. pp 617, 619
16 Neuman, T., 1828, *The London Gazette Part 1*. pp910
17 Miss Weeton's journal of a governess, 1807-1825, 2 vols., ed. by E. Hall
    (Newton Abbot: David & Charles (Holdings) Limited, 1969). Volume 2,
    pp225.

Appendix IV

Edward Pedder (1776-1835)

THE Pedder family had settled in Preston during the 17th Century and by the time of Edward's birth had become a prominent and influential family in the town. Between 1748 and 1777 Edward's grandfather, father and uncle were Mayors of Preston on six occasions. Edward's father was one of the founders in 1776 of Preston's first bank – Atherton, Greaves and Company. Edward, the first son and eldest child of Edward Pedder the elder, was born in Preston, Lancashire on 11 May 1776 and would become a man of independent means, owning property which he leased to tenants in and around Preston and Fulwood.

On 6 July 1797 Edward was appointed Captain in the 2nd Battalion of Supplementary Militia for the County of Lancaster[1] but resigned on 30 June 1798 and in August married Mary Gertrude Shawe, the twenty two year old daughter of William and Sarah Shawe of Preston[2] at Saint John's Parish Church, Preston. Their first child, Mary Gertrude, was born about 1800[3] and in 1803 Edward purchased for £6,100, the Darwen Bank estate from Ralph Asshton of Preston. On 18 July that year he was appointed Captain in the 3rd Regiment of the Lancashire Militia. Mary Gertrude (senior) died on 18 December 1807 and was buried on Christmas Eve at St John's Parish Church Preston. In 1809 Edward married Mary Robinson, the seventeen year old daughter of Bryan Robinson of Holmeshead near Ambleside.

Whilst Darwen Bank remained the family seat, in 1809 Edward leased Dove's Nest, Ambleside from its owner Mr John Benson. Miss Weeton writing from Dove's Nest stated that Edward had fallen in love with Mary Robinson, who had been employed by him as a dairymaid at Darwen Bank. Miss Weeton recounted that Mr Robinson, Mary's father, fearing his daughter might be seduced, sent for Mary to come home. However, Edward followed Mary, took her off to Gretna Green and married her[4]. There are no records to indicate if Mary Robinson was in Mr Pedder's employ prior to their marriage. Edward and Mary married on 7 August 1809 at the church of St Michael and All Angels in the village of Hawkshead[5], not at Gretna Green as recorded by Miss Weeton.

Records relating to the inquest into Mary Gertrude's death in 1810, simply records that the coroner charged £1 "to an inquisition

taken on view of the body of Mary Gertrude Pedder at Dove Nest"
and seven shillings and six pence for travelling a distance of ten
miles on 17 February 1810, the day of her death, to view the body[6].
The Lancaster Gazette (Saturday 24 February 1810) reported the
death 'On Tuesday last, at Doves-Nest, near Ambleside, aged
8, Miss Pedder, daughter of Edward Pedder, Esq. Her death was
occasioned by her cloaths [sic.] taking fire.'

Hall[7] states that Edward Pedder took Dove's Nest on a seven year
lease and vacated the property on the expiration of the lease in 1816.
However, in December 1811 and April 1812, Mr Thomas Benson
advertised in the Lancaster Gazette that Dove's Nest, occupied by
Edward Pedder, was to be let. On 11 September 1813, Dorothy
Wordsworth wrote an account of an auction sale of furniture and
household items at Dove's Nest. It was clearly a lengthy sale:

> We stayed the sale out to the very last and the beds were sold by
> candle-light and all walked home in the bright moonshine, I with
> a water decanter and glass in my hand and William and Mary
> with a large looking glass – oval with a gilt frame – to be hung
> in the best lodging room – very cheap 1£ 13s [sic]. Fanny went
> home with a loaded cart...[8]

The major sale of the contents of Dove's Nest suggest that the
Pedders left Dove's Nest about that time.

On 24 January 1822, Mary Pedder's father, Bryan Robinson,
died at Darwen Bank[9].

Edward and Mary had four children. Their three sons, Thomas
Edward, born in 1826, John Robinson, born in 1830 and Richard
Wallace, born in 1831 were born at Darwen Bank. In March 1833
their fourth child, Margaret Mary, was born at Bowness[10]. It is at this
time that Gale House Ambleside became their primary residence
and Darwen Bank was leased for £125 per annum, to Miles Rodget,
a cotton spinner.

Edward Pedder died on 19 January 1835 and was buried at St
John's Church Preston. Edward's will placed his estate into trust. It
made provision for his widow, Mary, to receive an annual allowance
of £400. Following the realisation of his property and goods his four
children received an equal share of his estate amounting to £9,639
19s 2d per child.

Edward and Mary's eldest son, Thomas Edward, became a
Captain in the 31st Regiment of Foot, he died in Ireland aged 28

years in 1853 and like his father, was buried at St John's Church Preston. The church contains a memorial tablet for Edward, Mary Gertrude, his first wife and their daughter Mary Gertrude. Hall[11] highlights the absence of 'the second Mrs Pedder's' name on the memorial 'slab'. During the thirty seven years between the deaths of Edward and Mary, the Pedders had suffered the humility of the 1861 banking scandal[12]. Edward and Mary's children were infants when their father died. By the time of their mother's death, the family had resided in Ambleside for thirty nine years and had witnessed the building and consecration of St Mary's Church in Ambleside. It is understandable that Mary was buried there, perhaps because her surviving family did not regard a memorial at Preston as being necessary.

In 1809, Miss Weeton described Mary Pedder's "ardent desire to improve." By April 1810 she wrote, "but for literature, Mrs P. has not the least taste. Her common lessons she submits to as tasks, with very great reluctance..." By November 1810 Miss Weeton states that Mrs Pedder has entirely given up her studies, "...she cannot bear books, nor even to hear one read." Hall highlights that Miss Weeton makes no reference to William Wordsworth in her letters or journals[13]. Whilst the young Mary had shown little interest in books, by the 1840s she had developed links with the poet Hartley Coleridge, eldest son of Samuel Taylor Coleridge. On 2 June 1841 Coleridge gave the eight year old Margaret Mary Pedder an unpublished sonnet. The second page of the document consists of notes on the sonnet handwritten by Mary Pedder[14].

By 1850 Mary was exchanging books with Mary Wordsworth, wife of the poet William Wordsworth. Residing in the rare book special collections of the National Library of Scotland is an 1850 copy of William Wordsworth's 'Select Pieces', which bears a brief dedication written by Mary Wordsworth: 'To Mary Pedder, With the thanks of Mary Wordsworth, for her kind acceptance of this Book, in exchange for One much more valuable, to them Both. Rydal Mount, Sept 17 1850'[15].

In 1857 Mary Pedder of Gale House, Ambleside, published a twelve page book containing the poem (first published in 1854) 'The Charge of the Light Brigade' by Alfred, Lord Tennyson.

Mary Pedder continued to reside at Gale House Ambleside until her death on 7 May 1872.

Andrew Heyes MA(Ed)

References/Notes:

1. The First and Second Supplementary Militia Regiments were raised in 1797 and later became the 2nd and 3rd Royal Lancashire Militia Regiments. In 1813 the latter was re-titled the 3rd Royal Lancashire Militia (The Prince Regent's Own).
2. The Shawes of Preston were also a prominent Preston family. William Shawe was an attorney-at-law and purchased the manor of Fishwick.
3. Mary Gertrude's birth and baptism do not appear to have been recorded. Miss Weeton describes her as being ten years old in 1809. A memorial Tablet in St John's Church Preston describes her as being ten years of age at the time of her death in 1810. Reporting her death the Lancaster Gazette (24th February 1810) states that she was aged eight.
4. Miss Weeton's journal of a governess, 1807-1825, 2 vols., ed. by E. Hall (Newton Abbot: David & Charles (Holdings) Limited, 1969). Volume 1 Page 218.
5. Source: Original Registers of St Michael and All Angels, Hawkshead, Lancashire, held at Kendal Record Office
6. Account of Robinson Cartmell, coroner, for taking inquisitions upon Robert Nelson, Thomas Brecks, Mary Gertrude Pedder and Jane Fallow (Cumbria Archive Service, Ref. WQ/SR/638/10)
7. Miss Weeton's journal of a governess, 1807-1825, 2 vols., ed. by E. Hall (Newton Abbot: David & Charles (Holdings) Limited, 1969). Volume 1 Pages 210 and 324.
8. De Selincourt, E., 1937, *The Letters of William and Dorothy Wordsworth: The middle years: pt. II.* Clarendon Press. Page 576.
9. Westmoreland Gazette, Saturday 16th February 1822.
10. Westmoreland Gazette, Saturday 30th March 1833. 'On Wednesday week, the lady of Edw. Pedder Esq. of Gale House, Ambleside, of a daughter.'
11. Miss Weeton's journal of a governess, 1807-1825, 2 vols., ed. by E. Hall (Newton Abbot: David & Charles (Holdings) Limited, 1969). Volume 1 Page 324.
12. During the financial crisis of the late 1700s the Bank of England suspended cash payments and about 300 banks across the country stopped payments to their customers. Pedder's bank, the only bank in Preston at the time, was one of only fifty banks nationally to stand firm and keep its doors open. As a result, 'As safe as Pedder's' was a common saying in Preston and district. By 1861 the bank was being run by Edward, a son of Edward Pedder's brother James, whilst another son, Henry Newsham Pedder, pursued a military career and was a silent partner in the bank. Following the sudden death of Edward, in March of that year, his brother, Henry, set up a committee to examine the accounts of the bank to settle Edward's estate. It transpired that up to date balance sheets had not been produced for several years. Whilst the bank had received deposits of £600,000 it had debts of £700,000. Edward had overdrawn his private account by £90,000 and had spent a further £70,000 on his estates. Additionally Henry owed the bank £40,000. Together the Pedder brothers had spent £200,000 of the bank's money on private expenditure. The collapse of the bank became a national scandal and rather than face legal proceedings Pedder property and estates were sold to pay off the debts. This must have been a major shock to the people of Preston, for whom the name Pedder had become synonymous with financial security. (Source: A Brief History of Pedder and Co,)

13. 13 Miss Weeton's journal of a governess, 1807-1825, 2 vols., ed. by E. Hall (Newton Abbot: David & Charles (Holdings) Limited, 1969). Volume 1 Pages 213, 254 and 324.
14. Hartley Coleridge Collection, Harry Ransom Center, The University of Texas at Austin: Manuscript Collection MS-0859 (Container 12.1)
15. The book, currently in the National Library of Scotland's rare book special collections (shelfmark: L.C.72), can be traced to a legacy bequeathed to Lady Margaret Hall at the University of Oxford by Margaret Mary Pedder following her death in 1883. Lady Margaret Hall College, was founded in 1878 and was the first women's college in Oxford. Its first principal was Elizabeth Wordsworth, the great-niece of William Wordsworth. Council Minutes for the college (vol. 1 1878-1884, Ref: GOV/1/1/1) contain a handwritten report of the year by Elizabeth Wordsworth inserted into the volume, titled ' April 23 1883', it is noted: "One or two kind gifts in money amounting to about £8 in all have been made to the Poor Students Fund and a legacy from Miss Pedder of Ambleside has been bequeathed to the Library, including prayer book said to have belonged to Charles I and three volumes of Ruskin's modern painters." (p.73).

Appendix V

Rev. Alexander Steill (1768-1832)

ALEXANDER Steill was born at Portsea, Hampshire, in February 1768. He responded to his call to ministry by first entering the Independent Academy at Gosport as one of its early students. He remained there for four years, during which time his theological studies brought about 'solidity and richness.' After preaching at Fareham, near Gosport, he moved to Winchester, where he settled and was ordained. He then ministered to the Congregational Church in the city. He remained at Winchester for five years, before receiving a call from the church at Kidderminster, where he ministered from 1798 to 1809. Then he ministered at various places in and around London, before removing to Wigan, Lancashire, after accepting a unanimous invitation from the congregation of St Paul's Independent Chapel, Standishgate.

As a minister, Steill was distinguished by sound learning, accurate theological knowledge and was skilled in Biblical criticism. His preaching was characterised by discriminating opinions on divine truth and was known for having 'solidity' rather than 'ornament.' His sermons were written to 'inform judgement and impress the heart,' rather than 'please the imagination and captivate the fancy.'

As a man, he was known for his extreme Calvinism and inflexible integrity, with a stern, uncompromising adherence to principles. He always said what he meant and abhorred any 'fawning and cringing.' It is said that his heart was seen on his face and his words represented the thoughts on his mind. Steill's resolute personality inevitably brought about conflict.

Despite his excellent standards, his theological learning and his powerful preaching, he was not an easy man to engage with. Equally forthright Miss Nelly Weeton described Steill as: 'A very worldly kind of man, haughty and overbearing, and of the most bitter temper, and not a fit companion for any inexperienced minister.'

Miss Weeton was far from alone in her unflattering appraisal of Steill. In the summer of 1810, a Mr Edmund Alston, who later became one of the first members of the new Hope Congregational Chapel in the town, had cause to record: 'Uneasiness among the congregation [at St Paul's] broke out in various forms . . . Many of the people had left the place for worship in rooms, and some to the Baptist Chapel.' As with most Independents of Steill's day, he would have had little in common with Presbyterians. The matter of doctrines and sectarian distinctions, more than likely being an equally important reason for the secessions from Steill's congregation. It should be noted that some who left St Paul's at that time were increasingly of the heretical Antinomian view, that Christians are by grace set free from any need to observe the moral law. Yet there were others in the congregation who were considered 'moderate' and 'scriptural.'

It is known that Steill was a great bibliophile and 'possessed one of the best private libraries in the Kingdom,' although it is not believed that he published anything himself, beyond a sermon. His library was large enough to require Wigan printer and publisher, J. Brown, to publish a catalogue of the contents of his library after his death, entitled: 'A Catalogue of the Library of the Late Alexander Steill,' (1833).

Steill's ministry appears to have been one of firm commitment. Under his pastoral oversight at St Paul's Chapel, attendance was good and the congregation 'attentive.' An 1829 Government Survey of non-conformist churches recorded St Paul's, Independent Chapel, Standishgate, Wigan, as having 1200 adherents.

Rev. Alexander Steill laboured at Wigan for 21 years. He died in March 1832, age 64. His wife, Mary, had died earlier, in April 1829, aged 60.

A.R.

References:

Evangelical Magazine (April 1833).
'Ebenezer' - St. Paul's Independent Chapel, Standishgate, Wigan. Compiled by Rev William Roaf (1847).
The Chronicle of St Paul's. Compiled by Ray L. Whittle (1977).
Miss Weeton's writings.

Appendix VI

Rev. John Holgate (1787-1850)

JOHN Holgate was born at Martin Top, located on the borders of Lancashire and Yorkshire, near Clitheroe. He was educated for the ministry at Idle Independent Academy, near Bradford. Rev William Vint was sole tutor at Idle, which was founded by him in his home in 1800. John Holgate completed his studies there in 1821 and soon afterwards began his ministry as a 'missionary' among impoverished and illiterate residents in the South Lancashire village of Far Moor (Orrell, near Wigan). Within two years of his arrival, Salem Independent Chapel was erected there in 1824 to replace an earlier structure. The Chapel at Far Moor was also the place of Holgate's ordination in November 1823.

The isolated village population consisted almost exclusively of self-employed nail makers and coal miners, working in the then famous Orrell Coalfield. At that time, frequent colliery explosions were the cause of many families losing their sole means of income. In Far Moor, this resulted in extensive destitution and a large number of orphans. One of Holgate's first priorities, therefore, was to embark on a personal mission to raise funds to build a village school. To realise his dream he travelled the length and breadth of Lancashire and into Cheshire on foot, preaching and begging wherever he went. Holgate's school was eventually opened in 1829 and was greatly appreciated by members of all denominations. The school offered a free education for all children, irrespective of 'class' or 'denomination', and records reveal that at one time no less than 55 orphans attended the school.

Holgate was known in the area to be a good, benevolent and humble man. He was referred to by his wife, Caroline, as 'ill-used' and he would often neglect his own welfare to ensure the well-being of others. He was never a wealthy man and was rarely comfortable. He never owned a horse, nor, according to Miss Weeton, did he own any books of substance; unlike his ministerial colleague, Rev Alexander Steill, at St Paul's Chapel, Wigan, whose personal library contained a large collection of theological classics.

In the circumstances it is unfortunate that Miss Weeton had an unhappy experience in her working association with Holgate, accusing him on one occasion of 'un-Christian behaviour'.

Allegedly, the direct result of Holgate acting on scurrilous comments with regard to her character. According to Miss Weeton, it seems that Steill had implied to Holgate that she 'would bring disgrace on the Society'. Yet at the same time, by way of contradiction, Miss Weeton also conceded that she believed Mr Holgate to be 'a most worthy man'.

In an effort to try to resolve the controversy, Holgate did his best to give Miss Weeton the benefit of the doubt, by calling at her home to give her a fair and impartial hearing. Sadly for both Miss Weeton and Holgate, irrespective of his personal opinion, he was not the final decision maker at Salem. Both he and Miss Weeton were subject to the opinions and subsequent votes of 12 'illiterate, coarse-looking, poor men and women' who, in a formal meeting, failed to vote unanimously that Miss Weeton should remain a teacher at the chapel. In the absence of a unanimous decision in her favour, Miss Weeton decided to leave Salem 'without any feelings of resentment.'

During Holgate's 30 years of labour, never having ministered other than in and around the village of Far Moor, he ended his ministry in the place where he began. Throughout his life he remained consistent in his attachment to the truths of the Gospel. His name was greatly revered and it became a household name well into the 20th century. A marble tablet in the church describes him as: 'A good and pious Christian, and in him his flock lost a good and faithful shepherd.'

Rev John Holgate died aged 63, in November 1850. His wife, Caroline, died aged 67, in September 1865. Both lie side by side in the graveyard of the chapel, now known as Salem United Reformed Church.

A.R.

References:

Nightingale, B. *Lancashire Nonconformity, Sketches, Historical and Descriptive – The Churches of Wigan, Warrington, St Helens, &c.*. Published by John Heywood, Manchester (1893).
Congregational Literary Register, 1850.
Miss Weeton's writings.

Appendix VII

Rev. William Marshall (1792-1861)

WILLIAM Marshall was born in Glasgow on 31 December 1792, where he was educated for the ministry at the University, although he does not appear to have graduated. On finishing his course he spent time in London, before accepting the pastorate of the Congregational Church in Macclesfield, Cheshire, where he served from 1815 to 1822. It was while at Macclesfield that he married Elizabeth, the daughter of Thomas and Mary Marsden, at Wigan Parish Church, on 10 April 1820. Thomas and Mary Marsden were prominent members of Hope Congregational Chapel, Wigan.

In 1812, the Rev John Ralph appeared in Wigan and was made 'the rallying point' by several who had left St Paul's Chapel, Standishgate, Wigan. By 1814 a 'regular organisation' had been formed and the new Hope Congregational Chapel was built. On the death of Ralph in September 1822, Marshall became minister there, having been a visiting preacher at Wigan for three years previously.

The prevailing religious atmosphere at Hope was not inspiring, as was the case in other non-conformist churches in the town. The small congregation at Hope had been burdened by a large debt and Marshall had to face continuing local opposition, which had accompanied his invitation to be their minister. Furthermore circumstances became exacerbated by the machinations of Rev. Alexander Steill, at St Paul's Chapel. Secession became the end result.

Historical details of actual reasons for conflict within Wigan's non-conformist congregations are not always made clear, but the ever-ready quill of Miss Weeton enables clear light to shine on some of the difficulties at Hope Chapel in the early days of Marshall's ministry. Her candid correspondence reveals that Lancashire Congregational Union had refused to nominate a minister for Hope Congregational Chapel, on the basis that 'they [Lancashire Congregational Union] would not encourage divisions and separations, and Mr Steill's Chapel was sufficient for the congregation.'

It should be noted that the secession from Hope had nothing to do with the character and personality of Rev William Marshall. At that time, and from the last quarter of the 18th century, congregations were often divided in their views. It was quite common to find Unitarian families worshipping with a Trinitarian society, or vice-versa. Hope Chapel member, Mr E. Alston, records that four members were "intent on doing interest at Hope Chapel all the mischief in their power . . . nothing could please but Antinomian doctrines."

Marshall's ministerial friends appear to have included many, who being Presbyterians like himself, were invited to preach from the Hope Chapel pulpit. As a result, customs of a Presbyterian character, both in government and discipline became the norm, before the passage of time brought about changes identified with modern Congregationalism.

It is clear from Miss Weeton's correspondence that she was most impressed by Rev. William Marshall. She opined: "Mr Marshall is a young man I esteem very highly. Having married Mr Marsden's daughter, my intimacy with Mrs Marsden has occasioned me to see much of him. His talents are considerable; but what I think of greater importance, is the Christian softness, forbearance, and benevolent liberality of his temper."

William Marshall was determined and committed in his ministry at Wigan. By 1827 he was able to write: "Time, that destroyer of all things, appears to deaden in a considerable degree that spirit of prejudice which was in being, with awful violence once, against poor Hope Chapel in the bosoms of not a few who call themselves Christians."

By 1829 a Government survey of non-conformist meetings and returns for Wigan, recorded that Hope Congregational Chapel, had 1,400 adherents.

Miss Weeton's high-opinion of Marshall, and her close friendship with his wife, Elizabeth and her parents, Thomas and Mary Marsden, ultimately proved to be the answer to an increasingly pressing dilemma which had troubled Miss Weeton as far back as 1810: To whom could she entrust her precious copy letter books and other autobiographical writings? Marshall proved to be the perfect answer. As instructed in her will, all her writings were left in his care.

It is evident that in the last five years of Rev William Marshall's life, he suffered ill-health and was unable to perform fully the duties of the pastorate. In July 1861, while on a visit to Shropshire, he was taken ill. He died 22 August while still in office. **A.R.**

References:

Horsman, J. Basil. *A History of Hope Congregational Church, Wigan, 1812-1962.* Thomas Wall and Sons Limited (1962).
Shaw, William B. *The Story of Presbyterianism in Wigan.* Sherratt and Hughes, Manchester (1912).
Miss Weeton's writings.

Appendix VIII

Miss Weeton as a poet

AMONGST the few extant poems that Miss Weeton wrote, one poem – "A Ramble in Dean Wood near Up Holland" contains enough subject matter to allow an informed opinion of her skill as a poet to be made. The poem consists of 105 quatrains linked by themes which are themselves loosely connected. If Miss Weeton deliberately included the theme of "rambling" with its double meaning for the style in which she wrote, then she was remarkably prescient.

The opening stanza sets the scene –

> *Dear are these hills and dear these vales*
> *but tenfold dear this wood*
> *where list'ning to the rustling gales*
> *full many an hour I've stood.*

She goes on to address the "*Great Power above*" and also to applaud "*Thou the great First Cause*". She is clearly in love with the place and refers to visiting the wood with her brother when she would listen to him playing his flute. But almost immediately she changes the poem's mood as she considers the hardships of local colliers who daily face the possibility of an early death -

> *How many toiling in those mines*
> *are crushed to instant death!*
> *their promised years, their fond design*
> *all dwindled to a breath.*

She then descends to ramble by the stream where she encounters some children playing and with delight joins in their fun as a passing collier laughs at her. "*Laugh on,*" she says,"*their harmless sports I'll join/dance, laugh or sing as they,*" and as she sees the flowers that the children twine into head dresses, she moralises on vanity, the blessedness of innocence and the delights of watching children mature. She seems now to have taken the children on board – "Well*! now my dears shall we proceed?*" This would come naturally to a schoolmistress given such an opportunity to pass on her own experiences to a younger generation. This she does at length, as she refers to significant trees and the varied colours of the landscape. These together cause her to muse on "*. . .the scenery of man's much* *chequer'd life."* Perhaps there is hint here of the vicissitudes of her own life. As she does so, she returns in verse to "*Those ragged children scrambling there/ . . ./do seem so happy and so gay/so sweetly innocent.*" As the children "*. . . in the streamlet wade/and sing their simple song,*" she cannot refrain from commenting "*. . .for sure your lot well might excite/the envy e'en of kings.*"

She soon reaches a cottage and presents us with portraits of the occupants – first a Captain and then a Lord and his Lady. These names are clearly soubriquets because Miss Weeton's subsequent descriptions leave us in no doubt as to their poverty. The Captain for example –"*his aged shoes are nought but soles/tied on with leather straps . . .,*" and then – "*My lord, decrepit, thin and old/hair silver, striped with jet,*" owns a wagon (not a carriage!) and pair, and she notes that each driver is also footman. Again she compares the poverty before her with the wealthy at whom she pokes fun, addressing them with the question – "*Can ye so drive and stand behind/ye lordly hair-brain'd race?*" Having dealt with "My lady's" attire –

> *The handkerchief around her neck*
> *so negligently cast*
> *in tatters dangles down her back*
> *as pendant from a mast.*

She considers her own attitude and regrets her sarcasm with another homily before saying farewell to the hills, vales and the wood, reprising the opening stanza - "*where list'ning to the rustling gales/so many hours I've stood.*"

To write a poem of one hundred and five stanzas maintaining a common metre (8,6,8,6) rhythm is an achievement by any standards. To provide at the same time a social document of some importance concerning rural life at the start of the nineteenth century is something more, especially when it also offers an insight into the mind of the writer. Miss Weeton, although contemporary with, was no Wordsworth, but she shared his love of, and insight into, nature and she expresses in this poem her own thoughts on beauty, wealth, poverty and the human condition. The departures from a regular beat and the occasional inversion or forced rhyme hardly detract from the sincerity of her writing. It was, and is, a poem written from the heart and anyone visiting Dean Wood today will find it much as Nelly Weeton described it.

Dr David Lythgoe

IN 1810 Miss Weeton was in her 34th year. Since December 1809 she had been experiencing life and work as a governess in the household of Edward Pedder, Esq., at the 'charming seat' of Dove's Nest, Ambleside. During the autumn of 1810, she was moved to write 'An Essay' in which she reflected on a society that denied the right of women to excel based on gender alone. With piercing foresight she recognised that as men 'rise in knowledge' and become 'truly enlightened,' respect for the female mind will bring with it equality of opportunity:

'An Essay'

We very often meet with authors of the present day, as well as with those of more ancient date, who speak with great contempt of women. However brilliant the talents of such may be, they must be greatly deficient, not only in liberality of opinion, but in justice of sentiment. Nay, even in common conversation, the severest sarcasms are still levelled at woman, as a distinct kind of being from man; and amongst men who profess a superior degree of refinement, it is often avowed that when they occasionally forbear direct expressions of contempt, their motive is – politeness! Is not such a reason more insulting to the sex they pretend to spare, than the coarser and more open attacks of meaner capacities? For they do not profess to forbear from a conviction of the injustice of such expressions; yet, on almost every other occasion they will, in the strongest and most decided manner, repeat – that general censures are not only illiberal, but extremely unjust.

Woman almost ever since the creation has been a humbled, degraded being indeed, when compared with a man. With as just a sense of right and wrong, as strong a feeling of liberty and oppression, the same warmth of gratitude and resentment, she has been treated as if her capacity were little above the level of a brute; as if her principal gratification was only – to do evil continually; and as if she were indeed little less than infernal! Has it not often been said, that she is the 'mother of all mischief?' Yes, coolly and deliberately, have such sentiments been often uttered by man, priding himself in superiority.

A candid mind, that one day hopes to inhabit a brighter region, that is enlightened by the smallest spark of the Heavenly ray, whatever form that mind now inhabits, will, on a serious reflection of expressions so shocking, and so evidently unjust, shudder with horror.

I would not be understood to argue that woman is superior to man, I should blush to advance so weak an opinion. I would only affirm that they are equal, and ought to be treated as such in every respect. For though their virtues and their vices, their mental and their corporeal qualifications necessarily differ greatly, yet, placed in opposition to each other, they would form so exact an equipoize, that a truly impartial mind, whatever kind a form encompassed it, could perceive not the smallest line of difference.

In proportion as the mind of man has been more cultivated, and become more refined, the intellect of woman has been more highly appreciated by him. He finds, when he begins to use his understanding, that he is not so much wiser, so much better, as he used to flatter himself he was; and as he still rises in knowledge, he more clearly perceives the equality of her whom he had been taught from infancy to look down upon.

In barbarous nations, strength of body is looked upon as the most admirable qualification – here, woman must sink in estimation; but in enlightened nations, where superiority of mind is most sought and most highly admired when found, woman will inevitably rise up to the level of man in wisdom, virtue and dignity. May it not then be justly inferred, that whoever censures woman as inferior to man, debases himself by it. If the censure is in a slight degree, he sinks a little below the level of a truly enlightened mind; and, in proportion as he is more severe, so much the nearer does he approach to the tyrant, the barbarian, and the savage.

E. Weeton,
18th October 1810

Index

Note: Miss Weeton's spellings of personal and place names have been corrected in the index where appropriate.
The letter n following a page number indicates an endnote.

Allonby, 119, 120–1, 123
Alston, Edmund, 351, 352
Alston, Mrs, 295, 299, 351
Ambleside, 144, 160
  Dove's Nest, 81, 83, 87, 90–2,
    111–12, 119, 131, 162
  Greens' home, 161
Appley Bridge, 49, 214, 283
Armitage, Emma, 203, 213, 276
Armitage, George (Joseph's
  father), 190–1, 201, 203, 230
Armitage, George (Joseph's son),
  193–4, 195, 203, 222, 223, 276
Armitage, Joseph, 178, 191, 192,
  196, 199, 204, 229, 230, 231
Armitage, Joseph (Joseph's son),
  203
  N.W.'s letter to, 276–7
Armitage, Marianne, 201, 208
Armitage, Miss C.: N.W.'s letter
  to, 280–1
Armitage, Mrs (Joseph's wife),
  192, 196, 199, 201, 207–9, 217,
  222, 230, 231
  N.W.'s letter to, 213
Armitage, Sarah Ann, 193–4, 195,
  235, 276
  N.W.'s letter to, 233–4
Armitage family, 190–1, 195, 201,
  203, 207, 216–17, 218, 230, 265
Askins, Mrs (Isle of Man) 183

Ball, Mr and Mrs (farmers), 264,
  266, 275, 290, 299, 334
balloons, 320
Bankes, Anne, 53–4
Bankes, Meyrick, 54, 231
Bannister, Mr (clergyman), 9

Barlow, James (apprentice), 302,
  304, 310, 311, 312, 313, 315,
  316, 323
Barlow family (London), 315–16
Barton, Margaret (née Rawlinson)
  (N.W.'s aunt), 3, 6, 12, 13, 21–2,
  39, 44–5, 49, 56, 60, 65, 97, 108,
  109, 121, 125, 184, 200, 204,
  208, 210, 212, 214–15, 220, 222,
  224–5, 226, 263n12
  N.W.'s letters to, 23–4, 24–5,
    28, 42, 47–8, 52–3, 62, 68,
    71, 74–5, 78–9, 94–7, 123,
    139–42
Barton, Mr (E. Pedder's steward),
  76–7, 83, 84, 86, 87, 101, 126
Barton, Thomas (N.W.'s uncle), 6,
  22, 49, 50, 58, 60, 62, 97, 200,
  208, 214, 215, 219, 220, 221,
  222, 223–4, 225–6, 235, 253
bathing, 61
Beacon's Gutter, 25–6, 29, 40
Benson, Mrs (London landlady),
  312, 313, 323
Billinge, 288, 304
Billington, Anthony (carrier),
  306n5, 324
Bingley, Rev William: North
  Wales Guide, 357
Bird, Catherine see Braithwaite,
  Catherine
Bird, Rev John, 350, 351
Bird, Mrs (Jane Weeton's sister),
  246
Bispham Hall, 234
Bolton, Col, 134, 135
Bolton, Miss, 17
Borrowdale, 136–7, 154

Boswell, James: A Journal of a Tour to the Hebrides with Dr Johnson, 147
Braithwaite, Mrs Anne, 13, 16, 19, 27–8, 49, 184, 215, 223, 224, 225, 258, 259, 265, 275, 278, 279, 280, 347
  N.W.'s letter to, 27–8
Braithwaite, Anne, 96
  N.W.'s letter to, 16–17
Braithwaite, Catherine (later Mrs Bird), 212, 225, 234, 265, 290, 292, 296, 298, 353, 355n13
  N.W.'s letters to, 44–6, 48–9, 196–8, 199–201, 202–3, 221–3, 229–31, 314–18, 319–24, 341–2
Braithwaite, Elisabeth, 265, 290, 292, 293, 296–8
Braithwaite, Rev John, 7, 45, 189
Braithwaite, Margaret see Jackson, Margaret
Braithwaite, Mary, 265, 333, 342
Braithwaite, Rev Richard, 7
Braithwaite family, 44, 96, 200–1, 266
Broadhead, Miss, 48
Bronte, Charlotte, 235n5
Brougham, Henry Peter, 1st Baron, 319
burns treatment, 98–100
butter making, 139, 140
Byron, George Gordon, 6th Baron: funeral, 325

Calvinism, 380
canals, 21, 22, 49, 50–1, 52, 283
Canning, George, 319
caravans, 339–40
Caroline, Princess (later Queen), 332n10
carts, 287, 302
Castlereagh, Robert Stewart, Viscount, 141

Charlotte Augusta, Princess, 141, 152
Chester, 64
Chesterfield, Philip Dormer Stanhope, 4th Earl of: Letters to his Son, 147–8
childbirth, 53–4
Chorley, Mary, 22, 24, 27, 31, 32–7, 39, 41, 47, 54, 89, 113–14, 184
  N.W.'s letters to, 18–19, 22–3
Chorley, Mr, 32–3, 37–8, 47–8, 265
Chorley, Mrs, 31–2, 35, 37, 47, 70, 77, 159, 265
  N.W.'s letters to, 88–92, 105–6, 120–1, 136–9
Chorley family, 22, 23, 24, 26, 27, 28–9, 41, 43
Christianity, 380
Clements, Mr, 38, 148
Coleridge, Samuel Taylor, 92
Congregationalism, 306nn2, 7, 380
Coniston, 154
cotton trade, 21
countryside: compared with town, 22–3, 55–6, 61
crafts, 109–10
crime and punishment, 188
Crosthwaite, P., 121
Cumberland
  Allonby, 119, 120–1, 123
  Borrowdale, 136–7, 154
  Keswick, 121, 138
  Skiddaw, 137–8

Dalrymple, Miss (Liverpool), 57, 276, 337, 358–9
  N.W.'s letters to, 273–4, 279–80, 287–8, 318–19, 362–3
Dannett, Margery, 58, 283, 299, 353
  N.W.'s letters to, 310–14, 349–51

Deeds of Separation, 259–60, 275, 288, 299, 376, 379
Dennett, Miss *see* Dannett, Margery
Dissenters *see* Congregationalism
Ditchfield, Elizabeth (née Rawlinson) (N.W.'s aunt), 3, 5
Ditchfield, Thomas (N.W.'s uncle), 3
divorce, 262n5, 332n10
Dodson, Mrs (née Prescott), 170–1, 177–8, 181, 184, 187, 197, 198, 265
    N.W.'s letters to, 194–6, 206–7
domestic violence, 118, 130–1, 134, 146, 156, 160, 241, 248, 257–9, 347

Edmondson, Mrs, 77, 161, 265
    N.W.'s letters to, 17, 122
Edwards, Mrs (Mrs Price's sister), 178, 211

fairs
    Greenwich, 318, 319, 321
    Wigan, 242
Far Moor (Orrell): Salem Independent (Congregational) Chapel, 269, 270–2, 273–4
farming, 139–40, 171–2
Fawel, Rev J., 80n16
ferries
    Menai Strait, 358, 360, 365–6
    Thames, 318–19
Fleming, Lady Diana, 142
Frederick, Duke of York, 324–5
'Friend, The' (newspaper), 92

Gaskell, James (musician), 307n17
Gaskell, Mr (solicitor), 259, 288, 304, 350
George III, King, 230
George IV, King, 324, 332nn10, 14
Gibson family (Birkland Barrow), 2

Gilbert, Hannah (Aaron Stock's step-daughter), 239, 247, 251, 252
governesses: status of, 171, 195–6, 199, 209
Green, Mrs, 146, 162, 265
    N.W.'s letters to, 147, 228–9
Green, William (artist), 94, 144–6, 151, 161, 229
Grundy, Mr (Parr Hall), 256, 257, 288–9, 300–1, 342, 343, 349, 351–2, 353
Grundy, Mrs (Parr Hall), 256, 257, 267, 293, 351
    N.W.'s letter to, 267–9

Hall, Edward: Miss Weeton's Journal of a Governess, 377, 379–80, 381
Hall, Miss (Liverpool), 69
Hampton, John, 165n18
Harris, Thomas (balloonist), 320
Hawarden, Dr, 247, 267, 277, 334, 336
Hawarden, Miss: N.W.'s letters to, 266–7, 338–40, 341, 351–2
Hawarden, Mrs, 278, 347
Hawarden family, 285–6
haymaking, 139
Hemans, Felicia Dorothea, 164n9
Henley-on-Thames, 328
Henshaw, Mrs (Mrs Armitage's mother), 216, 217
Hill, Rowland, 321
Hindley, William, 212, 223, 225
Hoghton family (Walton Hall), 3
Holgate, Rev John, 269, 270, 271–2, 274, 333
Honley, 190, 201
    High Royd, 192, 196, 207, 216, 217, 220, 229
honours system, 230
Huddersfield
    house fires, 223
    Luddite riots, 191, 196

Hudson family (London), 323,
326–7, 328
Hughes, Mrs (Wales), 364, 372–3
Huntriss, Mrs (Liverpool), 24–5, 29

Independency, 306n2
Irish immigrants, 330–1
Irving, Edward, 326, 327–8
Isle of Man, 168–89
    agriculture, 171–2
    Castletown, 179
    Douglas, 168, 169–70, 171,
        172, 175, 198
    fishing industry, 172
    food prices, 172
    Kirk Braddon, 173
    Kirk Conchan, 175–6
    Kirk Santon, 175
    laws, 188
    Laxey, 175, 177
    Manx language, 175
    Peel, 179, 188
    poverty, 174
    Ramsey, 183
    schools, 175
    Snaefell, 174, 177, 185, 382
    trade, 172
    Tynwald mount, 180
    West-Kella, 181, 182

Jackson, Margaret (née
    Braithwaite), 265, 287, 310, 311,
    325, 333–4
Jackson, Miss (Parr Hall teacher),
    342, 349, 352, 353, 354
Jackson, Mrs (née Hawarden), 140
Jackson, Richard (N.W.'s tenant),
    236n12
    N.W.'s letter to, 42–3
Jackson, Thomas Tellaw, 265, 333,
    334
Jackson family (Liverpool), 211
Johnson, Dr Samuel, 137, 147

Johnson, Mrs (London landlady),
    312
journeymen, 262n8

Keswick, 121, 138
knighthoods, 230

Lacy, Miss (Mrs Henshaw's grand-
    daughter), 216, 217
Lamberhead Green Methodist
    Chapel (Pemberton), 272
Lancashire Congregational Union,
    306n2, 7
Lancaster
    Captain Thomas Weeton
        honoured in, 2
    Lunatic Asylum, 377
    slave trade, 1
Lancaster, Joseph, 189n4
land prices, 138
Langdale Pikes, 154
Latham, Anne (Nanny) (N.W.'s
    cousin), 13, 94, 95, 110, 125,
    144, 162–3, 223, 225, 226–8, 350
Latham, Henry (N.W.'s nephew
    and Godchild), 42, 57, 62, 96,
    125, 140, 283, 350, 353
    N.W.'s letters to, 26, 142–4
Latham, J. (N.W.'s cousin), 78,
    258
Latham, Richard (N.W.'s
    nephew), 26, 42, 96, 125
Leamington, 329
Leigh, 18, 19, 49, 77–8, 253
Lewis, Mr (artist), 151
libraries, 36, 88, 114–15, 274, 364,
    365
Lichfield, 310, 315
Littler, Mrs, 347
Littler, Dr Thomas Caldwell,
    355n11
Lively (ship), 2, 4
Liverpool, 21, 55–6, 382
    business, 148
    Christ Church, 27, 48

exhibition of Androides (sic), 233
Great George Street Congregational Chapel, 306n7
Holy Trinity Parish Church, 237
Necropolis Cemetery, 377
stagecoaches from, 309
Liverpool Mercury, 309
Llandaff, Bishop of, 137–9, 142
Lodge, Miss J. (Liverpool), 57–8, 63–4
London, 316–28
British Museum, 323
Burlington Arcade, 321
Carlton Palace, 321
Doctors' Commons, 325
Fleet Street, 317–18
General Post Office, 316
Greenwich, 318–19, 321
Hatton Garden Chapel, 326, 327
Hyde Park, 324–5
Independent Chapel, Mile End Road, 321
Kensington Gardens, 323
Magdalen Hospital, St George's Fields, 323
maps of, 321
Paternoster Row, 321
Picture of London, The (guidebook), 309–10, 314, 321
public conveniences, lack of, 322
Ranelagh Gardens, 323
St Margaret's Church, 321
St Paul's Cathedral, 316, 317, 318
shops, 321–2
Smithfield Market, 321
Surrey Chapel, Blackfriars Road, 321, 323
Tower of London, 320

Whitechapel Church, 311
Longman, Hurst, Rees, Brown, and Orme's (publishers), 321
Lowe family (Southport), 283, 284
Luddites, 191, 192, 196, 202, 204
Lyon, George (criminal), 54

McAdam, John Loudon, 315
M'Cartney, William (N.W.'s agent), 38, 128–9, 148–9, 151, 154, 158, 161
Manchester, 191–2
Marsden, Mary, 265, 267, 283, 290, 334, 347
N.W.'s letter to, 269–72
Marsden, Thomas, 278, 279
Marsh, Mr (Magistrate), 259
Marshall, Rev William, 277, 376, 378
Martland, Mr (Liverpool), 48
Marwood, Miss (dressmaker), 135
Melling, Edward (carrier), 266, 282
Meols see North Meols
Methodism, 380
Meyrick, Rev Thomas, 45, 54, 355n13
Minerva Press, 206
Moneypenny, Mrs (Wales), 285–6, 287
Morris, Mrs, 299–300
music education, 336

Napoleonic Wars 231, 262n9
Peninsular Wars 264
Nelly (ship), 1
Newell, William (N.W.'s son-in-law), 377
Nicholson, Margaret (Peg), 230
North Meols, 18, 112
Norton, Caroline Elizabeth Sarah, 378–9
Orange, Prince of see William, Prince of Orange

Orrell *see* Far Moor
Ox House Heyes, 307n17
Oxford, 328–9

Park, Mungo, 179
Parr Hall Boarding Academy (St
  Helens), 256, 261, 281, 288–9,
  301, 303, 334, 342–3, 351–2, 382
patchwork, 335
Pedder, Edward, 75, 78, 81–2,
  83, 87, 88, 89, 90, 91, 94, 101,
  102, 104, 105–6, 110, 111, 114,
  115–19, 120, 121, 123, 124, 126,
  130–4, 140, 141, 146, 150–1, 152,
  153, 156, 157–8, 160, 161, 162
Pedder, Mary (née Robinson), 75,
  76, 81, 83, 84, 87, 88, 89–90,
  94, 101, 102, 104, 105, 106, 107,
  110, 111, 114, 115, 116, 117,
  118, 122, 123, 124, 126, 127,
  130–2, 133, 134, 146, 152, 155,
  157, 161, 162
Pedder, Mary Gertrude, 81, 84,
  87–8, 97–103, 104–5, 107
Peninsular Wars *see under*
  Napoleonic Wars
pens, 341
Perkins, Mr, 343, 352
Perkins, Mrs (N.W.'s sister-in-law),
  343, 346, 352
Platt, Mr, 318, 323–4
Plurality of Worlds doctrine, 40–1
Pollard, Mr, 211
postal service, 49–50, 316, 319
potatoes, 112
poverty, 27
Prescot, 333–54
Prescott, Miss, 55, 197
Prescott, Rev Richard, 10, 11–12
Preston, 78
Price, Bessy (née Winkley): N.W.'s
  letters to, 201–2, 207–8, 212,
  217–18, 231–3, 241–2, 243,
  244–8, 277
  see also Winkley, Bessy

Price, Mrs (Bessy Price's mother-in-
  law), 163, 287, 343
Pritchard family (Garth Ferry), 358
Protestantism 254; *see also*
  Methodism

Quakers, 1, 254
quills, 341

Radcliffe, Mr (magistrate), 203–4
Raffles, Rev Dr Thomas, 274
railways, 308, 355n8
Rawlinson, Abraham (ship owner),
  1, 2
Rawlinson, John (ship owner), 2
Rawlinson, Mary (née Smith)
  (N.W.'s grandmother), 6
Rawlinson, Richard (N.W.'s
  grandfather), 3, 228
Rawlinson, Thomas Hutton (ship
  owner), 1
Rawlinson family, 1
Reformers, 245–6
religious belief, 380
rents, 287, 288
Rhodes, Miss (niece of Mr Pedder's
  steward), 76, 86, 126, 127
Robinson, Bryan (Mrs Pedder's
  father), 88, 89, 153–4
Roby, Mrs, 351, 352
Roby, Rev William, 270, 272, 352
Roman Catholicism, 254
Roxburgh, Miss (Liverpool), 285

St George, Mr and Mrs (Isle of
  Man), 181–4
Saul, Rev Thomas, 119–20, 122,
  123, 157, 238
Schofield, John (farmer), 220, 232
schools
  Ambleside, 160
  dame, 7, 9
  Douglas (Isle of Man), 175

Parr Hall Boarding Academy (St Helens), 256, 281, 288–9, 301, 342–3, 351–2, 382
Sunday, 306n6
Up Holland, 7, 307n17
Wales, 363
Scott, Mrs (Jane Weeton's mother), 15, 21
shepherds, 136–7
Siddons, Sarah, 57
Singleton, W. (Mrs Dodson's first husband), 170, 198
slave trade, 1, 21, 46
Smith, Betty (Beacon's Gutter), 29, 40, 54, 59–60, 347
Smith, Edward (Beacon's Gutter), 24, 28, 40, 59
Smith, Henry (N.W.'s cousin), 49, 70
Smith, Miss M. (Henry Smith's daughter), 41
Smith, Rev Robert, 236n17
Southport, 54, 240
stagecoaches, 245, 278, 284–5, 305, 308–9, 310, 315, 328–31, 382
Standish, 302
steam packets, 357
Steele, Sir Richard: The Conscious Lovers, 28
Steill, Rev Alexander, 239, 257, 269, 270, 274
Stock, Aaron (N.W.'s husband), 237–9, 239–40, 241, 243, 247–9, 250–2, 256, 257–9, 267, 268, 269, 270, 274, 278, 281, 288, 290–1, 299, 302, 334, 340, 341, 346, 350–1, 376–7
    N.W.'s letters to, 239–40, 274–5, 281–2, 293–6, 343–5
Stock, Elizabeth (Aaron Stock's first wife), 250, 262n3
Stock, Hannah (Aaron Stock's step-daughter), 251, 252
Stock, Jane (Aaron Stock's step-daughter), 239, 278, 345

Stock, Margaret (Aaron Stock's niece), 283, 287, 290
Stock, Mary (N.W.'s daughter), 240, 241–2, 243, 246, 255–6, 264, 267, 268–9, 274–5, 279, 281, 282–3, 288–9, 293–4, 298–9, 301, 303, 304–5, 324, 334–5, 345, 346, 348–9, 351, 352, 353–4, 367, 377
    N.W.'s letters to, 256–7, 265–6, 275–6, 292–3, 304–5, 334–7, 338, 340–1, 342–3
Stock, Matthew (Aaron Stock's father), 290–1
Stock, William (Aaron Stock's brother), 283, 291
Stock, William (Aaron Stock's nephew), 301–2
Stopford, Ann, 304, 310, 311, 312, 313, 315, 316, 318, 323, 324, 347–8
Stopford, Mr, 275–6, 290, 323, 350
Stopford, Mrs, 290, 302
    N.W.'s letter to, 346–8
Stout, William, 189n1
superstitions, 104, 136–7
Sutton, Thomas, 339

Taylor, Mr (solicitor), 278
tea trade, 314
Tennyson, Alfred, Lord: 'In Memoriam,' 376
Thurtell, J. (murderer), 322
Toothill, Abraham, 143–4
Toothill, Rev John, 271, 272
tourism, 140–1
transport see canals; caravans; ferries; railways; stagecoaches; steam packets
Tunstal, Joshua, 271

Up Holland, 49, 53
    Grammar School, 307n17
    Mr Braithwaite's school for boys, 7

Parsonage, 355n13
The Priory, 13, 49
St Thomas the Martyr Church, 264, 269, 355n11
unmarried mothers, 54, 141
Weeton family home, 6–7

Wales
Bagillt, 285, 287
Bangor, 359, 363
Beaumaris, 358, 359
Carnarvon, 362–3
Conway, 361–2, 363
Holywell, 285, 287
language, 363
Menai Suspension Bridge, 358, 360, 363
Newborough, 366
Pont Aberglaslyn, 368
Rhuddlan, 286
St Asaph, 285–6
Snowdon, 360, 368–71
Walker, Adam (author and inventor), 112
Walker, Mrs (shopkeeper), 299, 300
Wallace, Mr (counsel), 288
Warwick, 329–30
Watmough, Mr and Mrs (Liverpool), 123
Watts, Dr Isaac, 382
Weeton, Edmund (N.W.'s uncle), 2
Weeton, Edward (N.W.'s brother), 2–3
Weeton, James (N.W.'s uncle), 2
Weeton, Jane (née Scott) (N.W.'s sister-in-law), 15, 16, 58–9, 65–8, 77, 93, 105, 111, 139, 178, 184, 197, 202, 260
Weeton, Margaret (N.W.'s sister), 3
Weeton, Mary (née Rawlinson) (N.W.'s mother)
  bereavements, 4–5
  character, 8, 38, 73

dame school, 7, 9
death, 11
and French language, 196, 224, 336
grave, 62–3, 291
health, 11
marriage, 2–3
N.W.'s obedience to, 200, 367
removal to Up Holland, 6
Will, 239, 335
Weeton, Nelly
and alcohol, 329
at Allonby, 119, 120–1, 123, 126
in Ambleside, 82, 87–163
  journey to, 81, 83, 85–7, 108
appearance, 93, 180, 222, 251, 360, 365; see also clothes
aunt's legacy, 125, 225–6, 227
on baths, 367
at Beacon's Gutter, 25–6, 28, 29, 40–9, 50–5, 60–5, 72
Birkenhead visit, 285
birth, 3
birthday, 84, 93
burial record, 377, 382
canal journeys, 21, 22, 49, 50–1, 52
character, 9, 11, 32–3, 50–1, 59–60, 62, 63, 86, 117, 174, 311, 350, 367, 378, 382
in Chester, 64
Christian name, 377
class consciousness, 72, 134, 136, 138–9, 174, 244, 245, 271–2, 357, 359
climbing, 127, 154, 173–4, 183, 368–71
clothes, 55, 119, 135, 201, 224, 305, 310, 327, 373–4
and corporal punishment, 218
and countryside, 22–3, 61, 122, 128, 137, 138, 154–5, 173, 179–80
daughter's birth, 240

and death of Mary Gertrude
Pedder, 97–102, 104–5, 107–8
and Deed of Separation, 376,
379
dental surgeon visit, 27
diary (Occasional Reflections,
A.D.1818), 248–9, 253–5,
378
on diet, 329
education, 7, 244
eyesight, 332n22, 338
and fashion, 43, 113, 135
father-in-law's funeral, 290–1
financial difficulties, 12, 14,
299, 323–4
and fires, 97–101, 259, 295
fortune-teller visit, 177
and gardens, 6–7, 8, 40, 43, 45,
72, 112, 220–1
gifts to, 109–10, 113
as a godmother, 151
and gossip, 53–4, 197, 232,
315, 356n15
as a governess, 76, 77, 82, 84,
88, 103, 107, 191, 192–4,
195–6, 199, 201, 203–4, 209,
213, 217–18, 222–3, 231
on grammar, 142–3
gravestone, 63
health 11, 13–14, 39, 56, 65,
104, 121, 125, 126, 207, 299,
303, 305, 340, 358, 360, 379;
see also under
eyesight; sea sickness; travel
sickness
at High Royd, 190–235, 238
on honours system, 230
as a housekeeper, 94, 107
at Huddersfield ball, 222
imprisonment, 258
income, 38–9, 41, 65–6, 77, 95,
158, 160–1, 237, 252, 261,
280, 344
and Irish immigrants, 330–1
Isle of Man visit, 163, 166–88,

198, 382
Journal, 30 9, 44, 55, 59–60,
65–8, 77–8, 92, 115–19,
129–33, 210, 218–20, 223–8,
234–5, 278, 282–7, 288–91,
293, 296–303, 305, 334, 336,
337–8, 342–3, 345–6, 348–9,
352–4, 358–62, 364–74, 382
in Kendal bookshop, 83
in Keswick, 138
and knowledge, 209–10
on Lake Windermere, 110–11,
120
in Leamington, 329
in Leigh, 18, 19, 49, 65–8
letter writing, 121, 125, 129–
30, 155, 161, 206, 212, 265
letters
    to Armitage, Miss C.,
        280–1
    to Armitage, Joseph Jnr,
        276–7
    to Armitage, Mrs, 213
    to Armitage, Sarah Ann,
        233–4
    to Barton, Margaret, 23–4,
        24–5, 28, 42, 47–8, 52–3,
        62, 68, 71, 74–5, 78–9,
        94–7, 123, 139–42
    to Bolton, Miss, 17
    to Braithwaite, Anne, 16–17
    to Braithwaite, Catherine,
        27–8, 44–6, 48–9, 196–8,
        199–201, 202–3, 221–3,
        229–31, 314–18, 319–24,
        341–2
    to Chorley, Mary, 17–19,
        22–3
    to Chorley, Mrs, 88–92,
        105–6, 120–1, 136–9
    to Dalrymple, Miss, 273–4,
        279–80, 287–8, 318–19,
        362–3
    to Dannett, Margery, 310–
        14, 349–51

to Dodson, Mrs, 194–6, 206–7
to Edmondson, Mrs, 17, 122
to Green, Mr and Mrs, 147, 228–9
to Grundy, Mrs, 267–9
to Hawarden, Miss, 266–7, 338–40, 341, 351–2
to Jackson, Richard, 42–3
to Latham, Henry, 26, 142–4
to Marsden, Mary, 269–72
to Price, Bessy, 201–2, 207–8, 212, 217–18, 231–3, 241–2, 243, 244–8, 277; see also under Winkley, Bessy
to Smith, Henry, 240
to Stock, Aaron, 239–40, 274–5, 281–2, 293–6, 343–5
to Stock, Mary, 256–7, 265–6, 275–6, 292–3, 304–5, 334–7, 338, 340–1, 342–3
to Stopford, Mrs, 346–8
to Weeton, Thomas Richard, 19, 21–2, 24, 28–30, 38–9, 41, 42, 43, 46–7, 49–52, 56–9, 62–5, 68–74, 75– 7, 82–4, 92–4, 97–103, 111–13, 123–5, 133–5, 144, 149–52, 154–6, 157–9, 220–1, 249–52, 258, 259–60
to Whitehead, Mrs, 17, 40–1, 53–4, 60–2, 113–15, 125, 152–4
to Winkley, Ann, 162, 163, 168–89, 198–9, 203–4, 208–10, 210–11, 213–17, 221, 238
to Winkley, Bessy, 84–8, 104–5, 106–11, 119–20, 125–9, 135, 148–9, 157, 159–61, 166–8, 191–4; see also under Price, Bessy
in Liverpool, 23–4, 31–9, 43, 54, 55–6, 68–77, 113, 161–2, 188–9, 212–13, 223, 233, 241, 254–5, 284–5, 287, 302, 331, 337
journeys to, 22–3, 81, 83, 96, 328–31, 212, 352
in London, 312–28, 382
journey to, 302, 304, 305, 309, 310, 314–15
Lytham visit, 283–4
in Manchester, 191–2
on manners, 136
on marriage, 104–5, 116, 148, 316, 364–5, 368
marriage of, 237, 239–40, 241, 243, 247–9, 250–2, 256, 257–9, 268, 281–2, 343–4
memorandum books, 378
on men and women, 179, 180
and music, 41, 62, 74, 151, 166, 167, 336, 337, 374
and natural history, 342
and needlework, 41, 45, 239, 335, 337, 367, 373
as an old maid, 59
on parents, 73
and playing cards, 113–14
and Plurality of Worlds doctrine, 40–1
and politics, 97
in Prescot, 75, 214, 333–54, 376
property ownership, 38, 42–3, 128–9, 148–9, 151, 154, 158–9, 161, 202, 204, 207, 221, 222, 231–2, 261
and rats, 90–2
as a reader, 7, 8, 40, 72, 114–15, 129, 155, 161, 204–5, 337, 374

books read by, 147–8, 205–6, 309–10, 314, 321, 364, 365
relationship with brother, 7–8, 10, 12, 14–16, 44, 56, 57, 63–4, 65, 66–8, 71, 77–8, 103, 108, 110, 113, 115, 142, 144, 149–50, 153, 160, 162, 173, 178, 202, 204, 208, 210, 218, 219–20, 224, 234–5, 238, 258, 259, 279, 288, 338; *see also under* letters to Weeton, Thomas Richard
relationship with daughter, 240, 241–2, 243, 246, 255–6, 257, 261, 264, 265–8, 274–6, 279, 281–3, 288–9, 293–4, 296, 300–1, 324, 334, 340, 342–3, 351, 352, 353–4, 367; *see also under* letters to Stock, Mary
religious faith, 115, 117, 123–4, 196, 238, 241, 243, 248, 249, 254–5, 290, 298, 301, 304, 305, 322, 329–30, 360, 370, 372–3, 378, 379–80, 381, 382
religious instruction, 9
religious observance, 8, 30, 38, 46, 70–1, 271, 380, 381
and Roman Catholicism, 253–4, 285–6
romantic feelings, 119–20, 122, 157, 238
on sailing, 359
in St Helens, 278
sea sickness, 168, 194, 283
sense of humour, 49–50, 340
separation from husband, 260, 288, 299, 348, 350–1
servants' treatment of, 239, 241, 242, 247, 251, 252, 275
and shipwreck, 25–6
slander against, 108, 110, 113, 124–5, 141, 162–3, 196–7, 214–15, 224, 269–70, 271
social isolation, 10–11, 14, 16,

29, 56, 69–70, 103, 106, 132, 134, 139, 195–6, 200–1, 206, 210, 219, 229, 238, 247, 248, 249, 252, 264, 275, 279–80, 300, 322, 333, 339, 347, 359, 368, 374
Southport visit, 266, 283, 284
suitors, 63
as a Sunday School teacher, 269, 271, 273–4
as a teacher, 12, 18, 160, 350
theatre visit, 28, 57
on theatres, 121
travel sickness, 192, 216
in Up Holland, 6–19, 49–50, 53, 54, 56, 58, 65, 72, 212, 223, 227–8, 233, 253, 258, 259, 264–310, 379
Wales visits, 55, 285–7, 357–73, 382
walks, 55, 151, 171, 173–4, 175–81, 183–6, 244, 287, 303, 304, 308, 321, 323, 326, 333, 334, 336, 337, 352, 353, 354, 366–7
in Warwick, 329–30
and weather, 45–6
and Welsh language, 363, 365, 372
in Wigan, 59, 60, 239, 283, 287, 290, 301–2, 376, 377
Will and estate, 377–8
on women's attainments, 150, 244
on women's status, 72–4
as a writer, 72, 153, 300
Weeton, Captain Thomas (N.W.'s father), 1, 2, 3–4, 73, 335
Weeton, Thomas Richard (N.W.'s brother)
apprenticeship, 10
as an attorney, 249, 253, 259, 293, 338
and aunt's legacy, 225
birthday, 3, 340–1

childhood, 7–8
as a correspondent, 159–60
criticism of N. W., 108–9, 110,
    153, 202
Dove's Nest visit, 139
financial difficulties, 30
health, 68, 77–8
health of family, 105, 111
income, 165n22
and Lodge, Miss J., 57, 63–4
in London, 14–15
marriage, 15–16, 63
and mother's gravestone, 80n17
move to Leigh, 18
musical education, 9
and N.W.'s income, 160–1
N.W.'s letters to, 19, 21–2,
    24, 28–30, 38–9, 41, 42, 43,
    46–7, 49–52, 56–9, 62–5,
    68–71, 71–4, 75–7, 82–4,
    92–4, 97–103, 111–13, 123–5,
    133–5, 144, 149–52, 154–6,
    157–9, 220–1, 249–52, 258,
    259–60
and N.W.'s marriage, 249, 253,
    258, 259–60
N.W.'s relationship with, 7–8,
    10, 12, 14–16, 44, 56, 57,
    63–4, 65, 66–8, 71, 77–8,
    103, 108, 110, 113, 115, 142,
    144, 149–50, 153, 160, 162,
    173, 178, 202, 204, 208, 210,
    218, 219–20, 224, 234–5, 238,
    258, 259, 279, 288, 338
and N.W's separation, 275
profligacy, 14
riding accident, 61
and Stock, Aaron, 237, 238,
    239, 260
Weeton, Tom (N.W.'s nephew),
    42, 61, 151–2
Welsh language, 358, 363, 365,
    372
Wesley, John, 380
West Derby, 341

Westmoreland
    agriculture, 139–40
    Ambleside, 144, 160
    Coniston, 154
    Grasmere Church, 154
    Holms-Head Farm, 154
    housing, 137
    inhabitants' appearance, 136
    see also Windermere, Lake
Whitehead, Mrs, 17, 109, 110
    N.W.'s letters to, 17, 40–1, 53–
        4, 60–2, 113–15, 125, 152–4
Wigan
    Atherton's (organ builders),
        Queen Street, 302
    Catholic Chapel, 253–4
    debating society, 245–6
    Eagle Inn, 247
    Fair, 242
    Hope Independent
        (Congregational) Church,
        272, 277, 278, 279, 376
    N.W.'s criticism of, 60
    St John's R.C. Church,
        Standishgate, 253–4, 380–1
    St Paul's Independent
        (Congregational) Chapel,
        Standishgate, 239, 269
Wigan Examiner, 377
Wigan Times, 377
William, Prince of Orange, 141
Windermere, Lake
    accident on, 143–4
    proposed draining of, 138–9
    Regattas, 134–5, 141–2
    sailing on, 110–11
    in winter, 106
Windsor Castle, 328
Winkley, Ann, 62, 110, 265
    N.W.'s letters to, 162, 163, 168–
        89, 198–9, 203–4, 208–10,
        210–11, 213–17, 221, 238
Winkley, Bessy (later Mrs Price),
    27–8, 43, 62, 69–70, 74, 95, 110,
    159, 208

N.W.'s letters to, 84–8, 104–5,
106–11, 119 20, 125 9, 135,
148–9, 157, 159–61, 166–8,
191–4
Winkley, Mrs, 64–5, 68, 69–70,
75–6, 77, 95, 110, 148, 149, 158
Winkley family, 77
Winstanley, Rev T., 231
Winstanley Hall, 53, 80n12,
236n18
Winwick, 21
witches, 136
women
deserted, 368
and divorce, 262n5
education, 73
hospitality of, 179
Magdalen Hospital, London,
323
and marriage, 104, 116, 118,
130–1, 148, 156, 181–2, 237,
241
men's attitude to, 339–40, 364–
5; *see also* domestic violence
poor, 174
and separation, 261
and travel, 55
unmarried, 54, 59, 141, 339
Wordsworth, Dorothy, 164nn1, 3,
5, 165n19
writing paper, 212

York, Duke of *see* Frederick, Duke
of York